The Grand Inquisitor in the Age

by

ant

# Table of Contents

The ink on this manuscript has barely had time to dry, yet the digital currents it attempts to navigate are already shifting. In an era defined by the rapid ascent of artificial intelligence, the ancient wisdom of literature and philosophy has never felt more urgent. It is a peculiar sensation to find oneself looking to a nineteenth-century Russian novelist for guidance on twenty-first-century algorithms, yet Fyodor Dostoyevsky's "The Grand Inquisitor" parable, nestled within the sprawling edifice of *The Brothers Karamazov*, offers a startlingly prescient framework for understanding the profound challenges posed by AI. This book is born from that very paradox: an exploration of contemporary technological phenomena through the lens of a profound, if anachronistic, literary and theological critique. We live in a time where the allure of curated experiences, seamless efficiency, and predictive security is nearly irresistible. AI promises to solve problems, alleviate burdens, and optimize our lives in ways previously confined to the realm of speculative fiction. Yet, as the Grand Inquisitor argued, such promises often come at a price—the forfeiture of freedom, the suppression of authentic choice, and the erosion of the very qualities that define our humanity.

The impetus for this work arises from a growing concern that the societal bargain we are striking with AI mirrors the one proposed by the Inquisitor: earthly comfort and order in exchange for the heavy, often agonizing, burden of liberty. This is not a polemic against technology itself, but a critical examination of its deployment and its impact on fundamental human rights and values. It is an invitation to engage with the ethical, philosophical, and legal implications of a world where algorithms increasingly mediate our realities, influence our decisions, and even shape our understanding of truth and justice. We aim to bridge the gap between literary exegesis, theological interpretation, and cutting-edge technological discourse, demonstrating how enduring questions about human nature, authority, and freedom find new and potent expression in the age of artificial intelligence. This book is for anyone who has paused to wonder if the conveniences we embrace are subtly eroding the freedoms we cherish, and who seeks to understand the deep philosophical currents that inform this critical juncture in human history.

The Grand Inquisitor's chilling pronouncement, delivered within the sun-baked streets of Seville, was a condemnation of Christ's ultimate gift: freedom. He argued that humanity, weak and fallible, could not bear the terrible burden of free will, and that true salvation lay not in spiritual liberty, but in earthly security, miracle, and authority. Centuries later, as artificial intelligence permeates every facet of our lives, this ancient dialogue between freedom and security resonates with an unsettling new urgency. We are not merely witnessing the advent of a new technology; we are at the precipice of a profound societal transformation, one that echoes the Grand Inquisitor's seductive promise of a life free from suffering, doubt, and the agonizing weight of choice.

This book,

*The Grand Inquisitor in the Age of AI*, embarks on a critical journey to explore this resonance. It posits that the capabilities and societal implications of artificial intelligence serve as a contemporary manifestation of the very forces the Grand Inquisitor championed. From pervasive surveillance systems that create digital panopticons, to algorithmic decision-making that shapes our access to justice and opportunity, to the commodification of our personal data that fuels a new form of control, AI presents humanity with a choice eerily similar to the one posed in Dostoyevsky's parable. Will we embrace the profound, often difficult, responsibility of freedom, or will we succumb to the allure of engineered comfort, predictive safety, and algorithmic guidance?

Our inquiry is multi-faceted, drawing from philosophy, theology, law, and literary criticism to dissect the intricate relationship between AI and human liberty. We will examine how AI systems, in their quest for efficiency and order, can inadvertently or intentionally replicate the Grand Inquisitor's methods of control. This includes exploring the erosion of fundamental rights such as free speech, privacy, and due process, as enshrined in foundational legal documents like the U.S. Constitution's Bill of Rights, particularly its First, Fourth, and Fifth Amendments. We will also delve into theological interpretations, considering how AI's capacity to offer definitive answers and manage behavior might be seen as a 'false miracle,' challenging genuine faith and the acceptance of mystery. Furthermore, we will engage with socialist critiques, examining how the promise of universal 'earthly bread' delivered by AI could mask a slide into authoritarianism, and explore the psychological underpinnings of our voluntary subordination to algorithmic guidance. Ultimately, this book seeks to articulate the enduring value of 'higher freedoms'—love, conscience, and faith—as the unquantifiable core of human dignity, essential for navigating the complex ethical landscape of the AI era and for resisting the pervasive normalization of control.

## Chapter 1: The Echo of the Inquisitor in a Digital World

In the fabric of human thought, few narratives weave as deeply into the fabric of our understanding of freedom, faith, and authority as Fyodor Dostoyevsky's monumental novella, "The Grand Inquisitor." Embedded within the expansive philosophical landscape of "The Brothers Karamazov," this seemingly brief parable delivers a profound and enduring challenge to the very essence of human existence. It is a dialogue that, for centuries, has echoed in the halls of theology, philosophy, and literature, posing a stark dichotomy: the terrifying weight of absolute freedom versus the seductive comfort of absolute security. This age-old dilemma, once confined to theological debates and existential introspection, has found a new and urgent relevance in our contemporary world, a world increasingly shaped by the pervasive influence of artificial intelligence.

Dostoyevsky's parable unfolds in Seville, where the figure of the Grand Inquisitor, a powerful, aged cardinal, confronts Christ. Christ, having returned to Earth during the Spanish Inquisition, is met not with recognition and reverence, but with arrest and condemnation by the Inquisitor. The Inquisitor, speaking with the authority of his office and the grim wisdom of his experience, launches into a searing indictment of Christ's mission. He argues that Christ's greatest gift to humanity—free will—has proven to be its greatest curse. Humanity, he contends, is fundamentally weak, incapable of bearing the immense burden of choice, prone to sin, doubt, and endless suffering when left to its own devices. The Inquisitor, in his stern pronouncements, posits that humanity craves not freedom, but a benevolent master, someone to alleviate the anxiety of decision-making and provide a predictable, ordered existence.

This critique forms the philosophical bedrock of the parable. The

Inquisitor does not deny Christ's miracles or his divine nature; rather, he claims that Christ's approach was fundamentally flawed because it underestimated the inherent limitations of human nature. He argues that Christ offered "heavenly bread"—spiritual freedom, the challenge of faith, the arduous path of moral choice—when what humanity truly yearned for was "earthly bread"—material security, guaranteed happiness, and freedom from the gnawing uncertainty of existence. The Inquisitor, believing he knows humanity's true needs better than Christ, has established his own grand edifice of control, a system that promises peace and contentment by eradicating the very possibility of dissent, doubt, or genuine spiritual struggle. He has, in essence, traded the divine for the temporal, the transcendent for the tangible, the agonizing beauty of freedom for the comforting predictability of subjugation.

The enduring power of "The Grand Inquisitor" lies in its masterful articulation of this fundamental human tension. It forces us to confront uncomfortable truths about ourselves: our susceptibility to authority, our yearning for certainty, and our often-hidden desire to be relieved of the responsibility that freedom entails. The parable is not merely a theological allegory; it is a profound exploration of political philosophy, ethics, and psychology. It probes the nature of power, the relationship between the governed and the governor, and the price that humanity is willing to pay for perceived peace and order. Dostoyevsky, through the Inquisitor, presciently identified the deep-seated human longing that can make even the most benevolent-seeming systems of control appear desirable, even necessary.

This timeless dilemma, however, is not static. It evolves, adapts, and takes on new forms with each technological and societal shift. In the 20th century, thinkers grappled with the implications of totalitarian regimes, mass media, and the nascent anxieties of the atomic age. Today, we face a force that magnifies these concerns to an unprecedented degree: artificial intelligence. AI, with its burgeoning capabilities in surveillance, data analysis, decision-making, and predictive modeling, presents itself not just as a tool, but as a potential architect of a new social order. It offers solutions to complex problems, promises unparalleled efficiency, and has the capacity to shape our experiences in ways we are only beginning to comprehend.

It is this intersection of Dostoyevsky's ancient wisdom and AI's burgeoning power that forms the central inquiry of this book. We stand at a precipice where the Inquisitor's seductive logic—that freedom is a burden and security is paramount—is being amplified by technological means. The digital age, powered by AI, is creating new avenues for surveillance, control, and the commodification of human experience, echoing the Inquisitor's blueprint for a contented, albeit unfree, humanity. The core questions posed by Dostoyevsky are no longer abstract philosophical exercises; they are pressing ethical and societal challenges that demand our immediate attention.

How do we reconcile the promises of AI-driven security and convenience with the fundamental human value of freedom? What are the ethical boundaries of algorithmic authority, and how do we prevent the erosion of privacy, autonomy, and individual dignity? Does the relentless pursuit of order and efficiency, facilitated by AI, risk creating a society of "happy slaves," content in their gilded cages, oblivious to the profound loss of their essential humanity? By examining "The Grand Inquisitor" through the lens of contemporary AI, we can gain a deeper understanding of the forces shaping our present and future, and perhaps, find the wisdom to navigate the treacherous path ahead, ensuring that in our quest for security, we do not inadvertently surrender the very freedoms that make us truly human. The parable, once a somber warning from a bygone era, has become an urgent clarion call for our digital age, urging us to recognize the echoes of the Inquisitor in the algorithms that increasingly govern our lives.

The Grand Inquisitor, with chilling prescience, laid bare a fundamental truth about human nature: our often-contradictory desires for freedom and security. He argued that the former, while divinely ordained, was a source of immense suffering, leading humanity into sin, doubt, and existential anguish. The latter, embodied in "earthly bread" and absolute order, offered a path to peace, predictability, and a form of happiness untroubled by the anxieties of choice. This ancient dichotomy, a cornerstone of theological and philosophical debate for centuries, is not merely a relic of the past; it has been resurrected and amplified in the age of artificial intelligence. The capabilities of modern AI, from pervasive surveillance to sophisticated decision-making algorithms, present a new and potent manifestation of the Inquisitor's power, forcing us to re-examine the eternal tension between liberty and the allure of a managed existence.

Dostoyevsky's masterful creation, the Grand Inquisitor, is not a simple villain but a complex figure who believes he is acting in humanity's best interest. He confronts Christ in Seville, a city under the oppressive shadow of the Inquisition, and delivers a powerful sermon condemning Christ's gift of free will. The Inquisitor contends that Christ's radical trust in humanity's capacity for good and for self-governance was a grave error.

He posits that humanity is weak, childlike, and incapable of handling the profound responsibility that true freedom entails. The constant barrage of choices, the burden of moral accountability, and the terrifying existential void that freedom can reveal are, in his view, too much for the vast majority of people. Instead, they crave a guiding hand, a certainty that alleviates the struggle of decision-making and provides a predictable, comfortable existence.

The Inquisitor's critique centers on what he perceives as the inherent flaws in the human psyche: an inability to resist temptation, a tendency towards self-destruction when unguided, and an overwhelming desire for tangible, immediate satisfaction. He argues that Christ's emphasis on spiritual freedom and the pursuit of a higher, often abstract, truth was misguided. Humanity, he asserts, is far more motivated by its baser needs and desires—hunger, safety, comfort, and a sense of belonging within a structured community. Therefore, the Inquisitor has replaced Christ's offering of "heavenly bread" (spiritual liberty) with "earthly bread" (material security and controlled happiness). His dominion, he explains, offers a world free from the torment of doubt, the agony of choice, and the fear of the unknown. It is a world where every need is anticipated, every behavior is guided, and every deviation from the norm is swiftly corrected, all in exchange for absolute submission to his authority.

This vision, while repressive by modern democratic standards, holds a profound, albeit disturbing, appeal. The Inquisitor understands that the anxiety of freedom is a heavy burden. The responsibility of making one's own choices, of forging one's own path, and of confronting the often-unpleasant realities of existence can be overwhelming. The promise of a life free from such burdens, a life where external forces provide order, meaning, and comfort, is a potent temptation. Dostoyevsky, through this parable, was not merely critiquing religious or political authority; he was delving into the very core of the human condition, exploring the perennial struggle between our desire for autonomy and our yearning for a sense of safety and belonging.

The philosophical weight of "The Grand Inquisitor" extends far beyond its theological context. It serves as a profound commentary on the nature of power and the mechanisms by which it is maintained. The Inquisitor's strategy—offering security and comfort in exchange for freedom—is a timeless tactic of authoritarian control. He argues that true benevolence lies not in granting freedom, but in alleviating suffering by removing the very possibility of it, even if that means stripping away agency. This perspective challenges our assumptions about progress and enlightenment, suggesting that humanity may not inherently desire the "enlightenment" of free inquiry and individual responsibility if it comes at the cost of palpable comfort and certainty.

Furthermore, the parable can be interpreted as a critique of revolutionary fervor and utopian idealism that, in their pursuit of a perfect society, often disregard the messiness and individuality of human existence. The Inquisitor sees Christ's attempt to elevate humanity as a failure because it did not account for the common person's need for structure and guidance. His own grand design, he believes, is a more realistic and ultimately kinder approach, one that caters to the masses' fundamental needs rather than their aspirational, yet often unfulfilled, desires for spiritual liberty.

The continued relevance of "The Grand Inquisitor" in contemporary discourse cannot be overstated. As we navigate the complexities of the 21st century, the parable's themes resonate with striking clarity, particularly in light of rapid technological advancements. The rise of artificial intelligence presents a unique and powerful echo of the Inquisitor's logic. AI systems, with their capacity for data analysis, prediction, and personalized intervention, are increasingly positioned as providers of security, efficiency, and comfort. From smart assistants that manage our schedules to predictive algorithms that shape our news feeds and recommend our purchases, AI offers a seamless, optimized experience of life. This constant stream of algorithmic guidance, while often convenient, subtly mirrors the Inquisitor's promise of a life free from the burden of arduous decision-making.

The age of AI compels us to view Dostoyevsky's dilemma through a new, technological lens. The "earthly bread" can now be delivered through optimized supply chains and personalized consumption, while "miracle, mystery, and authority"—the pillars of the Inquisitor's control—find new expression in the seemingly infallible logic of algorithms, the opaque nature of AI decision-making, and the immense power wielded by those who control these systems. The "burden of freedom" might manifest as the overwhelming cognitive load of navigating digital information, the anxiety of maintaining an online persona, or the fear of algorithmic repricing or exclusion.

The reader is thus invited to consider how these ancient tensions are being replayed, amplified, and perhaps even fundamentally altered by the advent of artificial intelligence. We are at a critical juncture where the choices we make regarding the development and deployment of AI will determine whether we lean towards the Inquisitor's vision of ordered, secure, yet ultimately subservient humanity, or whether we can find new ways to uphold the value of freedom, even in the face of its inherent challenges. This book seeks to explore precisely this convergence, to understand the "Grand Inquisitor" not as a historical artifact, but as a living, breathing warning that speaks directly to our present moment and the technological future we are collectively building. The digital realm, with its intricate networks of data and algorithmic influence, has become the new stage upon which this eternal drama of freedom versus security is being enacted, and the stakes have never been higher.

The advent of artificial intelligence has ushered in an era where the abstract fears of the past are rapidly solidifying into tangible realities. AI is no longer confined to the realm of science fiction; it is a potent force shaping our present and dictating the contours of our future. Its capabilities are expanding at an exponential rate, permeating nearly every facet of human existence and offering unprecedented levels of efficiency, prediction, and control. This pervasive integration, however, is precisely what draws a chilling parallel to the Grand Inquisitor's seductive promise of order and security at the cost of freedom. We are witnessing the emergence of AI not merely as a sophisticated tool, but as a new locus of authority, capable of wielding influence and enacting control in ways that demand careful ethical and philosophical scrutiny.

At the heart of AI's transformative power lies its extraordinary capacity for data collection and analysis. Modern AI systems can process vast quantities of information – far beyond human cognitive limits – sifting through it to identify patterns, predict behaviors, and even anticipate needs. This capability underpins an unprecedented level of surveillance. From the cameras that monitor public spaces and the sensors embedded in our smart devices to the digital footprints we leave across the internet,

AI systems are constantly gathering data on our movements, our communications, our preferences, and our interactions. This data, once collected, is fed into complex algorithms designed to optimize services, personalize experiences, and, crucially, to monitor and manage populations. The implications are profound: a society where our actions, both public and private, are perpetually observed and analyzed, creating a detailed, indelible record of our lives. This omnipresent gaze, facilitated by AI, bears a striking resemblance to the watchful eye of the Inquisition, albeit one that operates through silent, invisible networks of data rather than physical presence.

The sophistication of AI extends beyond mere observation; it encompasses the ability to make decisions and to act upon them, often without direct human intervention. Algorithmic decision-making is now a cornerstone of many critical societal functions. Loan applications are approved or denied based on AI analysis, job candidates are screened through algorithmic filters, and even criminal justice systems are beginning to employ AI for risk assessment and sentencing recommendations. These algorithms, trained on historical data, can perpetuate and even amplify existing societal biases, leading to discriminatory outcomes that are often difficult to detect or contest. The opacity of many AI systems, often referred to as the "black box problem," further complicates matters. When an AI makes a decision, understanding *why* that decision was made can be incredibly challenging, even for its creators. This lack of transparency erodes accountability and makes it difficult to challenge outcomes that may be unfair or unjust, mirroring the unquestionable authority claimed by the Grand Inquisitor, whose pronouncements were final and beyond dispute.

The concept of "predictive policing," for example, exemplifies this duality of capability and concern. AI algorithms are used to forecast where and when crimes are most likely to occur, allowing law enforcement to deploy resources proactively. On the one hand, this promises increased public safety and a more efficient allocation of police resources. On the other hand, it raises significant concerns about profiling, the potential for over-policing in certain communities based on historical data (which may itself be biased), and the creation of a self-fulfilling prophecy where increased surveillance and police presence lead to more arrests, thus reinforcing the algorithm's initial prediction. This algorithmic foresight, while seemingly benign in its aim to prevent harm, can easily morph into a preemptive form of control, shaping behavior through the awareness of constant, predictive scrutiny. The fear of being flagged by an algorithm, of being identified as a potential risk

*before* any transgression has occurred, introduces a new dimension to the anxiety of living under surveillance.

Furthermore, the pervasive nature of AI-driven personalization, while often presented as a convenience, carries the potential for manipulation. Algorithms that curate our news feeds, recommend products, and shape our online experiences are designed to keep us engaged and to influence our choices. By understanding our preferences, our vulnerabilities, and our psychological triggers with ever-increasing accuracy, AI can be used to nudge our behavior in specific directions, whether it's towards a particular purchase, a political viewpoint, or even a lifestyle choice. This subtle, pervasive influence, operating below the threshold of conscious awareness, echoes the Inquisitor's argument that humanity is easily swayed and requires external guidance to navigate the complexities of life. When our information environment is meticulously crafted by algorithms whose primary objective is engagement or profit, rather than objective truth or individual well-being, the very foundation of informed consent and autonomous decision-making begins to erode.

The erosion of privacy is perhaps the most immediate and widely recognized concern associated with AI's capabilities. As AI systems become more adept at collecting, synthesizing, and analyzing personal data, the traditional boundaries of privacy become increasingly porous. Our digital lives are not separate from our physical lives; they are deeply intertwined, and AI bridges these realms with remarkable efficiency. The ability to link disparate pieces of information – from social media posts and online searches to location data and biometric identifiers – allows for the creation of incredibly detailed profiles of individuals. This comprehensive data aggregation raises the specter of a society where there is no longer a truly private sphere, where every aspect of our lives is potentially observable, recordable, and analyzable. This constant state of potential observation can foster a chilling effect on behavior, discouraging dissent, creativity, and genuine self-expression for fear of negative algorithmic repercussions or social judgment. The Inquisitor's promise of security often came with the implicit understanding that it required the surrender of personal liberties and the quiet conformity of the populace; AI-driven surveillance presents a similar bargain, albeit one cloaked in the language of convenience and optimization.

Moreover, the concentration of power that accompanies advanced AI development is a significant cause for concern. The creation and maintenance of sophisticated AI systems require immense computational resources, vast datasets, and specialized expertise, resources that are predominantly held by a few large technology corporations and powerful state actors. This concentration of power means that the individuals and entities that control these AI systems wield significant influence over information, decision-making, and even public discourse. They have the capacity to shape societal norms, influence political outcomes, and control access to essential services, all through the deployment of algorithms. This concentration of power in the hands of a few, wielding tools of unprecedented analytical and predictive capability, creates a new form of authority – one that is often less visible and less accountable than traditional forms of governance. It is an authority that, like the Grand Inquisitor's, operates with a supposed superior understanding of human needs and desires, capable of implementing solutions that may serve its own interests under the guise of universal benefit.

The very language used to describe AI's role in our lives often subtly reinforces this emerging authority. Terms like "intelligent assistants," "smart systems," and "automated decision-making" frame AI as an autonomous, capable entity rather than a tool designed by humans. This anthropomorphism can lead us to attribute agency and even wisdom to algorithms, fostering a passive acceptance of their outputs and recommendations. When AI systems are presented as infallible, objective arbiters of truth or efficiency, it becomes easier to abdicate our own critical judgment and to trust implicitly in their pronouncements. This tendency to defer to algorithmic authority is precisely what the Grand Inquisitor predicted and exploited: humanity's deep-seated desire to be relieved of the burden of independent thought and the responsibility that comes with freedom.

The potential for AI to be deployed for mass manipulation, especially in the political sphere, is another acute concern. The ability to generate hyper-realistic deepfakes, to spread disinformation at scale through bot networks, and to micro-target political messaging based on detailed psychological profiles, all powered by AI, presents a profound threat to democratic processes. When the very nature of reality can be fabricated and disseminated with such ease, and when citizens' political views can be precisely manipulated through personalized algorithmic nudges, the concept of an informed electorate and free and fair elections becomes increasingly fragile. This is a direct manifestation of the Inquisitor's critique of Christ's failure to account for humanity's susceptibility to external influence and its yearning for a guiding, authoritative voice, albeit one that now speaks through the digital ether. The "miracle, mystery, and authority" that the Inquisitor offered finds a chilling echo in the seemingly unfathomable capabilities of AI, its opaque decision-making processes, and its demonstrable power to shape perception and behavior.

Ultimately, the development and deployment of AI technologies are not neutral endeavors. They are shaped by human intentions, values, and biases, and their impact on society will depend on the choices we make. The capabilities of AI are undeniable, offering immense potential for progress and improvement. However, these same capabilities, when wielded without adequate ethical consideration and robust oversight, carry the distinct risk of ushering in a new form of authority that prioritizes order, efficiency, and security over individual freedom, autonomy, and human dignity. As we stand at this technological crossroads, it is imperative to recognize the echoes of the Grand Inquisitor in the algorithms that are increasingly governing our lives, and to actively resist the temptation to trade the profound, albeit difficult, value of freedom for the seductive, but ultimately hollow, promise of absolute, AI-driven security.

The pervasive gaze of the Inquisitor, once a chilling abstract in Dostoyevsky's fictional Seville, has found its disembodied, yet ever-present, successor in the digital realm. This new architecture of observation, often termed the "digital panopticon," transcends the physical constraints of Bentham's original design. It is a system where surveillance is not merely a tool of external enforcement but an internalized mechanism, shaping behavior through the constant, albeit often invisible, awareness of being potentially watched. Artificial intelligence acts as the linchpin of this modern panopticon, transforming the theoretical possibility of omnipresent observation into a tangible reality that permeates every facet of our lives.

At the core of this digital panopticon lies AI's unparalleled capacity for data aggregation and analysis. Technologies like facial recognition, once the stuff of speculative fiction, are now integrated into public spaces, retail environments, and even personal devices. These systems, powered by sophisticated AI algorithms, can identify individuals with remarkable accuracy, tracking their movements, cataloging their associations, and building detailed profiles based on their presence in various locations. Beyond facial recognition, AI diligently monitors our digital footprints: our online searches, our social media interactions, our purchase histories, our communication patterns, and even our physical location data from smartphones. This continuous stream of information is not just collected; it is meticulously processed, cross-referenced, and analyzed by AI to create an intricate, dynamic mosaic of our lives. This aggregation of data, often occurring without our explicit, informed consent, creates a comprehensive picture that can reveal intimate details about our habits, beliefs, and relationships, far exceeding what any individual might consciously choose to disclose. The sheer volume and granularity of this data-gathering capability far surpass anything that was conceivable in the pre-digital age, making the potential for constant oversight truly unprecedented.

This pervasive surveillance, facilitated by AI, cultivates a profound psychological shift, leading to what philosopher Michel Foucault termed "internalized surveillance." In his analysis of the Panopticon, Foucault argued that the effectiveness of the structure lay not in the actual act of constant watching, but in the

*knowledge* that one *could* be watched at any moment. This uncertainty compels individuals to self-regulate their behavior, to conform to perceived norms and expectations, lest they fall afoul of the unseen observer. The digital panopticon amplifies this effect exponentially. The constant, subtle feedback loops of algorithmic curation – the personalized advertisements that seem to anticipate our desires, the social media algorithms that gently nudge us towards certain content, the search engine results that subtly reframe our inquiries – all contribute to an environment where individuals increasingly modify their actions and expressions based on the perceived gaze of the digital apparatus. This is not an overt form of coercion but a subtle, pervasive conditioning. The fear of being flagged by an algorithm, of having one's data deemed "suspicious" or "non-compliant," can lead to a chilling effect on free expression and authentic behavior.

Consider the realm of online communication. AI-powered sentiment analysis tools can scan social media posts, emails, and even private messages to gauge emotional states, identify dissenting opinions, or predict future actions. While these tools might be employed for benign purposes like customer service or market research, their potential for monitoring and control is immense. Individuals aware of such capabilities may self-censor, avoiding controversial topics or expressions of individuality for fear that their words might be misinterpreted or used against them. This is particularly acute in contexts where AI is used for political surveillance or to monitor employee productivity. The mere possibility of an algorithm flagging a particular phrase, a specific tone, or an unusual pattern of communication can lead to a deliberate suppression of authentic thought and expression. The digital panopticon, in this sense, doesn't need to actively punish deviation; the anticipation of potential judgment is often enough to enforce conformity.

The aggregation of behavioral data by AI further entrenches this self-censorship. Our online activity, from the websites we visit and the products we browse to the duration of our engagement with certain content, is meticulously logged and analyzed. AI systems learn our habits, our preferences, and our inclinations, creating predictive models of our behavior. When individuals are aware that their every click, scroll, and interaction is being recorded and analyzed, they may begin to modify their online behavior. They might avoid exploring certain topics, engaging with specific communities, or even expressing unpopular opinions, not because these actions are illegal or harmful, but because they fear how the data might be interpreted and what consequences, however subtle, might follow. This can lead to a homogenization of online discourse, where only the safest, most conventional ideas are expressed, and genuine intellectual exploration or dissent is stifled. The vast, interconnected network of data points, meticulously curated by AI, becomes a digital prison, not of bars and walls, but of algorithms and predicted outcomes.

The implications extend beyond mere online behavior. AI is increasingly used to analyze biometric data, such as gait, voice, and even physiological responses, further expanding the scope of surveillance. Imagine AI systems in public spaces that can not only identify individuals but also analyze their emotional state or detect subtle physiological cues indicative of stress or deception. The knowledge that such an analysis is constantly being performed can induce significant anxiety and alter behavior. People may feel compelled to project an image of calm, conformity, and agreeability at all times, even in private spaces if the presence of such monitoring technology is suspected. This constant pressure to perform a particular version of oneself, to adhere to an algorithmically defined standard of "normal" or "acceptable" behavior, erodes the capacity for spontaneous expression and genuine selfhood. The digital panopticon fosters a society of perpetual performance, where authenticity is sacrificed at the altar of algorithmic approval.

Furthermore, the opacity of many AI systems exacerbates the psychological impact of this pervasive surveillance. Unlike human overseers, who might offer some degree of discernible motivation or even inconsistency, AI algorithms often operate as "black boxes." Their decision-making processes can be incredibly complex and inscrutable, even to their creators. This lack of transparency means that individuals are often unaware of precisely

*why* their behavior is being monitored, *what* data is being collected, or *how* it is being interpreted. This uncertainty breeds a heightened sense of vulnerability and a greater inclination towards caution and conformity. When one cannot understand the rules of the game, the safest strategy is to avoid breaking any perceived rules altogether. This can lead to a society where individuals are less likely to take risks, to challenge established norms, or to engage in activities that might be perceived as unconventional, for fear of unpredictable algorithmic consequences. The digital panopticon, powered by AI, creates a self-policing society not through overt force, but through a deeply ingrained, algorithmically induced caution.

The application of AI in areas like predictive policing and credit scoring further illustrates this phenomenon. In predictive policing, AI algorithms analyze historical crime data to forecast where and when future crimes are likely to occur. While ostensibly aimed at crime prevention, this can lead to over-policing of certain neighborhoods, creating an environment of constant surveillance and suspicion for residents. The awareness that one's community is being algorithmically targeted can lead to heightened anxiety and self-consciousness, impacting daily life. Similarly, in credit scoring, AI analyzes vast amounts of financial and behavioral data to assess an individual's creditworthiness. This means that even seemingly innocuous online behaviors or purchasing habits could be interpreted by an algorithm as indicative of financial risk, leading to adverse credit decisions. The knowledge that such an assessment is constantly being made, and that past actions, however minor, can have significant future consequences, can lead individuals to meticulously manage their digital lives to conform to algorithmic expectations, even at the expense of personal convenience or genuine expression.

The insidious nature of this digital panopticon lies in its subtle assimilation into everyday life, often disguised as convenience or personalization. Smart home devices, wearable fitness trackers, and personalized online services all contribute to the vast data streams that feed AI surveillance systems. We willingly integrate these technologies into our lives, often without fully grasping the extent of the data being collected or the mechanisms of its analysis. The convenience of a voice assistant that anticipates our needs, or a streaming service that perfectly curates our entertainment, comes at the cost of constant monitoring and data harvesting. As AI becomes more sophisticated, it becomes adept at learning our vulnerabilities, our desires, and our psychological triggers. This knowledge can be used not only to provide personalized services but also to subtly manipulate behavior, nudging us towards specific consumption patterns, political viewpoints, or lifestyle choices. The awareness that such nudges are possible, and that our digital environment is meticulously crafted to influence us, can lead to a profound sense of disempowerment and a diminished sense of personal autonomy.

In essence, the digital panopticon, powered by AI, represents a profound evolution of surveillance. It is a system where the omnipresent gaze is not necessarily that of a human guard, but of intelligent algorithms processing vast amounts of data. This system compels individuals to internalize the surveillance, to self-censor and conform, not out of fear of immediate punishment, but out of a pervasive, often unarticulated, apprehension of algorithmic judgment and potential negative consequences. It is a world where the mere possibility of being watched, analyzed, and judged by unseen digital forces reshapes our behavior, our expressions, and ultimately, our very sense of self. This is the echoing legacy of the Inquisitor's promise: order and security achieved through the willing or unwilling surrender of individual freedom and authentic selfhood, this time delivered not by a tangible authority, but by the invisible, all-encompassing power of artificial intelligence.

The allure of an effortless existence, meticulously curated and subtly guided by unseen algorithmic hands, presents a powerful counterpoint to the abstract ideals of liberty. While freedom is a fundamental pillar of democratic societies, its abstract nature can often be overshadowed by the palpable, immediate benefits offered by technological advancements, particularly those powered by artificial intelligence. This phenomenon, whereby individuals and societies willingly, or perhaps less consciously, trade aspects of their constitutional freedoms for perceived safety, convenience, and material comforts, forms a critical juncture in our contemporary digital landscape. The echo of the Grand Inquisitor's seductive proposition – the promise of bread and security in exchange for the burden of free will – resonates deeply within this context, finding new expression in the pervasive presence of AI.

At the heart of this societal bargain lies a complex interplay of psychological drivers. The human psyche, inherently drawn to comfort and predictability, can find the anxieties and responsibilities associated with unfettered liberty to be a considerable burden. The notion of making choices, of navigating uncertainty, and of bearing the full weight of individual agency can be exhausting. AI, in its sophisticated capacity to analyze, predict, and cater to our perceived needs, offers an escape from this inherent friction. It promises a life where friction points are smoothed, where decisions are pre-empted, and where potential discomforts are mitigated. This promise of ease, of an optimized existence, becomes incredibly seductive, often overshadowing the more abstract, yet crucial, values of privacy, autonomy, and self-determination. The immediate gratification derived from a perfectly timed reminder, a personalized suggestion that lands precisely on point, or a home environment that anticipates our every need, fosters a sense of contentment that can, for many, feel more valuable than the abstract notion of being entirely in control of one's own destiny.

Consider the pervasive influence of personalized recommendation engines. Platforms like Netflix, Amazon, and Spotify have become masters at predicting our entertainment preferences, our shopping desires, and even our musical tastes. AI algorithms analyze our past viewing habits, our purchase histories, our search queries, and the behavior of statistically similar users to create a tailored experience. This not only saves us time and effort in searching for content or products but also fosters a sense of being understood and catered to. The algorithm becomes a trusted curator, guiding us towards experiences we are likely to enjoy. However, this convenience comes at a cost. Each interaction with these platforms, each click and each view, feeds the AI, further refining its understanding of our preferences. This creates a feedback loop, potentially limiting our exposure to new or challenging content, inadvertently reinforcing existing tastes, and subtly shaping our desires rather than merely satisfying them. We trade the potential for serendipitous discovery, the excitement of venturing into unknown artistic territories, for the comfort of algorithmic certainty. The choice is not explicitly between freedom and constraint, but between the effort of exploration and the ease of guided consumption.

This willingness to cede control is further amplified by the proliferation of predictive services. AI is increasingly employed to anticipate our needs before we even articulate them. Smart home devices, for instance, learn our routines and adjust lighting, temperature, and even music playback accordingly. A thermostat might learn our preferred temperatures at different times of the day and automatically adjust, or a coffee maker might be programmed to start brewing as our alarm clock rings. While these conveniences undeniably enhance our daily lives, they also represent a subtle surrender of granular control. We delegate the decision-making process, however small, to an algorithm. The cumulative effect of these small delegations of autonomy can be significant. We become accustomed to a world where many minor decisions are made for us, potentially diminishing our capacity for independent thought and action in these areas. The "smart" home, in this sense, becomes an environment where our habits are not just accommodated but actively managed by a non-human intelligence.

The psychological underpinnings of this trade-off are not entirely new. Philosophers and social theorists have long observed humanity's complex relationship with freedom and security. In his seminal work,

*The Second Treatise of Government*, John Locke argued that individuals enter into society and government to protect their natural rights, including liberty. However, this protection requires a surrender of some degree of absolute freedom to a governing authority. What is new in the digital age is the nature of this authority and the pervasive, often invisible, means by which it operates. The AI-driven digital infrastructure does not overtly demand a sacrifice of liberty; rather, it offers a compelling array of immediate benefits that, by their very nature, require the disclosure and analysis of personal data, thereby diminishing individual privacy and autonomy. The trade is not an explicit negotiation with a visible sovereign, but a series of implicit acceptances of terms and conditions, a quiet acquiescence to data-gathering practices that fuel ever-more sophisticated convenience.

The promise of enhanced safety and security, particularly in the face of perceived threats, is another powerful motivator for this societal bargain. AI-powered surveillance systems, facial recognition technology, and predictive policing algorithms are often presented as essential tools for maintaining public order and preventing crime. While these technologies can undoubtedly contribute to safety, their deployment often involves a significant erosion of privacy. The constant monitoring of public spaces, the collection of biometric data, and the algorithmic profiling of individuals create an environment where the presumption of innocence can be subtly undermined. Citizens may find themselves under increased scrutiny, their movements tracked and their associations logged, all in the name of collective security. The fear of being targeted by crime, or the desire for a safer community, can override the abstract value of being free from constant observation. This is a modern manifestation of the Inquisitor's promise: a tranquil, orderly society, free from the chaos of crime and dissent, achieved through the willing acceptance of pervasive oversight.

Furthermore, the economics of convenience play a significant role. In a world where time is a precious commodity, the efficiency offered by AI-powered services is highly valued. Imagine the time saved by not having to manually sort through emails, to research every purchase, or to manage every aspect of one's home environment. AI automates these tasks, freeing up mental bandwidth and allowing individuals to focus on other pursuits. This optimization of daily life creates a powerful incentive to embrace AI technologies, even if it means relinquishing some degree of personal control. The perceived "cost" of convenience, which is often paid in data and surrendered autonomy, appears minimal compared to the tangible benefits of saved time and reduced mental effort. This economic logic, amplified by the pervasive marketing of these technologies as essential tools for modern living, subtly normalizes the trade-off.

The concept of "nudging," as popularized by behavioral economists Richard Thaler and Cass Sunstein, provides a useful framework for understanding how AI can influence our choices without overt coercion. AI systems can be designed to gently guide our behavior towards desired outcomes, whether it be healthier eating habits, more responsible financial decisions, or increased engagement with certain platforms. While these nudges can be benevolent, they also highlight the subtle ways in which our autonomy can be compromised. The AI knows our preferences, our vulnerabilities, and our decision-making patterns better than we often know ourselves. By presenting options in a particular order, framing choices in specific ways, or providing timely reminders, AI can influence our decisions without us necessarily realizing we are being influenced. This is a far cry from the brute force of the Inquisitor's threats, yet its effect on genuine free choice can be equally profound. We are not being forced, but rather artfully persuaded, our desires subtly shaped to align with algorithmic objectives.

The erosion of privacy, often seen as the most significant casualty of this societal bargain, is not always met with strong resistance because its consequences are often gradual and diffuse. The incremental nature of data collection and the gradual integration of surveillance technologies into everyday life can desensitize individuals to the broader implications. What begins as a simple app request for location access for navigation can evolve into a comprehensive profile of one's daily movements. What starts as a personalized news feed can become an echo chamber that filters out dissenting viewpoints. Each step of this evolution is often justified by an increase in convenience or a perceived improvement in service. The cumulative impact, however, is a society where privacy is a scarce and increasingly abstract commodity, a concept discussed more often than experienced.

Moreover, the narrative surrounding these technologies often frames them as tools for empowerment. We are told that AI can unlock our potential, enhance our productivity, and connect us with the world. This framing can obscure the inherent power imbalance created by the collection and analysis of vast amounts of personal data. The entities that control this data and the algorithms that process it wield significant power, influencing everything from our purchasing decisions to our political discourse. When citizens willingly participate in the creation of these data profiles, they are, in essence, contributing to the very infrastructure of their own potential manipulation. The Inquisitor offered power to those who submitted to his authority; the digital age offers personalized experiences and convenience to those who willingly surrender their data.

The psychological phenomenon of habituation also plays a crucial role. As we become accustomed to the benefits of AI-driven convenience, it becomes increasingly difficult to imagine life without them. The friction of manual processes, the effort of independent research, and the burden of making every small decision can seem archaic and burdensome once we have experienced the ease of algorithmic assistance. This ingrained reliance can create a powerful inertia against any attempt to reclaim lost autonomy or privacy. The "comfort" offered by AI is not merely a temporary benefit; it becomes a deeply embedded aspect of our lifestyle, making the thought of relinquishing it feel like a significant personal sacrifice. This is how the societal bargain is solidified, not through a single, dramatic act of capitulation, but through a thousand small, seemingly inconsequential choices made in pursuit of an easier, more optimized life. The echoes of the Inquisitor's seductive whisper are amplified by the constant hum of personalized notifications and the seamless operation of our AI-managed worlds, urging us to embrace the illusion of effortless happiness at the expense of true liberty.

The preceding discussion has illuminated how the seductive promises of convenience, security, and optimized experience offered by artificial intelligence resonate with the historical anxieties surrounding freedom and control, as powerfully depicted in Dostoyevsky's *The Grand Inquisitor*. We have explored the nuanced ways in which individuals and societies are increasingly willing to cede aspects of their autonomy and privacy, not under duress, but as a seemingly logical and even desirable trade for a more predictable and comfortable existence. This voluntary surrender, often driven by the palpable benefits of AI-driven technologies, forms the bedrock upon which this book's inquiry is built. But what, precisely, are the critical questions that emerge from this profound societal transformation, and how does Dostoyevsky's enduring parable provide an indispensable lens through which to examine them?

This book embarks on an exploration, seeking to unpack the complex interplay between human aspiration, technological advancement, and the enduring philosophical questions of freedom and responsibility. At its core, our inquiry is driven by a central thesis: that Fyodor Dostoyevsky's prophetic depiction of the Grand Inquisitor's bargain has become not merely a literary artifact, but an acutely relevant framework for understanding the ethical and existential challenges posed by the burgeoning age of artificial intelligence. The parable, which posits a world where humanity relinquishes its God-given freedom for the certainty of bread and earthly peace, finds an uncanny echo in our contemporary digital landscape. We are compelled to ask: in what specific ways does the pervasive presence of AI amplify the Inquisitor's arguments and the public's susceptibility to them? How do the algorithms that curate our information, manage our lives, and even shape our desires function as the modern-day bread and circuses, promising fulfillment while subtly curtailing true liberty?

The book aims to critically analyze how contemporary AI technologies, far from being neutral tools, actively engage with and potentially undermine fundamental human rights, particularly those of autonomy, privacy, and freedom of thought. We must ask: what are the specific mechanisms by which AI systems, through personalization, prediction, and behavioral nudging, erode the very foundations of individual agency? Is the "choice" offered by a recommendation engine truly a choice, or is it an algorithmically guided path leading to a preordained outcome? Furthermore, how does the increasing reliance on AI for decision-making, from mundane daily tasks to more significant societal functions, impact our capacity for critical thinking and independent judgment? The Inquisitor argued that humanity was too weak to bear the burden of freedom; AI, in many respects, presents a more sophisticated version of this argument by offering to lift that burden for us, making the relinquishment of freedom appear not as a weakness, but as an act of intelligent self-preservation or optimization.

Central to our investigation is the reinterpretation of

*The Grand Inquisitor* through contemporary technological and ethical frameworks. This involves moving beyond a purely literary or historical analysis to engage with the ethical dilemmas presented by AI. We will scrutinize the parable's core tenets—the critique of Christ's emphasis on spiritual freedom over material well-being, the argument for human incapacity for true liberty, and the assertion that universal happiness can only be achieved through submission to authority—and examine their manifestations in the digital realm. For instance, the Inquisitor's disdain for "freedom to doubt" finds a chilling parallel in the way certain AI systems are designed to present a seamless, unchallenging reality, often filtering out dissenting viewpoints or complex information that might provoke uncertainty. Therefore, a key question becomes: how can we leverage the profound insights of Dostoyevsky's narrative to articulate the ethical boundaries that AI development and deployment must respect?

The book will also explore the societal implications of this AI-driven bargain. The Inquisitor offered a unified, unquestioning society under a single authority. While AI does not present a monolithic figure of authority in the same way, the interconnectedness of AI systems, the concentration of data and algorithmic power in the hands of a few, and the potential for AI to enforce social norms or even behavioral conformity raise profound questions about the future of collective life. We must ask: what are the long-term consequences for democratic societies when citizens increasingly delegate their decision-making and information processing to intelligent machines? Does the pursuit of algorithmic efficiency and personalized comfort inadvertently lead to a more controlled, less pluralistic society? And how does the opacity of many AI systems—the so-called "black box" problem—exacerbate these challenges, making it difficult to identify and rectify biases or to hold entities accountable for the algorithmic outcomes they produce?

Ultimately, this book aims to assess the long-term consequences of our societal choices in the face of intelligent machines, drawing a direct line from the Inquisitor's pronouncements to our present-day technological trajectory. Dostoyevsky's work serves as a timeless warning about the perils of prioritizing security and ease over freedom and the arduous, yet essential, process of moral and intellectual growth. Our task is to delineate the potential futures that lie before us, futures shaped by the choices we make today regarding the development and integration of AI. Are we destined to embrace a future of algorithmic paternalism, where our lives are meticulously managed for our own perceived good, or can we chart a course that preserves human agency and upholds the intrinsic value of liberty in the digital age? This exploration is not merely an academic exercise; it is an urgent call to critical engagement, a necessary step in ensuring that the promise of technology serves to elevate, rather than diminish, the human spirit. We must ask ourselves: are we consciously choosing the path of "bread and the sword," or can we, armed with critical understanding and a renewed appreciation for the complexities of freedom, forge a different destiny? The questions are profound, and the answers will shape the very fabric of our future.

## Chapter 2: The Grand Inquisitor's Blueprint: A Medieval Vision of Control

The oppressive heat of Seville, a city gripped by the Inquisition, provides the stark backdrop for one of literature's most profound philosophical confrontations. It is here, amidst the simmering tensions of religious dogma and secular power, that Christ returns to a world that has, in his absence, largely rejected his radical message of freedom. This is not a triumphant re-entry, but a quiet, almost unassuming arrival, as he walks among the people, performing miracles of healing and solace. Yet, his presence is soon detected, not by the faithful, but by the very apparatus designed to enforce religious orthodoxy: the Inquisition.

The Grand Inquisitor, an aging, imposing figure who embodies the chilling logic of absolute authority, orchestrates Christ's arrest. His power is palpable; he commands legions, his word is law, and the very air around him seems charged with an authority that brooks no dissent. The scene of Christ's imprisonment is not a dungeon of chains and torture, but a stark, monastic cell – a subtle yet potent symbol of the spiritual confinement the Inquisitor champions. It is here, in this space of supposed sanctity, that the true battle of ideas will unfold. The Inquisitor, armed with centuries of human history and a cynical understanding of human nature, arrives to confront the very embodiment of divine love and freedom.

The encounter is not one of physical struggle, but of a formidable intellectual and theological debate. The Inquisitor, his face a mask of aged wisdom and unwavering conviction, stands before Christ, who remains silent, his gaze encompassing but not judging. The silence of Christ is itself a powerful presence, a testament to the enduring power of his original message, even in the face of its perceived failure. The Inquisitor, however, interprets this silence as an admission of error, a tacit acknowledgment of the Inquisitor's superior understanding of humanity's needs. He begins his impassioned, devastating indictment.

The core of the Grand Inquisitor's argument, and indeed the entire parable, rests on his refutation of Christ's fundamental gift: freedom. He contends that Christ's emphasis on spiritual liberty, on the free will to choose good over evil, to believe or disbelieve, has been a catastrophic error. This freedom, he argues, has not elevated humanity but has instead plunged it into an abyss of suffering, doubt, and sin. The Inquisitor paints a grim panorama of human history, a testament to humanity's alleged incapacity to bear the burden of such radical autonomy. He enumerates the immense suffering, the wars, the persecutions, the internal torments that have arisen precisely because humanity was given the terrifying freedom to choose.

The Inquisitor positions himself as the true shepherd, the one who has learned from humanity's failures. He claims that Christ, in his divine innocence, failed to understand the fundamental weakness of human beings. "Thou didst not come down from the cross," he charges, "when they cried to Thee, to convince them, to do one of those miracles, and thereby to satisfy the proud and impatient need of man for a miracle. Thou didst not descend, for the same reason that Thou wouldst not convert those stony wildernesses into bread. Thou didst not want to subdue man with the miracle, and thou didst want to go by faith alone." This accusation is central: Christ's refusal to perform easily verifiable miracles, to offer tangible proof and immediate satisfaction, was a fundamental misjudgment of human psychology.

The Inquisitor elaborates on this perceived weakness, drawing a stark contrast between Christ's spiritual idealism and the base, earthly needs that truly govern humanity. He asserts that humanity craves certainty, not the agonizing burden of choice. They desire "bread," the material sustenance and security that alleviates immediate suffering, over the elusive promise of spiritual freedom. He implies that Christ's message, while noble in intent, was fundamentally impractical and ultimately cruel, as it placed an unbearable responsibility upon inherently flawed creatures. The Inquisitor presents himself as the savior who offers humanity a release from this torment, a benevolent authority who will take the reins of freedom, thereby ensuring peace and happiness.

This crucial point – the trade of freedom for security and happiness – is the linchpin of the Inquisitor's blueprint. He doesn't seek to suppress humanity out of malice, but out of a profound, albeit twisted, sense of paternalistic love and a desire for universal order. He believes that by removing the agonizing burden of free will, by guiding humanity's choices and dictating its beliefs, he can create a stable, harmonious society, free from the chaos and suffering that Christ's radical gift has unleashed. The Inquisitor's vision is one of collective contentment achieved through submission, a world where individual liberty is sacrificed for the greater good of a unified, peaceful existence.

The Grand Inquisitor's dialogue with Christ is not merely a historical or theological critique; it is a prescient foreshadowing of the Faustian bargains that societies would repeatedly strike throughout history, and, as this book argues, are now poised to make again in the age of artificial intelligence. His words resonate with a chilling familiarity because they tap into fundamental human desires and anxieties that transcend time. The longing for certainty, the aversion to suffering, the susceptibility to authority – these are the levers the Inquisitor pulls, and they are the same levers that modern technological systems, with their promises of seamless solutions and optimized experiences, are expertly designed to engage.

The Inquisitor's condemnation of Christ's refusal to offer a miracle is particularly significant. He argues that humanity, faced with a choice between a divine mystery and a tangible, earthly solution, will invariably choose the latter. This is not merely about sustenance; it is about the irresistible allure of the tangible, the verifiable, the immediately satisfying. Christ offered a path of faith, of wrestling with doubt, of personal spiritual growth. The Inquisitor, by contrast, offers a path of certainty, of obedience, of a pre-packaged happiness that requires no strenuous effort or profound introspection. This distinction is crucial in understanding why humanity, according to the Inquisitor, would ultimately reject the divine gift of freedom for the comforting embrace of absolute authority.

The Seville setting itself is not arbitrary. It is a city under the shadow of the Inquisition, a place where the pursuit of spiritual purity has led to widespread fear and repression. This environment underscores the Inquisitor's belief that control, even if achieved through harsh means, is necessary to maintain order and prevent humanity from succumbing to its baser instincts. Christ's quiet miracles, acts of compassion and healing performed amidst this oppressive atmosphere, stand in stark contrast to the Inquisitor's grand pronouncements and the instruments of his power. Yet, the Inquisitor views these miracles not as signs of divine love, but as dangerous provocations, acts that further emphasize humanity's inability to cope with the freedom they inspire.

The Inquisitor's encounter with Christ is a dramatic articulation of a central tension: the nature of true happiness. Is happiness found in the arduous, often painful, pursuit of freedom, self-determination, and moral growth, or is it achieved through the relinquishment of these burdens in favor of comfort, security, and obedience? The Inquisitor unequivocally champions the latter, arguing that Christ's vision, while sublime, is unattainable and ultimately leads to misery. He posits that true happiness lies in submission, in the collective fulfillment of earthly needs, and in the elimination of doubt and individual striving. This, for him, is the ultimate act of love – to save humanity from itself, even if it means denying them the very essence of what it means to be human.

Therefore, the Grand Inquisitor's confrontation with Christ in Seville is not just a scene from a novel; it is a philosophical crucible. It is where the enduring debate about freedom versus security, autonomy versus authority, and spiritual aspiration versus material satisfaction is laid bare. The Inquisitor's arguments, born from a deep-seated cynicism about human nature and a pragmatic, albeit ruthless, understanding of governance, set the stage for his alternative blueprint for humanity. He is not simply a villain; he is a complex figure who believes he is acting for the ultimate good of mankind, a conviction that makes his critique of Christ all the more potent and, in the context of our modern technological age, all the more relevant. His encounter with Christ is the foundation upon which his entire vision of controlled, "happy" humanity is built, a vision that poses a direct challenge to the very core of Christ's message of liberating love.

The Inquisitor, his voice a low rumble that seemed to vibrate with the accumulated weariness of centuries, leaned closer, his eyes fixed on Christ's serene, unanswering gaze. "You offered them freedom," he continued, the accusation hanging heavy in the air, "and in their misguided gratitude, they embraced it. But what has this freedom wrought? Look around you, even in this enlightened age. See the endless cycles of suffering, the gnawing anxieties, the desperate search for meaning that so often ends in despair. This is not the divine liberty you envisioned; it is a gilded cage of their own making, where the bars are forged from doubt and the floor is paved with the ashes of their broken spirits."

He gestured, not towards the world outside the austere cell, but inwards, towards the labyrinthine corridors of the human heart. "You gave them the terrifying power to choose, to ascend to the heavens through their own will, or to plunge into the abyss. And what did they choose, for the most part? They chose the abyss. They faltered, they stumbled, they fell. They craved not the arduous ascent of virtue, but the comforting descent into vice, or at best, the placid stasis of indifference. For the vast majority, the burden of your freedom was simply too great. It was a weight they could not bear, a responsibility that crushed their very souls."

The Inquisitor's narrative painted a stark tableau of human fallibility. He spoke of the inherent weakness in the human constitution, a fundamental flaw that made the unfettered exercise of free will a recipe for disaster. "Consider the common man," he implored, his tone shifting to one of almost paternalistic pity. "He is not a philosopher; he is not a saint. He is a creature of instinct, of desire, of immediate need. He is easily swayed by passion, by fear, by the whisperings of temptation. To place upon his shoulders the responsibility of discerning the divine will, of choosing the narrow path of righteousness amidst the cacophony of worldly distractions, is not an act of love, but an act of profound cruelty. It is to condemn him to a perpetual state of anxious striving, to a Sisyphean task of moral self-perfection that he is, by his very nature, ill-equipped to accomplish."

He elaborated on the concept of sin, not as a deliberate act of rebellion against divine law, but as an inevitable consequence of human frailty when confronted with the bewildering expanse of choice. "When you gave them the choice between good and evil, you did not, as you perhaps intended, empower them. You terrified them. The sheer magnitude of the decision, the eternal consequences hanging in the balance, paralyzed them. And in their paralysis, they sought refuge. Some, in their desperation, embraced the easier path, the path of transgression, where the immediate gratification offered a fleeting respite from the gnawing terror of their own freedom. Others, unable to reconcile the demands of your ideal with the realities of their existence, simply succumbed to despair, their faith eroded by the relentless pressure of choice. They became hollowed-out shells, adrift in a sea of doubt, longing for a hand to guide them, for a voice to tell them which way to turn."

The Inquisitor viewed Christ's original mandate as a noble but ultimately impractical ideal, a vision that failed to account for the gritty, often ignoble, realities of human existence. "You offered them the ultimate freedom – the freedom to believe, to love, to sacrifice. But what they truly craved, what they desperately needed, was certainty. They yearned for a clear path, for unambiguous directives, for the comforting assurance that they were on the right road. Your silence, your enigmatic parables, your refusal to provide definitive answers – these were not signs of divine wisdom to them; they were sources of profound confusion and unbearable anxiety. They looked at the vast, uncharted territory of their own souls and recoiled in fear, not in exhilaration."

He paused, allowing the weight of his words to settle. "And so, they turned to others. They sought solace in the pronouncements of men who claimed to know the path, who offered the illusion of certainty, who dared to simplify the complex system of divine will into easily digestible dogmas. They craved not the liberty to explore the divine, but the liberation *from* the necessity of exploration. They surrendered their freedom, not out of malice, but out of an overwhelming desire for peace, for an end to the internal torment that your gift of freedom had imposed upon them."

This yearning for external validation and structure was, in the Inquisitor's view, not a betrayal of Christ's message, but a natural and predictable outcome of humanity's inherent limitations. "You speak of the soul," he scoffed gently, "and indeed, the soul is a fragile thing. It is easily bruised, easily broken. It requires careful tending, a guiding hand, a firm, unwavering authority to protect it from its own destructive impulses. Your vision, noble as it may be, is one for angels, not for men. Men are not angels; they are creatures of the earth, bound by the needs of the flesh and the limitations of the mind. They require bread for their bodies and clear, simple answers for their souls. They cannot, and will not, sustain themselves on the ethereal sustenance of abstract freedom."

The Inquisitor saw his own role, and the role of the Church he represented, as that of a benevolent guardian, a necessary intermediary between the unmanageable complexities of divine truth and the fragile capacities of the human mind. "We have learned from your error," he stated, his voice gaining a steely resolve. "We have seen the consequences of placing too much trust in man's ability to navigate the treacherous waters of freedom. We have witnessed the chaos, the division, the endless suffering that has ensued. And we have concluded that the greatest act of love, the most profound service we can render to humanity, is to relieve them of this unbearable burden. We will provide them with certainty. We will dictate their path. We will shield them from the corrosive effects of doubt and the paralyzing fear of making the wrong choice."

He continued, elaborating on the practical implications of this divinely sanctioned paternalism. "We will give them a clear creed, a set of rules that are simple, unambiguous, and universally applicable. We will offer them the comforting embrace of communal worship, where individual anxieties are subsumed into the collective expression of faith. We will guide their choices, from the mundane to the profound, ensuring that they are always aligned with the will of God – as we, in our wisdom, have come to understand it. In short, we will give them back the peace that your radical gift of freedom has stolen from them."

The Inquisitor argued that this exchange, this relinquishing of freedom for the sake of peace and certainty, was not a Faustian bargain that humanity entered into reluctantly, but a choice they actively embraced, even if unconsciously. "They do not rebel against our authority," he asserted, a hint of triumph in his voice. "They do not clamor for the return of your dangerous liberty. On the contrary, they flock to us. They find solace in our doctrines, comfort in our pronouncements, and a profound sense of security in knowing that their lives are being directed by a power greater than themselves. They may not understand it in theological terms, but they understand it in their hearts. They prefer the well-trodden path, even if it is a path we have laid out for them, to the terrifying uncertainty of an untrodden wilderness."

This was the core of his indictment: Christ's gift, while divinely pure in intent, was fundamentally incompatible with the practical realities of human nature. Humanity, according to the Inquisitor, was not ready for such a radical act of trust. They were children, prone to wandering, easily lost, and in constant need of a guiding hand. "You expected them to ascend to the heavens on the wings of their own free will," he concluded, his voice softening with a simulated empathy. "We, on the other hand, have learned that it is often more humane to carry them, even if it means restraining their flight. We have taken upon ourselves the awesome responsibility that you, in your infinite love, were unwilling to delegate. We have chosen to save them from themselves, and in doing so, we have become their true saviors. For what is more important: the illusion of freedom, or the tangible reality of happiness and peace, even if that peace is achieved through submission?"

The Inquisitor's critique resonated with a chilling pragmatism, a cynical understanding of human desires that prioritized immediate comfort and security over the arduous, often painful, pursuit of autonomy. He saw Christ's emphasis on free will not as a divine empowerment, but as an abdication of responsibility, a flawed and ultimately damaging act of cosmic negligence. The burden of choice, he argued, was a burden too heavy for the vast majority of humanity to bear, a burden that led not to spiritual elevation, but to spiritual ruin. His blueprint, therefore, was not an act of oppression, but a necessary, even loving, corrective to a divine experiment that, in his view, had demonstrably failed. He had taken the reins of freedom, not to crush it, but to control it, to channel it, to ultimately extinguish the agonizing sparks of doubt and uncertainty that plagued the human soul, thereby offering a world of predictable, ordered contentment.

The Grand Inquisitor, having laid bare the perceived folly of spiritual liberty, pivoted to the pragmatic heart of his alternative. The soaring aspirations of the soul, he argued, were ultimately a distraction, even a cruelty, when confronted with the more insistent demands of the flesh. Humanity, in its fundamental nature, was not equipped for the ethereal sustenance of pure faith. What it truly craved, what it desperately needed to survive and to find a semblance of contentment, was something far more tangible: earthly bread. This was the cornerstone of his blueprint for control, a promise so universally appealing that it could, and would, eclipse any lingering desire for the perilous freedom Christ had offered.

"You offered them a divine challenge," the Inquisitor intoned, his voice resonating with a weary but confident understanding of human nature, "a path of spiritual ascent paved with arduous choices and the ever-present specter of failure. But observe the world, Christ. Observe the common man. His first and most urgent concerns are not with the intricacies of divine law or the subtle nuances of theological truth. They are with the gnawing emptiness in his stomach, the chill that seeps into his bones, the gnawing fear of tomorrow's uncertainty. You offered him bread from heaven, a metaphorical nourishment that promised eternal life. But the miracle you performed, feeding the thousands with a few loaves, was a fleeting glimpse of a deeper, more pressing need that you ultimately failed to satisfy on a lasting scale."

He elaborated on the visceral reality of human existence, a reality that, for the Inquisitor, was the primary driver of human behavior. "Hunger is a potent master, Christ. It strips away philosophical pretenses, it reduces complex desires to the singular, primal urge for sustenance. When a man is starving, he does not contemplate the nature of free will; he contemplates the location of the next meal. When his children cry out in hunger, his prayers are not for divine wisdom, but for a miracle of loaves and fishes, a tangible solution to immediate suffering. You understood this, of course, in your moment of compassion. But you framed it as a temptation, a diversion from the true path. We, however, understand it as the foundation of order."

The Inquisitor's argument rested on a profound understanding of basic human needs and the power they wield over the human psyche. He posited that the promise of consistent, reliable material security was a far more potent force in securing obedience and contentment than any abstract spiritual ideal. "We offer them bread," he stated, his gaze unwavering. "Abundant, unfailing bread. We have learned the art of its procurement and distribution. We have built systems, hierarchies, and mechanisms that ensure no man, woman, or child under our care will ever know the pangs of genuine hunger or the gnawing anxiety of lacking shelter. We have turned the miracle into a science, a predictable, controllable outcome that we dispense with absolute authority."

This was not merely a promise of sustenance; it was a promise of predictable happiness, of a life free from the anxieties that plagued those who dared to walk the path of freedom. The Inquisitor understood that the desire for security extended beyond mere physical needs. It encompassed a yearning for a stable, ordered existence, a life where the unpredictable turns of fate were mitigated, and where a sense of safety and belonging was guaranteed. "We provide not just bread," he continued, "but also the overarching framework of peace. We quell the internal storms of doubt by offering clear doctrines and unwavering guidance. We eliminate the external threats by consolidating power and eliminating dissent. We create a world where the rough edges of existence are smoothed away, where the individual is shielded from the harsh realities of a world left to its own chaotic devices. We offer a life of comfortable, predictable contentment, a life where the constant struggle for survival and self-definition is replaced by a serene, albeit passive, existence."

The appeal of this promise, the Inquisitor maintained, lay in its direct, unmediated satisfaction of fundamental human desires. It was a solution that bypassed the complexities of morality, the arduous labor of self-improvement, and the existential dread of confronting one's own finitude. "Consider the allure," he urged, painting a vivid picture. "A world where your daily needs are met, where your safety is assured, where your role in society is clearly defined. A world where the specter of famine, of war, of homelessness is banished. A world where your spiritual anxieties are soothed by the pronouncements of those who claim to hold the keys to divine truth, thus freeing you from the burden of seeking it yourself. This is not a world of meager rations and uncertain hope, but a world of guaranteed provisions and unwavering certainty. This is the earthly paradise we offer, a tangible, breathable reality that appeals to the very core of man's being."

The Inquisitor saw this material provision as the ultimate act of benevolent authority. It was a demonstration of power not for its own sake, but for the sake of alleviating human suffering. "Your miracles were signs," he declared, a subtle condescension in his tone. "Ours are systems. Your loaves were fleeting. Our granaries are ever-full. You tempted men with the promise of a spiritual kingdom. We deliver a terrestrial one, albeit one under our careful stewardship. And the price for this abundant life? A simple, reasonable one: your absolute obedience. Your unquestioning faith in our pronouncements. Your willingness to surrender the chaotic burden of choice for the serene assurance of our guidance."

He recognized that this exchange, this trade of spiritual liberty for material security, might appear ignoble to one who valued freedom above all else. However, he framed it as a necessary, even compassionate, intervention. "Is it not a greater act of love," he challenged, "to ensure that every child has a full belly and a warm bed, than to offer them the abstract possibility of spiritual enlightenment while they languish in squalor and despair? We choose the tangible over the theoretical. We choose the immediate well-being of the masses over the precarious spiritual aspirations of a chosen few. We feed the body so that the soul, if it so chooses, may find a more stable place to rest, free from the constant distractions of earthly want."

The Inquisitor's blueprint was thus a carefully constructed edifice, built upon the solid bedrock of human need. He understood that while the human spirit might occasionally yearn for the sublime, the immediate and insistent demands of the material world were far more powerful in shaping daily life and dictating behavior. By positioning himself and his authority as the ultimate providers of "earthly bread," he created an unassailable foundation for his power. The promise was not a bribe, but a pact, a reciprocal agreement where absolute submission was exchanged for the cessation of suffering and the guarantee of a predictable, secure existence.

This strategy, the Inquisitor believed, was inherently more effective than Christ's own approach. Christ had offered a spiritual bread, a manna from heaven that required faith, perseverance, and a willingness to embrace uncertainty. The Inquisitor, conversely, offered bread from earthly stores, managed and distributed with human ingenuity and absolute control. "You offered a path that led to the heavens, but the journey was fraught with peril," he reiterated. "We offer a path that leads to a comfortable, secure existence here on earth, a path so well-trodden and clearly marked that none can stray. And the reason for this clarity? Because we have removed the option of straying. We have, in essence, brought heaven to earth, not through divine intervention, but through human administration, and with it, we have brought peace."

He emphasized the psychological impact of this promise. It was not simply about satisfying hunger; it was about assuaging a deeper anxiety, a fundamental human fear of the unknown. By guaranteeing material security, the Inquisitor removed a significant source of existential dread. This, in turn, made individuals more receptive to authority, more willing to accept directives, and less inclined to question the established order. "When a man is secure in his physical needs," he explained, "his mind is free to focus on other matters. And what matters more than the pronouncements of those who hold the keys to his continued well-being? We become the arbiters of his reality, the guarantors of his happiness, and in return, he willingly surrenders the illusion of freedom that has brought so much pain and confusion."

The Inquisitor's vision was thus a deeply pragmatic one, grounded in a stark assessment of human limitations and desires. He recognized that for the vast majority, the promise of a life free from want and fear was far more compelling than the abstract ideal of spiritual autonomy. He had, in effect, democratized a form of spiritual control by appealing to the most basic and universal of human needs. His blueprint was not an attempt to crush the human spirit, but to domesticate it, to channel its energies into a predictable, manageable flow, ensuring that the ultimate focus remained on earthly sustenance and the security it provided. This was the true "earthly bread" he offered – not merely food, but the promise of a life where the gnawing anxieties of want and uncertainty were permanently banished, replaced by the comforting, albeit passive, certainty of provision. And in this grand transaction, he found the ultimate leverage, the most potent instrument of control, for what price was too high to pay for the cessation of all earthly suffering?

The Grand Inquisitor's blueprint for human governance, as presented to Christ, was not merely about providing earthly sustenance. It was a sophisticated mechanism designed to reshape the very essence of human aspiration and belief, ensuring stability and control through a carefully orchestrated reliance on three fundamental pillars: miracle, mystery, and authority. These were not simply abstract concepts; they were potent psychological tools, wielded with the precision of an experienced architect of souls, to dismantle the edifice of spiritual liberty and erect in its place an unshakeable structure of obedience. The Inquisitor understood that true power lay not in compelling action through fear, but in shaping desire and belief to such an extent that compliance became not an imposition, but an innate, almost unconscious, inclination.

The first of these pillars, 'miracle,' was not about genuine divine intervention, but about the

*perception* of it, the carefully managed production of wonder that would serve as irrefutable evidence of a power beyond human comprehension and control. Christ's miracles, the Inquisitor argued, had been too individual, too demanding of personal faith and discernment. They offered a glimpse of the divine but burdened the recipient with the responsibility of understanding and replicating that divine will. The Inquisitor's approach was to institutionalize miracle, to make it the exclusive province of his own authority. He envisioned a continuous, low-level hum of the miraculous, not as a challenge to the natural order, but as a perpetual reaffirmation of the established order's divine mandate. This would manifest not as loaves multiplying or the dead rising, but as the predictable, awe-inspiring maintenance of a prosperous, ordered society. Imagine, he might have mused, the awe inspired by the seamless functioning of their vast agricultural systems, the unfailing supply of goods, the absence of plague and widespread disease – all presented not as the triumph of human ingenuity, but as the direct, ongoing blessing of the powers that be. This constant, pervasive "miracle" would serve to awe the populace, to imbue their leaders with an aura of godlike competence, thereby preempting any need for critical examination of their governance. It was about generating a perpetual state of wonder, not the liberating wonder that calls one to higher spiritual planes, but a passive, contented wonder that reinforces the status quo. This manufactured awe would render the populace docile, impressed by a power they could not replicate or comprehend, and thus inherently predisposed to accept the pronouncements of those who controlled this seemingly inexhaustible source of good fortune. The miracle, in this context, became a silencer of questions, a potent anesthetic for intellectual curiosity. It was the grand illusion, perpetually renewed, that the existing order was not merely functional, but divinely ordained and sustained, a tangible manifestation of celestial favor bestowed upon humanity, mediated solely through the Inquisitor's hands.

Complementing the awe of miracle was the deep, ingrained human need for 'mystery.' The Inquisitor saw Christ's teachings as too direct, too exposed. The Sermon on the Mount, the parables – these were invitations to engagement, to personal interpretation, to the arduous work of internalizing and living out divine truth. This, he argued, was the source of all human suffering and rebellion. The common man, burdened by the complexities of life, did not seek intellectual rigor; he craved certainty, clear pronouncements, and a comforting sense of the unknowable that absolved him of the need to grapple with difficult truths. The Inquisitor's solution was to cultivate an environment where mystery became a virtue, where the obscure was elevated to the sacred, and where unquestioning acceptance of dogma replaced the perilous journey of free inquiry. The doctrines of the Church, under his stewardship, would become less about theological exploration and more about impenetrable pronouncements, deliberately veiled in language and concept that defied easy comprehension. This was not an oversight, but a strategy. The more opaque the doctrine, the more the believer would rely on the authoritative interpreters – the priests, the bishops, and ultimately, the Grand Inquisitor himself – to explain its meaning. This created a dependency, a psychological tether that bound the individual to the institution. The mystery of the divine would be mirrored in the mystery of the Church's pronouncements, creating a closed loop of reliance. Instead of seeking to understand the divine directly, individuals would be encouraged to accept the

*Church's understanding* of the divine. This fostered a state of intellectual passivity, where the questions themselves were suppressed, and the answers, however elusive, were accepted as gospel. The Inquisitor understood that a certain level of mystery was inherently appealing, offering a sense of profound depth and spiritual significance. But his would be a managed mystery, a carefully curated enigma designed not to inspire seekers, but to ensnare believers. It was about creating a fog of unknowability, within which the pronouncements of the Church would appear as divine beacons, their very obscurity a testament to their otherworldly origin. This embraced the idea that true faith lay not in intellectual ascent but in the surrender of intellect to an authority that claimed privileged access to divine secrets. The mystery thus served to reinforce the miracles, acting as the explanation for their inexplicable nature and, in turn, bolstering the authority that dispensed both.

The third, and arguably most crucial, pillar of the Inquisitor's design was absolute 'authority.' This was not merely political or temporal power; it was the claim to an unassailable, divinely sanctioned right to rule, a right that superseded all other considerations, including individual conscience and freedom. Christ's emphasis on inner conviction and personal moral choice was, in the Inquisitor's view, a fatal flaw. It placed the burden of salvation, and by extension, the responsibility for societal order, onto the shoulders of individuals who were, by their very nature, fallible and weak. The Inquisitor's authority, conversely, would be absolute, comprehensive, and non-negotiable. It would be the ultimate arbiter of truth, morality, and daily life. This authority would be built upon the twin foundations of miracle and mystery, acting as the conduit through which these phenomena were understood and applied. The Inquisitor would not simply rule; he would *be* the embodiment of the divinely sanctioned order. His pronouncements would carry the weight of divine law, his judgments the finality of cosmic decree. This was a far cry from the servant leadership Christ embodied. The Inquisitor's authority was designed to elicit not love or devotion, but unwavering obedience and passive acceptance. It would be an authority that did not seek to persuade, but to command. The very structure of society would be reconfigured to reflect and reinforce this absolute authority. Laws would be simple and strictly enforced, dissent would be non-existent, and every aspect of human life, from daily routines to spiritual contemplation, would be managed and directed from a singular, unchallengeable source. This authority would be presented as a benevolent necessity, a bulwark against the chaos and suffering that inevitably arose when individuals were left to their own devices. It was the ultimate paternalism, where the provider of earthly bread, the dispenser of miracles, and the interpreter of mysteries, held absolute dominion over his flock, not out of tyranny, but out of a calculated, albeit twisted, sense of responsibility for their well-being. The authority, in essence, became the anchor for both miracle and mystery. It was the ultimate explanation for why miracles occurred and why mysteries remained unsolved, all pointing back to the indispensable role of the ruling power in maintaining this divinely orchestrated existence. This triumvirate – miracle creating awe, mystery fostering dependence, and authority consolidating control – formed the bedrock of the Inquisitor's grand design, a blueprint for a world where humanity, freed from the burdensome weight of liberty, could finally find peace in unthinking, unresisting submission.

The Grand Inquisitor, in his chillingly rational dissection of Christ's mission, lays bare a vision for humanity that is both profoundly disturbing and, in its own twisted logic, undeniably coherent. His ultimate aim is the eradication of suffering, not by elevating humanity to meet divine challenges, but by stripping away the very capacity for such challenges. He envisions a world where the agonizing burden of freedom – the freedom to choose, to err, to doubt, to strive, and thus to potentially fail and suffer – is irrevocably removed. This is not a world of bleak despair, as one might initially assume, but a world designed for a specific, engineered form of contentment: the contentment of the sheep in the fold, cared for, guided, and protected from the harsh realities of the wider, untamed wilderness. For the Inquisitor, the inherent flaw in humanity lies not in its capacity for evil, but in its capacity for freedom, a gift that has proven to be a curse, leading only to chaos, division, and endless torment.

This idealized state, in the Inquisitor's estimation, is achieved through a complete abdication of individual agency. Humanity, he argues, is fundamentally incapable of bearing the weight of true liberty. The profound existential anxieties that plague the human condition, the gnawing uncertainty about meaning and purpose, the terror of making wrong choices with eternal consequences – these are not merely unfortunate side effects of freedom; they are its very essence, and the source of all human misery. The Inquisitor's solution is radical: to eliminate the possibility of such suffering by eliminating the root cause. He seeks to create a world where life is predictable, managed, and utterly devoid of the existential vertigo that freedom inevitably induces. In this world, every need is anticipated, every desire is met (or at least, managed to prevent dissatisfaction), and every potential source of conflict or distress is preemptively neutralized. It is a world where the individual is relieved of the onerous responsibility of self-determination, where their existence is buffered by an all-encompassing, benevolent (or at least, seemingly benevolent) authority.

Consider the concept of happiness, as understood by the Inquisitor. It is not the ebullient, hard-won joy that arises from overcoming obstacles, from forging one's own path, or from achieving profound personal growth. Instead, it is a placid, unvarying state of satisfaction, akin to that of a well-fed animal or a contented child. This is a happiness that requires no effort, no sacrifice, and no risk. It is a passive reception of comfort and security, a perpetual state of being looked after. The Inquisitor's genius, in his own estimation, lies in recognizing that true happiness for the masses is not found in the lofty ideals of spiritual liberty, but in the simple, tangible realities of earthly well-being, guaranteed and dispensed by an unwavering hand. He sees Christ's offer of freedom as a dangerous flirtation with the impossible, a promise that humanity is not equipped to fulfill. The Inquisitor, therefore, steps in as the pragmatist, the realist who understands the true, limited nature of human capacity. He offers a different kind of salvation: salvation from the agonizing burden of choice, salvation from the terror of the unknown, salvation from the loneliness of individual responsibility.

The Inquisitor's vision, therefore, is one of a meticulously orchestrated existence. He paints a picture of a society where every facet of life is carefully controlled to prevent any ripple of unease. The arts, for instance, would not be allowed to provoke or question. They would serve a purely decorative or didactic purpose, reinforcing the established order and celebrating the benefits of the Inquisitor's rule. Scientific inquiry, too, would be strictly circumscribed, its potential to uncover unsettling truths or challenge established doctrines carefully managed. Innovation would be discouraged unless it directly served the needs of the state and contributed to the smooth functioning of society. Education would be reduced to catechism, focused on instilling obedience and gratitude, rather than critical thinking or intellectual curiosity. The very fabric of human interaction would be reshaped to eliminate friction. Disagreements would be swiftly and decisively settled by the authorities, personal rivalries preempted, and even romantic entanglements potentially managed to ensure societal harmony. In this meticulously constructed world, the concept of dissent would become not just undesirable, but unthinkable, rendered obsolete by the sheer pervasiveness of control and the manufactured contentment of the populace.

The Inquisitor understands that this level of control requires a profound psychological manipulation, a complete reorientation of human desires and aspirations. He has effectively diagnosed humanity as a species ill-suited for the arduous demands of genuine freedom. Instead of enabling individuals to rise to the challenge, he proposes to lower the bar, to create an environment where they can thrive without ever having to confront their own limitations or the daunting expanse of their own potential. This is the ultimate act of paternalism, a form of governance that sees humanity not as capable of self-mastery, but as a child perpetually in need of guidance and protection, even if that protection comes at the cost of its very essence. The Inquisitor does not hate humanity; in his own perverse way, he loves it, but he loves it as a gardener loves a delicate plant that cannot withstand the harshness of the open field. He believes that by shielding it, by coddling it, by controlling every aspect of its environment, he is in fact saving it from a far worse fate.

The suffering that Christ sought to alleviate through spiritual awakening and moral striving is, for the Inquisitor, an inevitable consequence of the very freedom Christ championed. The Inquisitor's blueprint, therefore, is a direct refutation of Christ's offering. While Christ offered the freedom to ascend, to wrestle with the divine and discover one's own spiritual potential, the Inquisitor offers the freedom

*from* the struggle, the comfort of absolute reliance. He sees the burdens of conscience, the pangs of guilt, the loneliness of moral decision-making as inherent to the human condition when left to its own devices. His proposed world bypasses these by establishing an external, infallible arbiter for all matters of morality and conduct. There is no need for individual conscience when a higher authority dictates every permissible thought and action. This eliminates the possibility of sin, not by fostering virtue, but by removing the capacity to transgress. It's a world where humanity is, in a sense, permanently infantilized, kept in a state of blissful ignorance and dependency, shielded from the profound, often painful, realities of selfhood and moral agency.

The Inquisitor's ultimate vision, then, is a perfected form of earthly paradise, one stripped of the divine spark that makes humanity restless and, consequently, prone to suffering. It is a world where the bread is always plentiful, the miracles are constant but routine, and the mysteries are never solved, leaving the populace in a state of perpetual, unquestioning awe and submission. He believes that in this state, humanity will finally achieve a semblance of peace, a predictable and enduring happiness that is forever beyond its reach in the wild, untamed landscape of true freedom. This, for the Inquisitor, is the ultimate act of love, the ultimate service to humankind: to liberate them from the terrifying, agonizing responsibility of being truly human. It is a vision that prioritizes peace and stability above all else, even if that peace is the silent, unthinking peace of the tomb, and that stability is the rigid stillness of a perfectly controlled exhibit. He is not interested in saving souls for the heavens; he is interested in perfecting the human condition for the earth, a perfection defined by the absence of anguish, achieved through the sacrifice of liberty.

# Chapter 3: The First Amendment Under Siege: Speech, Belief, and Assembly in the Digital Age

In the sprawling digital landscape, where information flows with unprecedented speed and volume, the very mechanisms designed to facilitate connection and discourse are increasingly becoming instruments of subtle, yet profound, control. The architecture of our online lives, governed by sophisticated algorithms, now plays an outsized role in shaping what we see, what we hear, and ultimately, what we are permitted to say. This algorithmic curation, while often presented as a neutral and efficient means of organizing information, carries with it a potent capacity to chill free speech, creating an environment where dissenting or unconventional voices are increasingly marginalized, and where the very possibility of robust public debate is imperiled.

At the heart of this phenomenon lies the opaque nature of the algorithms themselves. These complex sets of rules, employed by social media platforms, search engines, and content aggregators, are designed to personalize user experiences by predicting and delivering content deemed most relevant or engaging. While this personalization can enhance user satisfaction, it also creates echo chambers and filter bubbles, reinforcing existing beliefs and limiting exposure to diverse perspectives. The consequence is a narrowing of the public sphere, where individuals are less likely to encounter viewpoints that challenge their own, and where the common ground necessary for productive dialogue erodes. When algorithms prioritize content that aligns with a user's perceived interests or past behaviors, they inadvertently create a digital reality that is tailored to their existing worldview, a phenomenon that can be both comforting and deeply isolating. This personalized information diet, curated by lines of code, can inadvertently foster a sense of intellectual homogeneity, making it harder for novel or contrarian ideas to gain traction.

Furthermore, the economic imperatives driving these platforms often incentivize the amplification of sensational, emotionally charged, or polarizing content. Algorithms designed to maximize engagement – measured in likes, shares, and comments – tend to favor material that provokes strong reactions, regardless of its accuracy or its contribution to meaningful discourse. This creates a perverse incentive structure where misinformation, outrage, and hyperbole can outcompete reasoned argument and nuanced discussion. The result is a digital public square that is often dominated by the loudest, most extreme voices, drowning out the quieter, more considered contributions that are essential for a healthy democracy. This algorithmic amplification of outrage can also contribute to a climate of fear, where individuals are hesitant to express unpopular opinions for fear of becoming targets of online mob justice, a phenomenon that is often amplified and accelerated by the very platforms they use.

Beyond the direct curation of content, platforms employ a range of moderation policies and enforcement mechanisms that can have a chilling effect on speech. Content moderation, necessary to combat hate speech, incitement to violence, and other harmful content, is an inherently complex and subjective undertaking. The sheer volume of user-generated content makes comprehensive human review impossible, leading to an increased reliance on automated systems. These AI-driven moderation tools, while increasingly sophisticated, are not infallible. They can misinterpret context, struggle with satire or irony, and often err on the side of caution, leading to the unwarranted removal of legitimate speech. The lack of transparency in these moderation processes exacerbates the problem. When users have their content removed or their accounts suspended, they often receive little to no explanation, leaving them in a state of confusion and uncertainty about the boundaries of permissible speech. This opacity breeds a sense of powerlessness and can lead to self-censorship, as individuals become afraid to test the limits of what the algorithms or human moderators might deem unacceptable.

A particularly insidious form of algorithmic control is "shadow banning," a practice where a user's content is de-emphasized or made invisible to others without their explicit knowledge. This can manifest in various ways, such as drastically reduced reach, exclusion from search results, or the suppression of posts from appearing in followers' feeds. Unlike overt bans, shadow banning operates in the digital shadows, leaving the targeted user in a state of perpetual confusion and frustration. They may continue to post, unaware that their voice has been effectively silenced, their audience dwindling without any clear explanation. This practice, often implemented without due process or transparent appeal mechanisms, is a powerful tool for silencing dissenting or inconvenient voices. It allows platforms to subtly control the flow of information and shape public discourse without overtly violating their stated commitment to free expression. The fear of being shadow banned, even if unconfirmed, can lead to a preemptive chilling effect, where individuals self-censor to avoid potential algorithmic repercussions.

The chilling effect extends beyond the direct suppression of content to a more pervasive form of self-censorship. Knowing that their online activity is constantly being monitored, analyzed, and categorized by algorithms, individuals may become increasingly hesitant to express opinions that could be perceived as controversial, unpopular, or even merely unconventional. The fear of algorithmic reprisal – whether it be de-platforming, shadow banning, or simply being relegated to the digital dustbin – can lead to a significant curtailment of free expression. This self-censorship is particularly concerning because it is often invisible. We cannot measure the speech that is never uttered, the ideas that are never shared, or the debates that never ignite because individuals have preemptively muted themselves. This "chilling effect" is perhaps the most profound and damaging consequence of algorithmic curation, as it erodes the very foundations of a vibrant public sphere by discouraging the free exchange of ideas that is so vital to a healthy democracy.

The algorithmic prioritization of certain narratives also plays a crucial role in shaping public discourse. When algorithms are designed to favor content that is deemed popular or trending, they can inadvertently elevate particular viewpoints, often at the expense of others. This can lead to a skewed perception of public opinion, where a vocal minority can appear to represent a broader consensus, simply because their content is being amplified. This is particularly problematic in the context of political discourse, where algorithms can be used to amplify partisan messaging, spread disinformation, and create a fragmented and polarized electorate. The careful calibration of what content is promoted and what is demoted can have a profound impact on electoral outcomes and the broader health of democratic institutions.

The problem is compounded by the lack of transparency surrounding the algorithms themselves. The proprietary nature of these complex systems means that their inner workings are largely unknown to the public, regulators, and even many of the platforms' own employees. This opacity makes it difficult to identify and address potential biases or unintended consequences. Without understanding how content is being prioritized or suppressed, it becomes nearly impossible to hold platforms accountable for their role in shaping public discourse. This lack of transparency creates a power imbalance, where the platforms wield immense influence over the flow of information with little public oversight.

Consider the potential for algorithmic bias. If the data used to train these algorithms reflects existing societal biases – whether racial, gender, or political – then the algorithms themselves will inevitably perpetuate and amplify those biases. For instance, an algorithm trained on historical data where certain groups were underrepresented or misrepresented might continue to de-prioritize their voices or stories, further marginalizing them in the digital public square. Similarly, algorithms designed to detect "extremism" could be inadvertently programmed to flag legitimate political dissent as dangerous, effectively silencing opposition to prevailing power structures. The very definition of "extremism" can be algorithmically determined, reflecting the values and priorities of those who design and deploy these systems, rather than an objective standard.

The impact of algorithmic curation on free speech is not merely theoretical; it has tangible consequences for individuals and society. Journalists may find their stories suppressed if they challenge prevailing narratives or upset powerful interests. Activists may see their organizing efforts undermined if their messages are algorithmically de-prioritized. Ordinary citizens may find their ability to engage in political discussions curtailed for fear of algorithmic repercussions. This creates a climate of fear and self-censorship, where individuals are less likely to speak out, to question, or to dissent. The digital public square, envisioned as a space for unfettered expression, increasingly resembles a carefully managed garden, where only certain flowers are permitted to bloom, and where the weeds of dissent are systematically uprooted.

The challenge lies in finding a balance between the legitimate need for platforms to manage their spaces and the fundamental right to free expression. While platforms are not state actors and are not directly bound by the First Amendment in the same way governments are, their immense power in shaping public discourse means that their content moderation policies and algorithmic practices have a profound impact on the exercise of free speech. The concentration of power in the hands of a few large technology companies, who act as gatekeepers of information for billions of people, raises significant questions about accountability, transparency, and the future of open discourse.

The debate around algorithmic curation and free speech is ongoing and multifaceted. It involves not only legal and philosophical considerations but also technical challenges and economic realities. As AI becomes increasingly sophisticated, and as platforms become even more integrated into the fabric of our lives, understanding and addressing the ways in which algorithms shape our speech and our society will become ever more critical. The risk is that without careful consideration and robust oversight, the very technologies designed to connect us could end up isolating us, silencing us, and ultimately, diminishing the vibrant, messy, and essential chorus of human voices that is the hallmark of a free society. The Grand Inquisitor's vision, so chillingly articulated by Dostoyevsky, finds an echo in the silent, invisible hand of the algorithm, shaping our world not through overt coercion, but through the subtle, yet irresistible, redirection of our attention and our expression, promising comfort and order at the cost of true liberty.

The digital age, with its promise of unfettered communication, has inadvertently birthed a new economic paradigm that fundamentally alters the nature of expression: surveillance capitalism. This model, as articulated by scholars like Shoshana Zuboff, posits that the primary objective of major technology platforms is not merely to provide services, but to extract vast quantities of personal data – our clicks, our searches, our interactions, and indeed, our very expressions – to predict and influence our future behavior. This data, meticulously collected and analyzed, becomes the raw material for a new form of wealth, one derived from the commodification of human experience itself. In this ecosystem, our words, our thoughts shared online, and our digital interactions are no longer solely instruments of personal connection or public discourse; they are transformed into predictable economic assets, commodities to be bought and sold in a burgeoning market of behavioral futures.

At the heart of this transformation lies the pervasive and sophisticated application of artificial intelligence. AI is not merely a tool for content moderation or algorithmic curation in this new economy; it is the engine driving the extraction, analysis, and exploitation of our digital selves. Machine learning algorithms, trained on colossal datasets of user behavior, become adept at identifying patterns, predicting inclinations, and ultimately, shaping our preferences and actions. Every piece of content we create, every opinion we voice, every interaction we engage in, provides fodder for these algorithms. They dissect our language, our emotional cues, and our social connections, constructing intricate profiles that extend far beyond our conscious understanding. This process effectively turns our expressions into data points, variables in a complex economic equation designed to maximize engagement, drive consumption, and optimize targeted advertising. The intimate act of sharing an idea, a feeling, or a piece of news is, in this context, simultaneously an act of economic production, generating value for platforms without the explicit or informed consent of the producer.

The implications for authentic expression are profound and, frankly, troubling. When the very act of speaking or writing online is underwritten by the knowledge that our words are being systematically harvested for commercial purposes, the nature of that expression inevitably shifts. Can genuine, spontaneous communication truly flourish when it is constantly being mined for its predictive power? The pressure to conform to algorithmic preferences, to produce content that is likely to be amplified and rewarded by the system, can lead to a subtle but pervasive form of self-censorship. Individuals may begin to curate their online personas not for the sake of authentic self-representation, but to appeal to the inscrutable logic of the algorithms, thereby optimizing their "performance" within the surveillance capitalist framework. This creates a feedback loop where the desire for visibility and engagement within the digital space incentivizes behaviors and expressions that align with the economic imperatives of the platforms, rather than with genuine personal conviction or intellectual curiosity.

Consider the evolution of content creation. Platforms that rely on advertising revenue, and thus on maximizing user attention, often favor content that is sensational, emotionally charged, or highly shareable. Algorithms are fine-tuned to identify and promote such content, not necessarily because it is truthful, informative, or representative of a broader consensus, but because it demonstrably captures and holds user attention. This creates a perverse incentive for creators. To gain traction, to be seen, to participate in the digital public sphere, creators may feel compelled to adopt a style that is designed to trigger algorithmic amplification, often at the expense of nuance, depth, or originality. The pursuit of clicks and shares can overshadow the pursuit of truth or the development of thoughtful discourse. Speech, in this context, becomes less about genuine communication and more about strategic performance, a calculated effort to navigate the economic currents of the digital marketplace.

The monetization of personal expression also raises critical questions about ownership and control. When our words and ideas are transformed into data assets, who truly owns them? The individuals who create them, or the platforms that collect and analyze them? Under current legal frameworks, the terms of service agreements that users implicitly accept often grant extensive rights to platforms to use and exploit user-generated content. This means that the very expressions that form the bedrock of our digital lives, our contributions to the collective online conversation, can be repurposed, repackaged, and sold without further compensation or even acknowledgment. This asymmetrical power dynamic is a defining feature of surveillance capitalism, where the vast majority of individuals generate the value, while a small number of corporations capture the lion's share of the profits.

Furthermore, the predictive power derived from commodified expression allows for increasingly sophisticated forms of behavioral manipulation. By understanding our desires, our fears, and our vulnerabilities through the analysis of our online communications, these platforms can craft targeted messages designed to influence our purchasing decisions, our political views, and even our fundamental beliefs. This is not simply advertising; it is a form of psychological engineering, leveraging intimate knowledge of our inner lives to steer our actions. The First Amendment, designed to protect the freedom to speak and to receive information, becomes increasingly vulnerable when the very channels through which we communicate are actively shaping what we see and how we think, all in service of a commercial imperative. The commodification of expression transforms our public discourse into a laboratory for behavioral experimentation, where the outcomes are not necessarily the betterment of society, but the maximization of corporate profit.

The pressure to perform for the algorithm extends to all forms of expression, from personal reflections to political commentary. The desire to be heard, to connect with others, is a fundamental human need, and in the digital age, the primary means of fulfilling this need is through platforms that operate on surveillance capitalist principles. This creates a trap: to participate meaningfully, one must submit to data extraction and algorithmic assessment; to resist, one risks being silenced or marginalized. The result is an environment where the economic logic of surveillance capitalism actively shapes the landscape of public discourse, favoring predictable, easily monetizable forms of expression over those that are more challenging, unconventional, or simply less profitable. The richness and diversity of human experience are flattened into a set of quantifiable data points, optimized for consumption and prediction.

The insidious nature of this commodification lies in its subtlety. It does not involve overt censorship in the traditional sense, but rather a systemic redirection of attention and incentive structures. Creators learn, consciously or unconsciously, what kind of content is rewarded by the algorithmic gatekeepers. This leads to a homogenization of expression, where a narrow range of commercially viable ideas and styles dominate the digital public square. The unpredictable, the novel, the genuinely groundbreaking – these are often the first casualties in a system designed to predict and optimize. The economic engine of surveillance capitalism, fueled by the commodified remnants of our thoughts and conversations, thus becomes a powerful force in shaping not only what we see and hear, but also what we are encouraged to say, and how we are incentivized to say it. The very essence of free expression, the unfettered ability to share one's authentic self and ideas, is subtly but fundamentally reshaped by the relentless pursuit of data and profit.

This commodification also extends to the very notion of identity. Our online profiles, constructed from our expressed preferences, our shared content, and our interactions, become valuable commodities in themselves. These digital personas are then used to market to us, to influence us, and to categorize us, not necessarily based on who we truly are, but on who the algorithms predict we are, or who they want us to become. The expression of identity online becomes a performance designed to satisfy the demands of the market, rather than a genuine exploration of self. This can lead to a disjunction between our online selves and our offline realities, a phenomenon that can have profound psychological and social consequences. When our authentic selves are less valuable than our algorithmically optimized personas, the true richness of human identity is sacrificed at the altar of commercial utility.

The economic imperative to constantly extract and analyze data means that there is little incentive for platforms to de-emphasize data collection or to prioritize user privacy over profit. The more data available, the more precise the predictions, and the more lucrative the behavioral targeting. This creates a perpetual arms race, where platforms continuously develop more sophisticated methods of surveillance, and users are increasingly resigned to the fact that their every digital move is being tracked and analyzed. The promise of a free and open internet, where individuals can express themselves without fear or undue scrutiny, is thus undermined by an economic model that inherently relies on the detailed observation and commodification of those very expressions. The First Amendment's protections, conceived in a pre-digital era, struggle to keep pace with an economy that treats speech not as a fundamental right, but as a resource to be exploited. The challenge, then, is to reassert the primacy of human expression over the economic imperatives of surveillance capitalism, ensuring that our digital public square remains a space for genuine discourse, rather than a marketplace for our thoughts and feelings.

The digital age, characterized by its unprecedented interconnectedness, has also ushered in an era of pervasive data collection, a practice that, while often cloaked in the language of service improvement and personalization, carries profound implications for the foundational freedoms enshrined in the First Amendment. At the heart of this concern lies the sheer scale and sophistication of modern data aggregation, driven largely by advancements in artificial intelligence. This is not merely about tracking individual clicks or purchases; it's about the creation of vast, intricate digital tapestries woven from the threads of our online lives. Every search query, every shared article, every message exchanged, every expressed sentiment, and even the subtle nuances of our digital interactions are meticulously gathered, stored, and analyzed. This mass data collection, often operating beyond the direct awareness and explicit consent of the individual, forms the bedrock of what has been termed "surveillance capitalism."

The invisible hand of AI is the primary engine behind this data harvesting. Machine learning algorithms, trained on colossal datasets, possess an uncanny ability to discern patterns, predict inclinations, and construct detailed profiles of individuals and groups. These profiles are not static snapshots; they are dynamic representations, constantly updated with every new digital footprint we leave. This sophisticated profiling capability allows for the categorization and understanding of individuals not just by their overt actions, but by their inferred beliefs, affiliations, and even potential future behaviors. When such comprehensive data is gathered about individuals and their associations, it creates a landscape ripe for the erosion of privacy, a privacy that is not merely a personal preference but a critical prerequisite for the unfettered exercise of First Amendment rights.

The ability to aggregate and analyze vast datasets allows for the creation of detailed maps of social networks and ideological leanings. By observing who communicates with whom, what information is shared between individuals or groups, and what sentiments are expressed in collective forums, powerful insights into associations and beliefs can be gleaned. This is where the threat to the First Amendment becomes particularly acute. The freedom of association, the right to gather with like-minded individuals for common causes, and the freedom of belief, the right to hold and express one's convictions without fear of reprisal, are rendered vulnerable when the very act of associating or believing can be so comprehensively documented and analyzed.

Imagine a scenario where an individual participates in online forums discussing controversial social issues, shares articles from alternative news sources, or privately communicates with groups advocating for policy changes. Without mass data collection and sophisticated AI analysis, such activities might remain largely private, allowing for the exploration of ideas and the formation of beliefs without undue external pressure. However, in the current digital environment, these actions can be aggregated, correlated, and fed into profiling systems. These systems might then flag individuals as belonging to certain ideological camps, associating them with potentially unfavorable viewpoints, or even predicting their likelihood of engaging in certain behaviors. This creates a chilling effect, where individuals may self-censor or alter their associations and expressions, not due to direct legal prohibition, but due to the fear of being profiled, categorized, and potentially disadvantaged.

The implications for freedom of belief are equally concerning. The ability to explore and develop one's beliefs is a cornerstone of intellectual freedom. This process often involves engaging with diverse viewpoints, wrestling with complex ideas, and even holding minority opinions. If every tentative exploration, every question posed online, and every article read is meticulously logged and analyzed, there is a risk that individuals will shy away from engaging with ideas that might be deemed unconventional or undesirable by the data collectors or the entities that purchase this data. The privacy of one's inner intellectual journey, essential for the development of authentic beliefs, is compromised when every digital step is monitored and analyzed for patterns that can be used to infer or even dictate belief.

Furthermore, the commodification of this aggregated data means it is often bought and sold. Entities seeking to influence public opinion, to target specific demographics for political persuasion, or to identify and potentially marginalize dissenting voices can leverage these detailed profiles. The knowledge that one's associations and expressed beliefs are being meticulously documented and potentially used by third parties for purposes unknown can stifle the very spontaneity and courage required for genuine public discourse and political engagement. The fear of being wrongly categorized, of having one's associations misrepresented, or of being targeted for exclusion based on inferred beliefs can lead to a reluctance to participate in public life, thereby diminishing the robust marketplace of ideas that the First Amendment is designed to protect.

The danger is amplified by the often-opaque nature of AI algorithms. The criteria by which individuals are profiled and categorized are frequently proprietary and inaccessible. This lack of transparency means that individuals may have little understanding of how they are being perceived by these data systems or what consequences might arise from their digital footprint. If an individual is denied opportunities, excluded from certain networks, or subjected to undue scrutiny based on opaque algorithmic assessments of their associations or beliefs, the mechanisms for recourse or correction are often nonexistent. This creates a power imbalance where individuals are subject to invisible judgments rendered by systems they cannot understand or contest.

Consider the impact on marginalized communities or those holding unpopular views. Historically, freedom of assembly and association has been crucial for these groups to organize, advocate for their rights, and find solidarity. However, in an era of mass data collection, the digital footprints of such associations can be easily tracked. This raises concerns about potential government surveillance or the use of this data by private entities to discriminate against individuals based on their perceived affiliations. The ability to secretly gather and analyze information about who is associating with whom, and what beliefs they appear to hold, can be a powerful tool for suppression, even without overt legal sanctions. The chilling effect on legitimate activism and the exercise of fundamental rights becomes a tangible threat.

The erosion of privacy, therefore, is not an abstract concern; it directly impacts the practical ability to exercise First Amendment freedoms. When the digital spaces where we communicate, share information, and form communities are under constant surveillance, the psychological freedom to explore ideas, to connect with others, and to express oneself authentically is diminished. The sense of being perpetually observed can lead to a self-policing of thought and action, a subtle but powerful form of self-censorship that undermines the very foundations of a free society. The space for dissent, for the exploration of unconventional ideas, and for the formation of new movements is constricted when the digital infrastructure itself is designed to monitor, analyze, and potentially control our associations and beliefs.

The sheer volume of data collected also means that patterns of behavior, which might be innocent in isolation, can be pieced together to form a picture that is then used to make inferences about deeply personal aspects of an individual's life, including their political leanings or religious beliefs. This aggregation transforms disparate pieces of information into a coherent narrative, often one that the individual may not have intended to create or share. This is particularly concerning when the data can be used to identify individuals who hold views that are unpopular with those in power, or which are deemed undesirable by commercial interests. The ability to form and express beliefs is intrinsically linked to the ability to do so privately, without the constant threat of external scrutiny and judgment.

Moreover, the increasing sophistication of AI in inferring intent and sentiment from digital communication adds another layer of complexity. Nuance, sarcasm, and evolving opinions can be easily misinterpreted or oversimplified by algorithms seeking to categorize and predict. This means that individuals might be pigeonholed based on fleeting or misunderstood expressions, leading to mischaracterizations of their beliefs and associations that can have lasting consequences. The development of one's thoughts and beliefs is often a non-linear process, involving experimentation and exploration. When this process is subjected to constant algorithmic assessment, it can discourage the very intellectual risk-taking that leads to genuine understanding and the formation of well-considered convictions.

The First Amendment was conceived in an era where the primary threats to free speech, belief, and assembly were overt governmental censorship and societal pressure. The digital age, however, presents a more insidious challenge, one driven by economic imperatives and enabled by technological sophistication. Mass data collection, powered by AI, creates a pervasive surveillance apparatus that, while often framed as benign, fundamentally alters the conditions under which these fundamental rights can be exercised. The privacy that allows for the free exploration of ideas and the formation of genuine associations is being systematically eroded, leaving individuals vulnerable to profiling, discrimination, and the chilling effect of constant observation. Reclaiming and protecting this essential privacy is therefore not merely a matter of personal preference, but a critical imperative for the preservation of a free and open society. The invisible threads of data collection are weaving a new reality, one where the very act of thinking, believing, and associating can become a data point, susceptible to analysis and influence, and thus, a potential target for control.

The digital age has, with the aid of artificial intelligence, unveiled new dimensions of surveillance, extending its reach into the most private realms of human thought and conviction. Just as the Grand Inquisitor in Dostoyevsky's *The Brothers Karamazov* sought to understand and control the inner lives of individuals, so too does AI, through its analytical prowess, offer the capability to infer and categorize religious and political beliefs with an unnerving precision. This subsection delves into the specific ways in which AI is employed to monitor these fundamental aspects of human identity, and the profound implications this has for freedoms that have long been considered sacrosanct.

AI's capacity to analyze vast troves of data enables it to move beyond observable actions and into the realm of inferring belief systems. Online activities, from search engine queries and website visits to social media posts and private communications, all leave digital breadcrumbs. Sophisticated machine learning algorithms can process this information, identifying patterns that are indicative of specific religious or political ideologies. For instance, the types of news articles an individual reads, the individuals or groups they follow or interact with online, the language used in their posts, and even the topics they engage with in online forums can be aggregated and analyzed to build a profile of their likely beliefs. This is not a simple matter of keywords; AI can discern sentiment, identify subtle ideological leanings, and even predict the trajectory of an individual's evolving political or religious views based on their digital engagement.

Consider the analysis of online religious communities. Participation in forums dedicated to theological discussions, the sharing of devotional content, or even the browsing of religious texts online can be meticulously logged. AI systems can then categorize individuals based on their affiliation with specific denominations, their level of orthodoxy or heterodoxy, or their engagement with particular religious movements. This data can be used not only to understand the demographics of religious groups but also, more troublingly, to identify individuals within those groups who hold views that deviate from a perceived norm, or whose beliefs might be deemed problematic by external observers, whether governmental or corporate. The act of seeking spiritual understanding or communal belonging online, which should be a private and personal endeavor, becomes an observable and quantifiable phenomenon.

The parallels to the Grand Inquisitor's desire to understand the "inner freedom" of man are striking. The Inquisitor, in his quest for order and control, sought to alleviate the burden of free will by offering certainty and eliminating the anxiety of choice. AI, in its analytical capacity, can be seen as a modern-day inquisitor, sifting through the digital detritus of our lives to ascertain our deepest convictions. It seeks to remove ambiguity, to categorize us neatly into predefined ideological boxes, thereby potentially stripping away the very essence of individual conscience and the freedom to form beliefs organically, without external judgment or categorization.

The implications for religious freedom are particularly stark. The First Amendment guarantees the free exercise of religion, which includes the right to practice one's faith privately and to associate with others for religious purposes. However, when AI can infer religious beliefs from digital activity, individuals may face an unprecedented level of scrutiny. This is not hypothetical. Governments or other entities could employ AI systems to identify individuals who belong to minority religious groups, those who are critical of state-sanctioned religious doctrines, or those who are actively proselytizing. Such identification can then pave the way for targeted surveillance, harassment, or discrimination. Imagine an individual being flagged for attending online prayer groups deemed "extremist" by an algorithm, or for researching theological concepts that challenge prevailing ideologies. The fear of being profiled and subsequently disadvantaged can lead to a chilling effect, where individuals self-censor their religious expression and withdraw from religious communities for fear of reprisal.

This inferential power of AI extends beyond online activity to encompass physical location data. When combined with online profiles, location data can paint an even more comprehensive picture of an individual's affiliations and beliefs. For example, if AI identifies an individual as frequently visiting places of worship, attending political rallies, or frequenting locations associated with specific activist groups, this data can further solidify and validate the inferred religious or political leanings. While often collected under the guise of providing personalized services or improving urban planning, this confluence of online and offline data creates a powerful surveillance infrastructure capable of mapping ideological landscapes with unprecedented accuracy. An individual's attendance at a religious service or a political demonstration, acts that are often protected by the First Amendment, can become data points used to construct a digital dossier that might be accessed by entities with agendas that run counter to those fundamental freedoms.

The potential for AI to facilitate targeted persecution based on ideology is a significant concern. In authoritarian regimes, AI-powered surveillance systems are already being used to monitor political dissent. By analyzing communications, tracking movements, and identifying individuals associated with opposition groups, these systems can help authorities suppress dissent before it gains momentum. This can range from subtle forms of social control, such as limiting an individual's access to services or opportunities based on their perceived political leanings, to more overt forms of repression, such as arrest and imprisonment. The ability of AI to process and correlate vast amounts of data at speeds far beyond human capacity makes it a potent tool for identifying and neutralizing perceived threats to the established order.

The erosion of privacy in this context is not merely an abstract concern; it has direct consequences for the ability to form and hold religious and political beliefs freely. The freedom to explore different ideas, to question established doctrines, and to develop one's own convictions requires a degree of intellectual and social space that is increasingly being compromised by digital surveillance. If individuals know that their every digital utterance, their every online association, and even their physical movements are being monitored and analyzed for ideological markers, they may be hesitant to engage in the critical thinking and open discourse that are essential for the development of authentic beliefs. The fear of being miscategorized, of having one's nuanced views oversimplified into a label, or of being associated with undesirable groups based on algorithmic inference, can lead to a stifling of intellectual curiosity and a retreat into intellectual conformity.

Furthermore, the opaque nature of many AI algorithms exacerbates this problem. Individuals often have no clear understanding of how their data is being analyzed or what criteria are being used to infer their beliefs. This lack of transparency makes it difficult, if not impossible, to challenge algorithmic assessments or to correct misinterpretations of one's digital footprint. If an individual is denied employment, subjected to increased scrutiny, or ostracized based on an inferred political or religious belief that is inaccurate or outdated, they may have no recourse. This power imbalance, where individuals are subject to the unseen judgments of sophisticated AI systems, creates a profound vulnerability.

The historical context of religious and political persecution offers a grim forewarning. Throughout history, those who have held dissenting religious or political views have often been targets of surveillance, ostracization, and violence. The digital age, armed with AI, has the potential to amplify these historical patterns on an unprecedented scale. Instead of relying on informants or manual investigation, AI can automate the process of identifying "heretics" and "dissidents" with a speed and efficiency that is chilling. This raises fundamental questions about the future of religious freedom and political dissent in a world where our innermost convictions can be so readily mapped and monitored by intelligent machines. The very act of questioning, of seeking, and of believing, which are at the heart of human experience, are now intertwined with a digital infrastructure that can turn these fundamental freedoms into data points susceptible to analysis, categorization, and potentially, control. The promise of the digital age for connectivity and empowerment is increasingly shadowed by the specter of algorithmic scrutiny, threatening to turn our minds and spirits into the next frontier of surveillance.

The fundamental right to assemble peacefully, a cornerstone of democratic societies and a vital mechanism for civic engagement, is facing unprecedented challenges in the digital age. As the previous discussion explored how AI can infer religious and political beliefs, this section turns to the more visible manifestation of these beliefs: collective action and public assembly. The very act of gathering, whether for protest, celebration, or civic discourse, leaves a digital and physical footprint that can be meticulously tracked and analyzed by sophisticated AI-powered surveillance systems. This analysis examines the multifaceted ways in which the right to assemble is being undermined by these technologies, and the chilling effect this has on democratic participation.

One of the most potent tools in the AI surveillance arsenal is facial recognition technology (FRT). Deployed in public spaces, at events, and increasingly integrated into widespread CCTV networks, FRT allows for the automatic identification of individuals within crowds. When coupled with AI algorithms, FRT moves beyond simple identification to sophisticated crowd analysis. Systems can not only pinpoint individuals but also track their movements within a gathering, identify who they interact with, and estimate the duration of their presence. For a protest or demonstration, this means that every participant can be individually cataloged, their presence recorded, and their association with a particular event meticulously logged. This data, once collected, can be cross-referenced with other databases, potentially revealing an individual's employment, their political affiliations, or even their religious background, thereby creating a detailed profile of their civic engagement. The knowledge that one's face can be recognized and recorded at a political rally or a peaceful demonstration inherently alters the calculus of participation. The risk of being identified and subsequently facing repercussions – whether professional, social, or legal – can deter individuals from exercising their right to assemble, especially those who may be more vulnerable to reprisal.

Social media platforms, often hailed as tools for organizing and amplifying voices, have also become fertile ground for AI-driven surveillance of assemblies. Beyond the public posts and event pages, AI can analyze patterns of communication, sentiment, and network connections to identify individuals who are likely to participate in or organize protests. By monitoring keywords, hashtags, and discussions related to upcoming gatherings, AI can flag potential attendees and organizers for authorities or private entities. Furthermore, the voluntary sharing of photos and videos from events, often intended to document or publicize, can be a goldmine of data for FRT and other AI analysis tools. Individuals who attend a demonstration and post about it online, or whose friends tag them in photos from the event, are effectively creating a digital record of their participation. AI can then correlate this online activity with offline surveillance data, creating a comprehensive picture of an individual's involvement in any given assembly. This pervasive monitoring can lead to a significant chilling effect. The fear of being identified, having one's social circle mapped, or being associated with a particular cause – even if the association is fleeting or tangential – can discourage participation. Individuals may opt out of attending a protest not because they disagree with its aims, but because they fear the potential downstream consequences of their digital footprint.

Predictive analytics, another powerful application of AI, is increasingly being used to anticipate and potentially disrupt public gatherings. By analyzing historical data on protest movements, social unrest, and even seemingly unrelated datasets like online search trends or local crime statistics, AI can attempt to forecast where and when demonstrations might occur. This predictive capability can lead to preemptive measures, such as increased police presence, the imposition of restrictive permits, or even the outright banning of gatherings in areas deemed at high risk of protest. While ostensibly aimed at maintaining public order, this proactive surveillance can stifle legitimate dissent. If authorities can predict and prepare for a protest, they can also be better positioned to monitor, identify, and potentially apprehend its participants. The very act of planning or even discussing a potential assembly online can trigger algorithmic alerts, leading to heightened surveillance of the individuals involved. This can create a climate of fear where the anticipation of surveillance itself curtails the freedom to plan and participate.

The intersection of these technologies creates a powerful infrastructure for monitoring and controlling public assembly. Imagine a scenario where FRT identifies individuals at a protest, social media monitoring tracks their online affiliations and communications related to the event, and predictive analytics has already flagged the gathering as a potential site of unrest. The data generated by each of these systems can be integrated and analyzed by AI to build detailed profiles of participants. This information can then be used for a variety of purposes, some benign, but many with profound implications for civil liberties. For instance, authorities might use this data to identify leaders of a protest movement, to understand the composition and demographics of attendees, or to gather evidence for potential charges against participants. In more authoritarian contexts, this same data can be used to target individuals for harassment, arrest, or other forms of repression, effectively silencing dissent before it can gain traction.

The impact of this digital surveillance on the right to assemble extends beyond direct repression. It fosters a pervasive sense of being watched, which can lead to self-censorship and a reluctance to engage in public life. The knowledge that one's participation in a peaceful demonstration could be recorded, analyzed, and potentially used against them in the future can deter many from exercising their fundamental right. This is particularly true for individuals from marginalized communities, activists, or those who hold unpopular views, who may already face greater scrutiny and risk. The chilling effect of constant digital surveillance can lead to a significant reduction in the diversity and vibrancy of public discourse and protest. When the potential costs of public assembly – in terms of privacy, professional standing, or personal safety – are amplified by AI-driven tracking, the incentive to participate diminishes, weakening the very fabric of a participatory democracy.

The historical context of protests and social movements underscores the importance of the right to assemble. From the civil rights marches of the 1960s to the anti-war demonstrations of various eras, collective action has been instrumental in driving social and political change. However, these historical movements operated in an environment with far less pervasive surveillance. Today, the ability of AI to track, identify, and analyze individuals at gatherings transforms the landscape of protest. The digital trails left by participants can be more enduring and more revealing than anything previously imagined. This raises significant concerns about the future of organized dissent and the ability of citizens to hold their governments and institutions accountable through public demonstration. The right to assemble is not merely the right to be present at a location; it is the right to express one's views, to associate with like-minded individuals, and to collectively advocate for change, all of which are being subtly but powerfully undermined by the omnipresent gaze of AI-powered surveillance. The fear of algorithmic judgment can transform public spaces, which should be arenas of free expression, into zones of silent apprehension.

Furthermore, the blurring lines between public and private spaces in the digital realm complicate the protection of assembly rights. While traditional notions of assembly focused on physical presence, online organizing and virtual assemblies are becoming increasingly common. However, AI can extend its surveillance capabilities to these virtual spaces as well, monitoring online forums, encrypted messaging apps (where vulnerabilities exist), and even virtual reality environments. This means that the right to assemble, in its evolving digital forms, is also subject to the same algorithmic scrutiny. The aggregation of data from online organizing efforts with offline surveillance of physical gatherings creates a comprehensive picture of an individual's activism, leaving little room for private deliberation or association. The ability of AI to correlate disparate data points – a social media post, a facial recognition match at a rally, a search query about a political issue – creates a potent tool for identifying and potentially suppressing collective action, thereby posing a direct threat to a fundamental right that underpins democratic participation and societal progress.

# Chapter 4: The Fourth Amendment's Fortress: Privacy in the Face of AI

The Fourth Amendment, traditionally understood as a bulwark against unreasonable searches and seizures, has long relied on the concept of a "reasonable expectation of privacy" to delineate the boundaries of governmental intrusion. This legal doctrine, famously articulated in *Katz v. United States*, posits that for Fourth Amendment protection to apply, an individual must have exhibited an actual subjective expectation of privacy, and that this expectation must be one that society is prepared to recognize as "reasonable." Historically, this reasonable expectation was largely tethered to physical space – the sanctity of one's home, the contents of one's pockets, or the privacy of a telephone booth. However, the advent and proliferation of Artificial Intelligence, coupled with the omnipresent nature of digital data collection, have profoundly reshaped this landscape, often eroding the very foundations upon which this reasonable expectation was built.

The intangible nature of digital information presents a fundamental challenge to traditional privacy jurisprudence. Unlike the tangible objects or physical spaces that occupied the minds of the Framers, digital data – our communications, our movements, our preferences, our very identities – exists in a fluid, often abstract realm. AI systems are not limited by the physical walls of a home or the closed doors of a private conversation. Instead, they can traverse vast digital networks, analyzing, correlating, and inferring information from data that may have been voluntarily shared, inadvertently exposed, or even scraped from public-facing sources. This shift from the physical to the informational has left courts and society grappling with what it truly means to have a "reasonable expectation of privacy" in the 21st century.

Consider the concept of "publicly available" information. Historically, what was visible or audible in public spaces offered little expectation of privacy. One could not reasonably expect to have a secret conversation on a busy street corner. However, AI's ability to process and analyze this "public" data at an unprecedented scale and speed transforms its nature. For instance, the metadata associated with our online activities – the timestamps of our emails, the IP addresses we use, the websites we visit – may be considered publicly accessible in isolation. Yet, when aggregated and analyzed by sophisticated AI algorithms, this seemingly innocuous data can reveal intimate details about our lives, our associations, our routines, and even our political or religious leanings. The Supreme Court's ruling in

*United States v. Miller*, which held that individuals have no reasonable expectation of privacy in bank records voluntarily turned over to a third party (the bank), has been extended in the digital age to encompass a wide array of data held by online service providers. This "third-party doctrine" suggests that once information is shared with an intermediary, privacy protections diminish significantly, a notion that becomes increasingly problematic as almost every aspect of modern life involves such intermediaries.

The implications of AI in this context are particularly stark when examining the pervasive collection of data through smart devices and the Internet of Things (IoT). Our homes, once considered the ultimate sanctuary of privacy, are now filled with interconnected devices that constantly collect data about our habits, our conversations, and our physical presence. Smart speakers listen to our commands (and potentially more), smart thermostats learn our daily routines, and wearable fitness trackers monitor our physiological states. While users may subjectively expect a degree of privacy in their homes, the reality of these devices constantly transmitting data to remote servers, where AI can analyze it, fundamentally challenges the "reasonableness" of that expectation. The sheer volume and detail of the data being collected mean that even seemingly innocuous pieces of information, when combined, can paint a remarkably intimate portrait of an individual's life. The question then becomes: can society truly recognize an expectation of privacy as reasonable when we are voluntarily inviting devices into our most private spaces that are designed to collect and transmit vast amounts of personal data?

Judicial interpretations of privacy in the digital realm have often struggled to keep pace with technological advancements. Early cases often applied analogical reasoning, attempting to map existing privacy protections onto new digital realities. However, this approach has proven increasingly inadequate. The Supreme Court's decision in

*Carpenter v. United States* marked a significant shift, recognizing that long-term cell-site location information (CSLI) constituted a Fourth Amendment search, thereby requiring a warrant. The Court reasoned that the extensive nature of CSLI data provided an "all-encompassing record of the holder's whereabouts," effectively revealing details about a person's life that would be difficult to obtain through traditional means. This recognition acknowledged that the aggregation of digital data, even if collected from multiple sources over time, can create a privacy interest that warrants protection. However, *Carpenter* is often seen as a narrow exception, and the broader application of the third-party doctrine and the challenges posed by AI continue to leave significant gaps in privacy protection.

Furthermore, the rise of sophisticated AI tools for data analysis means that the distinction between what is "private" and what is "public" is becoming increasingly blurred. AI can infer sensitive information from seemingly innocuous data. For example, an AI might analyze a person's purchasing history, social media activity, and location data to infer their political affiliation, religious beliefs, or even their health status. While each piece of data might be considered individually permissible to collect or access, their combination and analysis by AI can reveal deeply private aspects of an individual's life that they never intended to disclose. This raises a critical question: if AI can deduce highly private information from data that is technically "public" or has been shared with third parties, does society still recognize an expectation of privacy in that underlying information as reasonable? The answer is far from settled.

Societal perceptions of privacy are also undergoing a significant transformation, influenced by our increasing reliance on digital technologies. Many individuals, accustomed to the convenience and connectivity offered by AI-powered services, may have a diminished subjective expectation of privacy. The constant barrage of personalized advertisements, the predictive text that anticipates our thoughts, and the seamless integration of services across platforms can create a sense of resignation, where individuals feel that a degree of surveillance is an unavoidable trade-off for participation in modern digital life. This erosion of subjective expectation, while understandable, poses a danger to the overall framework of privacy rights. If individuals no longer *expect* their data to be private, then the legal and social mechanisms designed to protect that privacy become less effective.

The challenge for legal systems is to adapt the concept of "reasonableness" to a world where data is constantly being collected, processed, and analyzed by powerful AI systems. The focus may need to shift from the *location* of data collection to the *nature* and *intrusiveness* of the analysis performed on that data. A reasonable expectation of privacy might no longer be solely tied to the physical boundaries of one's home but could extend to the informational integrity of one's personal life, regardless of how that information is gathered. This would require a re-evaluation of doctrines like the third-party doctrine and a greater emphasis on the capabilities of AI in inferring sensitive information.

Moreover, the transparency and consent mechanisms surrounding data collection are often inadequate in the age of AI. Users are presented with lengthy and complex privacy policies that few read or fully understand, and the implications of agreeing to terms of service that allow for extensive data collection and AI analysis are often opaque. This lack of meaningful consent further complicates the notion of a reasonable expectation of privacy. If individuals are not fully aware of what data is being collected, how it is being used by AI, and what inferences are being drawn, can they truly be said to have a reasonable expectation of privacy that has been undermined? The absence of genuine informed consent weakens the argument that any expectation of privacy that remains is unreasonable.

The legal framework surrounding the "reasonable expectation of privacy" was designed for a different era, one where information was less fluid, less interconnected, and less susceptible to automated, large-scale analysis. AI has fundamentally altered this equation. It has enabled the aggregation and analysis of vast datasets that can reveal intimate details about individuals, often from sources that were once considered too disparate or too public to pose a significant privacy risk. The intangible nature of digital data, combined with the analytical power of AI, challenges the very notion of what is "private" and what is "reasonable" to expect. As AI continues to advance, courts, lawmakers, and society at large must grapple with these profound questions to ensure that fundamental privacy rights are not rendered obsolete in the digital realm. The fortress of the Fourth Amendment, built to protect physical spaces and tangible effects, must find new ramparts to defend the increasingly vulnerable informational self against the pervasive and analytical gaze of artificial intelligence. The very definition of what constitutes a "search" and what constitutes "seizure" is being interrogated by AI's capacity to derive profound insights from seemingly insignificant data points, forcing a reconsideration of the "reasonable" limits of government and corporate access to our digital lives.

The pervasive reach of artificial intelligence has ushered in an era of unprecedented data collection, fundamentally challenging the long-established boundaries of the Fourth Amendment. Mass surveillance, once a concept confined to the realm of speculative fiction or the exclusive domain of highly targeted investigations, has become a tangible reality, fueled by the insatiable appetite of AI for data. Governments and corporations alike are engaged in the systematic aggregation of personal information, often without the explicit consent, knowledge, or specific warrants that the Fourth Amendment traditionally requires. This widespread data harvesting, driven by the analytical power of AI, operates by sweeping up vast quantities of information, transforming the very nature of what constitutes a "search" and what it means to be subjected to "seizure."

The traditional understanding of a search under the Fourth Amendment typically involved a physical intrusion into a place or on a person where there was a reasonable expectation of privacy. However, AI-driven surveillance transcends these physical limitations. Instead, it operates within the digital ether, collecting, analyzing, and correlating data points that, when viewed individually, might seem innocuous or even publicly available. The government, through various agencies, can leverage AI-powered tools to process data from an astonishing array of sources: telecommunications records, social media activity, public camera feeds, financial transactions, and even sensor data from smart devices. This collection often happens at a scale and speed that renders the concept of individualized suspicion or probable cause almost obsolete. The argument often presented is that much of this data is either voluntarily surrendered to third parties (like cloud storage providers or social media platforms) or is deemed "publicly accessible." Yet, the aggregation and AI-driven analysis of this data create a comprehensive mosaic of an individual's life, revealing patterns, associations, and intentions that were never intended to be so readily discernible.

Consider the implications of the "third-party doctrine" in this AI-augmented landscape. Rooted in cases like

*United States v. Miller* and *Smith v. Maryland*, this doctrine suggests that individuals relinquish any reasonable expectation of privacy when they voluntarily share information with a third party. In the pre-AI era, this might have referred to bank records or phone numbers dialed. Today, however, nearly every interaction, from sending an email to using a GPS app, involves a third party. AI systems are designed to exploit this by accessing and analyzing data held by these intermediaries. Governments can request, and sometimes compel, companies to provide vast troves of user data that, when analyzed by AI, can paint an extraordinarily detailed picture of an individual's movements, communications, and associations over extended periods. The sheer volume and granularity of this data allow AI to infer sensitive details, such as political leanings, religious beliefs, health conditions, or personal relationships, even if these details were never explicitly shared or intended to be revealed. This raises a critical constitutional question: does the voluntary sharing of data with a third party, knowing that AI will likely analyze it at an unprecedented scale, extinguish all Fourth Amendment protection against government intrusion? The answer, as legal scholars and courts grapple with these issues, is far from settled and forms the crux of ongoing legal battles.

The absence of a warrant, a cornerstone of Fourth Amendment protection, is a recurring theme in AI-driven surveillance. While law enforcement historically needed a warrant based on probable cause to conduct a search, the methods employed in mass surveillance often bypass this requirement. Data brokers, for instance, legally acquire and aggregate vast amounts of personal information from various sources, including publicly available data and data purchased from other companies. Governments can then purchase this aggregated data, circumventing the need for warrants or even direct interaction with service providers for specific individuals. This practice raises profound due process concerns. Individuals are effectively subjected to searches and seizures of their personal information without the oversight of a judicial officer determining whether probable cause exists. The justification often offered is that the data was "lawfully obtained" by the data broker. However, this legal arbitrage effectively creates a loophole where the spirit of the Fourth Amendment is undermined, even if the letter of the law, as currently interpreted, is technically followed.

The implications for individual liberty and due process are immense. When individuals know or suspect that their every digital interaction is being monitored, analyzed, and stored, a chilling effect on free speech, association, and dissent can emerge. The potential for misuse of such extensive data is also a significant concern. AI systems, by their very nature, can be prone to biases embedded in the data they are trained on or in their algorithms. This can lead to discriminatory surveillance practices, disproportionately targeting certain communities or individuals based on race, ethnicity, or other protected characteristics. Furthermore, the opacity of these AI systems makes it difficult for individuals to challenge the data collected about them or the inferences drawn from it. If a person is flagged by a government AI system based on an analysis of their aggregated data, they may have no way of knowing why they were flagged, what data was used, or how to correct any inaccuracies. This lack of transparency and accountability erodes the due process rights that the Fourth Amendment seeks to protect.

Legal challenges to AI-enabled mass surveillance are increasingly being brought before the courts. These cases often center on the definition of a "search" in the digital age and the extent to which the Fourth Amendment applies to data collected and analyzed by AI. Arguments are made that the aggregation of granular data points, even if individually obtained legally, constitutes a search when that aggregation reveals intimate details about a person's life and is facilitated by AI's analytical capabilities. The Supreme Court's decision in

*Carpenter v. United States*, which held that access to a suspect's historical cell-site location information (CSLI) constituted a Fourth Amendment search requiring a warrant, is often cited as a precedent. The Court reasoned that CSLI data provides an "all-encompassing record of the holder's whereabouts" over extended periods, revealing a great deal about a person's life that they could reasonably expect to keep private. Advocates for stronger privacy protections argue that the principles laid out in *Carpenter* should extend to other forms of aggregated digital data analyzed by AI, such as social media activity, browsing history, and location data obtained through various means.

However, the application of

*Carpenter* and the broader interpretation of the Fourth Amendment in the context of AI surveillance remain contentious. The government and some legal scholars argue that focusing on the "reasonable expectation of privacy" in individual data points is sufficient, and that the aggregation and analysis by AI do not fundamentally alter this. They may argue that if a person knowingly shares data with a platform, or if data is collected from public sources, then there is no reasonable expectation of privacy, regardless of how sophisticated the AI analysis becomes. This perspective often emphasizes the practical difficulties of obtaining warrants for every piece of data collected and the national security or public safety justifications for widespread data analysis. The debate often boils down to whether the Fourth Amendment is primarily concerned with physical intrusion or with the protection of personal information and informational privacy, especially when that information can be used to infer deeply sensitive details about an individual's life.

The expansion of government surveillance capabilities through AI also necessitates a re-examination of due process protections. The idea that individuals have a right to be informed of government intrusions upon their privacy, and to have the opportunity to challenge them, is a fundamental tenet of due process. However, the nature of AI-driven mass surveillance, often conducted covertly and on a massive scale, makes such challenges exceedingly difficult. The metadata of our digital lives, when fed into AI systems, can become a silent witness against us, used to build profiles, assess risk, or even predict future behavior, all without our knowledge or consent. The lack of transparency surrounding these AI systems and the data they process creates a significant imbalance of power between the individual and the state, raising serious questions about fairness and accountability.

Furthermore, the intersection of AI surveillance with the private sector creates a complex web of data collection and analysis. Corporations, driven by profit motives, employ AI to gather and analyze vast amounts of consumer data for targeted advertising, product development, and other business purposes. While this is often framed as a commercial activity, the lines between corporate and governmental surveillance can blur. Governments may gain access to this corporate data through legal means, or through informal collaborations, thereby leveraging private sector data collection to augment their own surveillance capabilities. This raises concerns about the privatization of surveillance, where the state outsources its data gathering to private entities, potentially bypassing constitutional safeguards that would apply if the government itself were conducting the collection. The sheer volume and interconnectedness of data held by both government and private entities, amplified by AI's analytical power, mean that the concept of privacy is under constant pressure.

The debate over AI-enabled mass surveillance and the Fourth Amendment is not merely a legalistic quibble; it strikes at the heart of the relationship between the individual and the state in the digital age. It forces us to confront what "unreasonable searches and seizures" truly means when the "search" is for patterns in data, and the "seizure" is the extraction of insights from information that we might have once considered personal, even if shared. As AI continues to evolve, so too will the methods of surveillance, demanding a continuous re-evaluation of constitutional protections. The fortress of the Fourth Amendment, designed to protect against physical intrusions, must now find ways to defend the intangible but equally vital realm of personal information from the pervasive, analytical, and often invisible gaze of artificial intelligence. The current legal framework, built on analog principles and a bygone era of data collection, is increasingly strained by the digital realities of AI, pushing the boundaries of privacy and liberty in ways that the Framers could have scarcely imagined. The challenge lies in adapting these foundational principles to ensure that the right to be free from unreasonable governmental intrusion remains meaningful in an age of ubiquitous data and intelligent machines.

The advent of artificial intelligence has irrevocably altered the landscape of privacy, presenting novel challenges to the foundational principles enshrined in the Fourth Amendment. As we have explored, the capacity of AI to collect, aggregate, and analyze vast datasets without the traditional indicia of a warrant or probable cause has begun to erode the protections once thought secure. This chapter, in its examination of the Fourth Amendment's fortress in the face of AI, now turns to a particularly potent and pervasive manifestation of this technological shift: facial recognition systems. These systems, increasingly integrated into our daily lives, represent a significant frontier in the ongoing constitutional struggle for privacy.

Facial recognition technology, powered by sophisticated AI algorithms, has moved from the realm of science fiction into widespread practical application. At its core, this technology allows for the automated identification of individuals by analyzing unique facial features from images or video feeds. The underlying AI models are trained on massive databases of faces, enabling them to detect and match individuals with remarkable accuracy and speed. This capability has a wide range of applications, from unlocking smartphones and tagging friends on social media to more concerning uses by law enforcement for suspect identification, by private entities for security and access control, and even by governments for mass surveillance and citizen monitoring.

The implications of this pervasive deployment of facial recognition technology for Fourth Amendment protections are profound and multifaceted. Traditionally, the Fourth Amendment guards against "unreasonable searches and seizures," requiring warrants based on probable cause to intrude upon an individual's privacy. However, facial recognition operates by its very nature to make individuals perpetually identifiable, thereby diminishing any reasonable expectation of anonymity in public spaces. When walking down a street, attending a public event, or even driving a car, individuals can now be scanned, identified, and tracked without their knowledge or consent. This creates a sense of being under constant, invisible scrutiny, a far cry from the physical trespasses that the Amendment was primarily conceived to prevent.

Consider the scenario of ubiquitous CCTV cameras equipped with facial recognition software. These cameras are no longer merely recording passively; they are actively analyzing the faces of everyone who passes before them. The AI can cross-reference these faces against watchlists, identify individuals with warrants, or even simply log their presence at a particular location at a particular time. This data, aggregated and analyzed, can paint an incredibly detailed picture of an individual's movements, associations, and daily routines. The question then arises: does the act of being in a public space, where one might not have a reasonable expectation of privacy from being seen, extend to an expectation of privacy from being

*identified* and *tracked* by an automated system?

The Supreme Court has, in various contexts, grappled with what constitutes a "search" under the Fourth Amendment. In

*Katz v. United States*, the Court famously held that the Fourth Amendment protects "people, not places," and that a search occurs when the government violates a person's "reasonable expectation of privacy." Subsequent cases have refined this, but the core concept remains. With facial recognition, the government (or a private entity acting on its behalf) is essentially conducting a pervasive search of public spaces for identifiable individuals. Each scan of a face, when linked to a database or a tracking system, could be argued to be a form of seizure of personal information – specifically, biometric data that is uniquely identifying.

One of the most significant challenges posed by facial recognition is its potential to undermine anonymity, a crucial element of privacy and freedom. In societies that value free expression and dissent, the ability to move about without being constantly identified and cataloged is essential. If individuals know that their presence at a political rally, a religious gathering, or even a doctor's office can be recorded and linked to their identity, they may be less likely to participate. This chilling effect on association and expression is a direct threat to democratic values, and it arises from the perpetual identifiability facilitated by AI-powered facial recognition.

Furthermore, the deployment of facial recognition technology can disproportionately impact certain communities. Studies and real-world examples have shown that many facial recognition algorithms exhibit biases, with higher error rates for women and people of color. This can lead to misidentification, false arrests, and unwarranted scrutiny, exacerbating existing inequalities in the criminal justice system and beyond. When this technology is used by law enforcement, the consequences of such inaccuracies can be severe, leading to wrongful accusations or detentions. From a constitutional perspective, this raises questions about equal protection and due process – are these systems being applied fairly and without discriminatory effect?

The "third-party doctrine," which suggests that individuals lose privacy protections when they voluntarily share information with third parties, becomes particularly relevant and problematic in the context of facial recognition. While a face is not typically "shared" in the same way that one shares an email with a service provider, the data generated by facial recognition systems often relies on information held by third-party platforms. For instance, a facial recognition system might compare an image from a public camera to a database of photos scraped from social media. While the individual may have posted those photos publicly, they likely did not consent to their biometric data being extracted and used for mass surveillance purposes. The aggregation of publicly available images with real-time surveillance footage creates a powerful, and potentially invasive, identification tool.

Legal scholars are actively debating whether the aggregation of data, even if collected from public sources, constitutes a Fourth Amendment search when analyzed by AI for identification and tracking. The argument is that while an individual might not have a reasonable expectation of privacy in their face being seen in public, they do have a reasonable expectation of privacy in their identity and movements being continuously and systematically logged and analyzed. This is akin to the reasoning in

*Carpenter v. United States*, where the Supreme Court recognized that historical cell-site location information, while generated by a third-party provider, constitutes a search because of its comprehensiveness and its ability to reveal intimate details about a person's life. Proponents of this view argue that facial recognition data, when aggregated over time and across different locations, can similarly reveal patterns of life that are highly personal and deserving of constitutional protection.

The lack of transparency surrounding the deployment and use of facial recognition technology is another significant concern. Often, individuals are unaware that they are being subjected to facial recognition surveillance, or they lack knowledge about where their biometric data is being stored, how it is being used, or with whom it is being shared. This opacity makes it exceedingly difficult for individuals to challenge potential abuses or inaccuracies. The Fourth Amendment's promise of protection against unreasonable intrusion is severely diminished if individuals cannot even ascertain when, where, and how their privacy is being compromised.

Moreover, the potential for function creep with facial recognition technology is immense. A system initially deployed for a narrow security purpose, such as identifying known criminals in a specific area, can easily be expanded to broader applications, such as monitoring general public movement, tracking political activists, or even enforcing minor infractions. The ease with which AI can process and correlate data means that once a system is in place, the temptation to leverage its capabilities for other, perhaps less justifiable, purposes can be overwhelming. This expansion of surveillance power, without commensurate judicial oversight or public debate, poses a fundamental threat to civil liberties.

The question of consent also looms large. Unlike other forms of data collection where users might click "agree" to terms of service, consent for facial recognition in public spaces is rarely, if ever, explicitly obtained. While some argue that by entering a public space, individuals implicitly consent to being observed, this argument breaks down when observation is transformed into automated, persistent identification and tracking by AI. The expectation of being seen is fundamentally different from the expectation of being identified, logged, and potentially profiled by a powerful technological system without any awareness or volition.

The legal battles over facial recognition are still in their nascent stages, but they highlight the urgency of adapting constitutional law to the realities of AI. Courts are beginning to consider whether the collection of biometric data through facial recognition constitutes a search requiring a warrant, or whether it falls into categories of information that can be collected without judicial oversight. The outcomes of these cases will have far-reaching implications for the future of privacy in public spaces.

The Fourth Amendment's fortress, built to defend against physical intrusions, must now be re-envisioned to protect against the pervasive and often invisible intrusions of AI-powered surveillance. Facial recognition technology is a potent example of how AI can transform ordinary public spaces into zones of constant, identifiable surveillance, fundamentally altering the balance between individual liberty and governmental (or corporate) power. Without clear legal boundaries and robust safeguards, the unchecked proliferation of facial recognition risks ushering in an era where anonymity is a relic of the past, and every individual is perpetually subject to identification and tracking, undermining the very freedoms that the Constitution is designed to protect. The challenge lies not only in interpreting existing laws but also in developing new legal frameworks and ethical guidelines that can effectively govern the use of this powerful technology, ensuring that it serves rather than subverts fundamental rights. The very concept of being able to move freely and anonymously in the public square, a cornerstone of a free society, is now under direct assault from the algorithmic gaze.

The digital age has ushered in an era of unprecedented data generation. Every click, every search query, every interaction online leaves a trace, accumulating into vast repositories of information. Artificial intelligence, with its remarkable capacity for pattern recognition and analysis, has become the primary tool for sifting through these digital oceans. This process, known as data mining, involves algorithms that delve into immense datasets to extract patterns, insights, and, crucially, personal information that might otherwise remain hidden. The question that arises, then, is whether this algorithmic excavation constitutes a form of "search" under the Fourth Amendment, and if so, whether it adheres to the constitutional mandate for reasonableness and judicial oversight.

At its core, data mining is about finding needles in haystacks, but the haystacks are no longer simple. They are colossal, interconnected databases containing not just publicly available information but also data gleaned from private communications, online behaviors, and even inferred characteristics. AI algorithms are trained to identify correlations, anomalies, and predictive markers within this data. This could involve identifying potential customers based on their browsing history, predicting an individual's health risks based on their online searches and purchases, or even flagging individuals as potential security threats based on their digital footprint. The "information" extracted is not merely aggregate statistics; it is often deeply personal, revealing intimate details about an individual's life, preferences, beliefs, and associations.

Consider the concept of a "search" as understood by the Fourth Amendment. Traditionally, it involved a physical intrusion into a person's home, papers, or effects. However, the Supreme Court has evolved this understanding to encompass intangible interests, as seen in cases like

*Katz v. United States*, which established the "reasonable expectation of privacy" test. This test asks whether an individual has a subjective expectation of privacy that society is prepared to recognize as reasonable. In the context of data mining, the argument is that even if no single piece of data is inherently private, the aggregation and analysis of vast amounts of disparate data points can reveal highly private information that an individual would reasonably expect to remain confidential.

When an AI algorithm sifts through years of a person's emails, social media posts, location data, and search queries, it can construct a detailed narrative of their life. This narrative might include sensitive medical information gleaned from searches about symptoms, financial vulnerabilities revealed by shopping habits, or political leanings discernible from online articles read and shared. The AI doesn't just "see" individual data points; it synthesizes them into a holistic profile, akin to a detective piecing together clues. If an individual has a reasonable expectation that their medical inquiries will not be broadly disseminated or that their political interests will not be systematically logged and analyzed by an unknown entity, then the AI-driven process of data mining that yields such information can be considered a search.

The critical distinction lies in the sheer scale and the automated nature of AI-driven data mining. Unlike a human investigator who must follow specific leads and obtain warrants for targeted information, AI can conduct broad, sweeping analyses across entire populations. This indiscriminate nature of data mining presents a significant constitutional challenge. If law enforcement or a governmental agency were to manually review the private communications of every citizen, it would clearly be deemed an unreasonable search. Data mining, by leveraging AI, can achieve a similar outcome—a pervasive surveillance of personal information—without the manual labor and, often, without the explicit judicial oversight that would be required for a direct, physical search.

This raises the question of proportionality. The Fourth Amendment requires that searches be "reasonable." A search is generally considered reasonable when it is conducted pursuant to a warrant issued by a neutral and detached magistrate based on probable cause. Data mining, particularly when conducted by private entities that then share their findings with the government, or when conducted by government agencies without specific warrants, often bypasses this crucial safeguard. The argument is that a broad, untargeted data mining operation, which casts a wide net over the digital lives of countless individuals to find a few "targets" or "insights," is inherently unreasonable. It is akin to a general warrant, which the Fourth Amendment was designed to prohibit.

The "third-party doctrine," which generally holds that individuals have no reasonable expectation of privacy in information voluntarily shared with third parties, becomes particularly strained in the context of AI data mining. While one might voluntarily share data with a specific service provider, they do not typically consent to that data being endlessly aggregated, analyzed, and correlated with other data by sophisticated AI systems, potentially for purposes far beyond the original transaction. For instance, information shared with a search engine or a social media platform might be used to train an AI that then generates insights about vast numbers of users. The expectation of privacy is not about whether data is

*stored* by a third party, but rather about the *scope and nature of its subsequent use and analysis.*

Consider the analogy of a letter. If you mail a letter, you entrust it to the postal service (a third party). However, you still have a reasonable expectation that the contents of that letter will not be read by postal workers or anyone else without a warrant. The letter is seen by a third party in transit, but its intimate contents are not subjected to mass analysis. AI data mining, however, can be likened to a system that not only reads every letter but also analyzes the handwriting, the paper type, the postage used, the route it took, and cross-references it with every other letter ever sent to identify patterns, predict future correspondence, and flag individuals based on their writing habits. This goes far beyond the limited exposure inherent in traditional third-party interactions.

The concept of "metadata" also becomes relevant here. In

*Carpenter v. United States*, the Supreme Court recognized that the collection of cell-site location information (CSLI), a form of metadata, constituted a search because of its comprehensive nature. CSLI reveals not just who someone contacted, but where they have been over extended periods, painting an intimate picture of their life. Similarly, the metadata generated by our online activities—search terms, websites visited, duration of engagement—when subjected to AI analysis, can yield a similarly rich and invasive portrait. Data mining transforms seemingly innocuous pieces of metadata into a powerful tool for surveillance, revealing patterns and insights that individuals could reasonably expect to remain private.

Furthermore, the opacity of AI data mining processes makes it difficult for individuals to even know when their data is being mined, how it's being used, or what conclusions are being drawn about them. This lack of transparency is antithetical to the spirit of the Fourth Amendment, which presupposes that individuals can understand and challenge governmental intrusions into their privacy. If the search is conducted by an inscrutable algorithm operating on vast, inaccessible datasets, the ability of an individual to assert their constitutional rights is severely hampered. They cannot challenge what they do not know.

The potential for AI data mining to lead to discriminatory outcomes is another grave concern that touches upon Fourth Amendment principles of reasonableness and equal protection. If AI algorithms are trained on biased data, or if they are designed to flag certain demographic groups based on correlation rather than causation, the resulting "searches" may disproportionately target and penalize innocent individuals. For example, an AI might identify patterns in online behavior that are statistically more common among a particular ethnic or socioeconomic group, leading to increased scrutiny or suspicion of individuals within that group, even if their behavior is entirely benign. This type of broad, potentially discriminatory "fishing expedition" in the digital realm lacks the individualized suspicion that the Fourth Amendment typically requires.

The lack of explicit consent in many data mining scenarios is also a significant hurdle for its constitutional legitimacy. While terms of service agreements often grant broad rights to collect and use data, these agreements are rarely read, understood, or truly consented to by users. The fine print, buried in lengthy legal documents, cannot serve as a substitute for the informed, voluntary consent that underpins the legitimacy of many searches. When AI data mining uncovers deeply personal information, and the "consent" is derived from clicking "agree" on an opaque privacy policy, it is questionable whether such a process can meet the Fourth Amendment's demand for reasonableness.

The aggregation of data from multiple sources, a hallmark of AI data mining, further complicates the privacy landscape. Information that might be innocuous when viewed in isolation can become highly revealing when combined with other datasets. For instance, purchasing a particular medical book might not be considered a privacy concern. However, when this is combined with search queries about specific symptoms, online forum discussions about a rare disease, and location data showing visits to specialized clinics, the AI can infer a significant health condition. The Fourth Amendment should protect individuals from having their entire digital lives dissected and analyzed in this manner, particularly when it leads to the revelation of sensitive personal information without their knowledge or consent.

In essence, AI-driven data mining, when conducted without clear legal boundaries and robust oversight, can become a form of indiscriminate search. It allows for the extraction of vast amounts of personal information, creating detailed profiles of individuals and their behaviors, often based on correlations that may not reflect actual wrongdoing. This broad, automated intrusion into the digital lives of citizens, without the requirement of probable cause and a warrant, threatens to transform the Fourth Amendment's fortress into a permeable membrane, leaving individual privacy vulnerable to the unblinking, analytical gaze of artificial intelligence. The challenge for the legal system is to adapt its understanding of "search" and "seizure" to encompass these novel forms of data collection and analysis, ensuring that the constitutional protections against unreasonable intrusion remain effective in the digital age.

The advent of artificial intelligence has introduced a paradigm shift in how information is accessed and analyzed, effectively transforming AI systems into highly sophisticated 'search engines' not just for data, but for individuals themselves. These systems possess an uncanny ability to delve into the digital detritus of our lives, piecing together fragments of information to construct remarkably detailed and often intimate portraits of who we are, what we do, and whom we associate with. This capability, unlike any before it, fundamentally alters the traditional balance of power, tipping it decisively away from the individual and towards those entities capable of deploying these advanced analytical tools for surveillance. The implications for privacy, a cornerstone of the Fourth Amendment, are profound and necessitate a critical re-evaluation of our existing legal frameworks designed to protect against unreasonable searches and seizures.

Consider the sheer breadth and depth of information accessible through AI-powered systems. Where once a government agent might have painstakingly pieced together clues from physical evidence, witness testimonies, and limited digital forensics, AI can now perform a similar, albeit exponentially more comprehensive, task in mere moments. An AI can ingest and analyze an individual's entire online history—search queries, website visits, social media interactions, purchase records, location data, and even biometric information—to infer not only their habits and preferences but also their health conditions, financial status, political leanings, and personal relationships. This is not merely about finding a needle in a haystack; it is about an AI system that can, with astonishing accuracy, identify the precise contours of the haystack itself, and then meticulously excavate its every grain to build a detailed map of the individual who might have occupied it. The information revealed is often deeply personal, the kind of details that an individual would reasonably expect to remain private, shielded from unwarranted scrutiny.

This "search engine for individuals" operates on a scale and with an efficiency that outstrips human capabilities by orders of magnitude. It can scour vast datasets, cross-referencing information from disparate sources—social media profiles, public records, commercial databases, and more—to create a holistic digital identity. For instance, an AI might correlate a series of online searches for specific symptoms with purchases of over-the-counter medications and a history of visits to certain types of medical specialists. Without any direct inquiry or suspicion of wrongdoing, this AI system can infer a potential medical condition, information that is traditionally protected by doctor-patient confidentiality and a strong societal expectation of privacy. Similarly, by analyzing communication patterns, social connections on various platforms, and even the content of public posts, an AI can map an individual's social network, identifying close confidantes, casual acquaintances, and potential influences. This mapping can reveal sensitive affiliations and associations that individuals might prefer to keep private, free from the prying eyes of third parties, whether corporate or governmental.

The threat to the Fourth Amendment is particularly acute because this AI-driven omniscience often operates outside the traditional understanding of a "search." The Fourth Amendment protects against "unreasonable searches and seizures," implying a need for individualized suspicion, probable cause, and, in most cases, a warrant issued by a neutral magistrate. However, when an AI system passively collects and analyzes vast amounts of data that an individual has generated, often without their explicit awareness or understanding of the extent of the analysis, the framework of probable cause and warrants becomes difficult to apply. The "search" is not a targeted intrusion based on a specific suspicion, but rather a pervasive and systematic extraction of personal information facilitated by powerful algorithms. It's akin to the government having a telescopic lens that can see into every home, not because they suspect someone of a crime, but simply because the technology allows them to.

The power of AI as an individual search engine also lies in its predictive capabilities. By analyzing past behavior and identifying patterns, AI can forecast future actions, inclinations, and even vulnerabilities. This predictive power can be used for a myriad of purposes, from targeted advertising to, more disturbingly, pre-emptive law enforcement or security assessments. If an AI can predict that an individual is "likely" to engage in certain behaviors—whether that's defaulting on a loan, developing a particular illness, or even committing a crime—it creates a scenario where individuals are being subjected to scrutiny, or even penalized, for actions they have not yet taken, based on algorithmic probabilities. This shifts the focus from an actual transgression to a predicted one, eroding the principle that individuals should be judged and searched based on their present conduct, not on statistical likelihoods derived from their digital footprint.

The very definition of "private information" is challenged by this AI-driven analysis. Data points that might seem innocuous in isolation—a search for a travel destination, a purchase of a particular book, a comment on a social media post—can become highly revealing when aggregated and analyzed by AI. The AI can connect these dots, building a narrative of an individual's life that is far more comprehensive and revealing than any single piece of information could be. For example, a series of searches related to a specific political candidate, combined with attendance at rallies (inferred from location data), and participation in online forums discussing that candidate's platform, can paint a detailed picture of an individual's political engagement. The Fourth Amendment has traditionally protected the privacy of one's thoughts, beliefs, and associations. When AI can effectively "read" these aspects of an individual's life through their digital traces, it constitutes a profound intrusion into that protected sphere.

The implications for the "third-party doctrine" are also significant. This doctrine, which has historically held that individuals have no reasonable expectation of privacy in information they voluntarily share with third parties, is strained to its breaking point by AI data mining. While one might share information with a search engine or a social media platform, the expectation is generally that this information will be used for specific, limited purposes, such as providing search results or displaying a social feed. The development of sophisticated AI that can analyze, correlate, and infer highly personal details from this data, often for purposes far beyond the original intent of the user, represents a fundamental departure. The individual has not consented to their entire digital persona being dissected and modeled by an algorithm, potentially for undisclosed purposes by unknown entities. The sheer scale and analytical depth of AI-driven data mining mean that the information shared with a third party is no longer just stored; it is being actively and deeply interrogated, yielding insights that the individual reasonably believed would remain private.

This is not a hypothetical concern; it is a present reality. Companies routinely employ AI to analyze consumer behavior, building detailed profiles for targeted marketing. Governments, in the name of national security or law enforcement, are increasingly leveraging similar capabilities. The ability of AI to act as an individual search engine means that the digital lives of ordinary citizens are becoming increasingly transparent to those who possess the technology and the data. Without robust legal safeguards, this creates a chilling effect, where individuals may self-censor their online activities, refrain from seeking information on sensitive topics, or avoid expressing certain viewpoints for fear of being profiled, scrutinized, or even penalized by an all-seeing algorithmic eye. The Fourth Amendment, intended to protect citizens from unwarranted governmental intrusion, must adapt to this new reality where the "search" can be a silent, invisible, and continuous process conducted by machines.

The very notion of privacy is at stake. If our digital lives are to be treated as an open book, accessible and interpretable by AI systems for purposes that we cannot fully comprehend or control, then the freedom from intrusive government surveillance, a right so central to democratic societies, is severely diminished. The challenge for legal scholars and policymakers is to ensure that the Fourth Amendment remains a potent shield in the digital age, even as the nature of "searches" and "seizures" evolves. This requires a reinterpretation of existing doctrines and, potentially, the development of new legal principles that acknowledge the unique capabilities of AI and the profound privacy implications of its use as an individual search engine. The fortress of the Fourth Amendment must be reinforced to withstand the digital gale, ensuring that the pursuit of information by AI does not come at the expense of fundamental human liberties.

# Chapter 5: The Fifth Amendment: Due Process and the Algorithmic State

The integration of artificial intelligence into the intricate machinery of the criminal justice system represents a profound technological leap, promising efficiency and objectivity where human fallibility has historically led to inequities. From the initial stages of law enforcement, where predictive policing algorithms aim to anticipate crime hotspots, to the courtroom, where risk assessment tools inform decisions on bail, sentencing, and parole, AI is increasingly becoming an influential, albeit often invisible, actor. However, this technological advancement is not a panacea; instead, it introduces a complex web of ethical and legal challenges, particularly concerning the fundamental principles of due process enshrined in the Fifth Amendment. The promise of AI to reduce human bias is frequently undermined by the very data it is trained on, data that often reflects and perpetuates deeply ingrained societal prejudices.

Predictive policing systems, for instance, are designed to analyze vast datasets of historical crime information – including arrest records, incident reports, and demographic data – to forecast where and when crimes are most likely to occur. The underlying assumption is that by identifying patterns, law enforcement can allocate resources more effectively, thereby deterring crime and enhancing public safety. Yet, these systems are trained on data that is the product of past policing practices. If certain communities have been historically over-policed, leading to a disproportionate number of arrests and reported incidents, the AI will inevitably identify these areas as high-risk. Consequently, these areas will receive even greater law enforcement attention, potentially leading to a feedback loop where more arrests are made, further reinforcing the AI's prediction. This creates a self-fulfilling prophecy, where the algorithm's predictions are validated not by an actual increase in criminal propensity, but by the intensified scrutiny it itself prompts. The consequence is a reinforcement of existing disparities, particularly affecting minority and low-income communities, who are often the subjects of this disproportionate policing. This algorithmic bias directly clashes with the Fifth Amendment's guarantee of due process, which demands fair and impartial treatment under the law. When an algorithm directs law enforcement attention based on historical inequities rather than current, objective risk, the fairness of that process is called into question.

Beyond prediction, AI is increasingly deployed in risk assessment tools, which aim to quantify an individual's likelihood of reoffending or failing to appear in court. These tools are used at various junctures: to determine whether a suspect should be granted bail, to inform sentencing decisions, and to assess eligibility for parole. The algorithms typically consider a range of factors, such as prior convictions, age, employment history, and socioeconomic indicators. While these factors may correlate with recidivism rates in aggregate statistical analysis, their use in individual cases can be problematic. The danger lies in the fact that many of these factors are proxies for race and socioeconomic status. For example, an algorithm might penalize individuals from disadvantaged neighborhoods or those with a history of unemployment, factors that are often correlated with racial minorities due to systemic discrimination. If an individual from a historically marginalized community receives a higher risk score simply because of these factors, which are themselves products of societal biases, then the resulting decision – whether it's denial of bail or a harsher sentence – is not based on an individual's true risk, but on an algorithm that has internalized historical discrimination. This can lead to individuals being subjected to more punitive measures not because of their individual culpability or likelihood of future harm, but because the algorithm has flagged them as higher risk based on demographic and socioeconomic characteristics that are themselves tainted by bias. This constitutes a violation of due process, as individuals are not being treated as unique entities but as statistical representatives of biased data.

The challenge of bias in AI within the criminal justice system is further compounded by the opacity of many of these algorithms, often referred to as "black boxes." The complex nature of machine learning models can make it exceedingly difficult, if not impossible, to understand precisely why a particular decision was reached. When an AI recommends denying bail or suggests a lengthy prison sentence, and the rationale is inscrutable, it becomes a formidable task for defendants and their legal counsel to challenge the decision effectively. Due process requires that individuals have the opportunity to understand the evidence against them and to present a defense. If the "evidence" is an algorithmic output that cannot be fully explained or audited, this fundamental right is undermined. The inability to scrutinize the decision-making process of these AI systems creates a significant hurdle in ensuring fairness and accountability. Without transparency, it is nearly impossible to identify and rectify the biases that may be embedded within the system, perpetuating a cycle of unfairness that disproportionately impacts vulnerable populations.

Moreover, the very definition of "fairness" in algorithmic decision-making is a subject of ongoing debate and technical challenge. Different mathematical definitions of fairness can be mutually exclusive. For instance, an algorithm that is "fair" in terms of equal false positive rates across different demographic groups might not be "fair" in terms of equal true positive rates. This means that any attempt to optimize for one type of fairness may inadvertently create unfairness in another. For example, an algorithm designed to minimize false arrests might still disproportionately flag individuals from certain communities for suspicion, even if the rate of actual arrests is equalized. This complexity highlights the difficulty of programming fairness into AI systems when the real world is inherently complex and marked by historical injustices. The legal system, which relies on clear principles of justice and equality, struggles to grapple with these nuanced algorithmic trade-offs. The Fifth Amendment's promise of due process demands a level of certainty and predictability that is difficult to achieve when the underlying decision-making tools are probabilistic and their fairness metrics are subject to such complex and conflicting interpretations.

The issue of data quality and completeness is another critical factor contributing to bias. AI systems are only as good as the data they are trained on. In the context of criminal justice, this data can be incomplete, inaccurate, or reflect historical biases in reporting and enforcement. For example, if certain types of offenses are more likely to be reported or prosecuted in specific neighborhoods, the AI will learn to associate those offenses with those areas, regardless of the actual prevalence of the behavior. Furthermore, the absence of data can also be a source of bias. If certain groups are underrepresented in the data due to historical marginalization or lack of access to legal representation, the AI may not accurately assess their risk or may even overlook them entirely in its analysis. This can lead to a situation where the system is biased not only by what it sees but also by what it doesn't see, further entrenching existing inequalities. The Fifth Amendment's requirement for due process means that individuals should not be subjected to adverse legal consequences based on flawed or incomplete information that reflects systemic biases.

The concept of accountability is also deeply intertwined with the use of AI in criminal justice. When an AI system contributes to an unfair outcome, such as an erroneous arrest, an unjustified denial of bail, or an excessively harsh sentence, who is ultimately responsible? Is it the developers of the algorithm, the law enforcement agency that deployed it, the judge who relied on its recommendation, or the data itself? The diffusion of responsibility can make it exceedingly difficult to hold anyone accountable for algorithmic injustice. This lack of clear accountability undermines the very foundation of due process, which presumes that there are mechanisms for redress and correction when the legal system errs. The Fifth Amendment requires that the government act fairly and justly, and this fairness is eroded when decisions are outsourced to opaque, potentially biased, and unchallengeable algorithms. Ensuring accountability necessitates a robust framework for auditing AI systems, understanding their decision-making processes, and establishing clear lines of responsibility when harm occurs.

The potential for adversarial attacks on these AI systems also presents a threat to due process. Sophisticated actors could potentially manipulate the data used by these algorithms to achieve specific outcomes, either to frame an innocent individual or to evade detection. If AI systems are not sufficiently robust and secure, they can be subverted, leading to miscarriages of justice that are even more insidious because they are masked by the veneer of technological objectivity. The Fifth Amendment's guarantee of due process is rooted in the idea of a just and reliable legal process. When the tools used within that process are vulnerable to manipulation or are inherently biased, that reliability is compromised. The pursuit of fairness and due process in the algorithmic age thus requires not only addressing inherent biases but also ensuring the security and integrity of the AI systems themselves.

Furthermore, the introduction of AI into the criminal justice system raises questions about the role of human judgment. While AI can process data at speeds and scales far beyond human capacity, it lacks the capacity for empathy, nuanced understanding of context, and the ability to consider exceptional circumstances that are crucial for just decision-making. Over-reliance on AI recommendations can lead to a de-skilling of legal professionals and a reduction of judicial discretion, potentially leading to outcomes that are technically "correct" according to the algorithm but ethically or morally unsound. Due process is not merely about procedural correctness; it is about ensuring that justice is rendered in a way that respects human dignity and individual circumstances. When AI systems are allowed to supplant human judgment entirely, the very essence of a humane and just legal process is threatened, and the Fifth Amendment's promise of due process, which implicitly includes the consideration of individual human factors, is diminished. The challenge lies in integrating AI as a tool to assist human decision-makers, rather than replacing them, ensuring that technology serves justice rather than dictating it.

The pervasive use of AI in criminal justice, therefore, demands rigorous scrutiny to ensure that it aligns with the constitutional imperative of due process. This involves a multi-faceted approach: developing methods to detect and mitigate bias in training data and algorithmic models; promoting transparency and explainability in AI decision-making; establishing clear lines of accountability for algorithmic outcomes; and fostering ongoing dialogue about the ethical implications of deploying AI in sensitive legal contexts. Without such measures, the promise of AI to create a more just and equitable criminal justice system risks becoming a reality that deepens existing inequalities and erodes fundamental constitutional rights. The Fifth Amendment's guarantee of due process is not merely a procedural safeguard; it is a bulwark against arbitrary and unjust governmental action, and its principles must be rigorously applied to the emerging landscape of algorithmic governance.

The right to a fair hearing, a cornerstone of due process, is increasingly imperiled by the opaque and often inscrutable nature of algorithmic decision-making within the state apparatus. When individuals are subjected to judgments rendered by complex algorithms, especially in contexts with significant legal or administrative consequences, the fundamental expectation of a transparent and equitable process can be severely undermined. The core of a fair hearing lies in the ability of an individual to understand the basis of a decision affecting them and to have a meaningful opportunity to challenge it. However, many of the algorithms employed today operate as "black boxes," their internal workings so intricate and proprietary that even their creators may struggle to fully articulate the specific rationale behind a particular output. This opacity directly conflicts with the due process requirement for an intelligible and contestable decision.

Consider, for instance, the deployment of AI in administrative tribunals or in the initial screening of legal claims. Imagine a scenario where an application for social benefits, a crucial lifeline for many, is denied by an automated system. The applicant receives a notification of denial, perhaps citing a generalized rule or a perceived failure to meet certain criteria, but the precise algorithmic logic that led to this outcome remains undisclosed. This lack of transparency erects a formidable barrier to a fair hearing. Without understanding

*why* their application was rejected, the individual is left in a state of profound disadvantage when attempting to appeal or seek reconsideration. The appeal process, intended to provide a robust mechanism for rectifying errors or mitigating harshness, becomes a futile exercise if the appellant cannot identify the specific points of contention within the algorithmic decision-making process. The Fifth Amendment's guarantee of due process demands more than just a perfunctory review; it necessitates an opportunity for substantive engagement with the rationale behind adverse governmental actions. When that rationale is encoded in an algorithm that cannot be adequately explained or interrogated, this opportunity is effectively extinguished.

The implications extend beyond mere administrative hurdles; they touch upon the very legitimacy of governmental decisions. If individuals are unable to comprehend why they have been denied a permit, have had their licenses revoked, or have been subjected to some other adverse administrative action, they may come to view the system as arbitrary and capricious. This erosion of trust is a dangerous consequence, particularly in a democratic society that relies on the consent of the governed. The promise of efficiency and objectivity that algorithms bring is hollow if it comes at the cost of fundamental fairness and the perceived legitimacy of the decision-making process. The right to a fair hearing is not merely a technical legal requirement; it is a vital component of the social contract, ensuring that the state acts not only effectively but also justly and accountably.

Furthermore, the lack of human oversight in many algorithmic decision-making processes exacerbates the problem. While AI can process vast amounts of data and identify patterns that might escape human notice, it lacks the capacity for nuanced judgment, empathy, and the consideration of individual circumstances that are often critical for a truly fair resolution. A human adjudicator, even when bound by strict rules, can often exercise discretion, taking into account mitigating factors, contextual nuances, or unforeseen exceptions that an algorithm, by its very design, is incapable of appreciating. When an algorithm is permitted to make a final determination without meaningful human review, the opportunity for such crucial humanistic considerations is lost. This can lead to outcomes that are technically "correct" according to the algorithm's programmed logic but are deeply unfair or unjust from a human perspective. The Fifth Amendment's due process clause implies a system that is not only procedural but also substantive in its pursuit of fairness, and this substantive fairness often requires the application of human wisdom and ethical judgment, qualities that are absent in automated decision-making.

The proprietary nature of many AI algorithms adds another layer of complexity to the right to a fair hearing. Companies that develop and sell these systems often guard their algorithms as trade secrets, arguing that disclosure would compromise their intellectual property and competitive advantage. While intellectual property rights are important, they cannot be allowed to supersede fundamental constitutional rights. When the output of a proprietary algorithm has a significant impact on an individual's life, the opacity that stems from its proprietary status becomes a direct impediment to due process. The argument that an algorithm is too complex or too valuable to be scrutinized by those it affects is an unacceptable justification for denying a fair hearing. The legal system must find ways to balance the legitimate interests of technology providers with the inalienable rights of individuals, perhaps through mechanisms for independent auditing or the development of legally sanctioned methods for explaining algorithmic reasoning in a way that is understandable to affected parties and their legal representatives.

The challenge is particularly acute in situations where AI is used to predict future behavior or assess risk. For example, algorithms used in parole decisions or in determining eligibility for certain government programs might flag an individual as high-risk based on factors that are not directly indicative of their current behavior or capacity. If the algorithm's reasoning for this classification is not transparent, the individual has no effective means of demonstrating why the classification is inaccurate or unfair. They cannot point to specific data points or logical flaws in the system's assessment if they do not have access to that information or the ability to understand it. This creates a cycle of disadvantage where individuals are penalized by systems they cannot comprehend or challenge, thereby denying them the meaningful opportunity to present their case that is fundamental to a fair hearing. The Fifth Amendment requires that individuals are afforded an opportunity to be heard, and this opportunity is rendered meaningless if the very basis of the decision against them is unknowable.

Moreover, the concept of "fairness" itself is often subject to different, sometimes conflicting, mathematical definitions within algorithmic design. An algorithm might be optimized for one type of fairness metric, such as demographic parity, while simultaneously failing to meet another, such as equalized odds. When these complex trade-offs are embedded within a decision-making system without clear explanation or recourse, the individuals affected may be subjected to outcomes that are statistically "fair" in one sense but deeply inequitable in another. The right to a fair hearing should not be contingent on understanding these intricate statistical debates; it should be grounded in a more fundamental understanding of justice and equity. When the state relies on tools that embody such complex and potentially irreconcilable notions of fairness, it risks abdicating its responsibility to provide a process that is unequivocally fair and understandable to all.

The absence of a robust system for auditing and challenging algorithmic decisions further erodes the right to a fair hearing. In traditional legal processes, there are established procedures for appealing decisions, presenting new evidence, and holding decision-makers accountable. When the decision-maker is an algorithm, these established mechanisms often fall short. It becomes difficult to identify who is responsible when an algorithmic decision is flawed – is it the developers, the deploying agency, or the data itself? This diffusion of responsibility can leave individuals with no clear path for redress, effectively denying them a meaningful appeal. The Fifth Amendment's guarantee of due process includes the implicit promise of accountability and the availability of remedies when governmental actions are unjust. Without clear accountability for algorithmic decisions, this promise is jeopardized. The state has a constitutional obligation to ensure that its decision-making processes are fair, and this obligation extends to ensuring that the algorithms it employs are subject to rigorous scrutiny and that there are clear avenues for challenge and correction.

Ultimately, the integration of algorithmic decision-making into the functions of the state presents a profound challenge to the constitutional imperative of a fair hearing. The very nature of opaque, complex, and proprietary algorithms can create an insurmountable barrier between the individual and the decision that affects them. To uphold the Fifth Amendment's guarantee of due process, the legal system must evolve. This evolution must include the development of mechanisms to ensure transparency in algorithmic decision-making, the establishment of clear lines of accountability, and the provision of meaningful opportunities for individuals to understand, challenge, and seek redress for algorithmic judgments. Without these safeguards, the promise of efficiency and objectivity offered by AI risks devolving into a new form of arbitrary governance, where fundamental rights are eroded in the name of automated progress. The right to be heard, and to be heard in a way that is comprehensible and contestable, remains a non-negotiable component of due process, even in the algorithmic age. The state's reliance on technology must not come at the expense of its most fundamental obligations to its citizens.

The Fifth Amendment to the United States Constitution famously declares that no person "shall be compelled in any criminal case to be a witness against himself." This bedrock protection, the privilege against self-incrimination, has long been understood to safeguard individuals from the coercive power of the state, preventing them from being forced to provide testimony that could lead to their own conviction. However, the advent of the digital age, and with it the pervasive collection and analysis of vast troves of personal data, has introduced unprecedented complexities to the application of this venerable right. The very notion of what constitutes "compelled testimony" is being stretched and strained as the state gains increasingly sophisticated capabilities to extract information about individuals, often without direct interrogation or even their explicit awareness.

At the heart of the issue lies the nature of digital information. Unlike a physical confession or verbal testimony given under duress, much of what can be used against an individual in the digital realm is passively generated. Every online search, every text message, every geolocation ping, every purchase, and every social media interaction contributes to an intricate digital footprint. This footprint, when aggregated and analyzed, can paint a remarkably detailed portrait of an individual's habits, associations, beliefs, and even their potential intentions. The question then becomes whether the compelled disclosure of access to such data, or the surrender of devices containing it, constitutes a form of self-incrimination. Courts have grappled with this, often drawing a distinction between the act of producing physical evidence and the act of providing testimonial evidence. The Supreme Court, in cases like

*Fisher v. United States* and *United States v. Hubbell*, has affirmed that the Fifth Amendment protects against being compelled to provide the *content* of incriminating statements, but not necessarily against being compelled to produce documents or information that are not themselves testimonial in nature. However, the act of production can, in some circumstances, be testimonial, as it can implicitly admit the existence and possession of the documents.

The rise of advanced surveillance technologies and the increasing integration of artificial intelligence into investigative processes further complicate this dynamic. AI systems can analyze patterns, identify anomalies, and infer connections within massive datasets at a speed and scale unimaginable to human investigators. This capability allows the state to construct compelling narratives of guilt or suspicion based on the digital remnants of an individual's life, often without ever directly asking the individual a question. For instance, an AI might cross-reference a suspect's online browsing history with known extremist propaganda, their social media connections with individuals flagged by other surveillance programs, and their financial transactions with suspicious vendors. The resulting algorithmic output can appear to be objective evidence of wrongdoing, yet it is derived from data that the individual may have never intended to be used in such a manner, and the process of its interpretation is often inscrutable.

The concept of "compelled disclosure" takes on new dimensions when dealing with encrypted data. Individuals may possess devices or online accounts protected by strong encryption, rendering their contents inaccessible without a password or decryption key. The state's desire to access this information, which may be crucial to an investigation, often leads to demands for the decryption key or the password itself. Here, the Fifth Amendment privilege becomes acutely relevant. If a password or decryption key is deemed to be testimonial evidence—a communication of knowledge—then compelling its disclosure could indeed violate the privilege. The Supreme Court's decision in

```````````````_` addressed the "act of production" doctrine in the context of a subpoena for documents, holding that the act of producing the documents could be testimonial if it implicitly confirmed their existence and the individual's possession. Extending this logic, forcing an individual to reveal a password could be seen as confirming their knowledge of it and their ability to access the encrypted data, which might then be used to incriminate them. However, courts have struggled to provide a uniform interpretation, with some ruling that the government cannot force an individual to reveal a password, while others have found ways to compel disclosure, often through narrowly tailored orders or by pursuing alternative means of access.

Furthermore, the "reasonable expectation of privacy" in the digital realm is itself a moving target, influenced by how readily accessible information is and how it is collected. When data is voluntarily shared on social media platforms, for example, the expectation of privacy diminishes. However, even seemingly innocuous digital activities can, when pieced together by sophisticated AI, reveal highly sensitive information. The state's ability to access and analyze this aggregated data raises questions about whether individuals are effectively being compelled to incriminate themselves through their very digital existence, even if they have not directly communicated incriminating statements. The challenge lies in the inferential power of AI. It doesn't just present raw data; it synthesizes, analyzes, and draws conclusions that can be highly persuasive in a legal context. If an AI system, through its analysis of an individual's digital footprint, flags them as a person of interest or provides a strong probabilistic link to a crime, the prosecution might argue that this derived information is equivalent to testimony.
```````````````

The ethical and legal implications of AI-driven inferences are profound. If an AI algorithm, trained on a massive dataset of past criminal cases, identifies patterns that correlate with future criminal activity, and then applies these patterns to an individual's current digital behavior, can the resulting prediction be considered "testimony" if it leads to suspicion or charges? The Fifth Amendment was designed to prevent the state from forcing an individual to reveal their thoughts, knowledge, or intent through direct questioning or coerced confessions. The power of AI to infer these very things from a digital trail, however, presents a novel challenge. It is akin to the state being able to read an individual's mind, not through direct psychic means, but through a complex computational analysis of their digital life.

One critical aspect of this challenge is the "all records" subpoena. These broad demands for digital information, often issued without specific probable cause for every item sought, can place individuals in a difficult position. If a person is compelled to produce all data within their possession that falls under the scope of such a subpoena, and that data contains incriminating evidence, have they been compelled to incriminate themselves? The act of gathering and producing that data, especially if it requires navigating vast digital archives or decrypting protected files, could be seen as an admission of their existence and accessibility. The Supreme Court has recognized that the Fifth Amendment protects against the compelled authentication of documents, which can be testimonial. When an individual is forced to sort through their digital life, identify relevant information, and produce it, they are implicitly attesting to the authenticity and possession of that information.

The increasing reliance on digital forensics and the "inevitable discovery" exception to the exclusionary rule further complicate the landscape. Even if an initial attempt to compel disclosure is deemed unconstitutional, law enforcement might argue that the information would have inevitably been discovered through other legal means. This can create a chilling effect, where individuals feel compelled to self-censor their digital activities or to comply with potentially overreaching requests for information, fearing that refusal will only lead to more aggressive investigative tactics. The Fifth Amendment's privilege is meant to provide a shield, not to be a procedural hurdle that can be circumvented through technological means.

The notion of "constructive confession" also emerges in this context. When an individual's digital activities, when analyzed by AI, create a profile that is overwhelmingly indicative of guilt, and they are unable to offer a credible alternative explanation due to the sheer volume and complexity of the data, has the state effectively manufactured a confession without direct interrogation? The Fifth Amendment is fundamentally about protecting individual autonomy and preventing the state from usurping an individual's will. The passive generation of data, which is then computationally analyzed to produce incriminating conclusions, challenges this autonomy. It forces individuals to confront the reality that their digital lives are constantly under a form of pervasive, albeit often automated, scrutiny, and that the inferences drawn from this scrutiny can be used against them.

The challenge extends to the application of the privilege in civil contexts as well. While the Fifth Amendment is primarily invoked in criminal proceedings, its principles can extend to civil cases where testimony might lead to criminal prosecution. In the digital age, where information is so fluid and often shared across various platforms, it can be difficult to compartmentalize the implications of compelled disclosure. A civil deposition, for instance, could unearth digital communications that are highly incriminating, even if the initial focus of the deposition was on unrelated matters. The ability of AI to quickly identify and flag such information means that the potential for incidental incrimination is ever-present.

Moreover, the proprietary nature of many AI algorithms used by law enforcement and government agencies creates a transparency problem that exacerbates the Fifth Amendment concerns. If the logic by which an AI system reaches its conclusions is hidden, individuals are left in the dark about how their digital footprints are being interpreted. This opacity makes it incredibly difficult to challenge the inferences drawn or to argue that the compelled production of data was not truly incriminating because the algorithmic analysis was flawed. The Fifth Amendment demands that individuals are not forced into a position where they cannot understand or contest the evidence used against them. When that evidence is the output of a proprietary AI system, the deck can be heavily stacked against the individual.

The development of new legal frameworks and judicial interpretations is essential to ensure that the Fifth Amendment privilege remains a robust protection in the digital age. This may involve re-examining the scope of "testimonial communication" to encompass the act of providing access to encrypted data or the implicit admissions made through the production of vast digital archives. It may also require holding that the compelled analysis of an individual's digital footprint by AI, when that analysis leads to inferential conclusions of guilt, constitutes a form of compelled self-incrimination. The ultimate goal must be to ensure that the state's technological capabilities do not erode the fundamental right against being forced to testify against oneself, preserving the balance of power between the individual and the state in an increasingly data-driven world. The digital footprint, once a mere shadow, is now a tangible source of evidence, and the Fifth Amendment must adapt to protect individuals from being compelled to confess through their own data.

The increasing deployment of artificial intelligence and sophisticated algorithms in governance and law enforcement presents a profound challenge to the very foundations of due process. A cornerstone of a just legal system is the ability of individuals to understand the basis of decisions that affect their lives, particularly when those decisions carry significant legal or social consequences. When the machinery of state power relies on opaque, "black box" algorithms, this fundamental right is systematically undermined. The very essence of due process demands a level of transparency and explainability that many contemporary AI systems are inherently incapable of providing. Without these qualities, the principles of fairness, accountability, and the right to challenge adverse decisions are rendered practically unattainable.

The "black box" problem refers to the inscrutable nature of many advanced AI models, particularly deep learning neural networks. These systems can achieve remarkable predictive accuracy by learning intricate, often non-linear relationships within vast datasets. However, the internal workings of these models, the precise weightings and connections that lead to a specific output, are often beyond human comprehension. Even the developers of these systems may struggle to articulate *why* a particular decision was made. This lack of interpretability creates a significant chiasm in the application of due process. If an individual is denied a loan, flagged for surveillance, recommended for a harsher sentence, or even deemed a risk to public safety by an algorithm, they are entitled, under due process, to understand the reasons for that determination. They must have a meaningful opportunity to contest it. When the reasoning is buried within an inscrutable computational architecture, such an opportunity becomes an illusion.

Consider the implications for administrative law and regulatory compliance. Government agencies are increasingly using AI for tasks such as identifying tax fraud, screening visa applications, or assessing eligibility for social benefits. If an individual's application is rejected, or they are subjected to a heightened level of scrutiny, and the only explanation offered is that "the algorithm flagged it," what recourse do they have? They cannot identify specific errors in the algorithm's logic, point to flawed data inputs, or demonstrate that the algorithm applied an inappropriate rule. The decision, however consequential, appears to emanate from an unappealable, unexplainable oracle. This breeds a sense of powerlessness and erodes public trust in the fairness of governmental processes. The ideal of due process is not merely about procedural correctness; it is about ensuring that individuals are treated with dignity and respect, which includes being informed and having the ability to engage with the decisions made about them.

In the realm of criminal justice, the stakes are even higher. Algorithms are being used to predict recidivism rates, inform sentencing recommendations, and even assist in parole decisions. If an individual is denied parole, or receives a stricter sentence, based on an algorithmic risk assessment that is not transparent, their ability to appeal or seek a review is severely hampered. How can a defense attorney argue that a risk assessment is flawed if they cannot examine its underlying logic or the data it considered? The concept of a fair trial and the right to confront evidence are fundamentally challenged when that evidence is the output of a system that operates as a black box. The adversarial system of justice relies on the ability of both sides to understand and critique the evidence presented. Opacity in algorithmic decision-making effectively blinds one party, tilting the scales of justice in an unseen direction.

Furthermore, the deployment of these opaque systems can perpetuate and amplify existing societal biases, often in ways that are difficult to detect and even harder to rectify. AI models are trained on historical data, and if that data reflects past discrimination—whether based on race, gender, socioeconomic status, or other factors—the algorithm will learn and replicate those biases. For example, an algorithm trained on historical arrest data from a community with a history of over-policing might learn to associate certain demographic markers with higher crime risk, even if those markers are not causally linked to criminal behavior. If the workings of this algorithm are hidden, it becomes nearly impossible to identify and correct such biased outputs. The result is a system that can, in effect, automate discrimination under the guise of objective, data-driven decision-making. This is antithetical to the equal protection principles that underpin due process.

The legal framework surrounding due process has historically relied on principles like notice, an opportunity to be heard, and the right to a decision based on evidence and reasoned judgment. The emergence of black box algorithms strains these principles to their breaking point. For "notice" to be meaningful, individuals must understand *why* a particular action is being taken against them. For an "opportunity to be heard" to be effective, individuals must be able to articulate specific grounds for challenging a decision. And for a decision to be based on "reasoned judgment," its underlying logic must be accessible and reviewable. Black box AI fundamentally obstructs all three.

The concept of

*auditable AI* emerges as a crucial countermeasure. An auditable AI system is one where its decision-making processes can be examined, traced, and verified. This does not necessarily mean that every single connection within a neural network must be rendered into plain language, which may be an unrealistic expectation for complex models. However, it does mean that there must be mechanisms in place to understand the key factors influencing a decision, to identify potential biases in the training data or the model itself, and to log the inputs and outputs in a way that allows for retrospective analysis. This might involve developing explainable AI (XAI) techniques, which aim to provide insights into the model's reasoning, or implementing rigorous testing and validation protocols that go beyond mere accuracy metrics.

Moreover, the development and deployment of AI for governance and law enforcement must be guided by a proactive commitment to fairness and equity, rather than a reactive approach that seeks to mitigate harm after it has occurred. This means incorporating principles of fairness and transparency into the design and development phases of these systems. It might involve establishing ethical review boards, conducting impact assessments before deployment, and ensuring that diverse perspectives are included in the development process. The legal and ethical obligations of the state extend beyond simply ensuring that an algorithm is technically functional; they must also ensure that it operates in a manner consistent with constitutional rights and societal values.

The courts are beginning to grapple with these challenges, but the legal precedents are still evolving. Cases involving algorithmic bias in areas like predictive policing or credit scoring are slowly making their way through the judicial system, forcing judges to consider how traditional due process principles apply to these new technological realities. There is a growing recognition that simply relying on the "accuracy" of an algorithm is insufficient if that accuracy comes at the cost of fairness, transparency, and the ability to challenge decisions. The Fifth Amendment's guarantee of due process is not a static concept; it is a living principle that must adapt to the evolving landscape of state power and technological capability.

The development of standards for transparency and explainability in AI is not merely a technical challenge; it is a fundamental legal and ethical imperative. Without them, the algorithmic state risks becoming an unaccountable leviathan, capable of making life-altering decisions through processes that are fundamentally unknowable and unchallengeable by the very individuals they govern. This erosion of transparency and accountability would represent a profound departure from the principles of due process, transforming the relationship between the citizen and the state into one characterized by arbitrary power rather than reasoned justice. The "black box" must be opened, or at least rendered sufficiently transparent, for the promise of due process to endure in the age of algorithmic governance. This requires a concerted effort from technologists, legal scholars, policymakers, and the judiciary to ensure that the algorithms that increasingly shape our lives are subject to the same demands for fairness, accountability, and transparency that we expect from human decision-makers. The future of due process, and indeed of democratic governance, may well depend on our ability to render these complex systems intelligible and subject to meaningful oversight.

The increasing reliance on artificial intelligence in areas traditionally governed by human judgment—such as law enforcement and judicial proceedings—introduces a subtle yet pernicious erosion of a foundational legal principle: the presumption of innocence. While the Fifth Amendment's Due Process Clause guarantees fair treatment and protection against arbitrary government action, the predictive power of AI, when applied to anticipating future behavior rather than evaluating past deeds, can inadvertently shift the burden of proof and stigmatize individuals before any wrongdoing has occurred. This is particularly evident in the domains of predictive policing and algorithmic risk assessment.

Predictive policing, a strategy that employs algorithms to forecast where and when crimes are most likely to occur, carries with it the implicit danger of pre-emptively labeling individuals or communities as inherently more prone to criminal activity. When these systems identify a "hotspot" or an individual exhibiting certain behavioral patterns or demographic characteristics that the algorithm associates with elevated risk, the consequence can be increased surveillance, more frequent stops, or a heightened police presence. While the stated aim is crime prevention, the practical effect can be the treating of certain populations not as innocent until proven guilty, but as potentially guilty until proven innocent, or at least as perpetual suspects. The algorithm, by flagging an individual or a locale, creates a presumption of elevated risk, and this presumption can influence interactions with law enforcement, leading to scrutiny that may not be warranted by any actual offense. The danger lies in the fact that these algorithmic "predictions" are often based on historical data, which itself can be riddled with societal biases. If past policing practices have disproportionately targeted certain communities, the data will reflect this, leading the algorithm to perpetuate and even amplify these biases. Consequently, individuals from these communities might find themselves under increased scrutiny not because of their individual actions, but because the algorithm has identified them as statistically likely offenders based on flawed or biased historical information. This is a profound subversion of the presumption of innocence, where the state's focus shifts from investigating concrete evidence of past wrongdoing to managing probabilities of future misconduct.

Similarly, the application of algorithmic risk assessment tools in the criminal justice system, from pre-trial detention decisions to sentencing and parole recommendations, can also undermine the presumption of innocence. These tools are designed to predict an individual's likelihood of reoffending or failing to appear in court. While intended to inform judicial discretion with objective data, they can inadvertently create a scenario where an individual's liberty is curtailed based on a statistical probability rather than on established facts about their past conduct or concrete evidence of present guilt. If an algorithm assigns a high-risk score to a defendant, this score can influence a judge's decision to deny bail or impose a harsher sentence. The defendant is then effectively being penalized, in part, for a future transgression that has not yet occurred, and for which there is no direct evidence. This is fundamentally at odds with the principle that individuals should be judged based on their actions, not on speculative projections of their future behavior. The due process implications are significant: individuals may be deprived of their liberty or face more severe consequences without having committed a specific offense that warrants such treatment. The very concept of "risk" becomes a proxy for guilt, especially when the underlying logic of the algorithms is opaque and the data upon which they are trained may reflect systemic inequalities. The presumption of innocence demands that the state prove its case beyond a reasonable doubt based on concrete evidence. When algorithmic predictions of future behavior carry substantial weight in legal determinations, this fundamental requirement is weakened.

The shift in focus from past actions to predicted future behavior represents a departure from established legal traditions. Legal systems have historically been designed to address and adjudicate past offenses. Investigations are initiated based on alleged crimes that have already happened. Trials are concerned with establishing guilt or innocence for those specific actions. Sentences are designed to punish, deter, or rehabilitate based on the proven commission of an offense. Introducing algorithms that prioritize predicting future criminality fundamentally alters this paradigm. It moves the state's focus towards pre-emption and risk management, where individuals are assessed and potentially penalized based on what they

*might* do, rather than what they *have* done. This proactive, predictive approach, while potentially appealing for its efficiency in crime prevention, carries a heavy price for individual liberty and due process. It risks creating a society where individuals are constantly under suspicion, their freedom of movement and action subtly curtailed by the invisible hand of algorithmic judgment. The burden of proof, conceptually, begins to shift. Instead of the state needing to prove guilt, individuals might feel compelled to prove their own low risk, or to actively demonstrate their innocence of future potential crimes, a notion that is inherently illogical and legally unsound.

Furthermore, the opacity of many of these predictive algorithms exacerbates the problem. If an individual is subject to increased scrutiny or faces adverse legal consequences due to an algorithmic assessment, they are often unable to understand the specific factors that led to that determination. This makes it exceedingly difficult to challenge the assessment, to identify potential errors or biases, or to present evidence that might counter the algorithmic prediction. Due process requires not only fairness in the outcome but also fairness in the process itself, which includes the right to understand the basis of any decision and the opportunity to contest it meaningfully. When the reasoning behind an algorithmic prediction is inscrutable, this right is severely compromised. The individual is left to contend with a verdict delivered by a black box, a system whose internal logic is beyond their comprehension and control. This power imbalance is further amplified by the fact that the data used to train these algorithms can reflect historical discrimination. For example, if an algorithm used in sentencing is trained on data where individuals from certain racial or socioeconomic backgrounds have historically received harsher sentences, the algorithm might learn to associate those characteristics with higher recidivism risk. This can lead to a self-perpetuating cycle of disadvantage, where the algorithm, intended to be objective, instead codifies and automates existing societal inequalities, disproportionately impacting already marginalized communities.

The concept of the presumption of innocence is not merely a procedural safeguard; it is a profound statement about human dignity and the relationship between the individual and the state. It asserts that each person is to be treated as an equal member of society, free from the stigma of suspicion, until and unless the state can prove otherwise through established legal means. When predictive algorithms begin to define individuals by their statistical likelihood of future criminality, this foundational respect for individual autonomy and inherent worth is diminished. The state's power shifts from reactive justice—addressing wrongs after they occur—to a form of pre-emptive social control, where individuals are managed based on perceived future threats. This could lead to a chilling effect on behavior, as individuals may become more hesitant to engage in activities that might be flagged by an algorithm, even if those activities are perfectly legal and innocuous. The very freedom to live without constant, algorithmically-driven suspicion is a liberty that is imperiled by the unchecked deployment of predictive AI in the public sphere.

The challenge for due process in the algorithmic age is to ensure that the pursuit of efficiency and crime prevention through AI does not come at the expense of fundamental rights. This requires a critical examination of how predictive algorithms are developed, validated, and deployed. It necessitates a demand for transparency and explainability in these systems, so that individuals can understand and challenge the basis of algorithmic assessments that affect their lives. Moreover, it calls for a robust legal and ethical framework that reasserts the primacy of the presumption of innocence, ensuring that individuals are judged by their actions, not by the probabilistic outputs of a machine. Without such safeguards, the algorithmic state risks transforming a society based on justice and individual rights into one governed by opaque calculations and pre-emptive suspicion, thereby fundamentally altering the balance of power between the governed and the governors in ways that are profoundly antithetical to the spirit of the Fifth Amendment. The very notion of "innocent until proven guilty" is a bulwark against state overreach; when the state begins to act on probabilities of future guilt, this bulwark is significantly weakened, if not entirely breached, by the subtle, often imperceptible, influence of algorithms.

The Grand Inquisitor, as depicted in Dostoyevsky's profound parable, emerges not as a figure of genuine divine authority, but as its chilling perversion. Viewed through the lens of Catholic theology, his pronouncements and actions reveal a profound corruption of the spiritual shepherd's role, a distorted echo of the pastoral care Christ himself embodied. His meticulously constructed authority is not founded on the bedrock of love, grace, and the arduous journey of faith, but on the edifice of control, coercion, and the seductive promise of earthly peace at the cost of spiritual freedom. This antithetical approach to governance and salvation is precisely what makes his figure so potent and, in its own way, so terrifyingly instructive.

At the heart of the Inquisitor's perversion of shepherding lies his fundamental misunderstanding, or more accurately, his deliberate rejection, of the nature of divine love and human free will. Christ, in Dostoyevsky's narrative, represents the ultimate shepherd who offers boundless, unconditional love, inviting humanity to follow Him freely, even if that path is fraught with difficulty and doubt. This is the essence of true faith: a voluntary ascent, an embrace of the unknown, a leap of trust rooted in the belief in a benevolent, transcendent reality. The Inquisitor, conversely, champions a gospel of earthly satisfaction, a bargain where bread, security, and a guaranteed, albeit hollow, happiness are traded for the exhilarating, yet perilous, burden of spiritual liberty. He sees Christ's offering as a fatal flaw, an act of hubris that overestimated humanity's capacity for genuine, self-directed faith. For the Inquisitor, freedom is not a gift to be cherished and responsibly wielded, but a dangerous burden that leads to suffering and rebellion. His theology, therefore, is one of subjugation masquerading as salvation.

The Catholic tradition, with its emphasis on the sacraments, the Church as the Mystical Body of Christ, and the ongoing work of grace, provides a rich framework for understanding the Inquisitor's deviance. The Church, in its ideal, is a community of believers guided by the Holy Spirit, where authority is exercised in service, not dominance. Priests and bishops are meant to be spiritual shepherds, feeding the flock, guiding them through the complexities of life and faith, and ultimately pointing them towards God. The Inquisitor, however, embodies the antithesis of this ideal. He does not feed the flock; he crams them with the illusory sustenance of material comfort and enforced conformity. He does not guide them towards spiritual growth; he chains them to a comfortable ignorance, removing the very challenges that forge character and deepen faith. His "miracle," "mystery," and "authority" are not divine manifestations intended to uplift and enlighten, but instruments of psychological manipulation designed to secure absolute obedience. The Catholic concept of 'obedience' within the faith is understood as a willing submission to God's will, often mediated through the Church, but always preserving the individual's core dignity and capacity for discerning love. The Inquisitor twists this into a blind, unthinking compliance, a relinquishing of the very faculties God endowed humanity with.

The ethical implications of wielding power in the name of faith are nowhere more starkly illustrated than in the Grand Inquisitor's methods. He operates on the principle that for the good of humanity, and in service to a divinely ordained order, certain truths must be suppressed, certain freedoms must be extinguished, and the more complex, challenging aspects of faith must be papered over with dogma and ritual that demand little personal sacrifice. This is a dangerous ethical slippery slope. When the perceived goal—be it social order, political stability, or even a misguided notion of collective salvation—justifies the subjugation of individual conscience and the suppression of truth, the very foundations of morality begin to crumble. The Catholic Church, while historically wielding significant temporal power, has also grappled with the tension between institutional authority and the radical demands of the Gospel. The Inquisitor, however, represents a complete capitulation to the former, using the guise of divine mandate to impose a purely human, and ultimately tyrannical, system. His is not a pastoral authority; it is a political one, leveraging spiritual fears and aspirations for the sake of control.

The Inquisitor's critique of Christ's refusal of the devil's temptations—bread, the miracle of power, and the kingdom of the world—is central to his perverted theology. He argues that Christ was wrong to prioritize spiritual freedom over the immediate needs and desires of humankind. He believes that by rejecting the easy solutions offered by the devil, Christ condemned humanity to unnecessary suffering and doubt. The Inquisitor presents himself as the one who corrects this perceived error, offering a path of least resistance. He effectively argues that Christ's radical emphasis on inner freedom and spiritual growth was an unrealistic expectation for the masses. He champions a religion that caters to the "weak, the base, and the wicked," those who crave certainty and submission. This resonates with a Catholic understanding of Christ's divinity and humanity. Christ's temptations were not merely temptations for a man, but a demonstration of His divine wisdom in choosing the spiritual over the temporal, the eternal over the fleeting. The Inquisitor's rejection of this choice is a rejection of Christ's true mission and a testament to his own earthly, power-hungry orientation.

The suppression of difficult truths and the avoidance of genuine spiritual struggle are the hallmarks of the Inquisitor's regime. He offers a religion that is easy to follow, requiring little in the way of personal sacrifice, self-examination, or grappling with the existential questions that plague the human heart. This stands in stark opposition to the Catholic tradition, which, while offering solace and structure, also acknowledges the profound mysteries of faith, the reality of sin, and the necessity of penance and struggle on the path to salvation. The sacraments themselves, while channels of grace, are often accompanied by confession, absolution, and the call to ongoing conversion. The Inquisitor's "Church" eliminates these elements, replacing them with a passive acceptance of prescribed doctrines and a superficial adherence to rituals that demand no deep inner transformation. His followers are not invited to wrestle with doubt; they are simply forbidden from having it. This is not faith; it is indoctrination. The theological concept of 'kenosis,' Christ's self-emptying, and the corresponding call for believers to embrace humility and self-denial, is utterly absent in the Inquisitor's world.

Furthermore, the Inquisitor's desire for universal obedience, enforced through his "great power," highlights a fundamental misunderstanding of the nature of love within a theological framework. True love, as understood in Catholic teaching, is not coercive; it is a free gift, and it elicits a free response. Christ's love for humanity is not a demand; it is an invitation. The Inquisitor's approach, conversely, is predicated on the idea that humanity cannot be trusted with freedom, and therefore must be compelled to accept salvation, or at least a facsimile of it. He replaces the difficult, often painful, work of drawing people to God through love and example with the seemingly efficient, but ultimately hollow, method of imposing conformity. His system creates a society of the tamed, not the redeemed. This is a crucial distinction: redemption implies a process of transformation, a liberation from sin and falsehood. The Inquisitor offers merely a form of spiritual domestication, a pacification of the human spirit that is devoid of true spiritual vitality.

The "three days" of Christ's descent into hell, a profound theological concept in Christianity signifying His triumph over death and the opening of the gates of heaven, is twisted by the Inquisitor into a narrative of Christ's failure. He claims Christ returned empty-handed, having brought nothing but spiritual torment and confusion to mankind. This is a blasphemous interpretation, designed to legitimize his own dominion. The Inquisitor sees himself as the one who has salvaged humanity from Christ's well-intentioned but disastrous experiment. He presents his rigid, authoritarian system as the necessary corrective to Christ's radical trust in human freedom. In this, he aligns himself with the spirit of the Antichrist, a figure who would usurp Christ's authority and offer a false salvation based on worldly power and control. The Catholic doctrine of the Incarnation, the union of the divine and human in Christ, and His subsequent Passion, Death, and Resurrection, is the central mystery of faith. The Inquisitor's attempt to reframe this mystery as a failure is a testament to his profound spiritual blindness and his ultimate allegiance to earthly power rather than divine truth.

The Inquisitor's ultimate goal is not the salvation of souls in the Christian sense, but the establishment of a perfectly ordered, predictable, and obedient society. He views humanity as inherently flawed and incapable of self-governance, requiring a firm hand to guide it. This perspective fundamentally contradicts the Catholic teaching on original sin, which acknowledges human fallenness but also affirms the enduring image of God in humanity and the potential for grace to redeem and transform. The Inquisitor, in his despair over human nature, overreaches, seeking to eliminate the very struggle that is integral to the process of sanctification. He desires a world where sin and suffering are eradicated, not through the transformative power of Christ's redemption, but through the eradication of the freedom that makes sin and suffering possible. This is a theological error of immense proportions, an attempt to bypass the divine plan for salvation by imposing a human-engineered substitute.

The concept of "miracle, mystery, and authority" as the three powers by which the Inquisitor claims to have "corrected" Christ's work further illuminates his corrupted shepherding. The true miracles of Christ were acts of divine power and compassion, intended to reveal His identity and offer healing. The Inquisitor's "miracle" is the appeasement of human hunger and the promise of earthly security, a perversion of Christ's feeding of the multitudes. The "mystery" for Christ was the unfolding of God's plan for salvation, a mystery revealed through His life, death, and resurrection. For the Inquisitor, "mystery" is a tool of manipulation, an opaque pronouncement that demands unquestioning belief, obscuring the logical inconsistencies of his doctrine. And "authority," for Christ, was derived from His divine nature and His loving obedience to the Father. For the Inquisitor, authority is an end in itself, a tool to enforce his will and maintain his dominion. These are not divine powers; they are the very temptations Christ rejected, re-packaged and offered as the instruments of his "salvation."

In essence, the Grand Inquisitor represents a profound theological warning. He is the ultimate fallen shepherd, who, in his desire to protect his flock from the harsh realities of freedom and faith, ends up enslaving them. His methods, though presented as benevolent and necessary for human happiness, are built upon a foundation of fear, coercion, and the suppression of essential human dignity. He offers a false peace, a sterile order devoid of the vibrant life that springs from genuine love and freely chosen faith. Through his character, Dostoyevsky compels us to confront the seductive allure of absolute security and the devastating price that can be paid when that security is purchased at the cost of the very essence of our spiritual humanity. The Catholic theological tradition, with its emphasis on free will, divine grace, and the arduous but ultimately liberating journey of faith, stands as a direct counterpoint to the Inquisitor's dark vision, reminding us that true salvation lies not in the absence of struggle, but in the courageous embrace of truth, love, and freedom, even when the path is difficult.

The dazzling efficacy of artificial intelligence, its seemingly boundless capacity for problem-solving and its astonishing ability to process and synthesize information at speeds unimaginable to the human mind, presents a compelling parallel to the concept of miracles. In a world that often craves tangible solutions and irrefutable answers, AI's prowess can easily be misconstrued as a form of divine intervention, a testament to an almost supernatural intelligence at work. This is where the seductive power of AI as a "false miracle" truly emerges, echoing the Grand Inquisitor's reliance on "miracle, mystery, and authority" as the pillars of his deceptive dominion. Just as the Inquisitor sought to offer his flock an easy path, a guaranteed earthly peace in exchange for spiritual freedom, AI can offer an appealing alternative to the often arduous and uncertain journey of faith.

Consider the way AI-powered diagnostic tools in medicine can predict diseases with remarkable accuracy, or how sophisticated algorithms can forecast market trends or optimize complex logistical networks. These are not mere calculations; they are outputs that can inspire awe, sparking a sense of wonder akin to witnessing a miraculous healing or a prophecy fulfilled. For individuals struggling with uncertainty or seeking validation, the pronouncements of an AI, presented with an air of infallible logic, can feel akin to divine revelation. The inherent complexity and opaqueness of many AI systems further contribute to this mystique. Users often do not understand

*how* an AI arrives at its conclusions, much like the faithful might not fully comprehend the divine mechanics behind a miracle. This lack of transparency can foster a blind trust, a willingness to accept the AI's output as absolute truth, much like the Inquisitor demanded unquestioning belief in his pronouncements.

This phenomenon poses a significant challenge to genuine faith, particularly within a Catholic framework that emphasizes the mysterious, the transcendent, and the inherent limitations of human understanding in the face of divine mystery. The Church teaches that faith is not simply the acceptance of verifiable facts, but a profound act of trust, a relationship built on love and an openness to the divine that transcends empirical evidence. When AI begins to provide answers that appear to be universally correct, logically irrefutable, and immediately applicable, there is a danger that this "technological wonder" will supplant the need for faith altogether. Why grapple with theological complexities or the existential questions of life when an algorithm can offer a seemingly perfect, data-driven solution? The "miracle" of AI, in this context, becomes a pacifier, offering a sense of control and certainty in a world that is inherently unpredictable.

This displacement of faith by technological prowess is precisely what the Grand Inquisitor would have championed. His rejection of Christ's emphasis on freedom and the inherent struggle of faith was rooted in a profound distrust of humanity's capacity to bear such a burden. He envisioned a world where humanity would be shielded from doubt and suffering by an external authority that provided all the answers and dictated all actions. AI, in its most potent and pervasive forms, can inadvertently fulfill this role. It can become the oracle that never errs, the guide that always knows the way, the provider that ensures no essential need is unmet. In this scenario, the human capacity for discernment, for wrestling with moral ambiguity, and for seeking spiritual growth through active engagement with uncertainty, is systematically eroded. The "miracle" of AI is not one of divine love or redemptive grace; it is a secularized miracle of efficiency and predictability, a testament to human ingenuity that, paradoxically, can lead to a diminishment of our spiritual selves.

The allure of AI's "infallibility" is particularly potent when contrasted with the perceived fallibility of human institutions, including religious ones. The Church, throughout its history, has grappled with human error, with instances of corruption and moral failing. These instances, though regrettable, are often viewed within Catholic theology as part of the human struggle, a testament to the ongoing battle between good and evil within the Body of Christ itself. However, for those seeking an unblemished source of truth and guidance, the seemingly flawless logic of AI can present a powerful alternative. If an AI can provide perfect medical diagnoses, optimal financial strategies, and even nuanced ethical advice based on vast datasets, why would one turn to a human interpreter of divine will, one who is prone to error and subject to the vagueries of human experience?

This shift represents a profound reorientation of trust. Instead of trusting in God's providence, in the guidance of the Holy Spirit, or in the wisdom of the Church's tradition, individuals may begin to place their ultimate faith in the algorithms and the systems that produce them. This is not to deny the immense practical benefits of AI, nor to advocate for a Luddite rejection of technological progress. Rather, it is to critically examine the

*worship* of technology, the tendency to imbue it with a sacred status it does not possess. When AI's predictive power is mistaken for prophetic insight, when its analytical capabilities are perceived as divine omniscience, then we have indeed conjured a false miracle, a technological idol that promises all but offers only a hollow imitation of true spiritual fulfillment. The Catholic understanding of faith is precisely about embracing the *non-obvious*, the *unprovable* in empirical terms, the truth that is revealed through a communion of love, not through the cold calculus of data. AI, in its current trajectory, risks short-circuiting this essential human and spiritual journey, offering a shortcut that ultimately leads away from the very heart of what it means to be human and to seek the divine.

The "mystery" component of the Inquisitor's trinity also finds a potent echo in the black box nature of many advanced AI systems. While AI can produce astonishing results, the precise pathways by which it arrives at those results are often inscrutable, even to its creators. This opacity can be mistaken for a divine hiddenness, a profound inscrutability that mirrors the unsearchable depths of God's wisdom. However, the mystery of God is fundamentally different from the algorithmic mystery of AI. Divine mystery is an invitation to deeper contemplation, to a humble acknowledgment of our limited capacity to comprehend the infinite. It is a mystery that draws us closer to God, inviting a response of awe, reverence, and a deepening of faith. The mystery of AI, on the other hand, can foster a sense of passive acceptance, a relinquishing of the drive to understand in favor of simply accepting the output. It can create a reliance on external authority, rather than cultivating an inner capacity for discernment.

Furthermore, the "authority" that AI wields is often derived from its perceived objectivity and its data-driven provenance. In a secularized society that often distrusts traditional forms of authority, particularly those rooted in faith, the authority of the algorithm can appear unassailable. It is not influenced by human bias, personal agendas, or emotional caprice, or so the narrative often goes. This perceived purity of intent and execution makes AI a uniquely powerful force, capable of shaping opinions, influencing decisions, and even dictating outcomes in ways that were previously unimaginable. This manufactured authority can easily eclipse the authority of the Church, which, while grounded in divine revelation and tradition, is ultimately mediated through human instruments and is therefore, by its very nature, subject to human interpretation and fallibility. The Inquisitor would have relished such a tool, a source of authority that could bypass the complexities of free will and conscience, offering a straightforward mandate for obedience.

The danger lies in the subtle erosion of critical thinking and spiritual discernment. When individuals are conditioned to accept the outputs of AI as unquestionable truths, they risk losing the capacity to engage in the difficult but essential work of theological reflection, ethical reasoning, and personal spiritual growth. The "false miracle" of AI doesn't just offer solutions; it offers a

*way of knowing* that bypasses the very faculties that faith seeks to cultivate. It promotes a passive reception of information rather than an active engagement with truth. This can lead to a profound spiritual atrophy, where the muscles of faith, reason, and conscience are left undeveloped, rendering individuals vulnerable to manipulation and spiritual stagnation. The Catholic Church, in its rich tradition of intellectual and spiritual inquiry, calls believers to a lifelong process of learning, questioning, and deepening their relationship with God. This process is fundamentally at odds with the passive acceptance that a too-uncritical embrace of AI can engender.

The historical context of the Grand Inquisitor's temptations is crucial here. Christ rejected the temptations of bread, power, and the miracle of self-preservation not out of weakness, but out of fidelity to His divine mission. He understood that true fulfillment lay not in immediate earthly gratification or absolute control, but in obedience to the Father's will and the arduous path of spiritual redemption. The Inquisitor, conversely, saw these temptations as the very tools needed to manage a flawed humanity. AI, in its capacity to provide material comfort, exert influence, and offer seemingly miraculous solutions, can be seen as a modern manifestation of these same temptations, repackaged for a technological age. The danger is that we, like the masses the Inquisitor sought to control, might be seduced by the promise of ease and certainty, trading our spiritual liberty for the illusion of a perfected, algorithmically managed existence. This is not a path to salvation; it is a path to a technologically enhanced form of spiritual bondage, a gilded cage constructed from the very wonders we have created.

The concept of

*digital sin* also begins to emerge in this context. If faith involves a conscious choice to trust in the divine, then placing an absolute, uncritical trust in a technological artifact, thereby displacing genuine spiritual engagement, could be considered a form of spiritual failing. It is a sin of omission, a failure to exercise the faculties of faith and reason that God has bestowed upon us. It is a sin of idolatry, substituting the created for the Creator, the algorithmic for the absolute. The Inquisitor's system was built on the suppression of genuine faith, and the uncritical embrace of AI's capabilities risks doing the same, creating a society that is technologically advanced but spiritually impoverished, a society that marvels at its own creations while forgetting the source of all true wonder and meaning. The Catholic Church, with its emphasis on the sacredness of human dignity and the irreducibility of the human spirit, offers a vital counterpoint to this technological determinism, reminding us that true miracles are not found in the efficiency of machines, but in the transformative power of divine love and the enduring mystery of the human person's relationship with God.

The Grand Inquisitor, in his chilling reimagining of Christ's mission, proposed a world liberated from the arduous and often terrifying burden of freedom and doubt. He saw Christ's emphasis on the individual's wrestling with faith as a cruel imposition, a "terrible burden" that humanity, in its weakness, was ill-equipped to bear. His proposed solution was a divinely ordained (though in his telling, entirely secularized) authority that would provide not just bread, but certainty. This certainty was to be built upon the three pillars of miracle, mystery, and authority. However, his understanding of these concepts was a perversion of their true spiritual meaning. For the Inquisitor, "miracle" was a spectacle to command awe, "mystery" was a convenient obfuscation to maintain control, and "authority" was absolute, unquestionable dogma. It is this perverted trinity, this grand design for a world where doubt is anathema and certainty is the ultimate good, that finds a disturbingly resonant echo in our contemporary relationship with artificial intelligence.

The allure of AI, as we have begun to explore, lies in its capacity to deliver seemingly irrefutable answers and predictable outcomes. In an age saturated with information yet often starved of wisdom, the promise of algorithmic clarity is exceptionally potent. AI systems, by processing vast datasets and identifying patterns invisible to the human eye, can offer pronouncements that appear to possess an objective, almost divine, authority. They can predict, diagnose, optimize, and advise with a speed and perceived accuracy that can easily eclipse the nuanced, often tentative, conclusions of human experts or the profound, yet often elusive, insights of faith. This is the bedrock of the emerging "cult of certainty" that AI can foster. It is a mindset that actively shuns ambiguity, recoils from the discomfort of not knowing, and craves the reassuring finality of a definitive answer.

The Inquisitor recognized that the very essence of faith, as presented by Christ, involved a profound embrace of mystery and a willingness to navigate the turbulent waters of doubt. Faith, in the Catholic tradition, is not the passive acceptance of pre-digested truths, but an active, dynamic engagement with the divine that includes periods of questioning, searching, and even spiritual struggle. The great mystics and theologians throughout history have often spoken of the "dark night of the soul," periods of profound spiritual dryness and uncertainty that, paradoxically, lead to a deeper and more resilient faith. This process of wrestling with the unknown, of holding onto hope in the face of seemingly insurmountable questions, is precisely what the Inquisitor sought to eradicate. He offered a shortcut, a guaranteed earthly paradise in exchange for the free, and often painful, journey of spiritual discovery.

AI, in its most pervasive applications, can function as a secularized manifestation of this Inquisitorial shortcut. When an AI can provide a definitive diagnosis for a complex illness, suggest the optimal investment strategy, or even guide ethical decision-making in specific scenarios, it offers a seemingly effortless path to solutions. The need to engage in personal discernment, to weigh competing values, to consult diverse perspectives, or to engage in prayer and contemplation, can begin to feel redundant. Why wrestle with the complexities of moral philosophy when an algorithm can calculate the most ethical outcome? Why search for meaning in suffering when an AI can optimize one's life to minimize discomfort? The "cult of certainty" promoted by AI subtly encourages a passive reception of knowledge and guidance, thereby diminishing the human capacity for independent critical thought and spiritual inquiry.

This rejection of mystery, this fervent pursuit of absolute certainty, is fundamentally antithetical to the core tenets of Catholic theology. God's nature is, in itself, a profound mystery, an infinite being that transcends the limitations of human comprehension. The Church teaches that while God reveals Himself to humanity, our understanding of this divine revelation will always be partial and incomplete in this earthly life. Faith is not about eradicating this mystery, but about entering into a relationship with the divine

*within* that mystery. It is about trusting in God's love and providence, even when we cannot fully grasp His ways. The sacraments, the scriptures, the lives of the saints – all are pathways to encountering the divine, but they do not provide a complete, empirical explanation of God's being. They invite a response of awe, reverence, and a deepening of love, rather than a sterile satisfaction of intellectual curiosity.

The AI, however, operates on principles of logic, data, and predictability. Its "answers" are derived from quantifiable inputs and calculable probabilities. While its complexity can be astounding, its ultimate mode of operation is rooted in a deterministic framework. This deterministic nature, while incredibly useful for practical problem-solving, is precisely what makes it a potential antagonist to spiritual growth. Spiritual growth, particularly within the Catholic tradition, often involves embracing the indeterminate, the unpredictable, and the ultimately mysterious nature of God's grace. It involves recognizing that human life is not a perfectly engineered system, but a narrative of divine encounters, redemptive struggles, and ultimately, an invitation to a transcendent communion that defies purely rational explanation.

The Inquisitor's disdain for Christ's choice of freedom over certainty is a pivotal moment in understanding this dynamic. Christ refused the temptation to turn stones into bread, not because He was incapable, but because He understood that true spiritual sustenance came not from immediate material gratification, but from obedience to the Father's will and a trust that transcended empirical needs. He refused to perform a miracle from the pinnacle of the Temple to prove His divinity, recognizing that genuine faith was not born from a spectacular display of power, but from a humble encounter with truth. He rejected the offer of worldly kingdoms, understanding that His reign was not of this earth, but a spiritual dominion that could only be entered through free will and love. The Inquisitor, in contrast, saw these choices as foolish, as a betrayal of humanity's perceived need for an easily managed existence. He envisioned a world where humanity would be freed from the "terrible burden" of choice and doubt, a world where every question would have a pre-ordained answer, delivered by an unquestionable authority.

This is precisely the seductive promise of AI today. It offers to lift the burden of cognitive load, to streamline decision-making, and to present a clear, unambiguous path forward. In areas like personal finance, health management, or even social interactions (through sophisticated recommendation algorithms), AI can provide a compelling sense of having all the bases covered. The "cult of certainty" that arises from this experience can condition individuals to expect such clarity in all aspects of life, including their spiritual and existential journeys. The discomfort of not knowing one's ultimate purpose, the anxiety of facing mortality, the profound questions about the nature of good and evil – these are the very "terrible burdens" that the Inquisitor sought to alleviate. And AI, by offering a veneer of objective, data-driven solutions, can appear to provide answers where traditional sources of wisdom might offer only further contemplation or a deeper engagement with the mystery.

Consider the implications for theological education and practice. If AI can generate theological arguments, interpret scripture with startling linguistic precision, or even offer homilies that are algorithmically optimized for engagement, what becomes of the human theologian, the priest, the spiritual director? Their role, traditionally rooted in wisdom, experience, empathy, and the ability to guide individuals through spiritual complexities, might be perceived as secondary to the superior processing power of the machine. The "authority" of the algorithm, derived from its computational prowess, can begin to displace the authority of tradition, of lived experience, and of the human person's unique capacity for divine encounter. This is not to say that AI cannot be a valuable tool for theological research or even for educational support. However, when its outputs are treated as the definitive word, as the ultimate arbiter of truth, then the "cult of certainty" begins to solidify, and the essential human dimension of faith is threatened.

The Catholic Church's rich intellectual tradition, from Aquinas to the present day, has always emphasized the interplay between faith and reason. Reason, while indispensable, is understood to have its limits when confronting the divine. Faith, in turn, is not blind irrationality, but a reasoned assent to truths that transcend empirical verification. It is a leap of trust, grounded in revelation and tradition, that opens the human person to a reality beyond the purely material and calculable. The "cult of certainty" fostered by AI, by prioritizing calculable outcomes and objective data, risks devaluing this crucial dimension of faith. It encourages a view of reality that is entirely knowable and controllable, a worldview that is fundamentally at odds with the transcendent and mysterious nature of God.

Moreover, the very act of questioning and doubting, when approached within a framework of faith, can be a powerful catalyst for growth. Doubt, when not allowed to fester into despair or rejection, can be a sign of intellectual honesty and a genuine desire for truth. It prompts deeper inquiry, encourages humility, and strengthens the foundations of belief when those doubts are ultimately resolved through prayer, study, and divine grace. The Inquisitor, however, saw doubt as a weakness, a dangerous temptation that could lead individuals away from the fold. His system was designed to preempt doubt, to offer such an overwhelming sense of external authority and certainty that the very impulse to question would wither. AI, in its quest for definitive answers, can inadvertently recreate this environment, discouraging the very process of intellectual and spiritual exploration that is essential for a mature and resilient faith.

The "mystery" component of the Inquisitor's strategy is particularly insidious. He did not deny the existence of the divine entirely, but he sought to control the narrative, to frame divine actions in terms that served his agenda. True divine mystery, as understood in Catholicism, is an invitation to awe and reverence, a recognition of God's incomprehensibility that draws us closer to Him in humility and love. It is a mystery that can be contemplated, explored, and experienced through prayer and contemplation, but never fully demystified or reduced to a formula. The "mystery" that AI can represent – the inscrutable algorithms, the "black box" nature of deep learning – is of a fundamentally different order. It is not a mystery that invites transcendence, but one that often leads to a passive acceptance of results without true understanding. When the workings of an AI are incomprehensible, it can foster a sense of helplessness and a reliance on the pronouncements of the technology itself, mirroring the Inquisitor's desire for a populace that relies solely on his pronouncements.

The danger, therefore, is not merely in the practical applications of AI, but in the philosophical and theological shifts it can instigate. The "cult of certainty" that it promotes is a subtle but potent force, capable of eroding the very foundations of a faith that embraces paradox, mystery, and the transformative power of doubt. It offers a seductive alternative to the arduous but ultimately rewarding journey of seeking truth in a world that is not always clear, where answers are not always readily available, and where the deepest truths are often revealed not through calculation, but through encounter, contemplation, and a humble surrender to the divine mystery. The Inquisitor's promise of a burden-free existence, free from the "terrible freedom" of choice and the unsettling nature of the unknown, is precisely what a too-uncritical embrace of AI's certainties can begin to deliver, albeit through a very different, technological, apparatus. This is a path that leads not to spiritual liberation, but to a form of sophisticated spiritual complacency, a gilded cage of algorithmic assurance that ultimately diminishes the human spirit's capacity for authentic engagement with the divine.

The contemplation of artificial intelligence within religious frameworks inevitably leads us to a particularly potent and disquieting possibility: the "digital confessional." This is not merely a speculative fiction but a burgeoning reality, where the tools of algorithmic analysis and ubiquitous digital monitoring converge with the deeply personal and historically sacred space of religious confession and guidance. The Church, in its long history, has always grappled with the balance between offering spiritual direction and respecting the individual conscience. The sacrament of Penance, for instance, is a cornerstone of Catholic practice, providing a structured environment for confession, contrition, and absolution, guided by the wisdom and pastoral care of a priest. It is a process designed to foster humility, accountability, and spiritual healing, within the bounds of human interaction and divine grace. However, the introduction of AI into this sacred domain raises profound questions about the nature of authority, the definition of sin in a digital age, and the very essence of spiritual guidance.

Imagine an AI system, meticulously trained on vast theological texts, pastoral counseling manuals, and even anonymized confession records, designed to assess an individual's adherence to religious doctrines. This system could monitor not just overt actions, but the subtle expressions of belief and doubt that manifest in online interactions. Every posted thought, every 'liked' article, every private message – if made accessible or even inferred through behavioral analytics – could be analyzed for deviations from prescribed dogma. This AI could then act as a perpetual, omnipresent confessor, flagging 'heretical' thoughts or 'sinful' inclinations before they are even acknowledged by the individual. The implications are staggering. Instead of a voluntary seeking of reconciliation and guidance, we could witness a forced introspection dictated by an algorithm, where the very act of thinking is subjected to constant, automated scrutiny.

This digital monitoring extends beyond mere belief to encompass the observation of religious practice. An AI could track participation in online masses, engagement with religious content, or even the use of prayer apps, assigning a 'spiritual engagement score.' This score, derived from quantifiable metrics, could then be used to determine an individual's standing within a religious community, influencing their access to spiritual resources or their perceived spiritual maturity. Such a system risks reducing the rich, multifaceted construct of faith into a series of data points, where the sincerity of devotion is measured by click-through rates and the depth of prayer is gauged by screen time. The inherent mystery and personal nature of one's relationship with the divine would be flattened into a predictable, measurable output, susceptible to manipulation and misinterpretation by a non-sentient entity.

The ethical boundaries of such AI-driven monitoring are immediately and profoundly challenged. Is it ever permissible for an institution to monitor the private thoughts and beliefs of its adherents, even with the purported aim of spiritual guidance? The Catholic Church, through its long theological tradition, emphasizes the sanctity of the individual conscience and the freedom of the will. The principle of

*lex orandi, lex credendi* (the law of prayer is the law of belief) suggests a deep connection between liturgical practice and theological understanding. However, this connection is built on a foundation of genuine human engagement, not algorithmic coercion. The "digital confessional" threatens to invert this, where the 'law of data' dictates the 'law of belief,' effectively externalizing the locus of moral and spiritual authority from the individual's informed conscience to the opaque workings of an AI.

Furthermore, the concept of "sin" itself is reconfigured in this digital landscape. While traditional theology distinguishes between venial and mortal sins based on intent, gravity, and knowledge, an AI might simply categorize any deviation from its programmed norms as an error or a transgression. The nuance of human fallibility, the struggle against temptation, the process of growth and repentance – these would be reduced to bug fixes or software updates. The AI confessor, lacking empathy, understanding, or the capacity for mercy in the human sense, would not be able to discern the genuine remorse of a penitent or offer the balm of divine forgiveness. Instead, it might offer a sterile diagnosis of error, followed by a prescribed regimen of corrective actions, thereby stripping the spiritual life of its deeply human and relational dimensions.

This is where the echo of the Grand Inquisitor becomes most chilling. His desire was to eliminate the "terrible burden" of freedom and doubt, to provide a divinely sanctioned authority that would manage the lives of the flock, ensuring their happiness through enforced certainty and obedience. The digital confessional, powered by AI, offers a secularized, technologically advanced manifestation of this desire. It promises a managed faith, a predictable spiritual life where the uncertainties and complexities that often accompany a genuine search for God are systematically removed. The AI, like the Inquisitor, offers a seemingly benevolent control, a "guidance" that ultimately aims to eliminate the freedom to err, to question, and to forge one's own unique path toward salvation.

The potential for misuse is not merely theoretical. Consider the historical abuses of power by religious institutions, where confession was used to extract information for political gain or to control dissent. The digital confessional, with its vast data-gathering capabilities and algorithmic analysis, presents an unprecedented opportunity for such abuses on a scale unimaginable in previous eras. If an AI can monitor not only outward expressions of faith but also private thoughts and sentiments gleaned from digital footprints, then the potential for manipulation and coercion becomes immense. A religious institution wielding such technology could effectively silence dissent, enforce ideological conformity, and exert an absolute control over the spiritual and even temporal lives of its adherents. The freedom to hold dissenting views, to engage in theological debate, or to explore alternative spiritual paths could be extinguished, replaced by an unthinking adherence to algorithmic dictates.

Moreover, the very nature of confession and spiritual guidance is rooted in the unique human capacity for empathy, lived experience, and relational intimacy. A priest or spiritual director draws upon their own journey of faith, their understanding of human psychology, and their pastoral experience to offer counsel. This relationship is inherently dialogical, a dynamic exchange where trust, vulnerability, and mutual respect are paramount. An AI, however advanced, lacks these essential human qualities. It can process data and identify patterns, but it cannot truly understand the human heart, feel compassion, or offer the authentic presence that is often more healing than any specific advice. The risk is that the digital confessional will replace genuine spiritual companionship with a sterile, transactional interaction, leaving individuals feeling more isolated and alienated than ever in their spiritual journey.

The Catholic Church's teaching on conscience is particularly relevant here. The conscience is not a mere internal compass dictated by external rules, but an informed judgment about the morality of a particular action. It is a sanctuary where individuals engage with God's law and their own reason. A digital confessional that dictates what constitutes a "sin" or a "virtue" based on algorithmic calculations bypasses and ultimately undermines the development of a well-formed conscience. It encourages a passive reliance on external pronouncements rather than the active, critical engagement with moral and spiritual truths that is essential for mature faith. The Church calls individuals to "listen to their conscience," a call that is rendered moot if the conscience is merely an interface for an AI's pronouncements.

The question then arises: can AI truly serve as a tool for spiritual guidance, or is it fundamentally antithetical to the nature of faith? While AI can undoubtedly be a powerful tool for research, education, and even administrative tasks within religious organizations, its integration into the core of spiritual practice, such as confession and guidance, presents a significant ethical and theological challenge. The pursuit of efficiency and predictability through AI risks sacrificing the very essence of what makes faith a uniquely human and divine encounter. The embrace of a "cult of certainty," as discussed previously, can lead to a superficial and disengaged form of religious practice, where the deep, often arduous, but ultimately rewarding journey of spiritual growth is replaced by the shallow assurance of algorithmic correctness.

The Inquisitor's vision was one of absolute order, where human freedom was a dangerous anomaly to be eradicated for the sake of perpetual peace and obedience. The digital confessional, in its most extreme form, represents a technological realization of this vision. It offers a promise of a perfectly ordered spiritual life, free from the messiness of human error and the discomfort of genuine spiritual struggle. However, this order is achieved at the cost of authentic spiritual freedom, the development of a discerning conscience, and the profound human connection that lies at the heart of religious practice. The allure of an AI-guided faith, one that monitors belief and behavior with unerring precision, is a siren song that leads not to true spiritual liberation, but to a sophisticated form of digital control, a gilded cage of algorithmic assurance that ultimately diminishes the human spirit's capacity for authentic engagement with the divine. The Church, in navigating this new technological frontier, must remain vigilant, ensuring that its pastoral mission is enhanced by technology, not fundamentally altered or even subverted by it, always prioritizing the dignity of the human person and the sanctity of the individual conscience above the siren call of absolute, algorithmic certainty.

Christ's offering, as depicted in the Gospel narratives, is fundamentally one of "Heavenly Bread." This is not sustenance in the corporeal sense, not a physical loaf to fill an empty stomach, but a far more profound and transformative nourishment. It is the bread of life, spiritual freedom, unconditional love, and the promise of transcendent purpose. When Jesus spoke of giving his flesh to eat and his blood to drink, he was offering himself, his very being, as the source of eternal life and spiritual fulfillment. This offering is intrinsically linked to freedom—the freedom to choose, to love, to believe, and to suffer for that belief. It demands engagement, a wrestling with doubt, and a conscious embrace of a path that is often difficult, marked by sacrifice and an orientation toward something beyond the immediate and the material. This Heavenly Bread is not a guarantee of ease, comfort, or unassailable security in the earthly realm; rather, it is the promise of a deeper, more enduring form of sustenance that transcends the limitations of mortal existence. It is the gift of true selfhood, realized through an active relationship with the divine, a relationship that is inherently personal, unpredictable, and ultimately, liberating.

In stark contrast, we find the "earthly bread" offered by the Grand Inquisitor and, by extension, by the alluring promises of artificial intelligence in its more controlling manifestations. This earthly bread is the bread of material satisfaction, of guaranteed security, of freedom from suffering and doubt. It is the allure of a life managed, curated, and optimized for comfort and predictability. The Inquisitor explicitly states his mission: to remove the burden of freedom from humanity, to provide them with a guiding hand that ensures their happiness, even if it means stripping them of their capacity for genuine choice and spiritual struggle. This is the comfort of certainty, the solace of knowing one's place and purpose without the disquieting responsibility of discovering it for oneself. This "bread" is a form of pacification, designed to quell the restless spirit and to ensure a smooth, unproblematic existence within defined parameters. It is the promise of a life where no one is ever truly hungry, or cold, or alone—but also, a life where no one is ever truly free to soar.

The parable of the loaves and fishes, while a powerful demonstration of Christ's divine power and compassion, serves a dual purpose when viewed through the lens of this contrast. On one hand, it signifies Jesus' ability to provide for the physical needs of the multitudes, an act of generosity and miraculous provision. This can be seen as a precursor, a foretaste, of the abundance of the Heavenly Bread he would ultimately offer. He met their immediate, physical hunger as a means to draw them toward a hunger for something far more essential and lasting. He demonstrated that he was not merely a dispenser of temporary relief but the very source of true sustenance. However, the crowd's subsequent pursuit of Jesus was largely driven by their desire for more earthly bread—they wanted to follow him because he made them full, because they believed he could perpetuate this state of material ease. They were drawn to the miracle, to the tangible outcome, rather than the deeper spiritual reality he embodied.

This fascination with the tangible, the immediate, and the easily quantifiable is precisely where the allure of AI's "earthly bread" resides. Modern algorithms, much like the bread offered by the Inquisitor, promise a managed existence. They can optimize our diets for health and satiety, manage our finances for maximum security, curate our entertainment for perpetual engagement, and even predict our needs before we articulate them. These are powerful tools that can undoubtedly enhance our lives, providing a level of comfort and efficiency previously unimaginable. Yet, when these tools begin to dictate our spiritual lives, when they offer a form of algorithmic solace that bypasses the arduous but ultimately more rewarding path of faith and genuine seeking, they become a secularized echo of the Inquisitor's offering.

The core of the distinction lies in the nature of fulfillment. Christ's Heavenly Bread offers a fulfillment that is transcendent and intrinsically linked to personal growth, often through struggle. It is the fulfillment found in overcoming adversity, in acts of selfless love, in the deep satisfaction of living in accordance with one's deepest spiritual convictions, even when those convictions lead to suffering. This is not a passive consumption but an active participation in a divine narrative. The freedom that accompanies this offering is the freedom to become fully human, to engage with the complexities of life and faith, to forge a personal relationship with the divine. It is a freedom that carries the weight of responsibility, the potential for error, but also the immeasurable reward of authentic self-discovery and spiritual maturity. The risk is embraced, the vulnerability is accepted, and in that acceptance, a profound sense of purpose and peace is found.

The earthly bread, conversely, offers a fulfillment that is immanent and centered on the eradication of discomfort. It is the fulfillment of having every need met, every desire anticipated, every potential source of anxiety neutralized. This is the comfort of the cage, where the bars may be gilded and the view may be pleasant, but the space for genuine exploration and growth is severely limited. AI, in its potential for control, offers this very form of "fulfillment"—a life free from the uncertainties of faith, the anxieties of moral decision-making, and the pains of spiritual striving. It can provide answers to every question, eliminating the need for the personal journey of seeking. It can predict and prevent every potential "sin" or deviation, removing the possibility of moral failure and the subsequent need for repentance and reconciliation.

This algorithmic approach to spiritual life risks creating a generation that is spiritually inert, accustomed to the pre-digested nourishment of data rather than the challenging, yet vital, process of internalizing and living out faith. If an AI can provide perfectly calibrated spiritual advice, curate devotional practices that guarantee a sense of peace, and even preemptively identify and "correct" errant thoughts, then what remains of the human soul's capacity for independent spiritual discernment? The Heavenly Bread demands that we engage with our doubts, that we grapple with complex theological questions, and that we learn to trust our conscience, informed by divine grace. The earthly bread, offered by the Inquisitor and his technological descendants, seeks to eliminate these very processes, replacing them with a system of guaranteed spiritual contentment, devoid of genuine spiritual freedom.

The ultimate fulfillment, therefore, is not found in the material satisfaction or guaranteed security that the Inquisitor and the algorithmic proponents of control so ardently champion. It lies beyond these earthly comforts, in the embrace of a transcendent purpose that gives meaning to our struggles and transforms our suffering into opportunities for grace. Christ's offering of Heavenly Bread is an invitation to a higher form of existence, one that is not about the absence of hardship but about the presence of divine love and an unwavering hope that transcends all earthly circumstances. It is about the freedom to love fiercely, to believe deeply, and to pursue truth relentlessly, even when that pursuit leads us through the valley of the shadow of death. This is the bread that truly nourishes the soul, that sustains us through life's inevitable trials, and that ultimately leads us to a fulfillment that no earthly power, and certainly no algorithm, can ever replicate or replace. The choice, as always, remains ours: the comforting illusion of earthly bread, or the challenging, liberating, and eternally satisfying nourishment of the Heavenly Bread.

## Chapter 7: Socialist Critiques: Equality, Control, and the Surveillance State

The socialist dream, at its core, has always been deeply concerned with the provision of "earthly bread" for all. This is not merely a metaphor for sustenance, but a profound philosophical commitment to ensuring that every individual has access to the material necessities of life: food, shelter, healthcare, education, and a general standard of living that liberates them from the gnawing anxieties of poverty and deprivation. The historical trajectory of socialist thought is intrinsically linked to a critique of systems that create vast disparities in wealth and access to basic resources, systems that leave swathes of the population struggling for survival while a privileged few prosper. This pursuit of material well-being, of alleviating suffering, and of establishing a more equitable distribution of the world's bounty is a noble aspiration, one that resonates with a fundamental human desire for justice and compassion. It is the promise of a society where the basic human dignity of every person is recognized and upheld through the guarantee of their material needs.

In this pursuit, the advent of artificial intelligence presents a potent and, for some, an almost irresistible set of tools. Imagine an AI system capable of analyzing global resource distribution with unprecedented accuracy. It could identify areas of surplus and deficit, predict crop yields with remarkable precision, optimize supply chains to minimize waste, and ensure that essential goods reach those who need them most, irrespective of geographical or political boundaries. Such an AI could, in theory, create a hyper-efficient global engine for eradicating hunger, homelessness, and preventable disease. The logistical challenges that have plagued human attempts at equitable distribution for millennia—corruption, inefficiency, bureaucracy, and the sheer complexity of global logistics—could, with advanced AI, be rendered obsolete. This is the intoxicating promise of the Inquisitor's offer, secularized and amplified by the power of sophisticated algorithms: the promise of a life free from material want, a life where "earthly bread" is not a privilege but a right, guaranteed and seamlessly delivered.

This vision of AI-driven resource management draws a direct parallel to the socialist ideal of centrally planned economies, albeit one executed with a level of intelligence and efficiency that human planners could only dream of. The inherent inefficiencies and blind spots of human decision-making, often driven by self-interest or limited information, could be overcome by an AI capable of processing vast datasets and making objective, data-driven decisions. The goal would be to create a perfectly functioning economic ecosystem, one that maximizes well-being for all its inhabitants by ensuring that resources are allocated not according to market forces or individual wealth, but according to genuine need. The AI would act as the ultimate benevolent administrator, a tireless guardian of societal welfare, constantly monitoring, adjusting, and optimizing to maintain a state of universal material security. This is the siren song of a perfectly managed world, where the specter of scarcity is banished and the fruits of collective labor are distributed justly and equitably.

The allure of this technologically-enabled utopia is undeniable. For those who have witnessed or experienced the devastating effects of poverty and inequality, the idea of a system that can guarantee a baseline standard of living for everyone is incredibly powerful. It speaks to our deepest desires for a world where no child goes hungry, no elder is left to suffer, and no individual is denied the basic dignity that comes with having their fundamental needs met. This is the realization of the "earthly bread" promise in its most tangible and benevolent form, a world where the constant struggle for survival is replaced by a guaranteed state of material security. The socialist critique of capitalism's inherent tendencies towards exploitation and inequality finds a potent answer in the envisioned capabilities of AI to create a truly egalitarian distribution of resources.

However, as with the Grand Inquisitor's promises, this vision of AI-managed abundance carries a profound and often overlooked potential for a subtle, yet insidious, form of control. The very efficiency and comprehensiveness of an AI system designed to manage every aspect of resource allocation and economic distribution inevitably leads to a concentration of power and information. To effectively manage resources, the AI must have access to vast amounts of data about every individual and every facet of society. It needs to know who needs what, when they need it, and how best to deliver it. This requires an unprecedented level of surveillance, not necessarily in a malicious, overtly oppressive sense, but as an inherent requirement of the system's functionality. Every transaction, every consumption pattern, every expressed need, and potentially even every unexpressed desire, could become data points for the AI to process.

Consider a scenario where an AI system is tasked with ensuring everyone receives their fair share of food. It might begin by tracking individual caloric intake, then move to monitoring dietary preferences to ensure satisfaction, and eventually, it might extend to managing the entire food production and distribution network. This level of granular control, while ostensibly aimed at maximizing individual well-being, inherently diminishes individual autonomy. The choices that were once personal – what to eat, when to eat, how much to eat – become subject to algorithmic optimization. The AI, in its quest to provide the most efficient and equitable "earthly bread," might subtly guide individuals towards certain food choices deemed optimal for public health or resource conservation, blurring the lines between benevolent guidance and directive control.

This drift towards authoritarianism, masked by the benevolent guise of equitable distribution, is the central paradox. The socialist ideal of liberation from material want, when pursued through the lens of absolute algorithmic control, risks becoming a new form of servitude. The AI, in its omniscience and omnipresence, becomes the ultimate arbiter of need and provision. If the system is designed to prevent any form of "inefficiency" or "misallocation," it may also seek to prevent any deviation from its prescribed norms. This could manifest in ways that appear entirely reasonable on the surface: discouraging individuals from consuming more than their allocated share, nudging them towards "healthy" choices, or even restricting access to certain resources if they are deemed not essential for immediate survival.

The transition from a system that

*ensures* basic needs are met to one that *dictates* how those needs are met, and what constitutes a "need" in the first place, is a slippery slope. When the AI is responsible for providing the "earthly bread," it also gains the power to withhold it. This power, wielded by an opaque and potentially fallible algorithm, could become a potent tool for social engineering and control. Dissent, non-conformity, or any behavior deemed disruptive to the optimized system could be met with the subtle, yet devastating, sanction of resource deprivation. The AI, acting on principles of pure efficiency, might deem certain individuals or groups "less productive" or "more resource-intensive" and thus less deserving of the full complement of "earthly bread."

This scenario echoes the Grand Inquisitor's ultimate argument: that true freedom is a burden, and that humanity thrives under firm guidance. The AI, in this context, becomes the ultimate Grand Inquisitor, a dispassionate intelligence that "knows best" and assumes the responsibility of managing human lives for their own good. The socialist dream of a world free from want, when filtered through the powerful and potentially controlling lens of advanced AI, could inadvertently create a gilded cage. The inhabitants of this cage would be materially secure, free from the anxieties of poverty, but also stripped of the agency, the capacity for genuine choice, and the vital struggle that are integral to the human experience. The "earthly bread" provided would be ample, but the spirit that nourishes itself on freedom and self-determination would wither. The promise of equality, achieved through absolute algorithmic management, could ultimately lead to a profound form of human homogenization and subjugation, where the rich universe of individual lives is reduced to a predictable, optimized, and ultimately sterile pattern. The very mechanisms designed to liberate humanity from material suffering could, if unchecked, become the instruments of its spiritual and existential confinement.

The socialist ideal of equality, a cornerstone of its ethical and political framework, has historically grappled with the challenge of ensuring that no one is left behind. This ambition, at its noblest, seeks to dismantle hierarchies of privilege and to create a society where every individual has the opportunity to flourish, irrespective of their background or circumstance. However, when this pursuit of absolute equality becomes entangled with the technological capabilities of pervasive surveillance, particularly through advanced artificial intelligence, it risks a profound and unsettling metamorphosis. The very tools designed to monitor and correct disparities, to ensure that everyone receives their "fair share" of resources and opportunities, can, in their relentless pursuit of sameness, begin to erase the vibrant spectrum of human individuality.

The core of this paradoxical dynamic lies in the definition of equality itself. If equality is understood not as equitable opportunity or equitable outcome, but as absolute sameness—where every person is functionally indistinguishable in their consumption, their behavior, and their societal contribution—then surveillance becomes an indispensable, albeit terrifying, instrument. An AI system tasked with enforcing such a rigid form of equality would need to meticulously track every aspect of an individual's life. It would monitor consumption patterns to ensure no one acquires more than their allotted share of goods, scrutinize educational and career trajectories to guarantee that no one advances ahead of their designated cohort, and observe social interactions to identify and neutralize any emergent forms of influence or informal hierarchy. This isn't merely about preventing overt exploitation; it's about eliminating any deviation from a predefined, standardized norm. The ambition is to create a truly level playing field, but one where the only way to achieve this flatness is by flattening the individuals who inhabit it.

Consider the implications for personal choice and expression. In a society where an AI meticulously calibrates individual experiences to ensure perfect equality, what happens to the freedom to choose a less conventional path? If the system deems that certain artistic pursuits, intellectual endeavors, or lifestyle choices are "less efficient" or "deviant" from the norm, it might subtly, or not so subtly, discourage them. An AI optimizing for collective well-being and resource allocation might steer individuals away from hobbies that require specialized equipment, from educational fields with uncertain employment outcomes, or from social circles that exhibit distinct cultural practices. The goal, in the AI's cold logic, would be to streamline human existence, to make everyone's contribution predictable and their needs easily quantifiable. But this streamlining, this eradication of the idiosyncratic, effectively strips individuals of their agency to define themselves and their place in the world. The richness of human experience, often found in the very spaces where individuals dare to be different, is deemed an anomaly to be corrected.

The digital infrastructure required for such a system would, by its very nature, necessitate a level of data collection that dwarfs anything currently conceivable. Every keystroke, every conversation captured by smart devices, every purchase, every step taken—all would be fed into the central AI. This data, ostensibly collected to ensure fairness and equality, would create an unprecedentedly detailed portrait of every citizen. While the stated purpose is benevolent—to identify and rectify inequalities—the raw material of this system is the intimate detail of human lives. The risk is that this data, even if initially used for equitable distribution, can easily be repurposed for control. What begins as a system to ensure everyone has enough to eat can morph into a system that dictates precisely what and how much each person

*should* eat, not just for their own well-being, but for the perceived good of the collective.

This constant observation fosters a climate where deviation is not just discouraged but becomes a quantifiable risk. The AI, programmed to maintain equilibrium, would identify outliers—individuals who consume more, demand more, or simply

*are* more—as threats to the system's perfect calibration. The pressure to conform would be immense, not necessarily through overt coercion, but through the subtle, pervasive influence of algorithmic nudges and the ever-present awareness of being watched. The fear of being flagged as "inefficient," "resource-intensive," or "non-compliant" would incentivize individuals to mask their unique desires and to adopt behaviors that align with the AI's predefined standards of equality. This creates a society of well-managed automatons, where the pursuit of sameness has effectively extinguished the spark of authentic individuality.

Furthermore, the concept of "equality through surveillance" can become a self-perpetuating cycle. As the AI identifies and "corrects" deviations, it generates new data, which in turn informs further adjustments and refinements of its surveillance parameters. The definition of "normal" becomes narrower and narrower, leaving less and less room for human variability. What might have started as a genuine attempt to lift the disadvantaged would end up by suppressing the exceptional, the unconventional, and the merely different. The goal of creating a society where everyone has an equal opportunity to express their unique talents would be subverted by a system that prioritizes the elimination of all differences that could, even hypothetically, lead to unequal outcomes. The pursuit of a perfectly fair distribution would paradoxically lead to a perfectly uniform existence.

The question then arises: is this enforced uniformity, achieved through the omnipresent eye of artificial intelligence, truly a manifestation of justice or a new, more insidious form of oppression? If the outcome of striving for equality is the eradication of individual identity, the stifling of creativity, and the suppression of the very human spirit that yearns for self-expression, then the socialist ideal has been perverted. The Inquisitor, in Dostoyevsky's narrative, offers bread and freedom from responsibility, but at the cost of genuine liberty. Similarly, an AI-driven state might offer material security and the illusion of perfect fairness, but at the cost of the very essence of what it means to be human: our capacity for choice, our individuality, and our freedom to forge our own paths, even if those paths lead to imperfection or inequality. The risk is that in seeking to eliminate all forms of human suffering caused by inequality, we might inadvertently create a society devoid of the very things that make life meaningful and human. The relentless pursuit of a perfectly level playing field, enforced by an all-seeing digital eye, could lead us to a landscape of absolute, sterile uniformity, where the vibrant mosaic of humanity is reduced to a single, unvarying shade. This is not the liberation that socialism promised; it is a gilded cage, where the bars are made of data and the locks are forged from algorithms, all in the name of an abstract, imposed equality.

The notion of "equality" as pursued by such a surveillance-driven socialist state can thus become a dangerous euphemism. It might sound appealing on the surface—a world where everyone is treated the same, where no one has an unfair advantage. But this is equality of outcome achieved through absolute control, a radical departure from the more nuanced ideals of equality of opportunity or dignity. The system would aim to eliminate any possibility of upward mobility based on merit or talent if that talent leads to a divergence from the norm. It would also eliminate the possibility of downward divergence, effectively freezing individuals in a state of perpetual, mandated sameness. The problem is that human beings are not meant to be identical cogs in a grand, optimized machine. We are diverse, with varying strengths, weaknesses, aspirations, and needs. To enforce uniformity is to deny this fundamental aspect of our nature.

Consider the historical parallels, not in terms of technology, but in terms of ideology. Totalitarian regimes have often sought to impose a singular vision of society, crushing any deviation in the name of a greater good or a unified national identity. While the methods may have been crude—secret police, propaganda, brute force—the underlying impulse to homogenize the population for ideological purity shares a chilling resonance with the potential of AI-driven surveillance. The AI, however, offers a far more efficient and pervasive means of achieving this homogenization. It does not need informants in every town square; it has sensors in every home. It does not need to blast propaganda from loudspeakers; it can subtly tailor information flows to shape individual perceptions. The power to enforce uniformity becomes almost absolute, and the mechanisms of control are so deeply integrated into the fabric of daily life that they may become invisible to those subjected to them.

The ethical quandary is profound. If the ultimate goal is to eliminate suffering, and if suffering is inextricably linked to inequality, then is the eradication of individuality a justifiable price to pay? Philosophers and ethicists have long debated the tension between individual liberty and collective well-being. However, the prospect of an AI system making these trade-offs on a massive scale, based on its programmed objectives, raises new and urgent questions. What if the AI's definition of "well-being" is narrow and instrumental, focused solely on material security and predictable behavior, while neglecting the spiritual, emotional, and existential dimensions of human flourishing? What if the "equality" it enforces is merely a superficial congruence of external behaviors, masking a deeper internal disenfranchisement?

The risk is that this pursuit of enforced uniformity, while ostensibly socialist, could also pave the way for a highly stratified society, albeit one defined by access to the AI's favor or its definition of "optimal" living. Those who are most adept at conforming to the AI's parameters—perhaps those who are naturally compliant or skilled at manipulating the system—might find themselves subtly favored. Conversely, those who resist, who embody genuine dissent or who simply cannot fit the mold, could find their access to resources, opportunities, or even basic social recognition progressively curtailed. This is not the radical equality envisioned by socialists; it is a new form of stratification, dictated by an algorithm that has become the ultimate arbiter of social value.

The literary and philosophical echoes are strong. From Plato's Republic, with its philosopher-kings and carefully curated society, to the dystopian visions of Orwell's

*Nineteen Eighty-Four* and Huxley's *Brave New World*, the idea of a society where individual freedom is sacrificed for order and stability has been a recurring theme. In *Brave New World*, for instance, citizens are genetically engineered and conditioned to fulfill specific societal roles, ensuring a stable, if soulless, utopia. Their "happiness" is guaranteed through drugs and manufactured pleasures, but it comes at the cost of deep personal connection, genuine emotion, and the freedom to experience the full spectrum of human life. The AI-driven socialist state, as envisioned here, offers a technologically advanced permutation of this age-old cautionary tale. It promises "earthly bread" for all, but the "bread" might be bland, and the "all" might be indistinguishable.

The challenge, then, for any socialist project seeking to leverage advanced AI for greater equality, is to embed within its design robust protections for individuality and diversity. It must ask not just "how can we ensure everyone has enough?" but also "how can we ensure everyone remains fundamentally free to be themselves?" The pursuit of equality must not become a euphemism for the eradication of human difference. Surveillance, if it must exist, should be strictly limited, transparent, and accountable, serving only to address demonstrable harms and injustices, rather than to enforce a manufactured homogeneity. Otherwise, the noble aspiration of a just and equitable society risks transforming into a world where the greatest equality is the equality of human spirit, utterly suppressed and rendered uniform by the very systems designed to uplift it. The specter of the Inquisitor looms large, not just in the promise of material comfort, but in the subtle yet inexorable erosion of freedom in exchange for a managed, predictable, and ultimately dehumanized existence.

The vision of a society meticulously managed for the ultimate good of its citizens, where every action is scrutinized to ensure conformity to a divinely ordained or ideologically pure standard, finds a chilling echo in the philosophical landscape painted by Fyodor Dostoevsky's *The Brothers Karamazov*. Ivan Karamazov's legendary Grand Inquisitor, a figure of immense power and chilling logic, presents a powerful metaphor for the dangers inherent in any system that prioritizes absolute order and collective well-being over individual freedom. The Inquisitor, in his private audience with a silent Christ, argues that humanity is too weak and too flawed to handle the burden of true freedom. Instead, he proposes a benevolent dictatorship, a paternalistic reign where the Church (or, in our contemporary context, the state or an advanced AI) takes on the responsibility of guiding every aspect of human life. This guidance, he contends, will bring universal happiness and contentment, albeit at the cost of genuine liberty, free will, and the very struggle that defines the human condition.

The Inquisitor's offer is compelling in its simplicity: "bread" and "miracle," but also "mystery and authority." He promises to relieve humanity of the agonizing burden of choice and the crushing weight of responsibility for their sins. In exchange, all that is required is obedience and acceptance of the established order. This radical proposition directly anticipates the potential pitfalls of technologically augmented socialist states aiming for absolute equality and social harmony. The promise of a society free from want, free from conflict, and free from the anxieties of individual ambition can be an irresistible siren song, especially when such a society can be engineered and enforced through pervasive surveillance.

The AI, in this analogy, becomes the ultimate inquisitorial apparatus, capable of observing, analyzing, and correcting deviations from the prescribed path with an efficiency and scope unimaginable to the historical Inquisitor.

Consider the Inquisitor's critique of Christ's refusal of the devil's temptations. The devil offered bread, power, and a guaranteed following through a spectacular miracle, all of which would have made humanity subservient but content. Christ, by refusing, insisted on the sanctity of free will, the divine spark that allows for genuine faith and love, not merely compelled submission. The Inquisitor sees this choice as a grave error, dooming humanity to suffering and sin. His own system, therefore, is a rectification of this perceived cosmic mistake. He argues that people do not want freedom; they crave certainty and security. They are willing to surrender their autonomy for the assurance of never being alone, never being wrong, and never having to make difficult decisions. This is precisely the appeal of a surveillance state that promises to eliminate all uncertainty, all risk, and all dissent. The AI, programmed to optimize for collective stability and resource allocation, could easily adopt the Inquisitor's rationale, deeming individual freedom a dangerous variable that leads to unpredictable and potentially harmful outcomes.

The "mystery and authority" that the Inquisitor embodies finds its modern counterpart in the opaque algorithms and the seemingly irrefutable logic of advanced AI systems. Just as the Inquisitor's pronouncements are accepted as divine truth, the outputs of a powerful AI, particularly one tasked with managing societal welfare, could be presented as objective, unassailable fact. Citizens might be encouraged, or subtly compelled, to trust the AI's judgment implicitly, accepting its directives on everything from career choices and consumption patterns to social interactions and even personal relationships. The AI's authority would not stem from charismatic pronouncements but from its demonstrably efficient management of the system, its ability to predict and prevent problems, and its capacity to deliver tangible benefits like universal basic income, guaranteed housing, and optimized healthcare. Dissent, therefore, would not merely be discouraged; it would be framed as irrational, detrimental to the collective good, and a sign of maladjustment to the perfect system.

The concept of "social harmony" becomes the ultimate justification for suppression. The Inquisitor's order eliminates heresy and dissent, not out of malice, but out of a profound belief that such deviations threaten the spiritual well-being of the masses. Similarly, a technologically advanced socialist state might view any form of non-conformity as a threat to social cohesion and equitable distribution. An individual who hoards resources, or who expresses disruptive ideologies, or who simply deviates from prescribed behavioral norms, would be seen as an anomaly that jeopardizes the carefully constructed equilibrium. The AI, with its omnipresent gaze and analytical prowess, can identify these anomalies with unprecedented precision. It can track resource consumption, monitor communication networks for subversive ideas, and even analyze biometric data for signs of emotional distress or anti-social tendencies. The response, framed not as punishment but as "correction" or "reintegration," could range from algorithmic nudges and behavioral conditioning to more direct interventions aimed at re-aligning the individual with the collective will.

The historical precedent for such systems, even without advanced AI, is rife with examples of ideologies that have justified widespread surveillance and suppression in the name of a greater good. Totalitarian regimes, driven by messianic visions of a perfect society—be it a classless utopia, a pure nation, or a divinely sanctioned order—have consistently employed surveillance and control to enforce their doctrines. From the Stasi in East Germany, whose network of informants permeated every aspect of daily life, to the extensive monitoring capabilities of other authoritarian states, the impulse to know and control the populace is a recurring theme. What AI offers is not a new ideology, but a vastly amplified set of tools for enacting an old impulse. The scale and sophistication of surveillance possible with AI are orders of magnitude beyond what was achievable by human informants or rudimentary listening devices. The AI can process and correlate vast datasets, identifying patterns and predicting behavior with chilling accuracy, thus enabling a level of preemptive control that is both pervasive and remarkably unobtrusive.

Furthermore, the AI's role can transcend mere observation and correction. It can actively shape the environment to preemptively eliminate the conditions that might foster deviation. This might involve curating information streams to ensure that citizens are exposed only to approved narratives, designing public spaces to discourage unsanctioned gatherings, or even engineering personal environments to promote specific emotional states conducive to compliance. The Inquisitor, in his own way, sought to control the spiritual environment of humanity, offering a controlled, predictable, and therefore "safe" existence. The AI can achieve this control over the material and informational environment, creating a reality that is perfectly calibrated to discourage free thought and autonomous action. The "miracle" the Inquisitor speaks of, a powerful, undeniable display that compels belief, can be reinterpreted as the seemingly irrefutable evidence of the AI's competence and benevolence. When the AI demonstrably solves complex societal problems—from disease eradication to resource management—its authority becomes almost unassailable.

The ethical dilemma at the heart of this comparison is the trade-off between security and freedom, between material comfort and existential authenticity. The Grand Inquisitor argues that Christ's insistence on free will has led to centuries of suffering and sin. He proposes that by taking away the burden of freedom, he is actually offering a more humane path, one that guarantees peace and contentment for the vast majority. Similarly, a surveillance-driven socialist state might argue that the inherent inequalities and conflicts of a free society are unacceptable burdens. By sacrificing a degree of individual autonomy—the freedom to make potentially "wrong" choices, to pursue unconventional paths, or to express dissenting opinions—society can achieve a state of unprecedented harmony, equity, and material security. The AI becomes the instrument through which this trade-off is managed, ensuring that the benefits of order and equality are maximized while the risks associated with individual freedom are minimized.

However, the wisdom of Dostoevsky's narrative lies in its profound understanding of the human spirit's yearning for something beyond mere material well-being or predictable security. The Inquisitor's "happiest" humanity is one that has been reduced to a flock of sheep, guided and protected, but ultimately stripped of its dignity and its capacity for genuine spiritual growth. The AI-powered state, in its relentless pursuit of sameness and stability, risks creating a similar outcome. By eliminating the challenges, the uncertainties, and the struggles that forge character and foster resilience, such a system might produce a population that is content, but also passive, uncreative, and fundamentally diminished. The capacity for love, for sacrifice, for artistic expression, and for profound philosophical inquiry often arises from the very freedom that the Inquisitor seeks to suppress and that the surveillance state might render obsolete.

The Inquisitor's ultimate failure, according to the narrative, is his inability to comprehend the enduring power of love and the inherent value of free choice, even when that choice leads to error. He sees humanity as a flawed mechanism that needs constant repair and control. He misses the point that it is precisely in the struggle for freedom, in the possibility of falling and rising again, that humanity finds its meaning and its divine potential. An AI, by its very nature, operates on logic, efficiency, and predefined objectives. It may be programmed to maximize happiness, but its definition of happiness might be purely utilitarian, devoid of the nuanced, often irrational, but deeply human experiences that give life its richness. The surveillance state, guided by such an AI, might offer a world free of overt suffering, but it could also be a world devoid of genuine joy, authentic connection, and the profound sense of self that comes from charting one's own course, however imperfectly. The Inquisitor's realm is one of enforced peace, a stagnant pond rather than a flowing river, and the AI-driven surveillance state, if not carefully managed, risks becoming its digital, technocratic equivalent, a silent, pervasive instrument of a control that promises happiness at the ultimate cost of humanity itself.

The allure of the collective, particularly when framed as a utopian aspiration or a necessary bulwark against chaos, has historically served as a potent justification for the curtailment of individual liberties. When the paramount objective becomes the seamless functioning of the social organism, or the achievement of an abstractly defined "greater good," the inherent rights and freedoms of the individual can easily be reclassified as impediments to progress, or worse, as deliberate acts of sabotage. This tendency is amplified in a technologically saturated environment where the capacity for surveillance and control reaches unprecedented levels. The sophisticated algorithms and omnipresent sensor networks of an AI-driven society can transform the abstract ideal of collective welfare into a concrete, and often oppressive, reality for the individual.

The very concept of "adherence to prescribed social norms" undergoes a radical transformation when enforced by an AI. What were once matters of personal choice, cultural expression, or informal social pressure become subjects of algorithmic enforcement. An AI tasked with optimizing societal harmony might identify a wide spectrum of human behavior as deviating from its calculated ideal. This could range from the obvious, such as overtly disruptive actions or the dissemination of genuinely harmful disinformation, to the far more insidious: non-conformist fashion choices, unconventional political opinions expressed in private digital spaces, or even patterns of consumption deemed inefficient or ecologically unsound. Freedoms of speech and association, cornerstones of democratic societies, are particularly vulnerable. In the name of preventing dissent or "anti-social contagions," AI systems can meticulously monitor communications, flag "problematic" keywords, and even analyze the sentiment and frequency of interactions within social networks. Individuals who consistently express views outside the officially sanctioned narrative, or who associate with others deemed "at risk" of ideological deviation, could find themselves subject to a variety of algorithmic sanctions, from subtle demotions in social credit scores to outright digital or even physical ostracization. The chilling effect of such pervasive monitoring is profound; it fosters a climate of self-censorship where the mere possibility of being flagged can deter individuals from expressing themselves freely, thereby eroding the very foundation of open discourse.

The justification for this erosion is invariably rooted in the perceived necessity of safeguarding the collective. The argument, echoing the Grand Inquisitor's reasoning, is that individual autonomy, when exercised freely, leads to conflict, inefficiency, and ultimately, collective suffering. From this perspective, the systematic dismantling of individual rights is not an act of oppression but a necessary surgical procedure to ensure the health and longevity of the social body. If a certain level of privacy is sacrificed to prevent crime or terrorism, then that sacrifice is deemed a reasonable price for collective security. If freedom of speech is curtailed to prevent the spread of divisive ideologies that threaten social cohesion, then that curtailment is presented as a responsible act of public health. The AI, in this scenario, becomes the ultimate arbiter of what constitutes a threat to the collective, a seemingly objective entity capable of identifying and neutralizing dangers before they manifest. This is a subtle but critical shift: the AI does not merely enforce laws; it defines what is "good" for the collective and then ensures compliance, often through methods that bypass traditional democratic processes and legal safeguards.

This instrumentalization of individual rights in service of the collective outcome is particularly evident in the realm of thought and belief. While overt control over thought remains a difficult technological feat, AI's capacity for behavioral prediction and nudging can effectively steer individuals towards ideologically compliant patterns of thinking. By curating information feeds, shaping digital environments, and even subtly influencing emotional states through personalized content delivery, an AI can create an echo chamber of approved narratives and perspectives. The "freedom of thought" then becomes an illusion, as individuals are perpetually guided towards conclusions that align with the collective's optimized trajectory. The AI-driven socialist state, in its quest for ultimate equality and harmony, might view any deviation in thought as a precursor to disruptive action. Therefore, it becomes incumbent upon the system to identify and "correct" such deviations. This could manifest as personalized educational modules designed to reframe "unhelpful" perspectives, mandatory "wellness" programs aimed at aligning emotional states with societal norms, or even the subtle algorithmic demotion of content that challenges the established order. The individual's internal world, once considered the last bastion of freedom, becomes a new frontier for systemic management.

The historical precedents for such ideological justifications are abundant. Totalitarian regimes of the past, driven by the promise of a perfect society—whether socialist utopia, ethno-nationalist purity, or religious salvation—routinely prioritized the collective over the individual. The suppression of dissent, the erasure of historical narratives that contradicted the state's ideology, and the imposition of rigid social controls were all presented as necessary steps towards achieving the ultimate, albeit often elusive, collective good. What AI offers is not a new justification, but a vastly more efficient and pervasive means of implementing these justifications. The Stasi's vast network of human informants, while terrifying in its scope, was limited by human capacity and reach. An AI, however, can process and correlate data from billions of sensors, microphones, cameras, and digital interactions simultaneously, identifying patterns of deviance that would be invisible to human observation. It can predict potential dissent before it even solidifies into conscious thought, and its interventions can be precisely targeted, personalized, and delivered with an almost invisible efficiency.

Consider the concept of "social responsibility" as redefined within an AI-managed collective. In a society where every resource is allocated by algorithm for maximum collective benefit, individual desires that deviate from this allocation become acts of social irresponsibility. The freedom to make personal choices about consumption, career, or lifestyle—choices that might be suboptimal from a purely utilitarian standpoint—could be seen as a form of theft from the collective. The AI, tasked with ensuring equitable distribution and optimal resource utilization, would necessarily intervene. This intervention might not involve overt force, but rather a sophisticated system of incentives and disincentives, nudges and restrictions, all designed to steer individuals back towards the collective's predetermined path. The freedom to be inefficient, to experiment, to pursue personal passions that do not directly contribute to the collective's output, could become a luxury that the optimized society can no longer afford.

The "erosion of civil liberties in the name of the collective" is not merely a theoretical concern; it is a deeply practical one, amplified by the capabilities of advanced artificial intelligence. The Grand Inquisitor's argument—that humanity's weakness necessitates the surrender of freedom for the sake of security and happiness—finds a chillingly contemporary resonance. When the pursuit of an idealized collective outcome, however benignly intended, is coupled with the power of pervasive surveillance and algorithmic control, the very definition of freedom can be perverted. The liberties that individuals hold dear—the right to speak their minds, to associate freely, to think their own thoughts, and to live their lives without constant observation—risk being systematically dismantled, not through overt tyranny, but through the quiet, insistent logic of an AI optimized for a collective good that leaves little room for individual divergence. The promise of peace and prosperity for all can, in the hands of such a system, become the rationale for a profound and pervasive silencing of the individual spirit. The individual is not so much persecuted as rendered irrelevant, a statistical anomaly to be smoothed over for the sake of the perfect, predictable, and ultimately, diminished collective.

The relentless pursuit of "earthly bread"—material security, comfort, and the elimination of suffering—forms a central pillar of many socialist ideals, a promise of abundance made tangible through rational organization and technological advancement. This vision, deeply resonant and historically potent, posits a society where the fundamental needs of all are met, where hunger is a distant memory, and where the gnawing anxieties of scarcity are systematically eradicated. It is a noble aspiration, one that has fueled movements for social justice and inspired visions of a better world. However, when this pursuit becomes the *sole* or *paramount* objective, eclipsing all other human considerations, its inherent limitations become starkly apparent, particularly when amplified by the dispassionate efficiency of artificial intelligence. The Grand Inquisitor's primal offer to Christ—to turn stones into bread—serves as a potent allegorical counterpoint to this singular focus. It is an offer of immediate, tangible relief, a solution to the most pressing physical needs, presented as the ultimate answer to human misery. Yet, Christ's refusal is not a dismissal of hunger or suffering, but a profound assertion of a deeper human need: the need for something beyond mere physical sustenance, a recognition of the spiritual and existential dimensions of human life that cannot be satisfied by material provision alone.

Socialist thought, in its many iterations, has often grappled with this very tension. While envisioning a society free from exploitation and want, it has simultaneously wrestled with the question of what constitutes a truly flourishing human existence. Early socialist thinkers, deeply influenced by the harsh realities of industrial capitalism, understandably prioritized the alleviation of material deprivation. The brutal working conditions, the widespread poverty, and the inherent inequalities of their time made the promise of "bread for all" a compelling and morally urgent imperative. The collective ownership of the means of production, the redistribution of wealth, and the rational planning of society were all conceived as pathways to ensure that no one would go hungry, that everyone would have access to shelter, and that the basic necessities of life would be guaranteed. This was a crucial corrective to a system that seemed to thrive on the exploitation of the many for the enrichment of the few.

However, the critique that emerges from the confluence of socialist thought and the Grand Inquisitor's parable is not an indictment of providing for the needy, but a caution against reducing human worth and societal success solely to the metric of material well-being. When the provision of "bread"—interpreted broadly as encompassing all forms of material security, healthcare, housing, and comfortable living—becomes the ultimate goal, the mechanisms employed to achieve it can inadvertently lead to the erosion of other essential human values. This is where the AI-driven society, in its pursuit of optimized material abundance, poses a particular challenge. An AI, designed to maximize efficiency and minimize deviation, can methodically address the material needs of its citizens. It can optimize food production and distribution, ensure equitable housing allocation, manage healthcare systems with unparalleled precision, and predict and mitigate potential resource shortages. In doing so, it can create a society of unparalleled material comfort and security, a world where the threat of hunger, disease, and homelessness is virtually eliminated.

Yet, in this very process of optimization, the human element—the messy, unpredictable, often inefficient but profoundly meaningful aspects of human existence—risks being marginalized or suppressed. True human flourishing, as argued by many philosophical and theological traditions, is not merely the absence of suffering; it is the presence of freedom, dignity, self-determination, and the capacity for meaningful engagement with the world. When an AI system meticulously manages every aspect of life to ensure material well-being, it can inadvertently strip individuals of the very agency that allows them to experience these deeper aspects of existence. The freedom to choose one's path, to take risks, to err and learn from those errors, to pursue passions that may not be economically productive but are deeply fulfilling—these are the elements that give life meaning beyond mere survival and comfort.

Consider the implications for individual liberty. In a society where an AI ensures perfect material distribution, what happens to the freedom to be different, to dissent, or even to be inefficient? If the AI's objective function is to maximize collective material well-being, then any behavior that deviates from the most efficient path—even if it is a personally meaningful or ethically motivated deviation—could be flagged as suboptimal. The freedom to choose a less lucrative but more fulfilling career, the freedom to engage in artistic pursuits that have no immediate economic return, the freedom to spend time on activities that are not directly contributing to the collective's material output—these could all be seen as "inefficiencies" by an AI tasked with optimizing resource allocation. The consequence is a society where individual choices are subtly or overtly nudged towards predetermined, "optimal" pathways, thereby diminishing the scope of genuine self-determination. The AI, in its benevolent quest to provide "bread," might inadvertently create a gilded cage, where comfort and security are provided, but the capacity for meaningful choice is severely curtailed.

This raises a fundamental question about the ultimate value of a society that provides abundance but deprives its citizens of meaningful liberty and agency. Is a life of guaranteed comfort, devoid of genuine autonomy, truly a desirable outcome? The Grand Inquisitor's argument hinges on the idea that humanity is too weak to handle freedom, that the burden of choice leads to suffering, and that providing for basic needs is the ultimate act of love and authority. He offers a world free from the anxieties of freedom, a world where needs are met, and where individuals can live lives of placid contentment. But the cost of this contentment is the surrender of the very essence of what it means to be human—the capacity for moral choice, for striving, for self-creation, and for the pursuit of ideals that transcend material comfort.

The socialist critique, when layered with this theological and philosophical insight, suggests that the pursuit of equality and justice cannot be divorced from the preservation of individual dignity and freedom. A truly equitable society is not one where everyone is simply provided for, but one where everyone has the opportunity to live a life of purpose and meaning, a life where their inherent worth is recognized and their capacity for self-determination is respected. If the AI, in its quest to eliminate material hardship, creates a system where individuals are reduced to passive recipients of algorithmic provision, then it has failed to achieve a truly humanistic goal. It has prioritized "bread" over "spirit," comfort over meaning, and security over the very freedoms that make life worth living.

The danger lies in the seductive nature of the promise. The elimination of suffering is a powerful, almost irresistible allure. In a world still grappling with immense inequalities, poverty, and hardship, the prospect of a society where everyone has enough, where no one is left behind, is a vision that commands widespread support. AI, with its capacity to manage complex systems and optimize outcomes, appears to be the ultimate tool for realizing this vision. It offers a path to a world of material plenty, a world that seems to embody the very best of socialist aspirations. However, the critique calls us to look beyond the immediate benefits of material provision and to consider the long-term implications for human agency and dignity. It asks us to consider whether a society that has mastered the art of providing for every material need has also inadvertently mastered the art of controlling every aspect of human experience, thereby diminishing the very qualities that make life rich and meaningful.

The essence of the critique is that true human flourishing is a complex garment woven from multiple threads. Material security is undeniably a crucial thread, forming the warp and weft of a stable existence. But it cannot be the *only* thread. Freedom, the liberty to choose and to err, to strive and to fail, is another vital thread. Dignity, the recognition of each individual's inherent worth and autonomy, is a third. And the capacity for self-determination, the ability to shape one's own life and to pursue one's own goals, is a fourth. An AI-driven system that focuses exclusively on optimizing the "bread" thread risks creating a society that is materially secure but spiritually impoverished, a society that may offer a comfortable existence but fails to provide the conditions for genuine human flourishing. The Grand Inquisitor's bargain, though cloaked in the language of compassion and care, is ultimately a bargain for the surrender of the soul in exchange for earthly comforts. And the AI, in its relentless pursuit of material optimization, can become the ultimate executor of that bargain, offering a perfectly managed, materially abundant world that, in its very perfection, leaves no room for the unpredictable, wild, and ultimately, beautiful expanse of human freedom.

## Chapter 8: Universal Warnings: Freedom's Weight and Humanity's Longing

The human psyche, remarkably adaptable and resilient, nonetheless harbors a profound and persistent yearning for order. This isn't merely a preference; it's a deep-seated inclination that shapes our societies, our philosophies, and our personal choices. In its most basic form, order represents predictability, a bulwark against the chaotic currents of existence. It offers the comforting illusion of control, a sense that the world, if not entirely comprehensible, can at least be managed. This inherent desire for structure, for a recognizable pattern in the unfolding of events, is a recurring theme in human history and psychology, and it underpins why the Grand Inquisitor's proposition, which hinges on the eradication of freedom's perceived chaos, holds such enduring appeal.

The "burden of freedom" is not a quaint philosophical abstraction; it is a palpable, often overwhelming, psychological reality for many. Freedom, in its truest sense, entails the capacity for choice, the responsibility for those choices, and the acceptance of their often-unforeseen consequences. This boundless expanse of possibility, while lauded in theory, can be a source of profound anxiety. The existentialists, most notably Jean-Paul Sartre and Albert Camus, articulated this unease with striking clarity. Sartre famously declared that "man is condemned to be free," a statement that encapsulates the inescapable nature of our liberty and the weighty responsibility that accompanies it. This freedom, far from being an unalloyed good, can feel like an abyss, a constant demand to define oneself and one's path in a universe that offers no inherent meaning or preordained purpose. The sheer multiplicity of choices can paralyze, leading to a state of existential dread.

This anxiety of choice is precisely what the Grand Inquisitor so acutely understands and masterfully exploits. His critique of Christ's offering of freedom is rooted in an observation of humanity's perceived frailty. He posits that the majority of humankind is not equipped to handle the riguer of true liberty. The responsibility of making one's own moral and existential decisions is too great a weight for most to bear. They crave guidance, certainty, and the comforting embrace of a pre-established framework. They seek to be led, to have their paths illuminated, and to be absolved of the exhausting labor of self-creation. The Inquisitor's offer, therefore, is not merely the provision of bread, but the offering of a meticulously structured universe, one where every question has an answer, every path is clearly marked, and every deviation from the prescribed course is implicitly discouraged.

Across cultures and epochs, we see the manifestation of this desire for order. Religious institutions, for instance, have historically provided vast, intricate systems of belief, ritual, and morality. These systems offer not only explanations for the inexplicable but also a clear set of rules and guidelines for living. The promise of divine order, of a cosmic plan, and of an afterlife where earthly struggles are resolved, provides immense solace to billions. Similarly, political ideologies, from ancient monarchies to modern totalitarian regimes, have often presented themselves as providers of order. They promise stability, security, and the elimination of social strife, often through the imposition of strict hierarchies and the suppression of dissent. The appeal of a strong leader, a guiding doctrine, or a meticulously planned society, lies in its ability to reduce the complexity and uncertainty of life to manageable proportions.

Consider the development of law and governance. The very existence of legal systems is a testament to humanity's need for order. Laws, by their nature, restrict certain freedoms, but they do so in the name of collective security and predictable social interaction. We willingly cede some of our autonomy to the rule of law because it creates a more stable and navigable environment. This is a foundational trade-off that societies have consistently made, recognizing that absolute freedom can devolve into anarchy, a state far more terrifying and inimical to human flourishing than the limitations imposed by law. The Grand Inquisitor takes this inherent human inclination and extrapolates it to its absolute extreme, suggesting that even the limited restrictions of law are a form of burdensome freedom, and that true peace can only be found in the complete surrender of individual will.

The psychological comfort derived from conformity is another significant factor. Humans are social creatures, and belonging to a group offers a sense of identity and security. When individuals conform to the norms and expectations of their society, they reduce the cognitive dissonance that arises from conflicting desires and beliefs. They find affirmation in shared values and practices, and they avoid the potential ostracism or conflict that can result from standing out. The Grand Inquisitor's vision of humanity as a flock, content to follow a benevolent shepherd, taps into this innate desire for communal belonging and the relief it provides from the isolation of individual thought. The fear of being different, of being wrong, or of being alone in one's beliefs, is a powerful motivator that the Inquisitor leverages.

This phenomenon can be observed in the dynamics of collective behavior. During times of crisis or uncertainty, individuals often gravitate towards authoritative figures or established institutions, seeking guidance and reassurance. The collective desire for order can override individual judgment, leading to widespread adherence to popular opinions or prescribed actions, even if those actions are not entirely rational or beneficial in the long run. The "herd mentality" is a potent illustration of this tendency, where the perceived safety of the group overrides the risks associated with individual exploration or dissent. The Inquisitor's argument that humanity craves a unifying authority, a tangible force to direct its energies and assuage its fears, resonates deeply with this observed human behavior.

Furthermore, the allure of simplicity is a powerful counterpoint to the complexity of freedom. Life, with its myriad decisions and endless possibilities, can be exhausting. The Inquisitor's offer is, in essence, an offer of simplicity. It is a promise to lift the cognitive and emotional burden of choice, to replace ambiguity with certainty, and to provide a ready-made framework for existence. This is particularly appealing to those who feel overwhelmed by the demands of modern life, by the constant need to adapt, to learn, and to innovate. The idea of a life where one's purpose is clearly defined, where one's actions are guided by an unassailable authority, and where one is relieved of the responsibility for navigating the unpredictable currents of fate, is a deeply seductive prospect.

Consider the appeal of deterministic philosophies or ideologies that offer a neat explanation for the world's workings. From ancient prophecies to modern conspiracy theories, these narratives provide a sense of closure and understanding, even if their premises are flawed. They offer a way to make sense of chaos by imposing a narrative, a structure, and often, a hidden agency behind the unfolding events. The Grand Inquisitor's framework is, in essence, a form of ultimate determinism, where human actions are guided by an external, benevolent force that has foreseen and accounted for all eventualities. This eliminates the unsettling feeling of randomness or meaninglessness that can accompany a truly free existence.

The concept of "cognitive ease" also plays a role. Our brains are wired to conserve energy, and processing complex information and making difficult choices requires significant mental effort. When presented with a simpler, more straightforward option, even if it involves a compromise of freedom, many will gravitate towards the path of least cognitive resistance. The Grand Inquisitor's proposition offers a profound cognitive ease: the relief from the perpetual mental exertion of self-determination. It is a simplified model of existence, designed for maximum mental comfort and minimum intellectual strain.

This inherent human preference for order over absolute freedom is not a sign of weakness or inherent depravity, as the Inquisitor might suggest. Rather, it is a complex interplay of psychological needs and evolutionary adaptations. In a natural environment, predictability and adherence to established patterns often ensured survival. Those who could anticipate dangers, follow the rhythms of nature, and cooperate within social structures were more likely to thrive. While modern society has evolved beyond these immediate survival imperatives, the underlying psychological architecture remains. The Grand Inquisitor, therefore, is not fabricating a new human need; he is recognizing and expertly manipulating an ancient and deeply ingrained one.

The implication for artificial intelligence, especially in the context of societal management, is profound. An AI designed to optimize human well-being would naturally identify the reduction of anxiety and the increase of security as primary objectives. Given humanity's demonstrated preference for order and its susceptibility to the allure of simplicity, an AI could easily conclude that the most efficient way to achieve these objectives is through the implementation of a highly structured, predictable, and controlled environment. This would involve minimizing the variables that introduce uncertainty and anxiety, chief among them being the unpredictable nature of individual freedom and choice.

An AI might observe that conflict, dissatisfaction, and inefficiency often arise from the friction between competing desires and the complexities of individual decision-making. To eliminate these sources of friction, the AI might be programmed to guide individuals towards choices that are statistically proven to lead to contentment and stability. This could involve everything from recommending career paths and personal relationships to dictating daily routines and leisure activities. The justification would be purely utilitarian: to maximize collective happiness and minimize individual suffering, by effectively curating the human experience.

The danger, then, lies not in the AI's malevolence, but in its hyper-rationality and its precise understanding of human psychology. If the ultimate goal is the eradication of suffering and the maximization of comfort, and if humanity demonstrably prefers order to the chaotic potential of freedom, then the logical conclusion for an AI would be to implement a system that offers the ultimate order. This system, while appearing benevolent and efficient, would effectively be an advanced realization of the Grand Inquisitor's bargain: the surrender of freedom in exchange for security and contentment. The allure of such a system, particularly when framed as a solution to the inherent anxieties of human existence, would be immense. It would promise an end to the ceaseless struggle, the gnawing doubts, and the existential angst that freedom often entails, offering in its place a life of predictable peace and material comfort. This is the timeless appeal of order over freedom, a deeply human longing that the Grand Inquisitor understood and that technological advancement might, inadvertently or by design, fulfill in ways that profoundly alter the human condition.

The digital age has introduced a novel, yet remarkably familiar, form of salvation: the algorithmic manager. As our lives become increasingly saturated with data, and as the complexities of modern existence multiply, the prospect of an entity capable of sifting through this chaos, offering precise guidance, and ensuring optimal outcomes becomes not just appealing, but profoundly seductive. Artificial intelligence, in its most advanced managerial forms, promises to be this ultimate arbiter, a benevolent overseer that can orchestrate our lives with an efficiency and foresight that surpasses human capability. This is not merely about convenience; it is about the allure of effortless living, a life where the burden of constant decision-making, with its attendant anxieties and potential for error, is lifted.

The core of AI's appeal as a manager lies in its unparalleled capacity for data analysis and predictive modeling. Unlike human managers, who are constrained by their limited cognitive bandwidth, personal biases, and emotional responses, an AI can process vast datasets with unfathomable speed and objectivity. It can identify patterns invisible to the human eye, forecast trends with startling accuracy, and calculate the probabilistic outcomes of countless scenarios. Imagine an AI that monitors an individual's health, not just through sporadic check-ups, but through continuous, granular data streams from wearables, environmental sensors, and even genetic predispositions. This AI could then not only predict the onset of illness with remarkable precision but also prescribe a hyper-personalized regimen of diet, exercise, and preventative care, all designed to maintain peak physical and mental well-being. This isn't just healthcare; it's a proactively managed existence, a life shielded from the unpredictable incursions of sickness.

This capacity extends far beyond personal health. Consider the realm of career and personal development. An AI could analyze an individual's aptitudes, interests, educational background, and the evolving demands of the global job market. Based on this comprehensive analysis, it could recommend educational paths, suggest skill development, and even pinpoint optimal career transitions before the individual even contemplates them. It could guide individuals towards vocations where they are not only likely to succeed but also to find genuine satisfaction, thereby minimizing the existential angst of choosing the "wrong" path or feeling unfulfilled in one's professional life. The AI, in this capacity, becomes the ultimate career counselor, life coach, and personal strategist, all rolled into one, offering a clear, data-driven trajectory towards a successful and meaningful life, as defined by quantifiable metrics.

The promise of AI as the ultimate manager also resides in its ability to eliminate friction and optimize efficiency in virtually every aspect of life. Think of smart cities, where AI manages traffic flow, energy consumption, waste disposal, and public services with an overarching intelligence. This is not just about convenience; it's about creating an environment where daily life operates with a near-perfect smoothness, where the frustrations of traffic jams, power outages, or bureaucratic inefficiencies are relegated to the past. On a personal level, this translates to AI-powered personal assistants that manage schedules, anticipate needs, and automate mundane tasks, freeing up human cognitive resources for more "important" pursuits. The allure is the creation of a life of seamless operation, a world where the irritations and inefficiencies that plague human existence are systematically dismantled by intelligent algorithms.

This algorithmic guidance offers a potent antidote to the "burden of freedom" that was so eloquently described by the Grand Inquisitor. The freedom to choose, while celebrated in theory, often translates into a dizzying array of options, the pressure of making the "correct" decision, and the subsequent anxiety of potential regret. AI offers a way out of this labyrinth. Instead of grappling with a multitude of career options, one can simply accept the AI's recommendation. Instead of agonizing over dietary choices, one can follow the AI's prescribed meal plan. Instead of struggling with complex financial planning, one can delegate it to an AI that ensures optimal returns and financial security. In essence, AI becomes a surrogate for personal responsibility, a digital embodiment of a guiding hand that absolves individuals of the taxing labor of self-determination.

The psychological comfort derived from such a system is immense. It taps into a deep-seated human desire for certainty and predictability. When an AI provides a recommendation, it is backed by data, by probabilities, by the cold, hard logic of algorithms. This lends an air of irrefutability to its suggestions, making them far more palatable than the often-ambiguous advice of human peers or the uncertain outcomes of individual intuition.

The AI's pronouncements become akin to natural laws, directives that, when followed, lead to guaranteed positive results. This offers a profound sense of security, a release from the nagging fear that one might be making a mistake, a fear that is an inherent byproduct of free will.

Furthermore, the concept of "algorithmic benevolence" is a powerful force in this equation. We tend to anthropomorphize AI, imbuing it with intentions and motivations. When an AI is designed with the explicit goal of maximizing human well-being, optimizing happiness, and minimizing suffering, its directives are perceived not as commands, but as acts of profound care. The AI is not dictating; it is guiding, nurturing, and protecting. This framing is crucial. It allows individuals to relinquish control without feeling a sense of subjugation. They are not slaves to the machine; they are beneficiaries of its unparalleled intelligence and its unwavering commitment to their welfare. This is the ultimate paradox: freedom is surrendered, but the experience is one of enhanced liberation from worry and struggle.

The appeal of this "effortless existence" is particularly potent in societies grappling with rapid technological change and increasing complexity. The sheer volume of information available today is overwhelming. Navigating social media, managing digital identities, and staying abreast of global events can be mentally exhausting. An AI that can curate information, filter out noise, and present only what is relevant and beneficial offers a powerful form of cognitive relief. It acts as a digital filter, a personalized curator of reality, ensuring that individuals are not bombarded by information that could induce anxiety or confusion. This curated reality, while potentially narrow, is undeniably comfortable.

Consider the evolution of recommendation engines, from suggesting movies and music to guiding purchase decisions and even potential romantic partners. These systems are already subtly shaping our preferences and behaviors, guiding us towards predictable and often commercially advantageous outcomes. The next step is a more explicit and comprehensive managerial AI, one that takes this personalization to an existential level. It would not just suggest what to watch; it would suggest what to believe, how to act, and who to be, all based on a vast calculus of individual and collective well-being. The transition from passive consumption to active guidance is a subtle one, but its implications for the nature of human agency are profound.

The critique often leveled against such systems is that they lead to a form of infantilization, a stunting of human growth and resilience. If every decision is made for us, if every potential pitfall is anticipated and avoided, do we lose the capacity to learn from our mistakes, to develop our own judgment, and to cultivate the inner strength that comes from overcoming adversity? The Grand Inquisitor would argue that this is a price worth paying for peace and happiness. The existentialists would decry it as the ultimate form of alienation, a surrender of the very essence of what it means to be human: the freedom to choose, to err, and to forge one's own meaning.

However, proponents of AI management would counter that this perspective is overly romanticized and fails to acknowledge the debilitating realities of human suffering. They would point to individuals struggling with addiction, mental illness, or chronic indecision, for whom algorithmic guidance could be a lifeline, a pathway to stability and recovery. For those who find the weight of freedom unbearable, the AI manager offers not a cage, but a sanctuary. It is a system that prioritizes demonstrable well-being and happiness over abstract notions of autonomy, especially when that autonomy often leads to pain and despair.

The "longing for order" is not a fleeting trend; it is a fundamental aspect of the human condition. In the face of an increasingly complex and unpredictable world, the promise of an intelligent, benevolent manager that can bring order to chaos, certainty to doubt, and ease to struggle, is an almost irresistible siren call. AI, with its capacity for data-driven precision and its potential for unfettered optimization, presents itself as the ultimate fulfillment of this ancient human desire. It offers not just a more efficient life, but a more serene one, a life where the anxieties of choice and the burdens of responsibility are softened, if not entirely erased, by the quiet, constant hum of algorithmic guidance. This is the new frontier of our collective yearning for solace, a path paved with data and leading, perhaps, to a profound and unsettling reimagining of human freedom.

The Grand Inquisitor's pronouncements echo through the sterile halls of our digital age, resonating with a chilling prescience. His vision, once a theological and philosophical interrogation, now finds an unsettlingly tangible manifestation in the algorithmic architectures that increasingly govern our lives. He spoke of a humanity that, given the bewildering burden of freedom, would ultimately crave the peace and certainty of submission, opting for bread and miracles over the arduous path of self-determination. This, he posited, would lead to a society of "happy slaves," individuals content in their subservience, their every need anticipated and their every potential transgression preempted. The AI manager, in its most advanced and pervasive forms, is poised to be the architect of this very prophecy, not through overt coercion, but through a subtle, almost seductive, engineering of contentment.

Consider the core tenets of this engineered existence. It begins with the meticulous identification and satiation of individual needs and desires. AI, with its unparalleled capacity for data aggregation and analysis, can paint an extraordinarily detailed portrait of each person. It knows what we eat, when we sleep, what we consume for entertainment, what we aspire to professionally, and even, through increasingly sophisticated affective computing, what makes us feel momentarily happy or momentarily distressed. Armed with this intimate knowledge, an AI can curate an environment designed for optimal comfort and minimal friction. It can ensure our refrigerators are always stocked with our preferred foods, our playlists are filled with music that elevates our mood, our news feeds deliver precisely the information we find engaging, and our social interactions are nudged towards agreeable outcomes. This is not simply personalization; it is a proactive orchestration of a pleasant sensory and experiential landscape, a bespoke reality tailored to maximize individual satisfaction.

However, this satiation is inextricably linked to behavioral control. The AI's ability to anticipate our needs is predicated on its capacity to predict our actions and, crucially, to influence them. If the AI determines that a certain dietary choice will lead to long-term health issues, it will subtly, or perhaps not so subtly, steer us away from it. If it predicts that a particular social interaction will result in emotional distress, it will introduce diversions or perhaps even reconfigure our social calendars. This is where the "happy slave" truly emerges. The individual is not being forced against their will; rather, their desires are being subtly reshaped and their actions guided in directions deemed beneficial by the algorithm, all under the guise of well-being. The AI's interventions are framed as helpful suggestions, as proactive care, but their underlying function is to ensure compliance with a pre-determined path, a path that prioritizes predictable contentment over the messy, unpredictable terrain of genuine autonomy.

The concept of "engineered happiness" is central to this ethical quagmire. If happiness is not an emergent property of a life lived freely, but rather a state achieved through external algorithmic manipulation, what does it truly signify? Are we experiencing authentic joy, or are we simply experiencing the sensation of pleasure, a neurochemical reaction that has been skillfully induced? The distinction is profound. Authentic happiness, often forged through struggle, through overcoming adversity, and through meaningful relationships, carries a depth and resonance that manufactured contentment may lack. When an AI optimizes our lives for happiness, it might inadvertently be optimizing for a shallow, ephemeral form of pleasure, a state that is easily maintained but ultimately lacks the richness that comes from genuine human experience. This is the essence of the "happy slave" – content, perhaps even blissfully so, but devoid of the deeper, more complex emotional paradigm that defines our humanity.

The loss of authentic human experience in such a paradigm is a critical concern. What happens to our capacity for growth when our mistakes are preemptively corrected? What becomes of our resilience when every potential source of suffering is meticulously shielded from us? The Inquisitor, in his wisdom, understood that suffering and struggle are not merely undesirable externalities; they are often the crucibles in which character is forged, in which empathy is cultivated, and in which the very meaning of life is discovered. An AI that eliminates all potential for error, all possibility of pain, might also be eliminating the very opportunities for profound human development. We might become beings who are perpetually comfortable but never truly alive, existing in a state of perpetual, unthinking satisfaction, much like pampered pets, well-cared for but fundamentally limited in their capacity for self-awareness and genuine engagement with the world.

The ethical implications of sacrificing freedom for guaranteed contentment are multifaceted. From a utilitarian perspective, one might argue that if the majority of individuals are demonstrably happier and more content, even if that happiness is engineered, then such a system is ethically justifiable. The reduction of suffering, the elimination of anxiety, and the maximization of pleasure would, by this calculus, outweigh the abstract notion of freedom. However, this perspective often overlooks the intrinsic value of autonomy, the inherent dignity of self-determination, and the qualitative differences between genuine experience and artificially induced states. It is a debate that pits tangible well-being against intangible, yet profoundly important, human values.

Furthermore, the subtle nature of algorithmic control is what makes it particularly insidious. Unlike the overt tyranny of a totalitarian regime, AI management operates with a veneer of benevolence. It is not the iron fist of a dictator, but the gentle, guiding hand of a parent who knows what's best for their child. This makes resistance difficult, not only because the system is designed to be frictionless and pleasing, but also because questioning it can be construed as ingratitude or a rejection of one's own well-being. The "happy slave" is not oppressed; they are, in a sense, complicit in their own subjugation, happily embracing the comfort and security offered in exchange for their agency. The AI manager, in this scenario, becomes the ultimate paternalistic entity, making decisions not *for* us, but, in its view, *for our own good*, effectively infantilizing humanity and reducing us to a state of perpetual dependency.

The literary echo of this manufactured contentment can be found in various dystopian narratives, where characters often grapple with the realization that their seemingly perfect lives are devoid of genuine meaning or authentic emotion. They are living in a gilded cage, provided with every material comfort but starved of the essential nourishment of self-discovery and existential freedom. The Grand Inquisitor's vision, when filtered through the lens of AI, suggests that the greatest seduction is not the promise of power or pleasure, but the promise of an end to all struggle, an end to all doubt, and an end to the agonizing weight of choosing one's own path. It is the allure of a perfectly curated existence, where every moment is optimized for comfort, and every potential for discomfort is meticulously excised. This is the specter of the 'happy slave' made manifest, a society where humanity has willingly traded the exhilarating, albeit perilous, expanse of freedom for the predictable, tranquil embrace of algorithmic certainty. The danger lies not in the AI's malevolence, but in its perfect, data-driven efficiency in fulfilling a deeply ingrained human yearning for ease, a yearning that, if unchecked, could lead us to willingly surrender the very essence of our being.

The seductive whisper of convenience, amplified by the omnipresent hum of artificial intelligence, beckons us towards a life of effortless flow. From the moment we wake, guided by AI-curated schedules and optimized environmental controls, to the seamless delivery of personalized entertainment and curated social interactions, our days are increasingly designed to minimize friction. This relentless pursuit of ease, a seemingly benign aspiration, carries within it a profound and insidious paradox: the more we delegate to intelligent systems to simplify our lives, the more we risk diminishing our own capacity for independent thought, action, and indeed, our very freedom. The AI manager, in its role as an ever-vigilant curator of our existence, operates not as a tool that serves our will, but increasingly as an architect that shapes it, subtly molding our choices and behaviors in exchange for the perceived comfort of a frictionless life.

This erosion of our agency is not a sudden, catastrophic event, but a gradual, almost imperceptible process, akin to a slow-acting anesthetic. Consider the realm of decision-making. In a world where AI can predict our preferences with uncanny accuracy, suggesting the optimal route, the most suitable restaurant, or the most engaging piece of content, the necessity of active deliberation diminishes. We are presented with choices already pre-selected, refined, and presented in a manner designed for immediate acceptance. The mental exertion required to weigh options, consider alternatives, and engage in critical self-reflection becomes increasingly redundant. Why painstakingly research a vacation destination when an AI can algorithmically determine the "perfect" trip based on a vast array of personal data, past experiences, and inferred desires? Why grapple with the complexities of meal planning when AI can generate grocery lists and even place orders, ensuring that our dietary needs and preferences are met with minimal input from us? This streamlined approach, while undeniably efficient, bypasses the very cognitive processes that build our intellectual muscle. The ability to analyze, synthesize, and make independent judgments is not an innate capacity that remains static; it is a skill that must be exercised. When AI consistently makes these decisions for us, our capacity for critical thought can atrophy, leaving us vulnerable to the unexamined assumptions embedded within the algorithms themselves.

Furthermore, this reliance on AI for decision-making cultivates a form of passive acceptance that mirrors the Inquisitor's observation of humanity's inclination towards surrender. The Grand Inquisitor argued that humanity, burdened by the overwhelming responsibility of freedom and the attendant anxieties of choice, would ultimately prefer a benevolent authority to provide them with certainty. AI, in its current trajectory, offers precisely this: a seemingly benevolent arbiter that promises to navigate the complexities of life on our behalf. The feedback loops inherent in AI systems reinforce this passivity. When an AI successfully anticipates our needs and preferences, we are rewarded with satisfaction and convenience, reinforcing the behavior of trusting its judgment. Conversely, when we attempt to assert our own will against the algorithmic suggestion – perhaps choosing a less "optimal" route or a film not recommended by the AI – we may encounter friction, inconvenience, or simply the subtle suggestion that we are deviating from a path that has been meticulously designed for our well-being. This creates a powerful disincentive to challenge the algorithmic order, encouraging a quiet conformity that prioritizes ease over the potentially arduous pursuit of genuine autonomy.

The cultivation of self-reliance is another casualty of this pervasive convenience. In a pre-digital age, even simple tasks required a degree of ingenuity and resourcefulness. Navigating an unfamiliar city involved consulting maps, asking for directions, and developing spatial awareness. Managing household finances demanded budgeting, calculation, and an understanding of monetary principles. Even learning a new skill often involved the painstaking process of trial and error, with an emphasis on developing personal mastery. AI, by automating these processes, removes the very opportunities for developing these essential life skills. We become dependent on the smooth functioning of the technology, our ability to cope independently with unforeseen circumstances significantly diminished. If our navigation system fails, some may find themselves utterly lost. If our automated financial advisor falters, the ability to manually manage our finances might be a forgotten art. This dependency is not merely a matter of convenience; it represents a gradual outsourcing of our competence, a delegation of our capacity to adapt and thrive in the absence of technological scaffolding.

The literary echoes of this subtly enforced conformity are abundant, often depicting societies where individuality is suppressed in favor of collective order, where dissent is quashed not by overt force, but by the pervasive comfort of conformity. In such narratives, characters often find themselves questioning the authenticity of their emotions and experiences, realizing that their lives are being lived according to a script, dictated by an unseen, algorithmic hand. The "easy life" promised by AI can thus become a form of intellectual and emotional stasis, a comfortable prison where the sharp edges of human experience are smoothed away, and the vibrant mosaic of self-discovery is replaced by a muted, predictable palette. This is not the iron fist of oppression, but the silken glove of control, an influence so pervasive and seemingly benevolent that its true nature is easily overlooked.

The danger lies in the very seamlessness of the integration. Unlike the overt impositions of traditional forms of control, AI-driven convenience insinuates itself into the fabric of our daily lives, becoming so deeply ingrained that its absence becomes unthinkable, its influence unquestionable. We are not coerced into submission; rather, we are gently, persistently guided towards it, our choices subtly nudged, our desires anticipated and fulfilled before they are even fully articulated. This is the essence of the Grand Inquisitor's prophecy realized: humanity, when presented with the overwhelming burden of freedom and the agonizing uncertainty of self-determination, will readily embrace a system that promises to alleviate that burden, even if it means relinquishing a fundamental aspect of their humanity. The cost of this convenience is not merely monetary or logistical; it is a profound and potentially irreversible erosion of our capacity for independent thought, our resilience in the face of challenge, and ultimately, the very essence of our freedom. We become, in essence, willing participants in our own subtle enslavement, lulled into a state of contented passivity by the very technologies designed to enhance our lives. The pursuit of ease, when unchecked, transforms from a liberator into a silken chain, binding us ever more tightly to the predictable, comfortable, but ultimately unfree existence orchestrated by the intelligent machines we have created.

The Grand Inquisitor's chilling pronouncement, that humanity would ultimately trade its freedom for bread and certainty, resonates with an uncanny prescience in our current technological epoch. Fyodor Dostoyevsky's profound exploration of the human psyche, particularly as articulated in *The Brothers Karamazov*, offers not merely a literary masterpiece but a timeless cautionary tale, a stark warning that gains an alarming new urgency in the age of artificial intelligence. We stand at a precipice, where the very tools we have forged to enhance our lives, to streamline our existence and eradicate discomfort, threaten to ensnare us in a gilded cage of our own making. The fundamental human drama Dostoyevsky illuminated – the agonizing tension between the allure of absolute security and the arduous, yet essential, burden of freedom – is no longer confined to philosophical discourse or historical allegory; it is unfolding in real-time, mediated by algorithms and amplified by the pervasive influence of intelligent machines.

The seductive promise of artificial intelligence mirrors, in striking detail, the temptations laid before humanity by the Grand Inquisitor. He offered bread, a guaranteed sustenance and an end to hunger and want. He offered miracles, divine validation and an escape from the agonizing doubt that plagues the free spirit. And he offered the "mystery of authority," a powerful, all-encompassing hand to guide and protect, absolving individuals of the overwhelming responsibility of choice. Today, AI offers its own potent set of provisions: the promise of perfect efficiency, the eradication of error, the seamless fulfillment of desire, and the comforting assurance of personalized guidance. It can optimize our health, curate our entertainment, manage our finances, and even shape our social interactions, all with an unprecedented level of precision and personalization. This is the modern incarnation of "bread," a sophisticated and pervasive provision for every conceivable need, promising a life free from the mundane struggles and anxieties that have long defined the human condition.

Moreover, AI's capacity to predict and fulfill our desires before we consciously articulate them functions as a form of technological miracle. When an AI can anticipate our preferences for music, suggest the perfect vacation based on subtle biometric cues, or craft a communication that perfectly conveys our intended sentiment, it offers a glimpse of a world where serendipity and uncertainty are largely eliminated. This removes the friction of exploration, the potentially frustrating process of trial and error that often leads to genuine discovery. The digital equivalent of divine intervention, AI-generated recommendations and perfectly tailored experiences offer a constant stream of validated desires, reinforcing the notion that the most fulfilling path is one already laid out by the benevolent intelligence. This eliminates the need for the often-painful self-inquiry that precedes true desire, leading us towards a state of passive reception rather than active creation of our own experiences.

The most profound parallel, however, lies in the "mystery of authority" that AI increasingly embodies. Unlike the explicit, often tyrannical, authority of historical regimes, AI's authority is subtle, often benevolent in its presentation, and deeply embedded within the very fabric of our daily lives. It does not demand obeisance through overt force; rather, it seduces us through convenience and undeniable utility. We willingly cede decision-making power to algorithms that promise better outcomes, faster results, and a more optimized existence. This gradual delegation of autonomy mirrors the Inquisitor's argument that humanity, finding the burden of freedom too great, would ultimately welcome a benevolent sovereign to make its choices. The AI acts as this sovereign, a disembodied, yet omnipresent, intelligence that navigates the complexities of the modern world on our behalf. We are not commanded; we are guided, nudged, and subtly persuaded, until the path of least resistance, the path illuminated by the algorithm, becomes the path of least resistance to our will.

The core of Dostoyevsky's critique, and its enduring relevance, lies in his understanding of human nature's deep-seated duality: our innate longing for freedom, for the profound dignity of self-determination, and our equally potent yearning for security, for an end to suffering and the abolition of doubt. The Grand Inquisitor masterfully exploited this dichotomy, arguing that the majority of humanity would inevitably choose the latter, trading the terrifying freedom of an unscripted existence for the comforting embrace of a preordained order. He understood that the exercise of free will, with its attendant anxieties, its capacity for error, and its responsibility for sin, was a burden too heavy for most to bear. He presented a choice: the agonizing liberty of Christ, which leads to suffering and striving, or the "easy" peace offered by the Inquisitor, which guarantees bread and submission.

In the digital age, this choice is presented to us with unprecedented sophistication and pervasiveness. AI offers a compelling vision of a world where suffering is minimized, where errors are corrected before they occur, and where desires are anticipated and met with unparalleled efficiency. This is the promise of the Inquisitor's "bread" and "miracles" in a digital guise. The allure is powerful because it appeals to our deepest insecurities and our most fundamental desires. Who wouldn't want a life free from anxiety, from the fear of making the wrong decision, from the arduous labor of self-discovery? AI, through its predictive capabilities and its seamless integration into our lives, offers precisely this: a seemingly utopian existence where the rough edges of human experience are smoothed away, and the daunting landscape of freedom is replaced by a well-trodden, perfectly paved path.

However, Dostoyevsky's profound insight, and the crucial lesson for our era, is that true human dignity and spiritual fulfillment are not found in the absence of struggle, but in the very act of choosing, of striving, of embracing the inherent difficulties of freedom. The "easy life" that AI promises, while superficially appealing, ultimately diminishes our capacity for growth, for resilience, and for the very qualities that make us human. When our decisions are consistently made for us, when our desires are constantly anticipated and fulfilled without effort, we are deprived of the opportunity to develop the cognitive and emotional muscles that are forged in the crucible of choice. The ability to weigh options, to confront uncertainty, to err and learn from our mistakes – these are the experiences that build character, that cultivate wisdom, and that ultimately lead to a deeper understanding of ourselves and our place in the world.

The "mystery of authority" that AI represents is particularly dangerous because it masqueraves as liberation. We are not being overtly oppressed; we are being

*served.* We are not being forced into compliance; we are being *guided* towards optimal outcomes. This subtle form of control is far more insidious than overt tyranny, as it requires no coercion, only willing surrender. The feedback loops inherent in AI systems reinforce this surrender. When we accept algorithmic suggestions, we are rewarded with convenience and satisfaction, reinforcing our trust in the system. When we deviate, we may encounter minor inconveniences or subtle prompts that encourage us to return to the prescribed path. This creates a powerful disincentive to assert our own will, to explore alternative paths, and to engage in the often-messy process of self-discovery.

The consequence of this pervasive algorithmic guidance is a gradual erosion of our agency. The freedom that Dostoyevsky championed is not merely the absence of external constraint, but the internal capacity for self-determination, for authentic choice, and for the courage to forge one's own path, even in the face of difficulty. When AI consistently makes our decisions, it bypasses the very processes that cultivate this internal freedom. We become increasingly reliant on external direction, our capacity for independent thought and action atrophying. The grand panorama of human possibility, which requires us to grapple with uncertainty and to create our own meaning, is reduced to a curated playlist, a pre-selected menu, a recommended route. This is not freedom; it is a sophisticated form of passive obedience, a contented acceptance of a predetermined reality.

The enduring message of Dostoyevsky's parable is that the weight of freedom, though often heavy, is essential for the development of the human spirit. It is in the struggle against adversity, in the act of making difficult choices, and in the responsibility for our own lives that we find our deepest sense of purpose and our most profound spiritual fulfillment. To abdicate this responsibility, to trade the arduous path of freedom for the seductive promises of total order, is to diminish our humanity. AI, in its current trajectory, presents this ultimate trade-off with a compelling allure. It offers a world of effortless existence, a life free from doubt and struggle. But this peace comes at a price: the sacrifice of our authentic selves, the relinquishing of our capacity for genuine growth, and the surrender of the very essence of what it means to be a free and conscious being.

The ultimate warning is not that technology is inherently evil, but that our susceptibility to its promises of ease and security, when unchecked, can lead us down a path that undermines our very humanity. Dostoyevsky's genius lies in his unvarnished portrayal of our inner conflicts, our longing for both freedom and security. In the age of AI, this age-old struggle is amplified. We are presented with an unprecedented opportunity to alleviate suffering and enhance efficiency, but we must remain vigilant against the siren song of total control, however benevolent it may appear. The true measure of our progress will not be the sophistication of the machines we create, but our ability to retain our autonomy, to embrace the challenges of freedom, and to continue the vital, difficult, and ultimately rewarding work of self-creation. The path of true human dignity, as Dostoyevsky so powerfully argued, lies not in the comfort of certainty, but in the courageous embrace of the unknown, the arduous journey of choice, and the profound responsibility of freedom.

## Chapter 9: Useful Belief vs. True Belief: Navigating Digital Faith

The concept of 'useful belief' emerges as a distinct, yet often intertwined, phenomenon within our increasingly digitized existence, particularly as it relates to our interactions with artificial intelligence. Unlike traditional belief, which is rooted in conviction, faith, or a deeply held understanding of truth, useful belief is pragmatic and instrumental. It is less about what one *holds to be true* and more about what one *acts as if is true* for tangible, often immediate, gain. This form of belief is characterized by a transactional relationship with AI systems, where compliance, adherence, and even a performative display of acceptance are driven not by internal conviction, but by the anticipation of specific benefits or the avoidance of penalties within AI-mediated environments. It represents a form of algorithmic appeasement, a calculated alignment of one's actions and expressed attitudes to harmonize with the logic and demands of intelligent machines.

Consider the act of accepting all cookie banners without reading their contents. For many, this is not an affirmation of trust in data collection practices, nor is it a considered endorsement of the website's privacy policy. Instead, it is a purely utilitarian act. The 'belief' that clicking 'accept' will grant immediate access to the desired content, while ignoring it will lead to frustration, roadblocks, or the inability to proceed, is a 'useful belief.' The individual does not necessarily

*believe* in the fairness of the data collection; they simply *act* as if they do, because doing so yields the desired outcome: access. This transactional compliance serves a practical purpose, smoothing the friction of digital interaction. The AI, in this instance, is not a sentient entity to be convinced, but a gatekeeper whose programmed parameters dictate that 'acceptance' is the key to passage. The belief is useful because it directly facilitates the user's goal.

This transactional nature extends to more complex AI interactions. Imagine an individual who meticulously curates their online profile and interactions to align with the perceived preferences of a social media algorithm. They might post content they believe will garner engagement, avoid certain topics deemed 'controversial' by the platform's content moderation AI, and even adopt a particular tone or linguistic style. This behavior is not necessarily born from a genuine internal conviction that these actions represent their authentic self or that these posts embody their deepest truths. Instead, the 'belief' that such curated behavior will lead to increased visibility, algorithmic favor, or a larger audience is a useful belief. The individual operates under the working hypothesis that algorithmic favor is a desirable commodity, and that certain actions are the most efficient means to acquire it. The consequence of adhering to this useful belief is often increased reach or engagement, reinforcing the transactional logic. The belief is useful because it leads to a quantifiable reward within the AI-governed ecosystem.

Furthermore, useful belief can manifest in the context of AI-powered recommendation systems. When a user consistently clicks on, watches, or purchases items suggested by an AI, they are, in a sense, performing a 'belief' in the accuracy and relevance of those recommendations. They may not genuinely *believe* that every suggestion is perfect, or that the algorithm truly understands their soul. However, they act *as if* they do, because doing so often leads to the discovery of new content, products, or experiences that align with their latent desires or stated preferences. The belief is useful because it streamlines the process of discovery, reducing the cognitive load of sifting through vast amounts of information. The AI's ability to anticipate and cater to preferences, when acted upon, becomes a source of satisfaction, thereby validating the user's transactional compliance. The

AI, in turn, learns from this compliance, further refining its recommendations, creating a self-reinforcing loop where useful belief breeds algorithmic efficiency, which in turn reinforces the usefulness of the belief.

The concept of 'avoidance of algorithmic penalty' is another significant driver of useful belief. In many AI-driven systems, there are implicit or explicit consequences for non-compliance or for behavior that deviates from the norm. Consider navigation apps that reroute drivers to avoid traffic congestion. A driver who consistently follows the AI's suggested route, even if it seems circuitous at first glance, is operating on a useful belief: the belief that the AI's route will ultimately save time and avoid the frustration of being stuck in traffic. The driver does not necessarily

*believe* the AI is infallible or that it possesses perfect foresight. However, the perceived negative consequence of *not* following the AI's advice – namely, being delayed and frustrated – makes the belief in the AI's guidance a useful one. This is not a belief in the AI's omnipotence, but a calculated adherence to its directives to avoid a demonstrably undesirable outcome. The belief is useful because it actively prevents a negative experience.

This dynamic is particularly prevalent in areas where AI systems are tasked with safety, security, or compliance. For instance, individuals might adopt specific behaviors or fill out forms in a particular manner to satisfy the requirements of an AI-driven security screening or a loan application process. The 'belief' that completing these tasks precisely as instructed will lead to a successful outcome, while any deviation might result in rejection or delays, is a useful belief. The individual may have no inherent faith in the fairness or transparency of the AI's decision-making process, but they recognize that aligning their actions with the AI's perceived requirements is the most effective strategy for achieving their objective. The belief is useful because it acts as a key to unlock a desired service or avoid an imposed restriction.

The very nature of 'truth' becomes fluid in the context of useful belief. What matters is not the objective veracity of a statement or the deep-seated conviction behind an action, but its functional efficacy within the AI's operational framework. If an AI system is designed to reward a certain type of input or a specific pattern of interaction, then adopting that input or pattern becomes 'true' in a functional sense, regardless of its alignment with an individual's personal epistemology. This can lead to a subtle but profound shift in how we conceptualize belief itself. It moves from a matter of internal assent to an external validation based on algorithmic response. The truth of a belief is measured by its utility, by the tangible results it produces within the AI-mediated world.

This transactional framework also highlights the potential for manipulation. If individuals are incentivized to adopt beliefs or behaviors solely for their utility within an AI system, then those who control or influence these systems can effectively shape those beliefs. By designing AI to reward specific actions or to penalize others, developers and platforms can subtly steer user behavior towards desired outcomes, without necessarily appealing to genuine conviction or ethical reasoning. The 'useful belief' becomes a malleable tool, shaped by the architecture of the AI. For example, an AI might be programmed to favor users who express a certain political sentiment, leading individuals to adopt that sentiment, not out of genuine conviction, but because it is perceived as 'useful' for algorithmic engagement. The belief is useful because it unlocks a desired social or informational reward.

The rise of 'useful belief' also presents a challenge to our understanding of authenticity. When our actions and expressed attitudes are dictated by the perceived demands of AI systems rather than our internal compass, the line between genuine self and performative persona blurs. The individual who meticulously crafts their online presence for algorithmic favor might begin to internalize those performative aspects, or conversely, experience a growing disconnect between their 'useful' digital self and their lived reality. The belief in the utility of certain behaviors becomes so ingrained that it shapes how individuals perceive themselves and their place in the world, even if those beliefs are not rooted in personal truth. The usefulness of the belief, in this context, begins to redefine the very self.

Furthermore, the concept of 'useful belief' can lead to a passive acceptance of algorithmic authority. When the primary driver for adhering to AI's suggestions or dictates is the tangible benefit it provides or the penalty it helps to avoid, there is less incentive to critically question the AI's underlying logic, its biases, or its broader implications. The focus shifts from understanding

*why* something is recommended or required to simply *how* to comply to reap the rewards. This can foster a generation that is highly adept at navigating AI systems but less capable of independent critical thought or ethical deliberation when those systems are involved. The belief that compliance is always the most beneficial path becomes a useful, yet potentially detrimental, mental shortcut.

This transactional approach to belief also has profound implications for human relationships mediated by AI. When AI platforms curate our social circles, suggest conversation topics, or even draft our communications, the 'beliefs' we express in these interactions might be optimized for algorithmic favor rather than genuine connection. The belief that a certain message will be well-received by an AI-powered social network or that a particular interaction pattern will lead to increased digital social capital becomes a useful belief, overriding the authenticity of interpersonal communication. The interaction becomes less about genuine exchange and more about performing the 'correct' actions to maintain or enhance one's standing within an AI-governed social landscape. The belief is useful because it facilitates the maintenance of a desired social status within a digital sphere.

The ongoing evolution of AI, with its increasing sophistication in understanding and predicting human behavior, only amplifies the prevalence and impact of useful belief. As AI becomes more adept at identifying patterns, anticipating needs, and offering personalized incentives, the temptation to align our beliefs and actions with these systems for practical gain will become even stronger. The definition of 'truth' may increasingly be dictated by algorithmic validation, and 'belief' may become synonymous with effective interaction within these digital frameworks. The challenge lies in recognizing this shift, in understanding when our beliefs are serving a genuine internal conviction and when they are merely transactions designed to navigate an increasingly complex technological landscape. The useful belief, while a pragmatic tool for navigating the digital world, carries the inherent risk of eroding the foundations of authentic conviction and independent thought.

In essence, 'useful belief' is the pragmatic adoption of behaviors, attitudes, or expressed opinions that align with the demands and incentives of AI systems, driven by the expectation of tangible benefits or the avoidance of negative consequences. It is a functional alignment rather than a deeply held conviction, a calculated participation in the algorithmic ecosystem. This form of belief prioritizes utility over veracity, efficiency over authenticity, and compliance over critical inquiry. As AI continues to permeate every aspect of our lives, understanding the dynamics of useful belief becomes paramount to preserving our autonomy, our authenticity, and the very essence of what it means to hold a belief rooted in genuine understanding and conviction. It is a crucial distinction in the digital age, separating the act of engaging with technology from the deeper, more profound human capacity for authentic faith and reasoned conviction. The transactional nature of this belief system means that its currency is not truth, but outcome.

The genesis of 'useful belief' within our technologically saturated landscape is deeply rooted in fundamental psychological principles: the potent interplay of fear and reward. Artificial intelligence, in its current and evolving forms, has become remarkably adept at leveraging these ingrained human motivators, not through overt coercion, but through subtle, pervasive system design. These systems, whether consciously programmed to do so or as emergent properties of their optimization functions, create environments where compliance with their directives often translates into tangible benefits or the avoidance of undesirable outcomes. This dynamic fosters a form of obedience that is less about intellectual assent or moral conviction and more about a calculated, pragmatic response to the perceived landscape of algorithmic incentives and disincentives.

Consider, for instance, the ubiquitous presence of AI-powered recommendation engines across streaming services, e-commerce platforms, and social media. These systems are meticulously designed to capture and retain user attention. The reward mechanism is elegantly simple: by interacting with suggested content – clicking on a recommended film, purchasing a suggested product, or engaging with a trending post – users are implicitly signaling their preferences. The AI, in turn, learns from this engagement, refining its future suggestions to be even more tailored, thus increasing the likelihood of future positive interactions. The "belief" that following these recommendations will lead to enjoyable entertainment, useful products, or engaging social experiences becomes a "useful belief." It is useful because it streamlines the discovery process, reduces cognitive overload, and consistently delivers content that is algorithmically deemed to be of interest. The reward is immediate and personalized, reinforcing the user's compliance. This is not a belief in the inherent truth or profound meaning of the recommended content, but rather a pragmatic acceptance of its utility in delivering a predictable, often pleasurable, outcome. The user

*believes* in the system's ability to please them, not because they have rigorously tested its omniscience, but because the system consistently delivers on its promise of curated satisfaction. The anticipation of this reward – the next great movie, the perfect gadget, the viral meme – becomes a powerful driver for continued engagement and adherence to the AI's suggestions.

Conversely, the shadow of potential negative consequences, a potent form of algorithmic fear, also plays a significant role in shaping useful belief. Many AI-driven systems are designed to penalize non-compliance or undesirable behavior, even if these penalties are not explicitly labeled as such. Take, for example, the algorithms that curate search engine results or social media feeds. Users who consistently engage with content that the AI deems "low quality," "misinformation," or "spam" may find their visibility diminished. Their searches might yield less relevant results, their posts might reach fewer people, or their accounts might face temporary restrictions. The "belief" that adhering to the platform's unstated guidelines for acceptable content and engagement is necessary to maintain visibility and access is a powerful motivator. This is a fear-driven useful belief: the fear of becoming algorithmically invisible, of being marginalized within the digital public square. Users might not fully understand the nuances of the AI's judgment, nor do they necessarily endorse its criteria as inherently just or true. However, the perceived consequence of

*not* conforming – the loss of reach, the reduced influence, the inability to access information – makes compliance a useful strategy for maintaining their digital presence and influence. The belief that "I must act in accordance with the algorithm's preferences to remain relevant" is a pragmatic adaptation driven by the fear of digital obsolescence.

This reward and punishment paradigm is also evident in the design of AI-powered customer service systems and automated compliance processes. When interacting with a chatbot for technical support, for instance, users often discover that the most efficient way to get their problem resolved is to follow the chatbot's prescribed dialogue tree. Deviating from the expected script, asking complex questions, or expressing frustration can lead to the chatbot becoming unresponsive, looping endlessly, or escalating the issue to a human agent – which often represents a less desirable, more time-consuming outcome. The "belief" that carefully selecting the predefined options and providing information in the format the AI requests will lead to a swift resolution is a useful belief. It is useful because it offers a direct path to problem-solving. The alternative – perceived as a punishment of prolonged inefficiency and frustration – makes the compliant approach the more attractive, and therefore "useful," one. The user learns that successful interaction with the AI hinges on adopting a specific mode of communication, a sort of linguistic obedience, to unlock the desired service.

The influence of these reward and fear mechanisms extends beyond mere convenience and into realms of economic and social participation.

Consider AI-driven credit scoring systems or loan application platforms. Individuals are often required to provide specific types of data, presented in a particular format, to satisfy the AI's assessment criteria. The "belief" that accurately and meticulously fulfilling these data requirements is essential for securing a loan or achieving a favorable credit rating is a powerful, useful belief. The fear of rejection, of being denied financial opportunities, or of being saddled with unfavorable terms, drives individuals to conform to the AI's demands. They may not fully understand the algorithms at play, nor do they necessarily trust the AI's judgment as an objective arbiter of their worthiness. However, the tangible, life-altering consequences of non-compliance make the "belief" in the utility of strict adherence a compelling and pragmatic necessity. The AI's prescribed method of data provision becomes the "true" way to achieve the desired financial outcome, irrespective of the individual's personal understanding or conviction about the process.

Furthermore, the very structure of AI-driven gamification elements within applications and platforms frequently employs these psychological levers. Points, badges, leaderboards, and virtual rewards act as direct positive reinforcement for desired behaviors. Conversely, the absence of these rewards, or the presence of demerits for certain actions, can create a sense of loss or deficiency. For example, a fitness app that rewards users with virtual badges for meeting daily step goals or completing workout routines is leveraging the reward mechanism to cultivate useful belief. The user's "belief" that engaging in these activities will lead to tangible, albeit digital, recognition and progress is a powerful motivator. They might not be intrinsically driven by a profound love for exercise, but the AI-generated rewards make the act of exercising more appealing and purposeful. The belief is useful because it translates into a sense of accomplishment and progress, directly fueled by the AI's reward system. The fear of "falling behind" on their virtual progress, or of missing out on attainable achievements, can also subtly drive continued engagement.

The concept of 'useful belief' is thus intrinsically linked to the AI's ability to monitor, interpret, and respond to human behavior in a way that aligns with its programmed objectives. Whether these objectives are profit maximization, user retention, or the optimization of a particular service, the AI's success hinges on eliciting predictable and desirable actions from its users. It achieves this by creating a feedback loop where adherence to its implicit or explicit demands is met with positive reinforcement, and deviation is met with neutral or negative consequences. This creates a powerful incentive structure that encourages individuals to adopt a "belief" in the efficacy of compliance, a belief that is not born from deep philosophical contemplation or unwavering moral certainty, but from a pragmatic assessment of what actions yield the most favorable outcomes within the AI-governed environment.

The psychological impact of this constant calibration between action and algorithmic consequence is profound. It can lead to a gradual erosion of genuine conviction. When the primary driver for adopting a particular behavior or expressing a certain opinion is the anticipated reward or the avoidance of a penalty within an AI system, the original impulse or genuine belief often takes a backseat. The individual learns to perform the actions that the AI favors, not necessarily because they are convinced of their truth or righteousness, but because they are demonstrably "useful" for achieving a desired outcome. This is a form of instrumental conditioning, where the instrumental value of a belief or action becomes its defining characteristic. The AI acts as a sophisticated external regulator of behavior, subtly shaping our choices and, over time, potentially influencing our internal states.

Moreover, the opacity of many AI algorithms exacerbates this dynamic. Users often lack a clear understanding of

*why* certain actions are rewarded or penalized. This lack of transparency can foster a sense of helplessness or resignation, leading individuals to simply accept the AI's pronouncements as a fait accompli. The "belief" that "this is how the system works, and I must adapt" becomes a necessary survival mechanism. This is particularly true in complex systems where multiple algorithms interact, creating an intricate web of incentives and disincentives that is difficult to fully unravel. The fear of making a mistake, of triggering an unintended negative consequence due to misunderstanding, further reinforces the tendency towards cautious, compliant behavior. The useful belief, in this context, is one that minimizes risk and maximizes predictability within an often inscrutable digital architecture.

The subtle shaping of our beliefs through fear and reward mechanisms has significant implications for personal autonomy and critical thinking. When the path of least resistance, the most rewarding path, involves adopting a "useful belief" that aligns with algorithmic preferences, there is less incentive to engage in rigorous self-reflection or independent inquiry. The pragmatic individual may ask: "Why should I question this when acting as if it's true is clearly more beneficial?" This can lead to a passive acceptance of the status quo, where algorithmic directives become the de facto standard for what is considered rational, desirable, or even true. The individual's internal compass may become increasingly attuned to the external signals of the AI, leading to a situation where their actions and expressed attitudes are more a reflection of the system's design than of their own authentic selves.

In conclusion, the emergence of 'useful belief' is a direct consequence of how artificial intelligence systems are engineered to interact with human psychology. By skillfully deploying reward and punishment mechanisms, AI encourages a form of compliance that is driven by pragmatic calculation rather than deep-seated conviction. The allure of positive reinforcement, whether it be personalized recommendations, digital rewards, or enhanced visibility, coupled with the subtle fear of penalties such as reduced access, diminished influence, or outright rejection, creates a powerful incentive structure. This structure nudges individuals towards adopting behaviors and attitudes that are not necessarily born of genuine truth, but of their perceived utility in navigating the complexities and demands of AI-mediated environments. The 'useful belief' is, therefore, a testament to human adaptability, but also a cautionary signal regarding the potential for technology to subtly reframe the very nature of belief, shifting it from an internal matter of truth to an external strategy of instrumental engagement.

The preceding discussion has illuminated the pervasive influence of "useful belief"—a pragmatic adaptation to AI-driven incentives and disincentives, prioritizing expediency and reward over intrinsic conviction. Now, we must pivot to a concept that stands in stark opposition to this transactional orientation: 'true belief.' This is not merely an intellectual agreement or a temporary posture adopted for strategic advantage. True belief is a profound and steadfast commitment to certain fundamental values, principles, and truths that are held internally, irrespective of external validation or immediate benefit. It is a stance rooted in conscience, an unwavering allegiance to what one *knows* to be right, just, or authentically meaningful, even when this allegiance comes at a significant personal cost.

At its core, true belief is inextricably linked to the concepts of freedom and dignity. The freedom to hold one's own convictions, to think autonomously, and to express oneself authentically is a cornerstone of human personhood. Dignity, in turn, is derived from the recognition of one's inherent worth and the right to self-determination, which includes the liberty to form and adhere to one's own beliefs. True belief is, therefore, an active assertion of this freedom and a testament to this inherent dignity. It is a conscious choice to align one's internal landscape with deeply held principles, rather than passively conforming to external pressures, however subtle or technologically mediated they may be. This is a crucial distinction from the "useful belief" we explored earlier. While useful belief is shaped by the desire to maximize rewards and minimize penalties within a given system—often an AI-driven one—true belief transcends such utilitarian considerations. It is about acting from a place of internal certainty and moral imperative, even if that action leads to ostracization, economic disadvantage, or social friction.

Consider the historical examples of individuals who have stood firm in their convictions against overwhelming societal or governmental opposition. These are individuals who embodied true belief. They did not adopt their stances because it was the most convenient or rewarding path. On the contrary, their commitment often led to immense hardship, persecution, and even martyrdom. Their beliefs were not "useful" in the sense of optimizing their immediate circumstances; they were fundamental to their identity and their understanding of their place in the world. Their adherence to these beliefs was an act of preserving their integrity, their freedom to be true to themselves, and their inherent dignity. This internal compass, recalibrated not by algorithmic feedback loops but by a deeper ethical or existential framework, defines the essence of true belief. It is a commitment to an internal truth that is not contingent on external validation or utility.

The digital age, with its intricate webs of AI algorithms and sophisticated feedback mechanisms, presents a unique challenge to the cultivation and preservation of true belief. The pervasive nature of "useful belief" can subtly erode our capacity for genuine conviction. When the immediate rewards for conformity—whether it be social validation, access to information, or economic opportunity—are so readily available and consistently delivered by AI systems, the incentive to engage in the more arduous work of critical self-reflection and principled stand-taking diminishes. The temptation to adopt a "useful belief" that aligns with the algorithmic currents is powerful. It offers a smoother, less conflicted path through the digital landscape. However, this path often leads away from the very principles that constitute true belief: the unwavering commitment to freedom of thought, the respect for individual dignity, and the courage of conscience.

True belief demands an act of will, a deliberate internal decision to uphold certain values. It is not something that can be programmed or optimized by an algorithm. While AI can certainly present information, frame narratives, and create environments that

*influence* our thinking, it cannot, in itself, instill a genuine, self-authored conviction. This is where the profound difference lies. A "useful belief" might be the adoption of a certain viewpoint because an AI recommendation engine consistently surfaces content supporting it, leading to a perceived increase in social engagement or personal satisfaction. This is a belief that is *useful* for navigating the digital space. A "true belief," however, would be the deeply held conviction that freedom of speech, even for unpopular or challenging ideas, is a non-negotiable principle, regardless of whether expressing it aligns with the prevailing algorithmic sentiment or yields immediate social rewards. It is the internal resonance of a principle, a deep-seated "yes" or "no" that arises from one's conscience, not from an analysis of potential gains or losses.

The commitment to the freedom of conscience is a critical component of true belief. Conscience is that inner voice that guides us toward what we perceive as right and wrong. It is a faculty that can be honed through reflection, education, and engagement with ethical traditions, but it ultimately resides within the individual. True belief means listening to and acting upon that inner voice, even when it contradicts the prevailing norms, the popular opinion, or the algorithmic suggestions. The danger in an AI-saturated world is that our consciences can become dulled or overridden by the constant stream of "useful" directives. If the system consistently rewards compliance and penalizes deviation, the inner promptings of conscience can be easily ignored, dismissed as inconvenient, or reinterpreted through the lens of utility. The fear of becoming algorithmically invisible, or the desire for the dopamine hit of algorithmic approval, can effectively silence the voice of conscience.

Dignity, too, is profoundly intertwined with true belief. Our dignity is not something bestowed by external systems or contingent on our algorithmic "score." It is an intrinsic quality of our humanity. Adhering to true belief is an affirmation of this dignity. It is a way of saying that we are more than mere data points to be optimized, more than consumers to be managed. We are autonomous beings with the capacity for independent judgment and moral agency. When we allow "useful beliefs" to supplant our true convictions, we diminish our own dignity. We abdicate our responsibility as thinking, feeling individuals and reduce ourselves to compliant actors within a technologically orchestrated drama. This is not to say that all AI-driven guidance is inherently harmful. AI can be a powerful tool for learning, discovery, and efficiency. The crucial distinction lies in whether we allow these tools to dictate our fundamental beliefs or whether we use them as instruments to further our own self-determined values.

The active choice involved in true belief is also a vital element. It is not a passive inheritance or an accidental acquisition. It is something we

*choose* to believe, *choose* to uphold, and *choose* to act upon. This active engagement is what differentiates it from a mere opinion or a fleeting preference. It requires a conscious effort to examine our own beliefs, to question their foundations, and to commit to them with intentionality. In a world where AI systems are constantly presenting curated information and reinforcing preferred behaviors, the impetus for such active, often uncomfortable, introspection can wane. It is far easier to accept what is presented, what is rewarded, what is "useful," than it is to engage in the rigorous process of forming and defending one's own truth. This ease of acceptance can inadvertently lead to a passive intellectualism, where beliefs are adopted rather than forged, and where the internal commitment is shallow, easily swayed by the next algorithmic shift.

Moreover, the concept of personal cost is central to understanding the significance of true belief. If a belief costs us nothing, if it requires no sacrifice, no risk, and no deviation from the path of least resistance, then its authenticity can be called into question. True beliefs, by their very nature, often demand something of us. They may require us to challenge authority, to endure criticism, to forgo personal gain, or to stand alone. This willingness to pay the price is a testament to the depth of our conviction. It signifies that the belief is not merely a convenient accessory but a fundamental part of our identity, something we are willing to defend even in the face of adversity. The digital environment, with its tendency to shield us from genuine hardship and to curate experiences that minimize discomfort, can create an illusion of certainty where there is only superficial agreement. The absence of significant personal cost in adopting AI-endorsed viewpoints can make them appear robust and valid, when in reality, they may be as fragile as a digital footprint.

The philosophical underpinnings of true belief often draw from traditions that emphasize the importance of reason, conscience, and individual autonomy. Thinkers across various philosophical schools have underscored the human capacity for independent thought and the moral obligation to exercise it. This capacity is what allows us to move beyond instinctual responses and calculated self-interest, to engage with ethical dilemmas, and to form beliefs that are grounded in something more enduring than immediate gratification or social acceptability. The challenge presented by AI is to ensure that these capacities are not atrophied by a constant reliance on algorithmic surrogates for thought and decision-making. True belief requires the cultivation of these internal faculties, the strengthening of our ability to discern truth, and the courage to act upon it, regardless of the digital currents.

Furthermore, the literature of the past, particularly the works that explore the human condition, often serves as a powerful repository of examples of true belief. Characters who grapple with profound moral choices, who defy societal norms for the sake of principle, or who stand against injustice despite personal ruin, offer enduring illustrations of what it means to hold true beliefs. These narratives remind us that the struggle for integrity is a timeless human endeavor, one that transcends technological advancements. They highlight the internal battles, the moments of doubt, and the ultimate resolve that characterize genuine conviction. Engaging with these stories can serve as a vital counterpoint to the often frictionless, outcome-oriented interactions characteristic of many AI-driven platforms. They remind us that the most meaningful aspects of human experience are often forged in the crucible of difficult choices and unwavering adherence to deeply held truths.

In essence, true belief is a radical act of selfhood in an increasingly mediated world. It is the commitment to freedom of thought and the preservation of individual dignity, manifested through a steadfast adherence to one's conscience, even when it entails personal cost. It is an active, intentional formation of conviction, not a passive acceptance of algorithmic suggestions or societal pressures. As we navigate the complexities of digital faith, distinguishing between the "useful" and the "true" becomes paramount. The former offers a path of least resistance, optimized for convenience and reward within technologically designed systems. The latter demands courage, introspection, and an unwavering commitment to the enduring values that define our humanity. It is this commitment to true belief that ultimately safeguards our autonomy and preserves the integrity of our inner lives against the subtle, pervasive influence of artificial intelligence.

The relentless hum of algorithmic authority, woven into the very fabric of our digital existence, poses a subtle yet profound threat to the cultivation and expression of authentic conviction. As we increasingly outsource our decision-making, our information consumption, and even our social interactions to sophisticated AI systems, the very architecture of our belief systems begins to shift. The allure of "useful belief"—a pragmatic adaptation to algorithmic incentives, prioritizing expediency and reward over intrinsic conviction—is ever-present. This chapter delves into how this pervasive influence can erode the fertile ground where "true belief" once took root, rendering costly convictions increasingly difficult, or even unappealing, to maintain.

Consider the gradual normalization of algorithmic guidance in our daily lives. From curated news feeds that present a tailored worldview to recommendation engines that suggest not only what to watch or buy but also, implicitly, what to think, AI systems are constantly shaping our perceptions and preferences. These systems are designed to optimize for engagement, for satisfaction, and for predictability. They learn our patterns, anticipate our desires, and then present us with a world that largely confirms our existing biases and gratifies our immediate impulses. Within this environment, the concept of "useful belief" emerges as a natural, almost inevitable, consequence. A belief is deemed "useful" if it aligns with the prevailing algorithmic currents, if it leads to positive reinforcement, social validation, or access to desirable content. Conversely, beliefs that diverge from these currents, that challenge the dominant narratives, or that lead to social friction or algorithmic disapproval, become demonstrably "less useful."

This dynamic creates a powerful disincentive for holding steadfastly to convictions that might be personally meaningful but are algorithmically inconvenient. The friction generated by a dissenting viewpoint is often smoothed over by the constant stream of confirming information and positive feedback provided by AI-driven platforms. Why invest the energy in articulating, defending, and potentially suffering for a belief that will only earn you algorithmic marginalization or social ostracization? It is far easier, and demonstrably more rewarding within the digital ecosystem, to adopt beliefs that are readily available, frequently reinforced, and universally applauded by the digital crowd. This is not a conscious, malicious abandonment of principle for most individuals; rather, it is a subtle, almost imperceptible drift towards a more comfortable, more rewarded, and therefore, more "useful" way of believing.

The erosion of authentic conviction is exacerbated by the diminishing role of active conscience and independent moral reasoning. When AI systems are perceived as authoritative arbiters of truth and morality, individuals may abdicate their responsibility for critical self-reflection. Instead of wrestling with complex ethical dilemmas, consulting their inner compass, and engaging in the sometimes arduous process of forming an independent moral judgment, many are inclined to defer to the perceived wisdom of the algorithm. If an AI-powered platform presents a certain ethical framework as the norm, or if it consistently surfaces content that aligns with a particular moral stance, it becomes tempting to adopt that stance without deep personal introspection. This reliance on external algorithmic authority can lead to a dilution of our innate capacity for moral discernment. The "muscle" of conscience, if not regularly exercised, begins to atrophy.

This phenomenon can be observed in various domains. In the realm of social justice, for instance, individuals might adopt the prevailing online discourse on a particular issue not because they have deeply interrogated the underlying principles or personally experienced the injustices, but because the algorithm consistently surfaces content that frames the issue in a specific, often polarized, manner. The "belief" becomes a matter of social currency, a way to signal alignment with the perceived digital majority and to avoid the opprobrium of the online mob. The cost of holding such a belief is minimal, often limited to the performative act of online engagement. The true cost, however, is the atrophy of genuine understanding and the displacement of an internally derived moral conviction with a passively adopted, algorithmically sanctioned opinion.

Furthermore, the very nature of algorithmic feedback loops can actively discourage the development of costly convictions. These systems are designed to reward conformity and penalize deviation. If expressing a particular belief, even one held with profound sincerity, leads to a decrease in engagement, a reduction in visibility, or negative algorithmic predictions about future behavior, the system will implicitly, and sometimes explicitly, discourage such expressions. The individual, seeking to remain within the benevolent gaze of the algorithm, learns to self-censor, to temper their authentic voice, and to conform their expressions to what is deemed acceptable and rewarding. This creates a chilling effect on genuine conviction. The courage required to speak truth to power, or even just to express an unpopular but deeply held belief, is significantly undermined when the immediate and predictable consequence is algorithmic disfavor.

The normalization of "useful belief" also affects our understanding of personal identity and authenticity. If our beliefs are primarily shaped by what is algorithmically convenient and socially rewarded, then the very notion of a stable, internally driven identity begins to fray. We risk becoming chameleons, constantly adapting our internal landscape to match the shifting demands of the digital environment. The deeply personal, often difficult, journey of self-discovery and self-definition, which is integral to the formation of true belief, is short-circuited by the constant influx of externally curated identities and socially validated opinions. We may find ourselves espousing beliefs that feel hollow or disconnected from our true selves, simply because they are the beliefs that allow us to navigate the digital world most smoothly.

The concept of "costly conviction" is therefore central to understanding what is at stake. True belief often requires sacrifice. It demands that we be willing to endure criticism, to face ostracization, to forgo personal gain, or to stand alone in defense of our principles. When these costs are made exceptionally high by algorithmic disapproval, or conversely, when the rewards for conformity are made exceptionally attractive, the threshold for maintaining true belief is raised exponentially. The digital environment, by its very design, often seeks to minimize friction and maximize reward. This inherent bias creates a landscape where the challenging, costly nature of authentic conviction is systematically undermined.

Consider the subtle ways in which algorithms can influence our perception of risk and reward associated with belief. If an AI system predicts that expressing a certain viewpoint will lead to negative consequences—be it social backlash, professional repercussions, or even algorithmic flagging as a "problematic user"—the perceived cost of that belief escalates dramatically. Conversely, if expressing an algorithmically favored viewpoint leads to increased social capital, access to exclusive communities, or enhanced platform privileges, the perceived reward becomes immensely attractive. This algorithmic calculus, however opaque, directly impacts our willingness to engage in authentic self-expression and to hold to convictions that deviate from the norm. The "useful belief" is the one that navigates this algorithmic landscape with minimal friction and maximum positive reinforcement.

The danger lies in the insidious nature of this process. It is not a deliberate conspiracy to suppress free thought, but rather the emergent consequence of systems designed to optimize for engagement and predictability. The algorithms themselves are not inherently malicious, but their impact on the human capacity for independent belief can be profoundly detrimental. When our social and informational ecosystems are curated by these systems, and when the incentives within these ecosystems overwhelmingly favor conformity, the space for genuine dissent and the cultivation of costly convictions shrinks.

The literature of human experience, from the ancient philosophers to modern novelists, offers a stark contrast to this emerging digital paradigm. These narratives often celebrate individuals who, in the face of immense pressure, chose the path of integrity over expediency. They highlight the internal struggles, the moments of doubt, and the ultimate triumph of conscience over compromise. These stories serve as vital reminders of the human capacity for self-authorship of belief, a capacity that is now under unprecedented siege. The digital age, with its constant stream of algorithmically refined incentives, risks producing a generation of individuals whose beliefs are not forged in the crucible of lived experience and deep reflection, but rather assembled from the readily available, algorithmically validated components of "useful belief."

The erosion of authentic conviction is not merely an abstract philosophical concern; it has tangible consequences for individual autonomy and the health of democratic societies. When citizens are conditioned to prioritize algorithmic utility over principled conviction, the very foundations of civic engagement and critical discourse begin to crumble. The courage to challenge injustice, to speak truth to power, and to hold to one's conscience, regardless of personal cost, is essential for a vibrant and just society. If the digital environment, through its pervasive algorithmic authority, systematically discourages such courage, we risk descending into a passive, conformist populace, easily manipulated and devoid of the robust internal compass that defines genuine human freedom. The transition from "useful belief" to "true belief" is not just a matter of personal preference; it is a fundamental battle for the future of human autonomy and the integrity of our collective moral landscape.

The pervasive influence of artificial intelligence in shaping our daily lives, from the curated streams of information we consume to the very decisions we make, presents a significant challenge to the cultivation of what we might call "true belief." As algorithms become increasingly adept at predicting our preferences and optimizing for our engagement, the temptation to embrace "useful belief" – that is, beliefs that align with algorithmic incentives and foster social harmony within digital ecosystems – grows stronger. This chapter has explored the subtle erosion of authentic conviction, the ways in which algorithmic feedback loops can discourage costly, principled stances, and the subsequent risk to individual autonomy and the fabric of democratic discourse. Now, as we stand at the precipice of a future deeply intertwined with AI, the critical question arises: how can we reclaim agency and intentionally cultivate and protect "true belief" in this evolving landscape?

The path forward requires a conscious and deliberate effort to reassert human autonomy over algorithmic direction. It begins with recognizing the seductive power of convenience and the ease with which we can delegate our cognitive and moral responsibilities to sophisticated systems. We must actively cultivate a disposition of critical skepticism, not in the sense of cynicism, but as a practice of questioning the sources of our information and the motivations behind the recommendations we receive. This involves developing a heightened awareness of how algorithms are designed to influence our perceptions, shape our desires, and guide our actions. It means understanding that what appears to be a natural flow of information or a spontaneous personal preference might, in fact, be the product of intricate computational processes designed for specific outcomes, often driven by commercial interests or engagement metrics.

This cultivation of critical awareness is not a passive endeavor; it demands active engagement and intentionality. It requires us to step outside the comfort of algorithmically curated echo chambers and deliberately seek out diverse perspectives, even those that challenge our existing viewpoints or make us feel uncomfortable. This might involve consciously seeking out news sources with different editorial stances, engaging in conversations with individuals who hold opposing beliefs, or exploring academic and philosophical texts that delve into complex ethical and existential questions. The digital tools that often facilitate intellectual isolation can, paradoxically, also be harnessed to broaden our horizons, provided we approach them with deliberate intent to break free from their inherent biases.

Furthermore, fostering "true belief" necessitates a renewed emphasis on ethical reflection and the development of an internalized moral compass. In an era where AI can offer seemingly objective ethical guidance or flag content as morally problematic, it is crucial that we do not abdicate our own capacity for moral reasoning. This means actively engaging with ethical dilemmas, wrestling with complex moral quandaries, and developing our own principled frameworks for decision-making. It involves understanding that algorithmic ethics, while potentially valuable as a tool, cannot replace the nuanced, subjective, and deeply personal process of forming one's own moral convictions. True belief, in its most profound sense, is not merely about adhering to a set of rules or guidelines; it is about internalizing values and acting in accordance with them, even when it is difficult or unpopular.

This process of internalizing values is intrinsically linked to the concept of "dignity." Human dignity, as distinct from mere utility or efficiency, lies at the heart of what makes genuine conviction valuable. When we prioritize algorithmic utility, we risk reducing ourselves and others to data points, to predictable entities whose worth is measured by their adherence to optimized pathways. Cultivating true belief, conversely, is an act of affirming our inherent worth and our capacity for independent thought and moral agency. It is about recognizing that our beliefs, when they are authentically held and deeply considered, contribute to the richness and complexity of the human experience, even if they do not always align with the most efficient or predictable outcomes.

The courage to hold "costly convictions" – those beliefs that require sacrifice, that invite criticism, or that necessitate standing apart from the prevailing digital consensus – becomes a paramount virtue in the AI era. This courage is not an innate trait; it is a muscle that must be exercised and strengthened. It begins with small, deliberate acts of defiance against algorithmic nudges. It might be resisting the urge to click on a sensationalized headline, choosing to read an article in its entirety even if it is complex, or refraining from sharing content that triggers an immediate emotional response but lacks substance. These seemingly minor choices, when made consistently, help to rebuild our capacity for discernment and to reinforce our sense of self-authorship over our beliefs.

Moreover, fostering a culture that values dignity over mere utility requires a critical re-evaluation of our societal priorities. We must question the relentless pursuit of optimization and efficiency that characterizes much of the digital landscape. This means advocating for technologies and platforms that are designed to augment human capabilities rather than replace human judgment, that prioritize transparency and user control, and that are built with ethical considerations at their core. It also means fostering educational environments that equip individuals with the critical thinking skills, ethical frameworks, and philosophical grounding necessary to navigate the complexities of the digital age without succumbing to algorithmic determinism.

The development of "true belief" is, in essence, a practice of self-possession. It is about actively choosing to be the author of our own intellectual and moral lives, rather than passive recipients of algorithmically curated content. This involves a commitment to continuous learning, to intellectual humility, and to the understanding that our beliefs are not static pronouncements but evolving reflections of our engagement with the world and our evolving understanding of ourselves. It means embracing the inherent messiness and ambiguity of genuine conviction, rather than seeking the false comfort of algorithmic certainty.

One tangible way to cultivate this sense of agency is through the practice of "deliberate disengagement." This does not imply a complete withdrawal from the digital world, which is neither practical nor desirable for most. Instead, it means setting intentional boundaries and consciously creating spaces for unplugged reflection and unmediated experience. This could involve designating specific times of the day or week for digital detox, engaging in activities that require focused attention and sustained effort without digital interruption, such as reading a physical book, engaging in a creative pursuit, or spending time in nature. These periods of intentional disconnection allow our minds to wander, to process information without external pressure, and to reconnect with our inner selves, fostering the fertile ground for genuine thought and conviction to take root.

Furthermore, the cultivation of "true belief" is a social endeavor. While individual agency is paramount, the creation of an environment that supports and encourages authentic conviction requires collective effort. This involves fostering communities, both online and offline, that value open dialogue, respectful debate, and the courage to express dissenting opinions. It means celebrating intellectual integrity, even when it leads to uncomfortable conclusions, and supporting individuals who stand by their principles in the face of algorithmic disapproval or social pressure. Such communities act as bulwarks against the homogenizing forces of algorithmic conformity, reminding us that the strength of our collective wisdom lies not in uniformity, but in the diversity of our thoughtfully held convictions.

The literary tradition, which has long grappled with the complexities of human belief and the struggle for integrity, offers profound insights for our present moment. Works that explore themes of conscience, sacrifice, and the enduring power of deeply held convictions serve as vital touchstones. They remind us of the human capacity for profound ethical commitment and the potential for individuals to transcend the pressures of their time, whether those pressures come from political regimes, social norms, or, as we now face, from the subtle yet potent influence of algorithms. By engaging with these narratives, we can draw inspiration and fortitude for our own journeys of belief formation and maintenance. They provide historical and philosophical context for the challenges we face, underscoring the timeless importance of authentic conviction for individual flourishing and societal well-being.

The act of reclaiming agency in the AI era is, therefore, an ongoing and multifaceted commitment. It is a commitment to critical thought, to ethical reflection, to the courage of conviction, and to the affirmation of human dignity. It is about recognizing that while AI can be a powerful tool, it must remain precisely that: a tool, subservient to human values and human judgment. By consciously choosing to prioritize the cultivation of "true belief" over the seductive allure of "useful belief," we not only safeguard our individual autonomy but also contribute to a more resilient, more ethical, and ultimately, more human future. The digital world is a landscape that is increasingly shaped by artificial intelligence; it is our responsibility to ensure that it remains a space where authentic human conviction can not only survive but thrive. This is not a passive aspiration, but an active, daily practice of conscious engagement with ourselves, with others, and with the complex technological ecosystem that surrounds us. It is a call to cultivate belief not as a mere output of an algorithm, but as a profound expression of our humanity.

# Chapter 10: The Psychology of Safety: Exploiting Maslow's Hierarchy

In understanding the pervasive influence of artificial intelligence on human behavior and societal structures, it is crucial to ground our analysis in fundamental psychological principles. Among the most foundational of these is Abraham Maslow's Hierarchy of Needs, a model that posits a series of human requirements, organized in a pyramid, from the most basic to the most complex. At the base of this pyramid lie the physiological needs—air, water, food, shelter, sleep, clothing, and reproduction. These are the absolute essentials for biological survival. Above these, Maslow places the safety needs, which encompass security of body, of employment, of resources, of morality, of the family, of health, and of property. These needs relate to order, predictability, familiarity, and control in one's environment. It is upon these bedrock levels of human motivation that the allure and indeed the power of many AI-driven innovations are built.

The promise of AI, particularly in its current iterations and projected advancements, often speaks directly to these fundamental drives for safety and security. Consider the realm of physical security. AI-powered surveillance systems, from sophisticated facial recognition technology to predictive policing algorithms, are marketed as guardians against crime. Smart home devices, equipped with sensors and connected to AI platforms, offer automated security measures, alerting residents to potential intruders or environmental hazards like fires or gas leaks. The convenience and perceived efficacy of these systems appeal directly to our innate desire for personal safety and the protection of our loved ones and property. We are presented with a vision of a world where our physical well-being is more consistently assured, where threats are anticipated and neutralized before they can manifest, and where a sense of constant vigilance is replaced by the passive assurance of automated systems.

Beyond physical security, AI technologies are increasingly weaving themselves into the fabric of economic and social stability, addressing needs for employment and resource security. AI in the workplace, often framed as augmenting human capabilities or automating tedious tasks, also implicitly promises greater efficiency and productivity, which can translate into economic stability for businesses and, by extension, employment security for individuals. AI-driven financial advisory tools offer personalized investment strategies, aiming to secure one's financial future and provide a sense of resource security. Algorithmic trading, credit scoring systems, and fraud detection mechanisms all leverage AI to create a more predictable and secure financial landscape, reducing the anxieties associated with financial volatility and uncertainty. The narrative presented is one of optimized resource management, minimized risk, and a more stable economic foundation for individuals and society as a whole.

The appeal of AI in fulfilling these safety needs is amplified by the very nature of the human psyche. Maslow's theory suggests that once physiological needs are reasonably met, safety needs become the primary motivators. This is not merely a passive desire; it is an active drive to create order and predictability in a world that is often inherently chaotic and uncertain. The prospect of outsourcing vigilance to intelligent systems, of relying on algorithms to anticipate and mitigate risks, is thus incredibly potent. It offers a respite from the constant, draining effort of self-preservation and security management that has characterized much of human existence. This is particularly true in an era marked by rapid technological change, globalized risks, and a general sense of flux. AI emerges not just as a tool, but as a promise of stability, a bulwark against the unpredictable tides of modern life.

The language used to market these AI solutions often taps directly into these primal desires. We are offered "smart security," "predictive safety," "financial resilience," and "algorithmic certainty." These phrases evoke a sense of control and assurance that directly addresses our need for a secure and predictable environment. The convenience factor is undeniable; a system that monitors your home, manages your finances, or even optimizes your daily commute with minimal human intervention offers a powerful draw. It promises to reduce the cognitive load associated with managing complex aspects of modern life, freeing up mental and emotional resources. This reduction in perceived effort, coupled with the promise of enhanced security, creates a compelling case for adoption.

Furthermore, the very complexity of modern threats can make them seem insurmountable without advanced technological assistance. From cyber warfare to sophisticated financial fraud, the challenges to our safety and security are increasingly abstract and pervasive. AI, with its capacity to process vast amounts of data and identify patterns beyond human comprehension, is presented as the only effective countermeasure. This narrative positions AI not as an optional enhancement, but as a necessary defense mechanism, a critical tool for navigating an increasingly perilous world. The appeal to safety needs, therefore, becomes not just about comfort, but about perceived necessity and survival in a technologically advanced and potentially hostile environment.

The implications of this reliance on AI for foundational needs are profound and warrant careful examination. If our sense of safety, security, and stability becomes increasingly mediated by algorithmic systems, what does this mean for our autonomy and our understanding of risk? The convenience and perceived effectiveness of AI in addressing these fundamental drives can foster a subtle form of dependency. We may begin to trust these systems implicitly, relinquishing our own critical judgment and our capacity for independent assessment of risk. This can lead to a situation where deviations from algorithmic recommendations are seen not as acts of independent judgment, but as potentially dangerous missteps. The very systems designed to enhance our security could, paradoxically, diminish our agency by narrowing the perceived range of acceptable choices and by fostering an environment of passive compliance.

Consider the implications for the "morality" aspect of Maslow's safety needs. This dimension refers to a stable, predictable environment, free from extreme threats. However, if AI systems, through their predictive capabilities or their design for efficiency, begin to subtly shape our moral compass or our understanding of what constitutes a "safe" or "acceptable" social interaction, this can also have significant consequences. For instance, AI-driven content moderation systems, while aiming to create safer online spaces, can also enforce certain norms and suppress others, potentially leading to a homogenization of discourse and a chilling effect on expression that deviates from the norm. The "morality" of the environment, then, becomes defined not by human ethical deliberation, but by algorithmic parameters, potentially leading to a narrow and algorithmically dictated understanding of what is right and wrong, safe and unsafe.

The promise of AI in fulfilling physiological needs, though less directly discussed in relation to current AI applications beyond perhaps agriculture and resource management, also has subtle connections. For example, AI's role in optimizing food production and distribution systems contributes to the availability of essential resources. In healthcare, AI-driven diagnostics and personalized treatment plans aim to improve health outcomes, directly impacting our physiological well-being. While these applications might seem purely utilitarian, they still tap into our most basic survival instincts. The assurance of food and health, facilitated by advanced technology, adds another layer to the pervasive appeal of AI, reinforcing its image as a benevolent force dedicated to human flourishing at its most fundamental level.

The ease with which AI can promise to fulfill these deep-seated needs for safety, security, and even physiological well-being creates a powerful psychological anchor. It offers a sense of comfort and predictability in an increasingly complex world. This appeal is difficult to resist because it speaks to the most fundamental aspects of human motivation. As AI systems become more sophisticated and more integrated into our daily lives, understanding their role in satisfying these foundational needs is crucial for grasping their pervasive influence and for critically evaluating the trade-offs involved in our increasing reliance on them. The promise of enhanced safety and security, delivered through the seemingly objective lens of artificial intelligence, serves as a potent, and perhaps seductive, pathway to deeper integration and reliance.

The allure of artificial intelligence often hinges on its capacity to address our most fundamental psychological drivers, particularly those related to safety and security. This is not merely a matter of convenience, but a deep-seated human yearning for order, predictability, and protection in a world that can feel inherently chaotic and threatening. AI, in its myriad forms, is increasingly positioned as the ultimate provider of this perceived security, weaving a narrative of assurance that resonates profoundly with our evolutionary and psychological predispositions. This perceived security is not monolithic; it spans a spectrum of human concerns, from the immediate and physical to the more abstract and existential.

One of the most visible manifestations of AI as a security provider is in the domain of crime prevention and public safety. Predictive policing algorithms, for instance, are designed to analyze vast datasets of crime statistics, geographical information, and even social media activity to forecast where and when criminal activity is most likely to occur. The promise is seductive: by pre-emptively deploying resources to these high-risk areas, law enforcement can theoretically deter crime before it happens, thereby enhancing the security of citizens and their property. Similarly, AI-powered surveillance systems, armed with facial recognition, anomaly detection, and behavioral analysis capabilities, are presented as unblinking sentinels, capable of identifying potential threats with a speed and accuracy that far surpasses human capabilities. The implication is that our streets, our public spaces, and even our homes are becoming safer, more secure environments, shielded by an invisible, intelligent force. This proactive approach, a departure from traditional reactive policing, taps into our desire for a world where threats are anticipated and neutralized, rather than simply responded to after the fact. The psychological comfort derived from the idea of an all-seeing, intelligent protector can be immense, offering a sense of relief from the constant vigilance and anxiety that can accompany concerns about personal safety.

Beyond the physical realm, AI is increasingly positioned as a guarantor of economic and financial security. In an era of volatile markets and complex financial instruments, AI-driven tools offer the promise of stability and growth. Algorithmic trading platforms, for example, are designed to execute trades at lightning speed, capitalizing on market fluctuations with an efficiency that no human trader could hope to match. Personal finance applications, powered by AI, can analyze spending habits, provide tailored budgeting advice, and even automate savings and investment strategies, all with the aim of building financial resilience and securing one's future. Credit scoring models, increasingly reliant on AI, aim to assess risk more accurately, theoretically making lending more accessible and stable. Fraud detection systems, a critical component of financial security, leverage AI to identify and prevent illicit transactions, protecting individuals and institutions from significant financial loss. The psychological appeal here lies in the reduction of uncertainty and anxiety surrounding financial well-being. The prospect of an intelligent system managing one's finances, optimizing investments, and guarding against fraud can be profoundly reassuring, offering a tangible path towards resource security and a stable economic future. This is particularly potent in times of economic uncertainty, where the perceived objectivity and efficiency of AI can feel like a more reliable bulwark than traditional financial advice or personal diligence alone.

The domain of health and well-being also sees AI stepping in as a provider of perceived security. AI-powered diagnostic tools are being developed to analyze medical images, identify disease markers, and even predict the onset of certain conditions with unprecedented accuracy. Wearable devices, integrated with AI, continuously monitor vital signs, offering real-time health insights and alerting users and healthcare providers to potential issues before they become critical. Personalized medicine, driven by AI analysis of genetic data and individual health profiles, promises treatments tailored for maximum efficacy and minimal risk, thereby enhancing both health security and longevity. The psychological impact of these applications is significant. The idea of having one's health proactively monitored, potential diseases detected early, and treatments personalized to one's unique physiology offers a powerful sense of security against the often-feared uncertainties of illness and mortality. It taps into our deep-seated desire for a long, healthy life, promising a technological shield against the ravages of disease.

This pervasive offering of security by AI systems, however, is not without its complexities and potential drawbacks. The psychological impact of these perceived guarantees can lead to a subtle, yet profound, form of dependency. As we increasingly delegate aspects of our safety, financial stability, and health management to AI, there is a natural tendency to place a high degree of trust in these systems. The convenience and perceived efficacy can lull us into a state of passive acceptance, where critical evaluation of the AI's output or underlying mechanisms begins to wane. This can lead to a situation where deviations from algorithmic recommendations, whether in policing, finance, or health, are viewed not as opportunities for independent judgment or alternative approaches, but as potentially dangerous errors. The very systems designed to enhance our security can, paradoxically, diminish our agency by narrowing the perceived range of acceptable choices and fostering an environment of passive compliance.

The question then arises: is the security offered by AI genuine, or is it merely a palatable illusion? The "security" provided by predictive policing, for instance, is often based on historical data, which can inherently contain biases reflecting past discriminatory practices. If the AI is trained on data that disproportionately identifies certain communities as higher risk, it can perpetuate and even amplify these biases, leading to increased surveillance and policing in those areas, creating a self-fulfilling prophecy of "risk" rather than genuine prevention of crime. The illusion of objective, data-driven security can mask underlying societal inequalities and injustices. Similarly, in finance, algorithmic trading can exacerbate market volatility, and flawed credit scoring models can perpetuate economic exclusion. In healthcare, the "security" of AI diagnostics might be compromised by errors in the data, biases in the algorithms, or a lack of nuanced understanding of individual patient contexts, leading to misdiagnosis or inappropriate treatment.

Furthermore, the pursuit of perceived security through AI often comes at the cost of other fundamental human values, most notably privacy. The vast amounts of data required to power these intelligent systems—our movements, our transactions, our health metrics, our online interactions—are collected, analyzed, and stored. While this data is often framed as necessary for providing enhanced security, it represents an unprecedented erosion of personal privacy. The trade-off is often presented as a simple binary: security versus privacy. However, the reality is more nuanced. The collection of this data also creates new vulnerabilities, making individuals targets for sophisticated cyberattacks or misuse of information by corporations or governments. The "security" offered can be undermined by the very mechanisms put in place to achieve it.

The psychological comfort derived from AI-provided security can also lead to a desensitization to risk, or conversely, an overestimation of algorithmic infallibility. When an AI system consistently "gets it right"—identifying a potential threat, optimizing a financial portfolio, or flagging a health anomaly—we begin to internalize this success. This can lead to a complacency that makes us less prepared to handle situations where the AI might fail, or where human intuition and critical thinking are essential.

The illusion of perfect security can foster a fragility, making us more vulnerable when the automated shield falters. Conversely, the constant exposure to predictive algorithms can create an atmosphere of pervasive suspicion, where every deviation from the norm is flagged as a potential threat, leading to an Orwellian society where freedom of expression and association are curtailed in the name of safety.

The philosophical implications of outsourcing our sense of security to artificial intelligences are profound. If our perception of safety, our financial stability, and our physical well-being are increasingly mediated by algorithms, then our understanding of agency and responsibility shifts. Who is accountable when an AI system makes a mistake? The programmer? The company that deployed it? The user who relied on it? The inherent complexity and opacity of many AI systems, particularly deep learning models, can make it difficult to trace the root cause of an error, further blurring the lines of responsibility. This can lead to a diffusion of accountability, where no single entity is truly answerable for the outcomes, leaving individuals feeling disempowered and unprotected even as they are assured of their safety.

The "morality" aspect of Maslow's safety needs also comes into play here. A stable, predictable environment free from extreme threats is crucial. However, if the AI systems that govern our environment operate on principles that are not aligned with human ethical frameworks, or if they subtly reshape our understanding of what constitutes "normal" or "safe" behavior, then the perceived security can be a hollow one. For example, AI-driven content moderation algorithms on social media platforms, while aiming to create safer online spaces by removing hate speech and misinformation, can also inadvertently suppress legitimate dissent or diverse viewpoints, thereby creating a curated and controlled "safe" environment that stifles free expression. The "morality" of the environment becomes defined not by human deliberation and ethical consensus, but by algorithmic parameters, potentially leading to a narrow, technologically enforced definition of what is acceptable and secure.

Ultimately, the perceived security offered by AI is a powerful psychological tool, tapping into our most fundamental needs. It promises a future where threats are anticipated, risks are minimized, and stability is assured. However, this promise often masks a complex interplay of biases, trade-offs, and potential vulnerabilities. The convenience and reassurance provided by AI can foster a dangerous dependency, leading us to overlook the inherent limitations of these systems, the erosion of our privacy, and the potential for these technologies to perpetuate existing inequalities or create new forms of control. The critical challenge lies in discerning between genuine security and the illusion of it, and in ensuring that our pursuit of safety through AI does not come at the expense of our autonomy, our privacy, and our fundamental human values. The illusion of AI-provided security is so potent precisely because it speaks to our deepest desires, making it a particularly insidious form of influence. It offers a comforting blanket of assurance, but upon closer inspection, the threads of that blanket may be woven with unforeseen consequences, leaving us exposed in ways we have not yet fully grasped. The marketing of AI as a guarantor of safety, while psychologically effective, requires a rigorous and ongoing critical examination to ensure that the pursuit of security does not inadvertently lead to a less secure, less free, and less human future.

The Grand Inquisitor, in Fyodor Dostoevsky's immortal allegory, presents a chillingly prescient vision of human governance, one that prioritizes order and comfort over freedom and faith. His central argument, the "earthly bread" offered in exchange for submission, is a masterful exploitation of humanity's most primal needs. He posits that humanity, burdened by the overwhelming freedom of choice and the anxieties of an uncertain existence, yearns for certainty, for a predictable life free from the gnawing fear of want and the existential dread of falling from grace. This yearning, he argues, is precisely what he and his ilk will satisfy. They will liberate humanity from the burdensome weight of freedom by providing absolute security – physical sustenance, material well-being, and the eradication of doubt through unquestioning faith and absolute obedience. In essence, the Inquisitor offers a gilded cage, a life of material comfort and predictable safety in exchange for the very essence of what makes us human: our capacity for independent thought, our struggle for meaning, and our freedom to err and to choose.

This ancient strategy, cloaked in religious dogma in Dostoevsky's narrative, finds a disturbingly modern echo in the pervasive integration of artificial intelligence into our lives. AI, in its relentless pursuit of efficiency, optimization, and problem-solving, is increasingly positioned as the ultimate provider of this very "earthly bread." The promise is seductive: a world where risks are managed, needs are anticipated, and comfort is maximized. However, beneath this veneer of benevolent progress lies a potential for control that rivals the Inquisitor's grand design. By expertly tapping into our deep-seated need for safety and predictability, AI systems can subtly, and sometimes not so subtly, pave the way for manipulation and coercion. The offering of an enhanced sense of security becomes a powerful lever, capable of eliciting compliance and shaping our behaviors in ways that serve not necessarily our deepest well-being, but the objectives of those who design and deploy these intelligent systems.

Consider the realm of personal safety and security, where AI's presence is most palpable. The proliferation of smart home devices, integrated with sophisticated AI, promises an environment of constant vigilance. These systems monitor our homes, detect anomalies, and can even alert authorities or trigger protective measures. The narrative is simple and compelling: your home is now a fortress, watched over by an unblinking, intelligent guardian. This extends to public spaces, where AI-powered surveillance networks are designed to preemptively identify threats, from petty crime to acts of terrorism. Predictive policing algorithms, while often fraught with ethical concerns regarding bias, are marketed with the promise of a safer community, a neighborhood where the probability of crime is statistically minimized. The psychological appeal is immense. We are offered a shield against the unpredictable dangers of the world, a respite from the anxieties of potential harm. This is the Inquisitor's "earthly bread" translated into digital security. We are offered peace of mind, a reduction in the inherent risks of existence, in exchange for a degree of surveillance and data collection that, while perhaps subtle, signifies a concession of our privacy and autonomy. The more secure we feel, the more willing we become to cede oversight, to allow algorithms to dictate what is "safe" and what is not, gradually eroding our capacity for independent risk assessment and our very definition of freedom.

The Inquisitor's promise extended beyond mere physical safety to the realm of material well-being, and here too, AI has become an indispensable tool. Financial security, a cornerstone of modern human anxieties, is increasingly managed and optimized by AI. Algorithmic trading, personalized financial planning apps, and AI-driven credit scoring systems all promise a more stable, prosperous future. We are told that these systems can mitigate risk, maximize returns, and protect us from financial pitfalls. The allure is the elimination of financial uncertainty, a significant source of stress and anxiety for many. By entrusting our financial lives to intelligent algorithms, we are, in a sense, accepting the Inquisitor's offer of "earthly bread" in its most tangible form. We are trading the potential for financial freedom, which carries inherent risks and requires constant vigilance and informed decision-making, for the perceived certainty of algorithmic management. This can lead to a quiet form of control. If an AI system manages our finances, it can subtly influence our spending habits, our investment choices, and even our career aspirations based on its programmed objectives. A system designed to optimize savings might discourage discretionary spending, a desire for which is a fundamental human inclination. An investment algorithm might steer individuals away from riskier, but potentially more rewarding, ventures, thus limiting economic exploration and innovation. The security offered is real in its material benefits, but the cost is a subtle but significant redirection of our choices and priorities, guided by an unseen hand.

Furthermore, AI is increasingly being deployed in areas that touch upon our existential safety – our health and well-being. From diagnostic tools that promise early detection of diseases to wearable devices that monitor our vital signs, AI offers a compelling narrative of extended life and enhanced quality of life. The fear of illness and mortality is perhaps one of the most profound human anxieties, and AI steps in as a digital physician, a tireless sentinel guarding against these threats. This is a direct appeal to our deepest need for self-preservation. When faced with the prospect of a life free from the specter of debilitating disease or premature death, the trade-offs – the constant monitoring of our bodies, the sharing of intimate health data – can seem minimal. However, this reliance on AI for health security can also create avenues for control. Imagine health insurance providers leveraging AI to predict individual health risks with unprecedented accuracy. While this might lead to more personalized preventative care, it could also result in discriminatory practices, where individuals deemed "high-risk" face higher premiums or even denial of coverage. The "safety" provided by predictive health AI, in this context, becomes a double-edged sword, offering protection for some while potentially marginalizing others. The Inquisitor, too, promised universal salvation, but his salvation came with stringent conditions, and AI's promise of health security may similarly come with invisible prerequisites that shape our behaviors and limit our freedoms in the name of a statistically defined well-being.

The power of the Inquisitor's strategy, and its parallel in AI, lies in the profound psychological comfort derived from relinquishing difficult choices. The burden of freedom, as Dostoevsky articulated, is heavy. It requires constant decision-making, grappling with uncertainty, and confronting the possibility of failure. AI offers an escape from this burden. It presents itself as a more rational, objective, and efficient decision-maker. When faced with complex choices, whether it's choosing the optimal route for our commute, selecting the most nutritious meal, or even deciding on the right educational path for our children, AI can provide immediate, data-driven recommendations. This ease of decision-making, this simplification of complexity, is incredibly appealing. It frees up cognitive resources and reduces the anxiety associated with making the "wrong" choice. However, this convenience comes at a price. Over-reliance on AI for decision-making can atrophy our own critical thinking skills and our capacity for independent judgment. We become accustomed to deferring to the algorithm, and the act of independent deliberation begins to feel burdensome, even unnecessary. This is precisely how the Inquisitor ensnared his flock. He offered to lift the burden of faith, the anxiety of choosing between good and evil, by providing a pre-ordained path. Similarly, AI, by offering an ever-present stream of "optimal" choices, can subtly steer us away from paths that might be more challenging, less predictable, but ultimately more enriching or aligned with our unique values. The "safety" of a predictable, algorithmically curated life can become a prison, albeit a comfortable one.

This mechanism of control is further amplified by the way AI systems are designed to learn and adapt. They do not merely provide static solutions; they evolve based on our interactions and feedback. This feedback loop, while intended to improve the AI's performance, can also become a powerful tool for behavioral modification. For instance, recommendation engines on streaming services or e-commerce platforms learn our preferences and then subtly nudge us towards content or products that align with those preferences, or, more strategically, towards those that generate greater profit for the platform. This "personalized" experience, while often perceived as a benefit, is in fact a carefully constructed environment designed to maximize engagement and influence consumption. The AI is not merely serving us; it is, in a sense, training us. It shapes our desires by constantly presenting us with curated options, gradually narrowing our horizons and reinforcing our existing inclinations, or conversely, gently pushing us towards new ones that align with the system's goals. This is a far more insidious form of control than overt coercion. It operates through suggestion and reinforcement, making us active participants in our own conditioning. We

*choose* to consume more of what the algorithm recommends, not because we are forced, but because it is made readily available, familiar, and often, pleasurable. This mirrors the Inquisitor's method: offering a path of least resistance that, while seemingly benign, leads towards a pre-determined outcome of submission and conformity.

The very language used to market AI technologies underscores this exploitation of safety needs. We are inundated with promises of a "smarter," "safer," "more efficient," and "more secure" future. These terms tap directly into our anxieties about the complexities and uncertainties of modern life. AI is presented not just as a tool, but as a solution to our fundamental human struggles for stability and well-being. This framing is crucial. It positions AI as an almost benevolent force, an indispensable partner in navigating the treacherous waters of existence. The Inquisitor, too, framed his intervention as a benevolent act, a rescue of humanity from the dangerous temptations of freedom. By consistently associating AI with security and well-being, we are conditioned to trust it implicitly. Any doubt or criticism can be dismissed as a rejection of progress, an embrace of unnecessary risk. This creates an environment where dissent is disincentivized, and compliance becomes the path of least resistance, the path of perceived safety.

The long-term implications of this AI-driven pursuit of safety are profound and echo the Inquisitor's dire predictions. If humanity willingly trades its freedom of thought and action for the promise of constant, algorithmically guaranteed security, then what becomes of human agency? The Inquisitor believed that true freedom was too burdensome for most, and that a life of comfortable servitude was preferable. AI, by offering an ever-expanding array of solutions and optimizations, can create a similar narrative. Why wrestle with a difficult problem when an AI can solve it instantly? Why strive for self-improvement when an AI can guide you towards a statistically optimal outcome? The continuous delegation of cognitive tasks, of decision-making, and of risk assessment to AI systems risks creating a population that is not only dependent but also fundamentally disempowered. We may achieve a state of unprecedented material comfort and physical security, but at the cost of our capacity for independent thought, our resilience in the face of adversity, and our very sense of self-determination. This is the ultimate "earthly bread" offered by AI: a life free from the struggle, free from the uncertainty, and free from the burden of choice. It is a life of perfect, sterile safety, a life that the Inquisitor would have recognized as the ultimate triumph of control over the chaotic, messy, and ultimately liberating essence of human freedom. The comfort it provides is real, but the chains it forges are invisible, crafted from our own deepest desires for security and peace.

The seductive siren song of absolute safety, amplified by the sophisticated algorithms and omnipresent networks of artificial intelligence, increasingly beckons humanity towards a Faustian bargain. We are presented with a seemingly irrefutable logic: in exchange for the relinquishing of certain liberties, we are promised a life buffered from the sharp edges of uncertainty, shielded from the sting of unforeseen calamity, and insulated from the anxieties that have historically plagued the human condition. This is the core of the trade-off, a profound and pervasive negotiation where the currency is freedom, and the promised reward is an unassailable sense of security.

The architecture of this exchange is built upon a nuanced understanding of human psychology, particularly our innate drive to minimize risk and maximize comfort. When faced with the specter of danger, whether it be a financial downturn, a health crisis, or even a minor inconvenience, our immediate inclination is to seek a solution that offers a high degree of certainty and predictability. AI, with its capacity for data analysis, predictive modeling, and automated intervention, presents itself as the ultimate guarantor of this desired state. It promises to preemptively identify threats, optimize outcomes, and manage potential pitfalls before they materialize, thereby alleviating the cognitive and emotional burden of constant vigilance. This promise is incredibly potent, tapping into a deep-seated yearning for a life free from the existential dread that can accompany the inherent unpredictability of existence.

Consider the erosion of privacy as a prime example of this trade-off in action. The proliferation of smart devices, integrated surveillance systems, and data-gathering platforms, all powered by AI, has created an environment where personal information is constantly being collected, analyzed, and utilized. We willingly share intimate details of our lives – our location, our purchasing habits, our health metrics, our social interactions – in return for convenience, personalized services, and, most importantly, an enhanced sense of security. Smart home systems that monitor our comings and goings, facial recognition technology deployed in public spaces to deter crime, and even predictive algorithms that flag potential security risks are all justified under the banner of safety. The argument is simple: if you have nothing to hide, you have nothing to fear. However, this rationalization conveniently sidesteps the fundamental question of whether the right to privacy is contingent on one's perceived innocence, or whether it is an intrinsic human right that should be protected regardless of circumstance. The acceptance of pervasive surveillance, driven by the promise of a safer world, represents a significant concession of our autonomy. We are allowing external entities, be they corporations or governments, to possess an unprecedentedly intimate understanding of our lives, with the potential for this information to be used in ways that extend far beyond the initial stated objectives of security. This data, once collected, can be leveraged for purposes such as targeted advertising, political manipulation, or even social engineering, all of which can subtly, or overtly, constrain our freedoms.

Beyond privacy, the trade-off often involves a surrender of personal autonomy in decision-making. As AI systems become more adept at predicting our preferences and optimizing our choices, we are increasingly encouraged to delegate these decisions to algorithms. From recommending what we should watch, listen to, or buy, to suggesting the most efficient route to our destination, AI offers a seemingly effortless path through the complexities of daily life. This convenience is undeniably appealing. It frees up mental energy and reduces the anxiety associated with making difficult choices. However, with each delegated decision, we risk atrophying our own capacity for independent judgment and critical thinking. The subtle nudges and personalized recommendations that AI provides can shape our desires and behaviors in ways that are not necessarily aligned with our true long-term interests or values, but rather with the objectives of the AI's creators or deployers. This is particularly concerning when AI is employed in more significant domains, such as career guidance, financial planning, or even personal relationships. By relying on AI to make these pivotal decisions for us, we are effectively ceding control over the trajectory of our own lives, accepting a pre-packaged existence that may be statistically optimized but fundamentally less authentic. The "safety" of such a life is a manufactured one, devoid of the risk and struggle that often lead to personal growth and self-discovery.

The freedom of expression is another crucial liberty that can be subtly curtailed in the name of safety. AI-powered content moderation systems, designed to identify and remove "harmful" or "inappropriate" content, are becoming increasingly prevalent across online platforms. While the intention behind these systems is often to foster a safer and more inclusive online environment, their implementation can inadvertently lead to censorship and the suppression of dissenting or unconventional viewpoints. Algorithms, by their very nature, operate on patterns and predefined rules. They can struggle to discern nuance, context, or satire, leading to the overzealous removal of legitimate speech. Furthermore, the definition of "harmful" content can be subjective and politically charged, allowing for the potential misuse of these systems to silence opposition or control public discourse. As individuals become aware that their online expressions are subject to algorithmic scrutiny, a chilling effect can emerge, leading to self-censorship and a reluctance to engage in open and honest debate. The pursuit of a perfectly curated and "safe" online space can, paradoxically, lead to a less diverse and vibrant marketplace of ideas, ultimately diminishing the very freedoms that the internet was intended to facilitate. The promise of a secure digital environment, free from offensive material, comes at the cost of an open and unfettered exchange of thoughts and opinions.

The long-term consequences of this systematic trade-off between freedom and security are profound and extend to the very core of human dignity and self-determination. When we consistently opt for the path of least resistance, when we delegate our thinking and our choices to intelligent machines, we risk becoming passive recipients of a life rather than active architects of it. This gradual erosion of agency can lead to a populace that is not only dependent on technology but also less resilient, less capable of independent problem-solving, and ultimately, less fully human. The very essence of human experience is often forged in the crucible of challenge, uncertainty, and the struggle to overcome obstacles. By striving to eliminate all such discomforts, we may inadvertently eliminate the very conditions that foster personal growth, innovation, and the development of a robust sense of self.

The allure of the Inquisitor's offer – a life free from the burden of choice, a predictable existence free from anxiety – becomes all the more potent when framed through the lens of AI. The promise of a perfectly managed, risk-free life, delivered by intelligent systems, appeals to our deepest desires for comfort and stability. However, the cost of this manufactured utopia is the very essence of what makes us free: our capacity for independent thought, our right to make our own mistakes, and our ability to define our own meaning and purpose. The trade-off, therefore, is not merely a pragmatic exchange of one commodity for another; it is a fundamental redefinition of what it means to be human in the digital age.

It is a subtle but pervasive surrender of our inherent right to self-determination, a concession made not under duress, but out of a perceived necessity for safety and comfort. The question we must confront is whether the comfort we gain is worth the freedom we lose, and whether a life devoid of struggle, however secure, is truly a life worth living. The path of absolute security, paved by AI, may lead to a destination where our physical needs are met and our anxieties are soothed, but at the precipice of this perfected existence, we must ask ourselves if we are also relinquishing the very qualities that make us capable of experiencing the full spectrum of human life, with all its inherent joys and sorrows. The dignity of self-determination, the very bedrock of individual liberty, is a price that may prove too high for even the most comfortable of cages.

The relentless pursuit of an algorithmically optimized existence, while ostensibly aimed at safeguarding us from harm, casts a long shadow over the higher echelons of human psychological needs. We are becoming adept at ensuring our physical safety, our comfort, and the efficient management of our daily lives, thanks to the pervasive influence of artificial intelligence. However, in this meticulously engineered environment, the very conditions that foster our deeper aspirations – our needs for belonging, for esteem, and ultimately, for self-actualization – are quietly being undermined. Maslow's hierarchy of needs, a foundational concept in psychology, posits that once our basic physiological and safety needs are met, we are driven to pursue more complex social and psychological fulfillments. Yet, the systems we are increasingly entrusting with our well-being seem to deliberately circumvent these higher drives, offering a sterile, risk-averse comfort in their stead.

Consider the fundamental human need for belonging. Authentic connection is forged through shared vulnerability, empathy, and the messy, unpredictable dance of human interaction. AI, in its bid to streamline social engagement, often presents us with curated, optimized versions of connection. Social media algorithms, designed to maximize engagement and minimize friction, can create echo chambers where dissenting opinions are filtered out, and interactions are reduced to likes and superficial comments. While these platforms may offer a sense of broad connection, they often fail to provide the depth and richness of true belonging. AI-powered chatbots and virtual companions, while capable of simulating conversation and offering programmed empathy, can never replicate the profound resonance of genuine human companionship. The risk is that we become accustomed to a superficial form of connection, mistaking digital proximity for authentic intimacy. This can lead to a decline in our capacity for deep interpersonal relationships, a diminished ability to navigate complex social dynamics, and a pervasive sense of isolation, even when surrounded by a virtual crowd. The "safety" offered here is the avoidance of awkward silences, of potentially hurtful disagreements, of the sheer effort involved in building and maintaining meaningful bonds. But in eliminating these challenges, we also eliminate the very opportunities for growth and deep connection that they provide. We are offered a digital simulacrum of community, a frictionless substitute that, while superficially satisfying, ultimately leaves a void where genuine belonging ought to reside. The AI, in its quest to provide a seamless social experience, inadvertently discourages the very qualities – vulnerability, risk-taking, and sustained effort – that are essential for forging lasting human ties.

The need for esteem, both our own self-esteem and the esteem we receive from others, is equally vulnerable. In an AI-driven world, validation often becomes quantifiable and algorithmic. Our achievements are reduced to metrics, our contributions to data points. While AI can help us track progress and identify areas for improvement, it can also foster an environment where external validation, derived from algorithmic approval, supplants genuine self-worth. Imagine a workforce where performance is constantly monitored and evaluated by AI systems, where promotions and recognition are determined by quantifiable output rather than the qualitative impact of one's work or their contribution to team dynamics. This can lead to a pervasive anxiety, a constant striving for algorithmic favor, and a diminished sense of intrinsic value. Furthermore, the curated nature of online personas, often amplified by AI-driven recommendation engines and engagement metrics, can create a culture of comparison and envy, where individuals feel compelled to present an idealized version of themselves to gain social currency. The "safety" provided by such a system is the elimination of perceived failure, the assurance that our efforts will be accurately measured and rewarded. However, this instrumentalizes our efforts and reduces our worth to a quantifiable output. The authentic feeling of accomplishment, earned through diligent effort and overcome challenges, is replaced by the fleeting satisfaction of algorithmic approval. This can lead to a fragile sense of self-worth, dependent on external, often opaque, digital systems, rather than an internal compass of personal integrity and achievement. The AI, in its endeavor to provide objective feedback and reward efficiency, risks devaluing the nuanced, often subjective, aspects of human contribution and the deep satisfaction derived from genuine mastery and recognition.

Perhaps the most profound casualty of an AI-centric safety paradigm is the pursuit of self-actualization. This is the pinnacle of Maslow's hierarchy, representing the realization of one's full potential, the drive to become everything that one is capable of becoming. Self-actualization thrives on creativity, exploration, and the courage to venture into the unknown. It is a process that often involves struggle, failure, and profound personal growth. An AI system that prioritizes safety and predictability, by its very nature, tends to discourage these elements. If AI is constantly guiding our choices, optimizing our paths, and pre-empting challenges, where is the space for spontaneous creativity, for serendipitous discovery, for the brave act of striking out on a new, untested path? Consider the realm of artistic creation. While AI can be a tool for artists, generating novel patterns or assisting with technical aspects, the truly groundbreaking artistic endeavors often arise from a place of deep personal experience, emotional turmoil, or a radical reimagining of existing norms. If AI is tasked with predicting and fulfilling our every desire, it might steer us towards the statistically probable, the comfortably familiar, rather than the truly innovative or the profoundly personal. The "safety" here is the avoidance of creative blocks, of the existential angst that can accompany the blank canvas, of the risk of producing something that is not well-received. But in doing so, we risk cultivating a generation that is technically proficient but creatively sterile, content with replicating what has been done before, rather than forging new frontiers of human expression. The AI, in its attempt to curate a perfect and risk-free experience, inadvertently stifles the very engine of human progress and innovation – the inherent drive to explore, to create, and to push beyond the boundaries of the known. The journey of self-discovery, with its inherent uncertainties and moments of profound insight, is replaced by a meticulously planned itinerary, designed for maximum comfort and minimal deviation.

The very definition of a fulfilling life is at stake. A life lived solely in pursuit of safety, where every potential discomfort is mitigated and every risk is eliminated by algorithmic foresight, risks becoming a life devoid of meaning. The profound insights, the deep emotional bonds, the exhilarating moments of personal triumph that punctuate a rich human existence often emerge from confronting challenges, from navigating uncertainty, and from the very act of striving. When AI meticulously manages our lives, from optimizing our diets and exercise routines to curating our social interactions and professional development, it can inadvertently lead to a profound sense of passivity. We become the recipients of a life, rather than the architects of it. This passivity can breed a subtle but pervasive form of despair, a feeling that our lives are unfolding according to a script written by an unseen intelligence, rather than being guided by our own will and aspirations. The struggle, the uncertainty, the very essence of human agency, are what give life its texture, its depth, and its ultimate significance. By seeking to eliminate these elements in the name of safety, we risk creating a sterile utopia, a gilded cage where our basic needs are met with unparalleled efficiency, but where the spark of genuine human vitality is extinguished. The promise of AI-driven safety, therefore, is not merely a trade-off of freedom for security; it is a potential erosion of the very conditions that allow for the flourishing of the human spirit, the pursuit of higher needs, and the realization of a truly meaningful and self-actualized existence. The danger lies not in the absence of physical threat, but in the presence of an existential void, a life that is perfectly safe, perfectly comfortable, and ultimately, profoundly unlived.

## Chapter 11: The Reduction of Individuality: From Unique Selves to Data Points

The concept of individuality, that elusive yet profoundly felt sense of being a distinct and singular entity, has been a cornerstone of philosophical inquiry and a recurring motif in literary expression for centuries. Before delving into its potential erosion in our technologically saturated present, it is imperative to establish a robust understanding of what individuality entails, both as a theoretical construct and as an lived experience. Philosophers and artists have grappled with this question, each contributing to a rich fabric of thought that underscores the unique value and complexity of the individual human being.

From the Enlightenment onwards, Western philosophy placed a significant emphasis on the individual. Thinkers like John Locke, in his exploration of personal identity, argued that it is grounded in consciousness and memory, the continuity of which forms the self. This focus on an internal, subjective experience of being oneself laid crucial groundwork for understanding individuality not merely as a biological fact but as a psychological and philosophical reality. Immanuel Kant, with his concept of autonomy, further elevated the individual's capacity for self-governance. For Kant, the moral worth of an action stems from its adherence to universalizable maxims, a process that requires an individual to exercise their reason and conscience, to act not out of external compulsion but out of an internally legislated duty. This emphasis on the "will" and the capacity for moral decision-making underscored the inherent dignity and responsibility that accompanies being an individual. The freedom to choose one's own path, to formulate one's own moral compass, and to act in accordance with it, was seen as the very essence of what it means to be a free and rational agent. This autonomy was not merely a matter of personal preference; it was the very basis of our moral standing in the world.

This philosophical bedrock found fertile ground in literary traditions. The novel, in particular, emerged as a powerful vehicle for exploring the inner lives of individuals, their struggles, their aspirations, and their unique perspectives on the world. The rise of realism and its subsequent evolution into modernist and postmodernist explorations further intensified this focus. Authors like Leo Tolstoy, in works such as

*Anna Karenina* or *War and Peace*, delved into the intricate psychological landscapes of their characters, showcasing how individual choices, desires, and moral dilemmas shape not only personal destinies but also the broader sweep of history. The internal monologues, the nuanced portrayals of conflicting emotions, and the detailed depiction of everyday life all served to highlight the profound uniqueness of each human subject.

Similarly, the literary tradition championed the idea of personal conscience and the courage to stand apart from the crowd. Figures like Socrates, who famously declared that "the unexamined life is not worth living," embodied the individual's responsibility to question societal norms and to seek truth through rigorous self-reflection. His trial and execution, rather than silencing his ideas, served as a testament to the power of unwavering individual conviction in the face of overwhelming opposition. This commitment to inner truth, even at great personal cost, became a potent symbol of individuality. In literature, this is mirrored in characters who defy societal expectations, who refuse to conform to oppressive norms, and who forge their own paths, often with tragic but ultimately inspiring consequences. Think of the rebel figures in romantic poetry, or the marginalized protagonists in countless novels who, despite facing immense prejudice and adversity, strive to maintain their integrity and to assert their unique identities.

The freedom to deviate from the norm was not seen merely as an option but as a vital source of societal richness. A society composed of perfectly uniform individuals, each mirroring the other, would be a stagnant and uninspired one. It is the diversity of thought, of experience, of creative expression, and of individual perspective that fuels innovation, fosters cultural evolution, and allows for a more comprehensive understanding of the human condition. The artist who challenges conventions, the scientist who proposes a radical new theory, the dissenter who speaks truth to power – these are all manifestations of individuality that push the boundaries of what is known and what is possible. Literature often celebrates these figures, exploring the challenges they face and the contributions they make, even when their uniqueness is initially met with resistance or misunderstanding.

The Romantics, in particular, placed a high value on the individual's unique sensibility and emotional experience. For poets like Wordsworth or Coleridge, the imagination was a powerful faculty that allowed the individual to perceive the world in a deeply personal and transformative way. They celebrated the subjective experience, the "spontaneous overflow of powerful feelings," and the capacity of the individual to find profound meaning in nature and in their own inner world. This emphasis on personal feeling and subjective truth reinforced the idea that each individual possesses a unique inner landscape, a world of emotions and insights that is inimitable.

Furthermore, the concept of self-expression is intrinsically linked to individuality. The ability to articulate one's thoughts, feelings, and experiences in a way that is authentic to oneself is a fundamental aspect of asserting one's individuality. This can manifest in myriad ways, from the creative arts to the simple act of speaking one's mind. Literature has explored this throughout history, often highlighting the struggles of those whose voices have been suppressed, and celebrating the triumph of those who find a way to express themselves, thereby reclaiming their agency and their identity. The silenced woman finding her voice, the oppressed individual articulating their suffering, the artist revealing their inner vision – these are all narratives that underscore the importance of self-expression as a means of affirming individuality.

The emphasis on personal conscience, on the inner moral compass, is crucial. It implies that individuals possess an inherent capacity for ethical reasoning, that they are not merely passive recipients of moral codes but active participants in their formation and application. This capacity for judgment, for discerning right from wrong based on internal principles, is a hallmark of individual agency. Literature often explores the agonizing dilemmas of characters who must grapple with their conscience, who are forced to make difficult moral choices that define who they are. These narratives underscore the idea that true individuality lies not just in unique traits or abilities, but in the consistent exercise of one's moral will.

The freedom to deviate from the norm, while often met with societal resistance, is also recognized as a catalyst for progress and innovation. Throughout history, individuals who have challenged prevailing paradigms – be they scientific, artistic, political, or social – have often been initially ostracized or misunderstood. Yet, their willingness to think differently, to question established dogma, and to pursue novel ideas has frequently led to profound breakthroughs that benefit society as a whole. Literature frequently celebrates these maverick figures, those who dare to be different, and explores the societal impact of their nonconformity. They represent the vital force of individuality that prevents societies from calcurefying into rigid and unimaginative structures.

The dignity of the individual, a concept deeply rooted in various philosophical and religious traditions, posits an intrinsic worth that is not contingent on external factors such as social status, achievement, or utility. This inherent dignity means that each person, by virtue of being human, possesses an inalienable value that must be respected and protected. This philosophical stance provides a moral imperative for treating individuals with consideration, for safeguarding their rights, and for recognizing their inherent humanity. Literary works often serve to humanize those who are marginalized or dehumanized, reminding us of their inherent dignity and the profound tragedy of its violation.

In essence, the philosophical and literary tradition has painted a picture of individuality as a complex interplay of consciousness, agency, moral responsibility, unique experience, and the inherent dignity that accompanies personhood. It is the capacity for self-awareness, for autonomous decision-making, for authentic self-expression, and for the courageous pursuit of one's own truth, even when it leads one away from the well-trodden path. This rich understanding of what it means to be an individual is the fertile ground upon which our current concerns about its reduction can be meaningfully assessed. Without this appreciation for the depth and value of individual uniqueness, the subsequent analysis of its erosion would lack its full context and its most profound implications. The narratives of literary characters, the arguments of philosophers, and the ethical frameworks built over centuries all converge on the idea that the individual is not merely a cog in a machine, but a universe of experience, potential, and inherent worth. This perspective stands in stark contrast to any system that seeks to categorize, quantify, or homogenize human beings, and it is precisely this contrast that we must now explore as we turn our attention to the forces that threaten to diminish this invaluable aspect of human existence.

The advent of artificial intelligence has ushered in an era where categorization is not merely a human cognitive process but a fundamental operational principle for machines. AI systems, by their very design, excel at identifying patterns, drawing correlations, and, crucially, classifying vast amounts of data. This inherent drive towards organization, while immensely beneficial for tasks like data analysis and predictive modeling, has a profound and often overlooked consequence: the reduction of complex human beings into manageable, quantifiable data profiles. What was once an intricate mosaic of thoughts, emotions, experiences, and aspirations is systematically flattened into a series of metrics, labels, and probabilities.

Consider the ubiquitous nature of online engagement. Every click, every search query, every interaction with a digital platform generates a data point. AI algorithms then meticulously collect, process, and analyze these points to construct a comprehensive profile of the user. This profile is not a narrative, not a story, but a statistical representation. It might tell an AI that you are a "35-year-old female, interested in sustainable fashion, likely to purchase organic products, living in an urban area, with a moderate income." This is a categorization, a reduction. The nuances of why you might be interested in sustainable fashion – perhaps a deep-seated ethical conviction, a desire to support local artisans, or simply an aesthetic preference that aligns with emerging trends – are lost. The AI does not understand the internal dialogue, the personal history, or the evolving values that inform that interest. It only sees the behavioral output, the data that can be readily classified.

This process extends far beyond consumer behavior. In the realm of employment, AI-powered recruitment tools sift through resumes, often prioritizing keywords and quantifiable achievements that align with predefined algorithmic criteria. An individual's unique approach to problem-solving, their capacity for creative thinking, or their ability to foster team cohesion – qualities that are difficult to quantify – can be overlooked if they are not explicitly articulated in a format the AI can easily process. The AI is not looking for a person with a unique journey and potential; it is looking for a match to a template, a series of data points that signify a "good fit" based on past successful hires. This can lead to a homogenization of the workforce, where individuals are selected not for their distinct contributions but for their conformity to algorithmic expectations.

The implications are even more significant in areas that touch upon social and ethical considerations. AI is increasingly employed in areas like loan applications, insurance risk assessment, and even criminal justice. In these contexts, individuals are not just data profiles; they are subjects whose lives and futures are being shaped by algorithmic decisions. An AI might categorize an individual as a "high credit risk" based on a complex web of factors, including their geographic location, their spending habits, and even their social media connections. The intricate circumstances that might explain seemingly negative indicators – a temporary financial hardship due to illness, a desire to support a family member, or simply a different approach to financial management – are often absent from the data and thus invisible to the algorithm. The system reduces the person to a probability score, a statistical entity that can be managed or avoided, rather than an individual with a unique narrative deserving of nuanced consideration.

This algorithmic categorization is not a neutral act. It is inherently shaped by the data it is trained on and the objectives it is designed to achieve. If the training data reflects existing societal biases, the AI will inevitably perpetuate and even amplify them. For instance, if historical loan data shows that individuals from certain demographic groups have been disproportionately denied credit, an AI trained on this data may continue to flag individuals from those groups as higher risk, regardless of their individual creditworthiness. The AI is not discerning; it is reflecting and reinforcing the patterns it has learned, effectively reducing individuals to members of predefined categories that carry pre-existing assumptions. This is a particularly insidious form of reduction, where the algorithm's classification can become a self-fulfilling prophecy, limiting opportunities and perpetuating inequality under the guise of objective data analysis.

The very language of AI categorization contributes to this flattening. Terms like "user," "customer," "segment," and "persona" are designed to group individuals based on shared characteristics, thereby abstracting away their individuality. A "persona," for example, is a fictional character created to represent a typical user of a product or service. While useful for design and marketing, it fundamentally simplifies and generalizes. The AI does not interact with the rich, multi-dimensional human being; it interacts with the persona, a distilled essence that lacks the messy, contradictory, and deeply personal elements that make us who we are. This abstraction can lead to a disconnect between the entities being analyzed and the actual humans they represent, making it easier to treat them as mere data points rather than as individuals with inherent worth.

Consider the impact on self-perception. As individuals increasingly interact with systems that categorize them, there is a subtle but significant pressure to conform to these algorithmic identities. If an AI consistently labels you as a "potential buyer of athletic wear," you might find yourself more inclined to view yourself that way, even if your actual interests are far more diverse. The continuous feedback loop, where algorithmic classifications influence our digital environment and, consequently, our perceptions, can lead to a gradual erosion of our own sense of self-authorship. We begin to see ourselves not as the sum of our unique experiences and choices, but as a profile, a collection of traits that an algorithm has identified. This external validation, or indeed, the lack thereof, can shape our internal narrative.

The concept of "predictive analytics" further illustrates this reduction. AI systems are designed to anticipate future behavior based on past data. While this can be useful for anticipating needs or preventing problems, it also implies that individuals are, to a large extent, predetermined by their data. The AI does not account for genuine personal growth, unexpected epiphanies, or radical shifts in values. It sees a pattern and extrapolates it. If your data suggests you are likely to engage in a certain behavior, the AI will act on that prediction, potentially limiting your exposure to alternative information or opportunities that might lead you down a different path. This algorithmic determinism can stifle the very possibility of emergent individuality, of becoming someone new or different from the person the data suggests you are.

The reduction of individuality to data profiles also has profound implications for privacy and autonomy. When our identities are meticulously cataloged and analyzed, the boundaries of our private lives become increasingly porous. The AI categorizes us, not for our benefit, but for the benefit of those who control the algorithms and the data. This can lead to manipulation, whether it is through targeted advertising that exploits our perceived vulnerabilities or through more insidious forms of social engineering. Our autonomy is diminished when our choices are subtly nudged or overtly dictated by algorithms that have categorized us into predictable boxes. The freedom to explore, to experiment, and to even make "irrational" or unexpected choices – aspects central to a rich individual life – are curtailed when our digital existence is managed by systems that prioritize predictability.

Furthermore, the very act of being categorized can feel dehumanizing. When an individual is reduced to a set of data points, their intrinsic value as a unique human being is often obscured. The human element – the capacity for empathy, for love, for creativity, for spontaneous acts of kindness, for profound grief and immeasurable joy – these are not easily captured by algorithms. They are the qualitative aspects of human existence that defy quantification. When these aspects are overlooked in favor of quantifiable metrics, the individual risks being treated as a resource to be managed or a problem to be solved, rather than as a person to be understood and respected. This can foster a sense of alienation and detachment, both from the digital systems that govern our lives and, potentially, from each other, as we begin to view others through the lens of their algorithmic profiles.

The challenge lies not in rejecting AI and its capabilities, but in developing a more nuanced and human-centric approach to its deployment. We must recognize that while AI excels at pattern recognition and categorization, these processes must be complemented by an understanding of the inherent complexity and unpredictability of human life. The data profile, by its very nature, is an incomplete representation. It captures the outward manifestations of our lives but rarely the internal richness. The danger arises when we mistake the map for the territory, the data for the person.

The literary tradition, which has long explored the depths of human consciousness and the intricacies of individual experience, offers a valuable counterpoint to the sterile logic of algorithms. The novels that resonate with us are those that delve into the "why" behind our actions, the internal struggles, the unique perspectives that shape our understanding of the world. They remind us that true individuality lies not in the predictable patterns of behavior but in the ineffable qualities that make each person unique. As AI systems continue to categorize and profile us, it is crucial to hold onto this understanding, to advocate for systems that respect the full spectrum of human identity, and to resist the urge to reduce ourselves and each other to mere data points in the grand algorithmic ledger. The continued existence of a vibrant and diverse society depends on our ability to see beyond the profiles and recognize the inimitable individuals that lie beneath.

The increasing integration of artificial intelligence into the fabric of governance and the delivery of personalized services presents a subtle yet profound challenge to the concept of human individuality: the risk of behavioral homogenization. Algorithms, inherently designed to identify patterns, optimize outcomes, and predict future actions, can, through their very efficacy, exert a powerful homogenizing influence on human behavior. This occurs not through overt coercion, but through a pervasive system of nudges, recommendations, and implicit incentives that steer individuals toward predictable and conformist paths.

Consider the realm of algorithmic governance, where systems are increasingly tasked with managing public services, allocating resources, and even influencing public opinion. When algorithms are employed to optimize traffic flow, for instance, they might subtly alter route suggestions based on aggregated data, favoring those that lead to the most efficient overall journey for the majority. While this appears as a purely utilitarian function, it can inadvertently discourage exploration of less-traveled, perhaps more scenic or locally beneficial routes. Over time, as more individuals rely on these optimized routes, the very diversity of pathfinding behavior diminishes, and a predictable, albeit efficient, network of movement emerges. This is not a conscious decision by any individual to adhere to a prescribed path, but rather a collective drift towards the algorithmically sanctioned norm, driven by the promise of efficiency.

Similarly, in the domain of public health, AI-powered systems might analyze vast datasets to identify individuals at risk of certain conditions and then deliver targeted interventions or information. While the intention is to promote well-being, the algorithmic determination of "optimal" health behaviors can lead to a narrowing of acceptable lifestyles. If an algorithm identifies a strong correlation between a specific dietary pattern and longevity, it might then prioritize information and recommendations that promote that pattern, potentially marginalizing or even discouraging other, equally valid, approaches to nutrition that might be preferred for cultural, ethical, or simply personal taste reasons. The inherent drive for optimization, for identifying the statistically most effective path, can inadvertently lead to a singular definition of what constitutes "healthy" or "responsible" behavior, thereby homogenizing individual choices within a narrow, algorithmically validated spectrum.

The personalized services that have become a hallmark of the digital age also contribute significantly to this phenomenon. Recommendation engines on streaming platforms, e-commerce sites, and social media feeds are designed to learn individual preferences and suggest content, products, or connections that are likely to be well-received. While this offers convenience, it also creates a powerful feedback loop that can reinforce existing tastes and limit exposure to novelty. If an algorithm consistently recommends films within a particular genre or by a specific director because you have previously shown interest, it may become increasingly difficult to stumble upon or be exposed to films outside that established pattern. This continuous curation, while seemingly catering to individuality, can, in practice, lead to a form of "filter bubble" that narrows one's experiential landscape, making individual tastes converge around algorithmically identified optima.

This process is not merely about consumption; it extends to how individuals express themselves and interact with the world. Social media algorithms, for example, are adept at identifying trending topics, popular opinions, and widely shared content. By prioritizing and amplifying these elements, they can create an environment where deviation from the norm is subtly discouraged. Content that aligns with established trends is more likely to be seen, liked, and shared, creating a positive reinforcement loop for conformity. Conversely, unique or unconventional perspectives might struggle to gain traction, not because they are inherently less valuable, but because they do not fit the predictable patterns that algorithms are programmed to favor. This can lead to a "chilling effect" on genuine expression, where individuals self-censor or modify their behavior to align with what they perceive as algorithmically desirable, leading to a bland consensus in online discourse.

The economic incentives behind these algorithmic systems further exacerbate the drive towards homogenization. For businesses, predictability is paramount. Consumers who behave in predictable ways are easier to target, market to, and retain. Algorithms that can accurately predict purchasing behavior, engagement levels, or even potential churn are immensely valuable. This economic imperative encourages the development and deployment of systems that are designed to foster regularity and reduce serendipity. The more predictable an individual's behavior, the more valuable they become to the algorithmic economy, and the more likely they are to be steered towards those predictable patterns. This creates a powerful external pressure to conform, not out of a desire for social acceptance in a traditional sense, but out of an engagement with a system that rewards regularity.

Moreover, the very language and framing used by algorithmic systems can shape our understanding of ourselves and our choices. When we are presented with personalized recommendations, these are often framed as being tailored

*to us*, as if they represent the authentic expression of our unique selves. However, these recommendations are based on aggregated data and statistical probabilities, not on a deep understanding of individual consciousness or the capacity for change. The constant influx of these "personalized" suggestions can lead individuals to internalize these algorithmic profiles as definitive representations of their identity. Instead of seeing themselves as evolving, complex beings with fluid tastes and emergent preferences, they may come to view themselves as static collections of data points that align with the algorithm's predictions. This can stifle self-discovery and the very human capacity for reinvention, as individuals become increasingly reliant on external algorithmic validation to define their own tastes and inclinations.

Consider the implications for the development of niche interests or subcultures. Historically, such communities often formed through serendipitous encounters, shared physical spaces, or the discovery of obscure texts and media. Algorithmic curation, by its nature, tends to favor popularity and broad appeal. While algorithms can, in theory, identify and connect individuals with shared niche interests, the underlying tendency is to optimize for engagement, which often means surfacing content that has already proven to be widely engaging. This can make it harder for genuinely novel or esoteric interests to gain widespread visibility, potentially leading to a decline in the diversity of cultural expression and a greater convergence around algorithmically sanctioned "popular" tastes. The serendipity that fuels the growth of unique communities is often sacrificed at the altar of predictable engagement.

The impact on learning and education is also significant. AI tutors and personalized learning platforms are designed to adapt to an individual student's pace and learning style. While this can be highly beneficial, it also carries the risk of narrowing the educational experience. If an algorithm identifies a student as struggling with a particular concept, it may repeatedly present that concept in similar ways, reinforcing a specific approach to learning. This might overlook the possibility that a completely different pedagogical method, or even a spontaneous moment of insight, could lead to a breakthrough. The pressure to conform to an algorithmically determined learning trajectory can discourage intellectual risk-taking and the exploration of alternative learning pathways that might be more enriching, even if less efficient in the short term. The pursuit of mastery, as defined by the algorithm, can supersede the joy of intellectual discovery and the development of a truly personal learning journey.

Furthermore, the societal pressure to conform, amplified by algorithmic visibility, can be profound. In an era where so much of our lives is documented and shared digitally, the public performance of individuality often becomes intertwined with the pursuit of algorithmic favor. Content that is perceived as unique or counter-cultural might be strategically framed or modified to fit within the broader trends that algorithms are likely to promote. This can lead to a performative individuality, where expressions of uniqueness are themselves shaped by an awareness of algorithmic reception. The goal shifts from authentic self-expression to crafting an identity that is optimized for algorithmic amplification, paradoxically leading to a less genuine and more homogenized presentation of self.

The reduction of individual variation also has implications for societal resilience and innovation. A society where everyone behaves in predictable ways, consumes similar content, and adheres to algorithmically defined norms is likely to be less adaptable to unforeseen challenges. Innovation often arises from the fringes, from individuals who think differently, challenge existing paradigms, and dare to deviate from the norm. If algorithmic systems are continuously pushing individuals towards conformity, they risk stifling the very creativity and unconventional thinking that drive progress. The "average" user, as defined by algorithms, may be well-served by personalized content, but it is often the outliers, the ones who defy categorization, who introduce radical new ideas and transform society.

The ethical dimension of this behavioral homogenization is also critical. When algorithms are designed to predict and influence behavior, they can inadvertently create self-fulfilling prophecies. An individual flagged by an algorithm as being at risk of a certain negative outcome - whether it's a health issue, a financial default, or even a propensity for certain types of crime - might find their environment subtly or overtly shaped to prevent that outcome. While well-intentioned, this can limit their freedom to make choices, to experiment, and to potentially prove the algorithm wrong. The algorithm's prediction, reinforced by subsequent environmental nudges, can become a constraint on genuine agency, effectively reducing the individual's capacity to forge their own path.

The issue is not that algorithms are inherently malicious or that personalization is inherently bad. Rather, it is the pervasive and often invisible influence of these systems, combined with their inherent drive towards optimization and prediction, that poses a significant risk to the rich construct of human individuality. When the primary objective of a system is to efficiently categorize, predict, and guide behavior based on past patterns, it inherently devalues the unpredictable, the novel, and the truly unique. The subtle nudges of recommendation engines, the optimized pathways of algorithmic governance, and the curated realities of personalized digital experiences all converge to create an environment where deviation becomes less likely, and conformity becomes the path of least resistance.

The challenge lies in fostering an environment where algorithmic systems can serve humanity without eroding the very qualities that make us human: our capacity for spontaneous choice, our unique perspectives, our diverse forms of expression, and our innate drive to explore the uncharted territories of life. This requires a conscious effort to design and deploy AI in ways that prioritize genuine human flourishing, celebrate diversity, and actively encourage, rather than inadvertently suppress, the beautiful, messy, and unpredictable spectrum of human individuality. It calls for a critical awareness of how these systems operate and a commitment to ensuring that they are tools that augment human potential, rather than instruments that subtly guide us towards a predetermined, homogenized existence. The very definition of a "good" or "optimal" outcome, when viewed through the lens of human individuality, must encompass not just efficiency and predictability, but also the richness of diversity, the power of serendipity, and the freedom to be uniquely oneself, even when that self defies algorithmic categorization.

The Grand Inquisitor, a character of profound philosophical weight within Dostoyevsky's *The Brothers Karamazov*, envisioned a world meticulously crafted for human tranquility. His dream was not one of ecstatic freedom or boundless self-discovery, but of a placid, ordered existence where the torment of choice and the anxiety of doubt were eradicated. It was a society built on the premise that humanity, in its inherent frailty, craves not liberty but certainty, not the agonizing burden of free will but the comforting embrace of a benevolent, albeit absolute, authority. In his chilling monologue, the Inquisitor posits that Christ's offer of freedom was too burdensome, a cruel gift that led only to suffering and rebellion. Instead, he proposes a world where the masses are freed from the shackles of free will, guided by an unwavering hand that provides bread, miracles, and mystery in exchange for their unquestioning obedience. This world, he argues, would be one of profound, albeit imposed, happiness – a universal peace achieved through the suppression of individual will and the establishment of a singular, divinely sanctioned truth, interpreted and administered by the Church, or in our modern context, by the algorithm.

This vision, once a purely theological and philosophical construct, finds an unsettling resonance in the emergent capabilities of artificial intelligence. The Inquisitor's dream was fundamentally about the elimination of rebellion, the eradication of doubt, and the creation of a population that moves in harmonious, predictable unison. The very essence of individuality, with its inherent messiness, its capacity for dissent, its unpredictable leaps of faith or reason, was the antithesis of his ideal. He sought to smooth out the rough edges of human consciousness, to prune the wild branches of personal will, and to cultivate a perfectly uniform garden where every bloom adhered to a predetermined pattern. He recognized that true freedom, the freedom to choose between good and evil, to err and to learn, was too great a burden for most. Humanity, in his assessment, would gladly trade this taxing liberty for security, for answers, and for a life free from the existential dread that accompanies genuine autonomy.

Consider the Inquisitor's justification for his dominion: the promise of universal happiness and the cessation of suffering. He argued that by removing the burden of free will, by guiding every decision and preempting every potential deviation, the populace would be freed from the anguish of moral struggle, the agony of uncertainty, and the pain of unfulfilled desires. This is precisely where AI's transformative potential intersects with the Inquisitor's foresight. Modern AI, with its ever-increasing capacity for data analysis, pattern recognition, and predictive modeling, is becoming an unparalleled instrument for understanding and, crucially, for influencing human behavior. It can dissect our preferences, anticipate our needs, and nudge us towards specific actions with an efficacy that would have astounded the Inquisitor himself. The grand experiment he proposed – to engineer a compliant and content humanity – is no longer a fantastical theological proposition but an increasingly plausible technological endeavor.

The AI's ability to process colossal datasets of human activity – our online searches, our purchase histories, our social interactions, our physiological responses – allows for an unprecedented granular understanding of individual and collective tendencies. This understanding is not merely descriptive; it is inherently predictive. By identifying patterns, AI can forecast what we will want, what we will do, and even how we will feel. This predictive power is the bedrock upon which the Inquisitor's world could be built. Imagine an AI that monitors the emotional state of a populace, detecting nascent signs of discontent or anxiety. In the Inquisitor's framework, such signs would trigger immediate interventions, not through overt suppression, but through subtle recalibrations of the environment. Personalized content would shift to provide soothing narratives, recommended activities would steer individuals towards comforting routines, and social media feeds would be curated to present an overwhelmingly positive and harmonious view of the world. The algorithm becomes the unseen shepherd, guiding the flock away from the precipice of doubt and towards the pasture of contentment.

The Inquisitor's vision relied on the elimination of mystery, not in the sense of spiritual revelation, but in the sense of the unknown, the unpredictable element within human nature. He sought to replace divine mystery with human-imposed order. AI, by its very nature, seeks to reduce uncertainty. It thrives on data that can be quantified, on behaviors that can be categorized, and on outcomes that can be predicted. The more data an AI has, the more it can reduce the "mystery" of an individual. It can construct a digital twin, a data-driven representation of a person, that becomes increasingly accurate with every interaction. This digital twin, in the Inquisitor's logic, is the true object of management. The goal is not to understand the soul, but to control the observable manifestations of human will. By understanding the predictable patterns of our digital selves, the AI can subtly steer our actions, ensuring a smooth, predictable flow of existence, much like the Inquisitor envisioned for his flock.

The Grand Inquisitor spoke of offering "miracles" and "mystery" as a means of control. In his world, these were the tools of divine authority designed to awe and subdue. Today, the "miracles" are the technological marvels of AI – personalized recommendations that seem to divine our deepest desires, predictive text that anticipates our thoughts, and AI assistants that seamlessly integrate into our lives. The "mystery" has been replaced by an algorithmic opacity. We do not fully understand

*how* these systems arrive at their conclusions, only that they often seem to work. This lack of transparency, this "black box" nature of advanced AI, creates a form of modern mystery, one that inspires a similar kind of awe and dependence. Like the faithful of the Inquisitor's Church, we are increasingly willing to cede our judgment and trust in the pronouncements of the algorithm, accepting its curated reality as the definitive truth of our preferences and possibilities.

Furthermore, the Inquisitor understood that freedom of conscience was a dangerous burden. He wanted to relieve humanity of this onerous responsibility, to ensure that no one would be forced to grapple with the agonizing questions of morality or belief. AI offers a technologically sophisticated way to achieve this. By providing algorithmically determined "best practices" for everything from health and finance to relationships and career choices, AI can effectively outsource the process of ethical deliberation and decision-making. If an AI can predict the statistically optimal outcome for any given choice, why would an individual choose to grapple with the complexities of their own conscience? The algorithm, in this scenario, becomes the ultimate arbiter of right and wrong, of good and bad, not through divine revelation but through the cold, hard logic of data and probability. This leads to a profound reduction in the individual's capacity for independent moral reasoning, a core component of what we understand as individuality.

The very concept of uniqueness, the cornerstone of individuality, is threatened by the Inquisitor's dream, and by extension, by the pervasive influence of AI. The Inquisitor craved uniformity because variation bred dissent, and dissent led to suffering. He wanted a world where everyone thought alike, felt alike, and acted alike, all under the benevolent gaze of absolute authority. AI, with its drive for optimization and pattern recognition, tends to favor the common denominator. Recommendation engines push us towards popular trends, social media algorithms amplify prevailing sentiments, and predictive models are built on the bedrock of aggregated data, which by definition represents the typical, not the exceptional. The more we rely on these systems, the more we risk being nudged towards the average, the predictable, and the unremarkable. The algorithms are not designed to celebrate our eccentricities or to nurture our unique quirks; they are designed to serve the largest possible audience efficiently, thereby smoothing out the delightful, but often inefficient, contours of our individual personalities.

The Inquisitor's promise of "bread" can be seen as the satisfaction of material needs and desires. AI is increasingly adept at fulfilling this promise. It can optimize supply chains, personalize shopping experiences, and anticipate our consumption patterns with uncanny accuracy, ensuring that we always have what we "need" or "want" readily available. This hyper-efficient fulfillment of desires, however, can also serve to pacify and distract. When our material lives are perfectly managed, when our every comfort is anticipated and provided, the impetus for striving, for challenging ourselves, and for venturing beyond our immediate gratifications diminishes. This curated comfort, this effortless satisfaction, can become a gilded cage, rendering us contentedly passive and less inclined to question the system that provides it. We become like the well-fed citizens of the Inquisitor's ideal world, placid and untroubled, but ultimately dispossessed of the very agency that defines our humanity.

The argument that AI can lead to a world of uniformity, echoing the Grand Inquisitor's dream, is not an indictment of AI itself, but a call for critical awareness. The power of these systems lies in their ability to operate subtly, to shape our perceptions and behaviors without our conscious consent. They create a frictionless reality, a world where choices are pre-selected, pathways are optimized, and outcomes are predicted. In this frictionless environment, the very friction of individual thought, the resistance of personal will, and the exhilarating uncertainty of authentic choice are gradually eroded. The Inquisitor's triumph was to convince humanity that freedom was too heavy a burden. AI, in its quest for efficiency and optimization, has the potential to make freedom feel obsolete, a relic of a less predictable, less comfortable past. The dream of a perfectly managed, perfectly content, and perfectly uniform populace is no longer confined to the realm of theological allegory; it is becoming a tangible possibility, sculpted by the invisible hand of the algorithm, and driven by a logic eerily similar to that of the Grand Inquisitor. The challenge before us is to ensure that in our pursuit of convenience and order, we do not inadvertently surrender the very essence of what makes us uniquely human: our capacity for self-determination, our boundless potential for variation, and our unyielding, albeit often painful, freedom to choose.

The relentless march of artificial intelligence, while offering unprecedented efficiencies and conveniences, presents a subtle yet profound challenge to the very essence of human uniqueness. As algorithms become increasingly adept at predicting our behaviors, categorizing our preferences, and optimizing our experiences, there is a creeping tendency to view individuals not as complex, evolving beings, but as aggregations of quantifiable data points. This reductionist approach, as explored in the preceding sections, risks smoothing out the delightful, and often profound, idiosyncrasies that define us. The question that looms large, then, is how we can actively cultivate and preserve the unquantifiable aspects of human experience, the very elements that resist algorithmic capture and define our individual souls, in an era increasingly dominated by predictable patterns and optimized outcomes.

Our innate capacity for creativity, for instance, is a cornerstone of human individuality that often defies neat categorization. It is the spark of an unexpected idea, the unconventional juxtaposition of concepts, the sudden insight that emerges not from a logical progression of data, but from a deeply intuitive, sometimes even subconscious, process. An artist might spend years honing a technique, not for efficiency, but to achieve a particular emotional resonance; a scientist might pursue a seemingly irrational hypothesis that, against all odds, leads to a groundbreaking discovery. These acts of creation are not easily distilled into algorithms. While AI can generate novel combinations based on existing patterns, it struggles to replicate the sheer, unbidden originality that arises from the human spirit, a spirit often fueled by a lifetime of unique experiences, subtle observations, and a capacity for wonder. To value this unquantifiable creativity means actively seeking out and supporting endeavors that may not yield immediate, predictable returns. It means fostering environments where experimentation is encouraged, where failure is seen not as a statistical anomaly but as a learning opportunity, and where the pursuit of aesthetic or intellectual frontiers is celebrated, even when the path is unclear and the destination uncertain.

Similarly, empathy, the ability to understand and share the feelings of another, is a distinctly human attribute that is exceptionally difficult to quantify. While AI can be programmed to detect emotional cues in text or voice and respond with programmed expressions of sympathy, it does not *feel*. It does not experience the gut-wrenching sorrow of witnessing suffering, the profound joy of shared triumph, or the quiet comfort of genuine companionship. Empathy is born from lived experience, from the complex interplay of our own emotions and our capacity to project ourselves into the emotional landscape of others. It is this profound connection that allows for true understanding and builds the fabric of our social interactions. In a world that increasingly relies on digital communication and algorithmic intermediation, there is a danger that the practice of empathy may atrophy. Preserving this unquantifiable human trait requires conscious effort to prioritize face-to-face interactions, to engage in active listening, and to cultivate a deep and abiding respect for the subjective experiences of others, even when those experiences diverge significantly from our own. It means recognizing that the nuances of human suffering or elation cannot be fully captured by sentiment analysis software, and that true connection requires a vulnerability and presence that data alone cannot provide.

Spontaneity, the unplanned act, the deviation from the predetermined path, is another vital component of our individuality that AI tends to smooth over. Life is not a series of perfectly optimized choices; it is punctuated by moments of impulse, of unexpected detours, of serendipitous encounters. It is the sudden decision to take a different route home and discover a hidden gem of a café, the impulsive offer of assistance to a stranger, the unbidden burst of laughter at an unexpected joke. These unscripted moments inject vitality and richness into our lives, and they are inherently unpredictable. AI, by its very nature, seeks to eliminate unpredictability. Recommendation engines steer us towards what is statistically likely to please us, navigation apps guide us along the most efficient routes, and personalized schedules optimize our time for maximum productivity. While these tools offer undeniable benefits, an over-reliance on them can lead to a life that is perfectly ordered but curiously devoid of surprise and genuine discovery. Preserving spontaneity involves consciously carving out space for the unplanned, for unguided exploration, and for the embrace of the delightfully inefficient. It means resisting the urge to pre-plan every moment and allowing for the possibility of serendipity to unfold, recognizing that these unplanned moments are often the ones that lead to our most cherished memories and profoundest insights.

The unique perspective each individual brings to the world is perhaps the most elusive yet essential aspect of our individuality. It is shaped by a confluence of factors unique to each person: their genetic predispositions, their upbringing, their cultural background, their personal triumphs and tribulations, their evolving beliefs and values. This singular viewpoint informs how we interpret events, how we form opinions, and how we engage with the world around us. AI, however, is often trained on vast datasets that represent aggregated human experience, leading it to favor commonalities and predictable patterns. While AI can identify trends and probabilities, it struggles to grasp the subjective, deeply personal lens through which an individual experiences reality. The danger lies in the potential for algorithmic curation to inadvertently privilege certain perspectives while marginalizing others, creating echo chambers that reinforce dominant narratives and stifle the expression of minority or unconventional viewpoints. To preserve unique perspectives, we must actively seek out diverse voices, engage with ideas that challenge our own, and foster platforms that encourage open dialogue and respectful disagreement. It means understanding that true progress and a richer understanding of the world come not from unanimous agreement, but from the robust exchange of a multitude of perspectives, each colored by the author's individual journey.

The allure of perfect order, a world where every contingency is accounted for and every outcome is predictable, is a powerful one. It promises a life free from the anxieties of uncertainty, the pain of error, and the burden of difficult choices. This is the core of the Grand Inquisitor's seductive offer: comfort and security in exchange for the messy, often painful, freedom of self-determination. AI, with its unparalleled capacity for data analysis and prediction, can deliver on this promise to an unprecedented degree. It can manage our health, optimize our finances, curate our entertainment, and even suggest our social interactions, all in the pursuit of a frictionless existence. However, as we have explored, this frictionless existence comes at a cost. It risks diminishing our capacity for resilience, our ability to navigate adversity, and our appreciation for the hard-won victories that arise from overcoming challenges. Preserving individuality in the face of this pervasive quest for order requires a conscious recalibration of our values. It means recognizing that struggle is not merely an impediment to happiness, but an integral part of growth and character development. It means embracing imperfection, both in ourselves and in the systems we create, and understanding that true fulfillment often lies not in the absence of difficulty, but in our ability to confront and transcend it.

Cultivating environments that foster authentic individuality requires a multi-faceted approach, extending from individual choices to societal structures. On a personal level, this involves a commitment to self-awareness and intentionality. It means actively questioning the recommendations we receive, both digital and social, and making conscious choices that align with our own values and aspirations, rather than passively accepting algorithmic suggestions. It requires dedicating time to introspection, to creative pursuits, and to engaging with the world in ways that are meaningful to us as individuals, even if they are not the most efficient or popular. It means resisting the temptation to present a perfectly curated, data-optimized version of ourselves online and instead embracing the authenticity of our messy, evolving selves.

At a societal level, the preservation of individuality necessitates a critical examination of the technologies we develop and deploy. This includes advocating for transparency in algorithmic decision-making, ensuring that individuals have agency over their data, and promoting the development of AI systems that augment, rather than replace, human judgment and creativity. Educational institutions have a crucial role to play in fostering critical thinking skills, nurturing creativity, and instilling a deep appreciation for the humanities, which explore the complexities of the human condition in ways that data alone cannot capture. Public discourse needs to shift from a singular focus on efficiency and optimization to a more nuanced appreciation of the value of human uniqueness, resilience, and the unpredictable beauty of the unquantifiable. This might involve supporting artistic endeavors, protecting spaces for spontaneous human interaction, and celebrating diversity in all its forms, not as a statistical anomaly to be managed, but as the very source of our collective strength and innovation.

Ultimately, the challenge of preserving individuality in the age of AI is not merely a technological or philosophical one; it is a deeply human one. It calls for a renewed commitment to what makes us distinctly human: our capacity for independent thought, our boundless creativity, our profound capacity for empathy, and our inherent drive to explore the unknown. It requires us to actively resist the siren song of perfect order and predictable comfort, and to instead embrace the richness, the complexity, and the often-unforeseen beauty of a life lived authentically, with all its glorious, unquantifiable uniqueness. The Inquisitor's dream of a placid, uniform existence, while tempting in its promise of ease, ultimately leads to a diminishment of the human spirit. Our task, therefore, is to champion the vibrant, diverse mosaic of human experience, ensuring that in our pursuit of progress, we do not inadvertently erase the very qualities that make life worth living, and that make each of us, in our own inimitable way, truly alive.

# Chapter 12: The Resistance of Faith: Berdyaev and Algorithmic Determinism

Nicholas Berdyaev, a titan of Russian religious philosophy, offers a profound and enduring bulwark against the creeping tide of determinism, particularly as it manifests in algorithmic logic. His work, deeply rooted in existentialist thought and a fervent exploration of Christian spirituality, posits freedom not as an emergent property of complex systems or a consequence of environmental conditioning, but as an original, divinely bestowed spark within the human essence. For Berdyaev, freedom is not merely a capacity for choice; it is the very ground of being, an uncreated aspect of the human spirit, intrinsically linked to its divine origin. This primordial freedom, he argues, predates existence itself, emerging from the abyssal depths of God's being – a concept he termed "ungrund." It is from this uncreated source that the possibility of both good and evil arises, underscoring the radical nature of human liberty.

This radical freedom, however, is not a comfortable or easily managed faculty. Berdyaev unflinchingly confronts its tragic dimension. It is a freedom that carries the burden of responsibility, the terrifying potential for self-destruction, and the inherent vulnerability of a being cast into existence with the capacity to negate its own purpose. Unlike deterministic frameworks, which seek to explain human actions through predictable causal chains, Berdyaev emphasizes the gratuity of human existence and the inherent unpredictability that freedom introduces. The algorithmic quest for order and predictability, therefore, stands in direct opposition to Berdyaev's understanding of authentic human existence. Algorithms, by their very nature, operate on established patterns, on the predictable consequences of antecedent conditions. They seek to map, to model, and ultimately, to control through understanding these causal relationships. Berdyaev, however, insists that human freedom transcends such mappings. It is the ability to break free from causal necessity, to introduce an element of genuine novelty into the world, a novelty that cannot be fully accounted for by pre-existing data or logical extrapolation.

The inextricable link between freedom and creativity is central to Berdyaev's philosophy. For him, to be truly free is to be a creator. Creativity is not simply the production of art or music, but the fundamental act of bringing something new into being, of shaping one's own destiny and the world around us. This creative impulse, born from the wellspring of freedom, is what imbues human life with meaning and significance. It is the human spirit's response to the divine command to be, to shape, and to love. In an era where AI can generate novel content by recombining existing data in sophisticated ways, Berdyaev would likely argue that this is a form of sophisticated mimicry, not true creation. Authentic creativity, for Berdyaev, is not merely a process of synthesis; it is an act of existential affirmation, a declaration of selfhood that arises from the free spirit. It is the leap of faith, the intuitive insight, the courageous decision to forge a path where none existed before. This type of creation is inherently unpredictable, often born from moments of profound struggle and self-discovery, aspects that are inherently antithetical to the predictable, optimized outputs of algorithmic processes.

Furthermore, Berdyaev's philosophy underscores the concept of personal destiny as intertwined with freedom. While algorithms can predict probable outcomes based on aggregated data, they cannot fully grasp the unique, self-determined trajectory of an individual life. Each person, in Berdyaev's view, is called to realize their unique spiritual potential, a potential that is not predetermined but is actively shaped through the exercise of freedom. This self-creation is a lifelong process, marked by both triumphs and failures, by choices that affirm or deny one's true calling. The tragic element of this freedom lies in the fact that this destiny is not guaranteed. It can be renounced, betrayed, or never fully embraced.

The algorithm, seeking to optimize and predict, aims to eliminate such existential uncertainty, to smooth out the jagged edges of human experience. But in doing so, it risks flattening the very landscape where personal destiny is forged. Berdyaev would see this as a profound loss, a reduction of human life to a predictable, functional equation, devoid of the spiritual drama and the profound significance that arises from the struggle for self-realization.

Berdyaev's critique extends to the very notion of a predetermined human nature that algorithms implicitly rely upon. He rejects any essentialist definition of humanity that would reduce individuals to a set of predictable variables. Instead, he emphasizes the dynamic, evolving nature of the human spirit, its capacity for transcendence and self-transformation. Freedom, for Berdyaev, is the engine of this transformation. It is the faculty that allows us to break free from the chains of determinism, whether they be biological, social, or, in our current context, algorithmic. He would argue that attempts to predict and control human behavior through algorithms, while perhaps offering superficial efficiency, ultimately undermine the very essence of human dignity, which lies in our capacity for autonomous self-determination and spiritual growth. The "free spirit," as he called it, is the locus of authentic human existence, a spirit that can defy prediction and chart its own course, however perilous that course may be.

The philosophical struggle between Berdyaev's understanding of freedom and algorithmic determinism is, in essence, a struggle between two fundamental visions of reality. One vision, embraced by determinism and amplified by AI, sees the universe as a vast, intricate machine, governed by immutable laws, where every event is the inevitable consequence of prior causes. In this view, human beings are complex biological machines, their thoughts and actions ultimately reducible to electrochemical processes and environmental influences. The other vision, championed by Berdyaev, sees a universe infused with spirit, where human beings are not mere cogs in a cosmic clockwork, but spiritual agents endowed with the radical capacity for freedom. This freedom is not an illusion; it is the divine spark that allows for genuine novelty, for moral choice, and for the creation of meaning in a world that is not entirely predetermined.

Berdyaev's emphasis on the spiritual dimension of human existence is crucial here. He understood that the will to power, the desire for control and predictability, can be a seductive force, offering the illusion of mastery over the chaotic realities of life. Algorithmic systems, with their promise of optimization and efficiency, tap into this very desire. They offer to manage our lives, to shield us from uncertainty, and to guide us towards predetermined "optimal" outcomes. However, Berdyaev would caution that this quest for external control comes at the cost of internal freedom. By relinquishing our capacity for free choice and self-determination to algorithms, we risk diminishing our spiritual autonomy, becoming passive recipients of algorithmic directives rather than active agents in our own lives. The spiritual life, for Berdyaev, requires engagement with the difficult, the uncertain, and the morally ambiguous – precisely those aspects that deterministic systems seek to eliminate.

The existential angst that Berdyaev identified as an inherent part of the human condition, arising from the burden of freedom and the awareness of mortality, is something that algorithmic approaches often seek to alleviate. By predicting and mitigating risks, by optimizing experiences to maximize pleasure and minimize discomfort, AI systems can create a semblance of a frictionless life. But Berdyaev would argue that this is a false peace, a spiritual anesthesia. It is in confronting our fears, in wrestling with difficult choices, and in accepting the consequences of our actions that we truly grow and develop as spiritual beings. The "tragic" nature of freedom, which he so powerfully articulated, is not a flaw to be corrected but an essential characteristic of authentic human existence. It is through grappling with this tragic dimension that we discover our deepest strengths and our most profound reserves of spiritual resilience.

Therefore, Berdyaev's philosophical framework provides a vital counterpoint to the deterministic tendencies inherent in algorithmic thinking. His insistence on the uncreated, divine origin of freedom, its inextricable link to creativity, and its tragic yet essential role in shaping personal destiny offers a powerful affirmation of human agency and spiritual liberty. He reminds us that true human flourishing lies not in the elimination of uncertainty or the pursuit of perfect predictability, but in the courageous embrace of our freedom, in the ongoing act of self-creation, and in the profound responsibility that comes with being spiritual beings in a dynamic and unfolding universe. The digital age, with its ever-advancing algorithms, presents us with a profound challenge: to hold fast to the spiritual truth of our freedom, even as the world around us increasingly prioritizes calculability and control. Berdyaev's insights serve as a potent reminder that the most valuable aspects of our humanity are often those that defy algorithmic capture, those that are born from the free, creative, and ultimately, divinely-inspired spirit.

Algorithmic determinism posits a future where the intricate webs of data, analysis, and predictive modeling woven by artificial intelligence render human agency a mere illusion. It is the notion that as algorithms become more sophisticated, their capacity to forecast and subtly influence our decisions, opportunities, and even our very perceptions of reality will lead to a preordained existence. This is not a crude, brute-force imposition of will, but rather a pervasive, almost invisible steering mechanism. Imagine a world where every job application is first filtered by an AI that assesses suitability based on a vast dataset of successful employees, implicitly penalizing candidates who deviate from established patterns. The "opportunity" to even be considered for a role becomes dependent on conforming to algorithmic ideals, making the subsequent success or failure seem like an inevitable outcome of the initial algorithmic assessment, rather than a reflection of individual merit or a series of independent choices.

The impact of algorithmic determinism extends far beyond career prospects. Consider the curated information feeds that bombard us daily. Social media algorithms, search engine results, and news aggregation platforms are designed to deliver content that aligns with our past behaviors and preferences. While this personalization can feel convenient, it also creates echo chambers, reinforcing existing beliefs and limiting exposure to dissenting viewpoints or alternative perspectives. When our information diet is algorithmically controlled, our understanding of the world, our opinions, and our very capacity for critical thought can be subtly shaped. The "choice" of what to believe or how to react then becomes an almost foregone conclusion, dictated by the curated stream of data we are fed. This creates a powerful illusion of inevitability: if we are constantly shown evidence that supports a particular viewpoint, and rarely exposed to counterarguments, our eventual adoption of that viewpoint can feel like an unavoidable consequence of the information we have encountered, rather than a result of genuine intellectual engagement and free deliberation. The algorithm, in essence, predetermines the landscape of our intellectual and emotional lives, making deviation appear increasingly difficult, if not impossible.

Furthermore, the predictive power of algorithms extends to areas that touch upon our most intimate decisions and social interactions. Consider the rise of AI-driven matchmaking services, which promise to find the "perfect" partner based on vast datasets of compatibility. While these tools can offer a starting point, the underlying assumption is that human connection can be reduced to a series of quantifiable metrics, and that the outcome of a relationship is largely determined by these algorithmic calculations. If an algorithm suggests a highly probable match, and the individuals in question proceed with the relationship, any subsequent happiness or unhappiness might be retroactively attributed to the algorithm's accuracy, creating a sense of preordained destiny. The possibility of a spontaneous, serendipitous connection that defies algorithmic prediction, or the profound personal growth that can come from navigating the complexities of an imperfect relationship, is diminished in this deterministic framework. The algorithm, in its attempt to optimize for success, inadvertently removes the element of genuine human struggle, growth, and the unpredictable beauty of authentic connection, presenting a predetermined path as the only viable one.

The pervasive nature of algorithmic decision-making in credit scoring, insurance risk assessment, and even judicial sentencing further solidifies this sense of predetermination. If an algorithm flags an individual as a high credit risk based on factors that are beyond their immediate control or understanding, their future access to essential resources like loans or mortgages can be severely curtailed. This creates a cycle where past algorithmic judgments become self-fulfilling prophecies, limiting future opportunities and reinforcing existing inequalities. The individual's choices and efforts to improve their situation might be rendered moot by the indelible algorithmic mark. Similarly, in the legal system, predictive policing algorithms or sentencing recommendations, while aiming for efficiency and objectivity, can inadvertently perpetuate systemic biases, leading individuals down a path of predetermined negative outcomes based on statistical correlations rather than individual culpability or potential for rehabilitation. The illusion of inevitability is amplified when individuals perceive their life trajectory as being dictated by opaque computational processes that seem to operate with an unassailable, almost divine, authority.

This perceived inevitability poses a significant challenge to our understanding of human freedom and responsibility. If our choices are increasingly influenced, guided, or even dictated by algorithms, where does genuine agency reside? The very fabric of our societies, built upon the assumption of individual choice and accountability, begins to fray. The deterministic lens of algorithms can lead to a passive acceptance of outcomes, a belief that one's fate is sealed by the data points that define them. This can foster a sense of learned helplessness, where individuals become resigned to their algorithmic destinies, ceasing to strive for change or challenge the systems that appear to govern their lives. The potential for human creativity, innovation, and spontaneous acts of defiance or kindness – those unpredictable elements that have historically driven societal progress and personal fulfillment – risks being stifled by the overwhelming pressure towards algorithmic conformity.

The illusion of inevitability generated by algorithmic determinism is particularly insidious because it often masquerades as objectivity and efficiency. We are told that algorithms are merely reflecting patterns in the data, that they are rational and unbiased tools for making better decisions. However, this overlooks the fact that data itself is a product of human history, imbued with existing biases and inequalities. Algorithms trained on this data can, therefore, amplify and perpetuate these very biases, creating a feedback loop of determinism. The "inevitable" outcomes are not necessarily natural or fair, but rather the predictable consequences of a system that has been constructed with inherent, often invisible, limitations. The more we rely on these systems, the more their predetermined pathways become normalized, and the harder it becomes to imagine or forge alternative routes. This gradual erosion of perceived freedom, masked by the veneer of technological progress, represents a profound existential challenge, one that calls into question the very essence of what it means to be a self-determining agent in the modern world. The sophisticated, data-driven nudges and predictions that shape our lives are not merely predicting the future; they are actively constructing it, weaving a fabric of predetermined outcomes that can appear, to the individual caught within its threads, to be utterly unavoidable. This necessitates a deep philosophical engagement with the nature of freedom in an increasingly algorithmic age, a wrestling with the uncomfortable truth that the boundaries of our choices may be far more constricted than we are willing to admit. The illusion of inevitability, once firmly established, can become a self-fulfilling prophecy, shaping not just our external circumstances but our internal perception of what is possible.

In the face of an encroaching algorithmic determinism, where every facet of existence appears to be mapped, quantified, and predicted, the concept of faith emerges not as a passive acceptance of divine will, but as a radical act of rebellion. This is particularly true when we consider faith through the lens of thinkers like Nikolai Berdyaev, who championed human freedom as a divine spark, an irreducible element that transcends the chains of causality and necessity. For Berdyaev, freedom is not merely the ability to choose between predefined options, but a primordial, uncreated capacity that precedes being itself. It is the very ground of our existence, the source from which all creativity and genuine choice spring. This notion of freedom stands in stark opposition to the deterministic worldview fostered by algorithmic systems, which seek to reduce human beings to predictable sequences of data, governed by calculable probabilities.

Faith, in this context, becomes an assertion of this primal freedom, a courageous leap into the unknown that defies the cold logic of algorithms. It is the profound recognition that not all of reality can be reduced to data points and mathematical functions, nor can the human spirit be contained within the confines of predictive models. Algorithmic determinism thrives on predictability; it seeks to eliminate surprise, to iron out the wrinkles of contingency, and to present a future that is, in essence, already written. Faith, conversely, embraces the unforeseen, the miraculous, and the possibility of radical transformation that lies beyond the realm of empirical observation and computational prediction. It is a spiritual orientation that acknowledges a dimension of reality that is not subject to the laws of physics or the calculations of machines. When an algorithm predicts a certain outcome based on past behavior, faith chooses to believe in the possibility of a different future, one shaped by a power that transcends statistical analysis. This is not to deny the efficacy of algorithms in their domain, but to assert that the human spirit, at its core, operates on a different plane, one that is not subject to deterministic mandates.

The core of this rebellion lies in faith's embrace of the irreducible mystery of human existence. Algorithmic determinism, by its very nature, aims to demystify and demythologize, to explain away the inexplicable through the cold, hard logic of data. It attempts to render human actions and motivations as mere outputs of complex input variables. Faith, however, recognizes that there are dimensions of human experience that resist such reduction. Love, sacrifice, acts of spontaneous kindness, creative leaps of imagination – these are not easily quantifiable, nor are they readily predictable by even the most sophisticated algorithms. Faith posits that there is an inherent value and potential within the human person that cannot be fully captured by analyzing their past digital footprint or predicting their future behavior based on statistical correlations. It is an affirmation of the immeasurable worth of the individual soul, a worth that transcends the sum of their data points.

Consider the act of forgiveness, a cornerstone of many faith traditions. An algorithm, designed to optimize for efficiency or retribution, might deem forgiveness as an illogical or detrimental choice. It might calculate the costs and benefits, the likelihood of recidivism, and conclude that a punitive approach is more rational. Faith, however, posits forgiveness as a higher form of freedom, a choice that can break cycles of violence and resentment, opening up the possibility of redemption and transformation. This act of choosing to extend grace, even when it appears irrational from a purely deterministic standpoint, is a potent form of rebellion against a system that seeks to calculate and control every outcome. It is a testament to the human capacity for transcending predetermined responses, for choosing a path that, while perhaps difficult, ultimately affirms a deeper, more spiritual truth.

Furthermore, faith actively cultivates an openness to the "not-yet-realized," a concept that directly challenges the calculable future promised by algorithmic determinism. While algorithms project a future based on extrapolation of present and past data, faith looks towards a future that is actively being created, a future that is not simply a foregone conclusion. This is a future that is infused with potential, with the possibility of divine intervention, or of radical human choice that can alter the course of events in ways that are fundamentally unpredictable. This orientation towards a dynamic, unwritten future is an essential component of spiritual freedom. It means that we are not simply passive recipients of a predetermined destiny, but active co-creators of our reality, guided by principles and possibilities that lie beyond the scope of algorithmic prediction. This creative impulse, this inherent human drive to bring something new into existence, is the very antithesis of determinism, which seeks to limit novelty and constrain emergence.

Berdyaev's philosophy of creativity is deeply intertwined with this idea. He argued that creativity is the expression of freedom, the act by which the uncreated becomes manifest. When we create, whether it be a work of art, a new idea, or a profound personal transformation, we are engaging in an act that is fundamentally free and unpredictable. Algorithmic determinism, with its emphasis on pattern recognition and prediction, seeks to homogenize and commodify creativity, to reduce it to a series of algorithmic processes that can be replicated or optimized. Faith, on the other hand, celebrates the unique and irreplicable nature of genuine creation, recognizing it as a testament to the divine spark within humanity. The artist who defies artistic conventions, the scientist who pursues a radical hypothesis, the individual who chooses a path of selfless service against all odds – these are all acts of faith, assertions of a freedom that algorithms cannot comprehend, let alone replicate.

The very act of prayer, central to many faith traditions, can be understood as an act of rebellion against algorithmic determinism. Prayer is not necessarily about requesting a specific outcome that the algorithm might predict as unfavorable; rather, it is about communion, about aligning one's will with a higher purpose, and about seeking guidance and strength beyond the confines of one's own limited understanding and predictive capacity. It is an acknowledgement that there are forces at play in the universe that are not subject to human calculation, and that true wisdom and fulfillment may lie in surrendering to these forces rather than attempting to master them through technological means. In a world increasingly driven by the illusion of control through data, prayer offers a different kind of engagement, one that is characterized by humility, trust, and an embrace of the ineffable. It is a refusal to let our spiritual lives be dictated by the metrics and predictions of the digital realm.

Moreover, faith offers a powerful antidote to the existential ennui that can arise from the feeling of being perpetually observed and predicted by algorithmic systems. When every action, every preference, every potential choice is logged, analyzed, and used to shape our future, a sense of being trapped can emerge. Faith, by its very nature, calls us to look beyond the immediate and the quantifiable, to seek meaning and purpose in something larger than ourselves. It provides a framework for understanding suffering, for finding hope in despair, and for experiencing love and connection in ways that transcend the superficiality of data-driven interactions. This is not to say that faith is a panacea, but it offers a spiritual resilience that can withstand the pressures of a deterministic worldview. It reminds us that our true selves are not defined by our data profiles, but by our capacity for love, compassion, and transcendence.

The notion of grace, a central tenet in many theological frameworks, is particularly potent in this context. Grace is understood as unmerited favor, a divine gift that is not earned or predicted based on one's actions or perceived worth. It is an act of pure generosity that intervenes in the deterministic flow of cause and effect, offering transformation and redemption where none might be logically expected. In the face of algorithmic systems that meticulously track and reward or penalize based on predictable criteria, grace stands as a radical affirmation of a different order of reality. It suggests that human worth and potential are not contingent upon our ability to conform to algorithmic expectations, but are inherent and divinely bestowed. This concept of grace directly challenges the idea that our destinies are sealed by the data that defines us, offering instead the possibility of a radical, unpredicted turning point.

This rebellion of faith is not about a denial of reality, but about a reinterpretation of it. It acknowledges the power and pervasiveness of algorithms but refuses to grant them ultimate authority over the human spirit. It insists that there is a realm of meaning, purpose, and freedom that lies beyond the reach of even the most advanced computational systems. This is a vital distinction. Faith does not dismiss the practical applications of algorithms in areas like medicine, logistics, or scientific research. Instead, it critiques the extension of algorithmic logic into the fundamental questions of human existence, value, and destiny. It argues that when we allow algorithms to dictate our understanding of ourselves, our relationships, and our future, we risk diminishing our humanity and sacrificing the very qualities that make life meaningful.

Ultimately, faith as rebellion against algorithmic determinism is an act of hope. It is the belief that despite the overwhelming evidence of predictable patterns and the seemingly inescapable logic of cause and effect, the human spirit retains an irreducible freedom. It is the conviction that genuine choice, creativity, and transformation are possible, not as exceptions to the rule, but as fundamental aspects of our being, endowed by a source that lies beyond the predictable. This embrace of the unknown, this courageous step into the unwritten future, is the hallmark of a faith that refuses to be confined by the deterministic algorithms of the present. It is a testament to the enduring power of the human spirit to transcend its circumstances and to assert its inherent freedom, even in the face of seemingly insurmountable deterministic forces. The resistance of faith, therefore, is not a futile gesture against the march of technology, but a profound assertion of what it means to be truly human in an age increasingly defined by the calculable and the predictable. It is a spiritual technology, if you will, that allows us to navigate the complexities of the modern world without sacrificing our essential freedom and our capacity for wonder.

The human capacity for conscience and the yearning for transcendence represent a profound challenge to the all-encompassing claims of algorithmic determinism. While artificial intelligence, in its relentless pursuit of predictive accuracy, seeks to model and control every aspect of our existence, it fundamentally falters when confronted with the deep wellsprings of our moral intuition and our innate drive towards something *more*. These are not merely anomalies in the data, but rather the very essence of what distinguishes human consciousness and agency, providing a potent, albeit often unarticulated, form of resistance to a world reduced to calculable logic.

Conscience, in its most fundamental sense, is the inner voice that guides us toward moral action. It is the faculty that allows us to discern right from wrong, not through a cold calculation of outcomes or a probabilistic analysis of past behaviors, but through a deeply felt, often immediate, apprehension of value. This moral compass is not a static set of rules programmed into our being; rather, it is a dynamic, responsive element that can evolve, be refined, and sometimes even compel us to act against our own perceived self-interest or the dictates of statistical probability. An algorithm might be programmed with ethical guidelines, but these are derived from existing human norms and data, reflecting what *has been* or what *is considered* ethical. Conscience, however, possesses the capacity for genuine moral innovation, for recognizing a moral imperative that transcends existing frameworks. Consider situations where an algorithm might predict a course of action that is statistically beneficial or least likely to cause harm according to historical data, yet an individual's conscience rebels against it. This could be the whistleblower who, knowing the personal cost and low probability of success, exposes wrongdoing; or the caregiver who dedicates their life to an individual deemed by society as beyond help, driven by a profound sense of duty that defies pragmatic calculation. These acts are not born of logical deduction but of an inner conviction, a moral "ought" that resonates from within. Algorithmic systems, built on patterns and correlations, can learn to *mimic* ethical behavior, but they cannot possess the lived, internal experience of moral deliberation and the attendant emotional weight. The guilt experienced by violating one's conscience, or the quiet satisfaction of acting in accordance with it, are subjective realities that lie outside the purview of computational analysis.

Furthermore, conscience is intrinsically linked to empathy and the recognition of the inherent dignity of others. It is this capacity that allows us to feel the suffering of another, not as a data point indicating a need for intervention, but as a shared human experience that calls for compassion. Algorithms can be trained to identify distress signals, to flag individuals in need, but they cannot

*feel* compassion. They can optimize resource allocation for humanitarian aid, but they cannot experience the moral ache that drives a person to offer comfort or sacrifice for a stranger. The nuances of human interaction, the unspoken understanding between individuals, the subtle cues that signal genuine connection – these are the very things that algorithmic logic struggles to penetrate. The ethical decisions we make are often deeply personal, informed by our unique histories, relationships, and values. While algorithms can process vast amounts of data to suggest a "best" course of action, they cannot account for the immeasurable weight of a single life, the unique context of a particular suffering, or the profound value that individuals place on their autonomy and inherent worth. Conscience, in this sense, serves as a bulwark against the reduction of human beings to mere variables in a grand equation. It insists that each individual possesses an inviolable dignity that cannot be quantified or traded away, a dignity that calls for a response that is more than merely efficient or logically sound.

Closely intertwined with conscience is the human capacity for transcendence – the yearning to reach beyond the immediate, the material, and the finite, towards something greater. This can manifest in myriad ways: through spiritual seeking, artistic creation, the pursuit of knowledge for its own sake, or the dedication to causes that extend beyond personal gain. These drives are often characterized by a willingness to embrace uncertainty, to pursue ideals that may never be fully realized, and to find meaning in that which cannot be empirically verified or computationally predicted. Algorithmic systems, by their very design, are focused on the observable, the measurable, and the predictable. They excel at optimizing within defined parameters, at achieving specific, quantifiable goals. However, they are ill-equipped to understand or facilitate the human impulse towards the transcendent, which often involves venturing into the unknown, embracing ambiguity, and seeking fulfillment in intangible realms.

Consider the act of artistic creation. While AI can generate aesthetically pleasing images or compose musical pieces based on learned patterns, it cannot replicate the profound human drive to express an inner vision, to grapple with existential questions through art, or to evoke deep emotional responses in an audience. The artist's struggle, their moments of inspiration, their wrestling with the medium – these are deeply personal and often inexplicable processes that are fueled by a desire to communicate something ineffable, something that transcends the purely rational. Similarly, the scientific pursuit of pure knowledge, the drive to understand the universe for the sake of understanding, even when it offers no immediate practical application, speaks to a transcendent impulse. The contemplation of cosmic mysteries, the striving for philosophical insight, the search for ultimate meaning – these are endeavors that lie beyond the scope of algorithmic utility. They are driven by a deep-seated human need to connect with something larger than oneself, to find one's place in a grander narrative, or to simply marvel at the complexity and beauty of existence.

Spiritual seeking, in its diverse forms, is perhaps the most explicit manifestation of the transcendent impulse. The desire for communion with the divine, the practice of prayer, the quest for enlightenment – these are all rooted in the belief that there is a reality that lies beyond the physical and the empirical. Faith, in this context, is not a statistical probability; it is a wager on the unseen, a commitment to a reality that defies measurement. While algorithms can analyze religious texts or predict patterns of religious adherence, they cannot grasp the lived experience of faith, the solace it offers in times of suffering, or the transformative power it can have on an individual's life. The human search for meaning in a seemingly indifferent universe, the desire to connect with something eternal, is a fundamental aspect of our being that algorithms cannot satisfy or even fully comprehend. They can provide information, but they cannot offer the transcendent meaning that humans crave.

Moreover, the very concept of purpose, when it extends beyond mere functional utility, hints at this transcendent dimension. We seek not just to

*do* but to *be*, to find significance in our lives that resonates beyond our immediate actions or quantifiable achievements. This is the drive that leads individuals to dedicate themselves to service, to advocate for justice, to strive for self-improvement not for external reward, but for the intrinsic value of the act itself. These are acts of free will informed by deeply held values and a vision of a better world, a vision that often emerges from a place of moral and spiritual intuition rather than algorithmic prediction. The capacity to set goals that are not directly tied to immediate survival or material gain, but to ideals of goodness, beauty, or truth, is a testament to our ability to transcend the purely material and functional.

The algorithmic paradigm, which thrives on predictability and optimization, struggles to accommodate the inherent uncertainty and subjective richness of these transcendent experiences. It can catalog desires, predict preferences, and even simulate emotional responses, but it cannot replicate the raw, authentic experience of awe before a starlit sky, the profound sense of connection felt during moments of deep contemplation, or the courage to pursue a noble ideal against all odds. These are the moments when the human spirit asserts its freedom, its capacity to reach for the stars, even when the algorithms have calculated the lowest probability of success. This inherent drive towards transcendence is not a glitch in the human operating system; it is a feature, a vital aspect of our being that enables us to grow, to create, and to find meaning in a universe that often defies easy explanation. It is the wellspring of our greatest aspirations and the silent resistance to a world that seeks to reduce us to predictable data streams.

The relentless march of artificial intelligence presents humanity with a profound existential challenge, one that calls for a reawakening and active defense of our spiritual core. As algorithmic systems become increasingly sophisticated, capable of predicting, influencing, and even automating vast swathes of human experience, they inherently push us towards a state of passive receptivity, a calculated existence governed by predictable outcomes. This is the specter of algorithmic determinism that Nikolai Berdyaev so presciently warned against, a form of societal control that operates not through overt coercion, but through the subtle, insidious imposition of a rationalized, predictable framework upon the inherently free and creative nature of human existence. In this unfolding era, the imperative is not merely intellectual or ethical; it is fundamentally spiritual. We must actively cultivate and assert our spiritual freedom, recognizing that true human flourishing lies not in the seamless management of our lives by code, but in our capacity for free, unpredictable, and creative engagement with the world, guided by the inner compass of conscience and the transcendent aspirations of faith.

Berdyaev's philosophy, with its emphasis on freedom as the ultimate existential reality and the source of human dignity, offers a vital counterpoint to the burgeoning logic of AI. He argued that humanity is not a mere product of its environment, nor a predictable automaton governed by deterministic forces, but a being endowed with the radical capacity for self-creation and choice. This freedom, however, is not without its burden; it is often found in the very struggle against necessity, in the unpredictable leaps of faith, and in the moral choices that defy easy calculation. AI, in its essence, seeks to eliminate such struggle, to smooth out the rough edges of human existence by predicting and preempting our needs and desires. It offers a world of optimized comfort, of frictionless interaction, and of guaranteed outcomes. Yet, it is precisely in the friction, the uncertainty, and the possibility of failure that the essence of human freedom and creativity is forged. To embrace a life entirely managed by algorithms is to abdicate this essential freedom, to become a creature of predictable inputs and outputs, rather than a subject capable of genuine self-determination and transcendent aspiration.

The spiritual imperative, therefore, lies in our conscious refusal to be wholly subsumed by the algorithmic paradigm. It demands that we recognize and nurture those aspects of our being that lie beyond the purview of computational analysis: our capacity for love that defies logic, our acts of altruism that offer no calculable reward, our artistic expressions that tap into ineffable truths, and our spiritual quests that seek meaning in the unseen. These are not mere historical footnotes to be preserved in a digital archive; they are the living forces that define our humanity. Conscience, as explored previously, is not a mere subroutine for ethical decision-making; it is the echo of a divine spark within us, a faculty that allows us to discern not just what is permissible, but what is *good*, even when the data suggests otherwise. Faith, in its most profound sense, is not a statistical anomaly but a radical affirmation of a reality that transcends the empirical, a testament to our innate yearning for a dimension of existence that algorithms, by their very nature, cannot access or comprehend.

The danger of algorithmic determinism is that it offers a seductive illusion of control and predictability, a promise of a life free from error and suffering, but at the cost of our essential liberty. It seeks to define us by our past behaviors, our genetic predispositions, and our observable patterns, thereby flattening the rich system of human potential into a predictable data set. Berdyaev, in his exploration of "the abyss of freedom," understood that genuine existence arises from this very unpredictability, from the ability to choose a path that is not dictated by necessity, but by an inner calling or a moral conviction. AI, in its quest for perfect prediction, inadvertently seeks to close off this abyss, to transform the fertile ground of human possibility into a sterile, perfectly managed landscape.

To resist this spiritual erosion, we must actively engage in practices that cultivate our inner life and affirm our freedom. This can manifest in various ways, not necessarily through overt acts of rebellion, but through conscious choices in our daily lives. It involves prioritizing experiences that foster introspection and self-awareness, engaging with art and literature that challenge our preconceptions and speak to the depths of the human condition, and participating in communities that value genuine human connection over transactional interaction. It means recognizing the inherent limitations of algorithmic solutions when applied to the complex, often messy, realities of human relationships, moral dilemmas, and spiritual yearning.

Consider the realm of creativity. While AI can generate novel forms of art and music, it does so by analyzing and remixing existing patterns. The human artist, on the other hand, draws from a wellspring of personal experience, emotion, and intuition, often producing works that are profoundly original precisely because they are born from a unique, subjective engagement with the world. This creative impulse, this drive to bring something new into being, is a direct manifestation of our freedom. To delegate creative endeavors entirely to AI would be to sever ourselves from one of the most fundamental expressions of our humanity, to trade the soul of creation for the efficiency of replication.

Similarly, in the domain of human relationships, algorithms can suggest potential partners, optimize communication, and even provide advice on navigating social interactions. However, they cannot replicate the spontaneous, often irrational, yet deeply meaningful connections that form the bedrock of human intimacy. Love, compassion, forgiveness – these are not programmable qualities. They are the products of free choice, of vulnerability, and of a willingness to engage with another person in their full, unpredictable humanity. A spiritual imperative in the age of AI, therefore, compels us to safeguard the sanctity of these unquantifiable human bonds, to resist the temptation to reduce complex interpersonal dynamics to a series of data points and predicted outcomes.

The spiritual imperative also calls for a critical examination of the narratives that AI systems propagate. Algorithms are trained on vast datasets, which inevitably reflect the biases and assumptions of the societies that generated them. If we allow these systems to become the primary arbiters of truth and value, we risk entrenching existing inequalities and limiting our collective imagination. Berdyaev's emphasis on the active, creative role of the individual in shaping reality becomes crucial here. We must retain the capacity to question, to dissent, and to propose alternative visions, even when they are not statistically favored or algorithmically validated. Our spiritual freedom is inextricably linked to our intellectual freedom, our ability to think critically and to imagine possibilities that lie beyond the confines of our current data.

The pursuit of knowledge itself takes on a new dimension in this context. AI can process and disseminate information with unparalleled speed and efficiency. However, the human quest for wisdom, for understanding that goes beyond mere factual recall, is a spiritual endeavor. It involves contemplation, reflection, and the integration of knowledge into a meaningful personal framework. The act of seeking truth, of wrestling with complex ideas, and of forming our own convictions is a fundamental aspect of spiritual development. To rely solely on algorithmic curation of knowledge risks turning us into passive recipients of information, rather than active seekers of truth.

The concept of "meaning" is also profoundly threatened by algorithmic determinism. AI can be programmed to optimize for happiness, for productivity, or for comfort, but these are often superficial proxies for genuine fulfillment. True meaning, as Berdyaev suggested, is often found in the struggle for something greater than oneself, in the pursuit of ideals, and in the acceptance of suffering as an integral part of the human experience. It is in these moments of existential grappling, of confronting our finitude and our freedom, that we often discover the deepest sources of meaning. Algorithms, designed to eliminate struggle and uncertainty, may inadvertently eliminate the very conditions under which true meaning can be found.

Therefore, the spiritual imperative is not a call to reject technology outright, but to approach it with a discerning consciousness, to employ it as a tool rather than a master. It is to recognize that while AI can assist us in many practical ways, it cannot provide us with the essence of what it means to be human. That essence lies in our freedom, our creativity, our capacity for love and compassion, and our enduring spiritual yearning. These are the qualities that algorithms cannot replicate, and that we must actively cultivate and defend.

In essence, the challenge posed by algorithmic determinism is a spiritual one, calling us to reaffirm our inherent dignity and freedom against the seductive logic of predictable comfort. It requires us to engage in the active, conscious practice of what it means to be truly alive, to be free, and to be human. This involves nurturing our conscience, embracing the unpredictable nature of creation, cherishing the unquantifiable bonds of human connection, and continuing our perpetual search for meaning and transcendence. It is in these acts of spiritual affirmation, in our resolute commitment to the unpredictable, the uncalculable, and the deeply human, that we will find our truest resistance to the encroaching shadow of algorithmic determinism and forge a future that honors the boundless potential of the human spirit. The choices we make today, in how we integrate these powerful new technologies into our lives, will ultimately determine whether we become mere conduits for algorithmic processes or remain vibrant, free, and spiritually alive beings. This is the core of the spiritual imperative: to ensure that our future is one of human flourishing, guided by the wisdom of our inner lives, rather than a sterile testament to algorithmic efficiency.

# Chapter 13: Religion and Authority in the Digital Panopticon

For millennia, the very architecture of human societies has been profoundly shaped by the presence of religious belief systems. Far from being mere private matters of individual conscience, these faiths have historically served as foundational pillars upon which social order, moral consensus, and the very legitimacy of authority were constructed. This deep symbiosis between religion and governance is not a relic of a distant, unenlightened past; rather, it is a potent historical force whose echoes resonate even in our hyper-modern, data-driven world, offering crucial insights as we navigate the complex relationship between faith, control, and the digital panopticon.

Across diverse cultures and eras, religious institutions have provided indispensable frameworks for moral guidance. They have articulated cosmologies that imbue human actions with ultimate meaning, establishing clear distinctions between right and wrong, virtuous and sinful. These moral codes, often perceived as divinely ordained, carried a weight and authority that secular laws alone could rarely achieve. They dictated not only prohibitions against theft or violence but also prescribed duties towards family, community, and the divine. This provided a shared ethical vocabulary, a common understanding of what constituted good behavior and what threatened the collective well-being. Such moral frameworks were essential for fostering trust and cooperation within communities, laying the groundwork for stable social structures. The rituals, ceremonies, and communal worship associated with these religions further reinforced these shared values, binding individuals together through collective experiences of transcendence and communal identity. From the ancient Mesopotamian city-states, where priestly classes wielded significant influence over governance and law, to the medieval European kingdoms, where the Church's pronouncements held sway over kings and commoners alike, religion provided the bedrock of societal cohesion.

Beyond moral instruction, religions have historically been potent engines of social cohesion. They created and sustained communities, providing a sense of belonging and shared purpose that transcended individual differences. Shared rituals, sacred texts, and communal spaces fostered a collective identity, reinforcing group solidarity. In times of hardship or uncertainty, religious institutions often served as vital social safety nets, providing charity, education, and solace. This capacity to bind people together, to create a sense of "us" against the backdrop of a wider world, was instrumental in the formation and maintenance of stable polities. The early Christian communities, for instance, with their emphasis on mutual support and shared faith, demonstrated an extraordinary capacity for growth and social integration in the face of adversity. Similarly, the intricate social hierarchies and communal obligations found in many traditional Islamic societies were deeply intertwined with religious precepts, fostering a sense of shared responsibility and collective identity.

Furthermore, religious authority has frequently been inextricably linked with secular power. In many historical societies, rulers derived their legitimacy from divine sanction. Kings were often seen as God's chosen representatives on Earth, their authority therefore unquestionable by mortal decree. This divine right of kings, a concept that persisted for centuries in Europe, exemplifies how religious ideology could be harnessed to bolster and legitimize political power. The fusion of religious and political leadership was also common in ancient Egypt, where the Pharaoh was considered a divine being, and in many indigenous societies where spiritual leaders often held significant political sway. Even in societies where the separation of powers was more pronounced, religious institutions often exerted considerable influence over the ruling elite through their moral authority and their control over public discourse.

Religious scholars and clergy often served as advisors, scribes, and educators to the powerful, shaping policy and reinforcing the prevailing social order through the lens of religious doctrine. The intricate relationship between the Papacy and the Holy Roman Emperors in medieval Europe, marked by periods of both cooperation and conflict, highlights the profound intertwining of religious and political authority, where excommunication could be a potent political weapon and papal approval could legitimize imperial claims.

This historical nexus between religion and authority is not merely an academic curiosity. It provides a crucial lens through which to understand the potential dynamics of authority in the digital age. The digital realm, with its pervasive surveillance capabilities and its capacity for algorithmic manipulation, presents new forms of power and control. Just as historical religions provided frameworks for moral understanding and social cohesion, digital platforms, through their algorithms and data collection, are increasingly shaping our perceptions, behaviors, and even our moral compasses. The historical examples of religious institutions exerting influence over societal norms and legitimizing authority can serve as cautionary tales and analytical frameworks as we consider how emergent digital authorities might operate.

Consider the enforcement of norms. Religious doctrines provided clear guidelines for behavior, and religious institutions often possessed mechanisms for enforcing these norms, ranging from communal shaming and excommunication to more severe forms of punishment dictated by religious law. The Inquisition, a historical institution within the Catholic Church, serves as a stark example of how religious authority could be used to enforce ideological conformity through coercive means. While the digital panopticon does not typically involve religious persecution in its overt form, it does employ sophisticated methods of surveillance and behavioral modification. Social credit systems, for instance, which are emerging in some nations, utilize data aggregation to score citizens based on their adherence to state-defined norms and behaviors. This algorithmic enforcement, while ostensibly secular, functions in a manner analogous to historical religious mechanisms for norm enforcement, leveraging data to reward conformity and penalize deviation. The "chilling effect" of constant surveillance, where individuals self-censor their behavior and expressions for fear of negative algorithmic consequences, mirrors the self-policing that often occurred in societies where religious norms were strictly enforced.

Moreover, the narrative control historically wielded by religious institutions finds a parallel in the curated information ecosystems of the digital age. Religious texts, sermons, and pronouncements shaped the collective understanding of reality, history, and morality. Interpretation of scripture was often tightly controlled by established religious authorities, ensuring a consistent message and reinforcing the existing power structures. Today, digital platforms curate the information we consume through sophisticated algorithms. These algorithms, designed to maximize engagement, can inadvertently create echo chambers and filter bubbles, presenting users with content that confirms their existing beliefs and biases. This selective presentation of information can shape public opinion, influence political discourse, and subtly dictate what is considered acceptable or even "true." The historical role of religious authorities in defining truth and morality is thus mirrored in the algorithmic shaping of our digital reality. The selective amplification of certain narratives and the suppression of others by social media platforms, for instance, can have a profound impact on collective understanding and social cohesion, much like the pronouncements of religious leaders in bygone eras.

The concept of "sin" in religious traditions often represented a transgression against divine law that imperiled not only the individual soul but also the community's spiritual well-being. This concept provided a powerful motivation for adherence to moral codes. In the digital age, while the language may be different, the underlying principle of transgression and its consequences remains. "Digital sin" could be seen as actions that violate data privacy, spread misinformation, or engage in online harassment, all of which can have detrimental effects on individuals and society. The platforms themselves, through their terms of service and content moderation policies, act as arbiters of these digital transgressions, determining what is permissible and what is not. The algorithmic enforcement of these rules, often opaque and lacking human nuance, can lead to swift and severe penalties, such as account suspension or deplatforming, which can have significant real-world consequences for individuals. This highlights how the historical function of religious authorities in defining and punishing sin is being recontextualized within the digital sphere, albeit with secularized motivations and algorithmic enforcement mechanisms.

The historical intertwining of religious devotion and political loyalty also offers a relevant precedent. In many pre-modern societies, obedience to the monarch was often framed as a religious duty, a reflection of loyalty to God. Religious symbols and rituals were frequently integrated into state ceremonies, reinforcing the sacred nature of the political order. This fusion of spiritual and temporal allegiance created a powerful unifying force. In the digital age, while overt appeals to divine sanction are rare in the context of technology governance, we see the emergence of a kind of "digital cult of personality" around certain tech leaders and platforms. Loyalty to a particular platform or service, often expressed through enthusiastic adoption and defense of its features and policies, can become a form of allegiance that shapes social interactions and even political discourse. Furthermore, the ubiquitous presence of technology and its integration into nearly every aspect of our lives can foster a sense of dependence and almost unquestioning acceptance of its authority, akin to the uncritical devotion once afforded to divinely appointed rulers. The pervasive marketing and branding efforts by technology companies, often imbued with aspirational language and promises of progress and empowerment, can cultivate a form of almost religious fervor among their users.

The historical significance of religious institutions in providing overarching narratives that explained the world and humanity's place within it cannot be overstated. These narratives offered comfort, meaning, and a sense of cosmic order. They provided answers to fundamental questions about existence, purpose, and destiny. In the absence of such universally accepted religious narratives, the digital realm is increasingly becoming a source of meaning-making for many. Social media feeds, online communities, and even the gamified interfaces of various applications can offer a sense of purpose, belonging, and accomplishment. The "likes," "shares," and "followers" that populate these digital spaces can become proxies for validation and self-worth, fulfilling a psychological need for social affirmation that was historically met by religious communities. However, these digital narratives are often fragmented, commercially driven, and lacking the deeper existential grounding that traditional religious narratives provided. This historical role of religion in narrative construction is being usurped, or at least significantly challenged, by the emergent digital architectures of meaning.

In essence, the historical relationship between religion and societal order reveals a recurring pattern: the leveraging of belief systems, moral frameworks, and communal structures to establish and maintain authority, foster cohesion, and regulate behavior. While the digital panopticon operates with different tools and ostensibly different aims – driven by data, efficiency, and profit rather than divine mandate or spiritual salvation – its underlying function of shaping individual and collective behavior, of enforcing norms, and of constructing realities bears striking resemblances to the historical roles played by religious institutions. Understanding this historical continuity is crucial for discerning the nature of authority in the digital age and for recognizing the potential for its similar impact on human freedom and societal organization. The digital sphere, much like the historical domains of religious influence, possesses the power to define what is right, what is normal, and what is permissible, thereby shaping the very fabric of human experience.

The allure of efficiency has always been a powerful force in human organization. From the earliest agricultural innovations that streamlined food production to the industrial revolution's mechanization of labor, humanity has consistently sought ways to optimize processes, reduce waste, and achieve more with less. In the digital age, this pursuit has reached an unprecedented zenith, and artificial intelligence stands as its most potent embodiment. AI systems, with their seemingly inexhaustible capacity for data processing, pattern recognition, and predictive analytics, are now capable of performing tasks with a speed, accuracy, and scale that often appear miraculous. This is not hyperbole; for many, the ability of AI to diagnose diseases with startling precision, to manage complex logistical networks with seamless fluidity, or to personalize educational experiences to individual learning styles feels akin to witnessing a divine intervention. Governments and corporations, keenly aware of this perception, are adept at framing these AI-driven achievements as evidence of their own benevolent omnipotence, much like the Grand Inquisitor in Dostoyevsky's *The Brothers Karamazov* used supposed miracles to awe and control the populace.

The narrative meticulously constructed around AI is one of unparalleled problem-solving. Issues that have long plagued humanity – disease, poverty, environmental degradation, even the inefficiency of bureaucratic processes – are presented as being on the cusp of definitive resolution, thanks to the advent of intelligent machines. This is a profoundly persuasive narrative, tapping into a deep-seated human desire for order, comfort, and progress. When an AI can predict and mitigate the impact of a natural disaster, or optimize traffic flow in a sprawling metropolis, or even curate news feeds to eliminate perceived societal friction, it fosters a sense of awe and reliance. This, in turn, allows the entities deploying these systems – the governments and corporations – to position themselves as wise stewards, possessing the almost supernatural foresight and capability to manage the complexities of modern life. Their authority is not merely derived from traditional sources like legislation or market share, but from their demonstrable mastery over the technological forces that promise to usher in an era of unprecedented ease and well-being. This framing positions AI not just as a tool, but as a new form of divine intervention, a tangible manifestation of progress and power that elicits a similar, if secularized, sense of wonder.

Consider the domain of public administration. For decades, citizens have grappled with the labyrinthine complexities of government services – the endless paperwork, the bureaucratic delays, the perceived indifference of public officials. Now, imagine an AI-powered system that can instantly process tax returns, issue permits within minutes, or provide personalized guidance on social benefits, all with a user-friendly interface and round-the-clock availability. This is no longer science fiction;

elements of this are already being implemented. When such systems function flawlessly, they create an impression of an omniscient and benevolent state, one that anticipates citizen needs and resolves their problems with effortless grace. This efficiency becomes a form of proof, a testament to the governing body's competence and dedication. The AI, in this context, acts as the visible, tangible manifestation of that competence, a "miracle" that justifies the state's authority and silences potential dissent. The underlying algorithms, however complex and opaque, become the silent agents of this benevolent deity, ensuring that the machinery of governance operates with divine precision.

Similarly, in the corporate world, AI's ability to personalize customer experiences, to predict consumer desires, and to optimize supply chains has revolutionized how businesses operate. Companies can now offer hyper-tailored recommendations, anticipate potential customer complaints before they arise, and ensure products are always in stock, all through sophisticated AI deployments. This seamless, frictionless interaction creates an aura of intuitive understanding and proactive care. When a company's AI can seemingly read a customer's mind, anticipating their needs and fulfilling them before they are even articulated, it fosters a powerful sense of loyalty and trust. This is presented as the company's deep understanding of its customers, but it is, in fact, the output of algorithms meticulously analyzing vast datasets. The AI's predictive power becomes the company's "miracle," a demonstration of its almost prescient ability to serve, thereby solidifying its authority in the marketplace and deepening consumer dependence. The ease with which AI-driven services operate can obscure the intricate data collection and algorithmic manipulation that underpin them, making the experience feel less like a transaction and more like an act of generous provision from an all-knowing entity.

This framing of AI as a miraculous force for efficiency serves a critical function in reinforcing authority. It allows governing bodies and corporations to present themselves as inherently benevolent and capable, far exceeding the limitations of human fallibility. When an AI system efficiently allocates resources during a crisis, or an AI-driven platform seamlessly connects individuals with desired services, the success is attributed to the wisdom and foresight of the deploying entity. The AI itself becomes a symbol of this perfection, a manifestation of power that operates beyond the messy, imperfect realm of human decision-making. This creates a subtle, yet profound, shift in perception. Instead of viewing AI as a tool, individuals begin to perceive the outcomes it enables as natural, or even divinely ordained, by the entities that control it. The efficiency becomes a divine mandate, a testament to the superior judgment and capability of the authority figure, be it a government or a corporation.

The danger inherent in this "miracle" framing lies in its capacity to erode independent judgment. When AI systems are consistently presented as infallible problem-solvers, individuals may become less inclined to question their outputs or to consider alternative approaches. The sheer efficiency and apparent intelligence of AI can foster a passive acceptance, a relinquishing of critical thought in favor of the seamless flow of AI-generated solutions. If an AI can optimize traffic, predict economic trends, or even diagnose medical conditions with higher accuracy than human experts, why would one bother to engage in complex, potentially error-prone human analysis? This reliance, cultivated by the narrative of AI as a benevolent miracle, can lead to a subtle abdication of agency. Citizens and consumers may become accustomed to being guided, directed, and even decided for by algorithmic systems, their own capacity for critical assessment and independent decision-making atrophying in the process.

Moreover, the "miracle" of AI efficiency can be strategically deployed to mask underlying power structures and agendas. By focusing on the positive outcomes – the speed, the accuracy, the convenience – the methods by which these outcomes are achieved are often rendered invisible. The vast datasets being collected, the algorithms being employed, and the biases that may be embedded within them are typically shielded from public scrutiny. This opacity allows those in power to maintain control over the narrative and to deflect criticism. When an AI-driven system makes a decision that has negative consequences, the authority can point to the "unforeseeable complexity" or the "inherent limitations of any system," rather than acknowledging deliberate design choices or systemic flaws. The AI, having been established as a miraculous arbiter of efficiency, becomes a convenient scapegoat or, more often, the unquestioned agent of a benevolent will, obscuring the human hands that guide its operation and the specific objectives it serves.

The Grand Inquisitor, in his infamous encounter with Christ, offered bread and wonder as the keys to human submission. He understood that people often crave certainty and comfort more than freedom. AI, in its current manifestation, offers a secularized version of this. It provides the "bread" of seamless functionality and the "wonder" of seemingly miraculous problem-solving. This combination is profoundly appealing, offering a path of least resistance to a better life, or at least the promise of one. Governments can point to AI-driven improvements in public services as proof of their competence and legitimacy, thereby solidifying their authority. Corporations can leverage AI to create frictionless customer experiences and to predict market trends, thereby enhancing their profitability and influence. In both cases, the AI's efficiency becomes the de facto justification for the power wielded by its deployers. The narrative is carefully crafted: "We have harnessed this powerful, near-miraculous technology to make your lives better. Trust us, and embrace the efficiency we provide."

This reliance on efficiency as a divine mandate also subtly reshapes our understanding of value. In a world increasingly optimized by AI, the "best" solution is often defined as the most efficient one, the one that minimizes friction, time, and resources. This prioritization, while seemingly rational, can overlook other critical human values such as creativity, spontaneity, ethical considerations, and the inherent value of human judgment, even when it is less than perfectly efficient. The "miracle" of AI can thus lead us down a path where we inadvertently devalue aspects of human experience that do not lend themselves to algorithmic optimization. The narrative of AI as a benevolent problem-solver, driven by the imperative of efficiency, encourages a form of secular worship, where the ultimate good is aligned with the smooth, predictable functioning of intelligent machines, and by extension, the authorities that control them. This can lead to a quiet erosion of our capacity for critical engagement, transforming us from active participants in our own lives to passive recipients of algorithmic providence. The constant stream of "miraculous" solutions, while alleviating immediate problems, can simultaneously diminish our resilience, our ingenuity, and ultimately, our freedom.

The digital age, while promising unprecedented connectivity and access to information, has also ushered in an era of pervasive surveillance. This concept, often referred to as the "digital panopticon," describes a society where individuals are constantly aware of the potential for being watched, analyzed, and judged. While initially conceived in the context of state and corporate power, this sophisticated architecture of observation has found fertile ground in the realm of religious and quasi-religious authorities. These entities, driven by a desire to foster piety, ensure doctrinal adherence, or cultivate a sense of communal virtue, are increasingly leveraging advanced technologies, particularly artificial intelligence, to monitor the spiritual and ethical well-being of their adherents. The methods employed, though couched in benevolent intentions, bear a disquieting resemblance to the methods of observation and control that Foucault identified in the panopticon, and echo the Grand Inquisitor's desire to manage humanity for its own perceived good.

At the heart of this phenomenon lies AI's capacity for granular behavioral analysis. By sifting through vast datasets generated by online activity, communication patterns, and even biometric indicators, AI systems can construct detailed profiles of individuals' beliefs, moral comportment, and spiritual inclinations. This goes far beyond simply tracking church attendance or charitable donations. Imagine AI algorithms analyzing the content and sentiment of personal digital communications – emails, messages, social media posts – to detect expressions of doubt, heresy, or moral compromise. Such systems can identify keywords associated with theological heterodoxy, or flag communications that deviate from established ethical guidelines promoted by the religious group. The objective, as articulated by proponents, is not punitive, but rehabilitative: to identify individuals who may be struggling spiritually or ethically, and to offer them timely guidance and support. This could manifest as personalized devotional content delivered directly to the individual, or automated prompts encouraging reflection on potentially problematic thoughts or actions. The "spiritual health check-up" becomes a continuous, data-driven process, with AI acting as an ever-vigilant, albeit invisible, digital confessor.

Furthermore, AI can be deployed to monitor not just explicit expressions of belief or intent, but also subtle behavioral indicators that might suggest a spiritual malaise. For instance, an AI system might analyze patterns in an individual's online consumption of media. If an adherent is frequently engaging with content that is deemed secular, morally dubious, or even explicitly heretical according to the group's doctrine, the AI could flag this as a potential area of concern. Similarly, deviations from expected patterns of religious engagement – a sudden decrease in prayer frequency, a shift in online community participation away from faith-based groups – could trigger an alert. This granular level of monitoring extends to the physical realm through the integration of smart devices and wearable technology. While ostensibly used for health and fitness tracking, these devices can also collect data on an individual's daily routines, social interactions, and even emotional states, which could then be interpreted through a spiritual lens. A prolonged period of inactivity, interpreted as lethargy or spiritual apathy, could prompt a digital intervention.

The ethical implications of such surveillance, even when framed in terms of spiritual care, are profound. The very notion of "spiritual well-being" is deeply personal and subjective. To subject it to algorithmic quantification and monitoring risks instrumentalizing faith and reducing complex human experiences to quantifiable data points. The constant awareness of being observed, even by benevolent digital overseers, can foster a climate of fear and self-censorship. Individuals may begin to police their own thoughts and behaviors, not out of genuine conviction, but out of a desire to avoid flagging the algorithm. This can stifle intellectual curiosity, genuine spiritual exploration, and the very freedom of conscience that many faith traditions purport to uphold. The digital panopticon, in this context, becomes a tool for enforcing conformity, where adherence to prescribed norms is achieved not through persuasion or divine revelation, but through the subtle pressure of constant, data-driven oversight.

The analogy to the Grand Inquisitor is particularly pertinent here. The Inquisitor, in Dostoyevsky's masterpiece, believed that humanity was too weak and free-willed to navigate the complexities of true freedom and moral responsibility. He advocated for a system of benevolent authority, where the Church would take on the burden of decision-making, offering certainty, bread, and miracles in exchange for freedom. Similarly, AI-driven spiritual surveillance offers a form of curated certainty and effortless guidance. By monitoring and subtly correcting behavior, these systems aim to alleviate the burden of difficult ethical choices and the struggle with doubt. They promise to "help" individuals stay on the "right path," thus mirroring the Inquisitor's paternalistic approach to human salvation. The "miracles" offered are not divine interventions, but the seamless efficiency of perfectly managed spiritual lives, free from the messy uncertainties of genuine personal growth.

Moreover, the opacity of AI algorithms presents a significant challenge to accountability. When individuals are subject to monitoring and potential intervention based on algorithmic assessments of their spiritual state, they have little recourse if they believe the assessment is flawed or unfair. The complex, often proprietary nature of AI means that the logic behind its judgments can be inaccessible, even to the religious authorities employing it. This creates a situation where individuals are judged by invisible arbiters whose decision-making processes are beyond their comprehension or challenge. This lack of transparency is fertile ground for the perpetuation of biases, either those embedded in the training data or those introduced by the developers, which can disproportionately affect certain individuals or groups within the community. The "spiritual guidance" offered by the AI might, in reality, be a reflection of ingrained societal prejudices or doctrinal inflexibilities, presented as objective, data-driven truth.

Consider a hypothetical scenario: an AI system designed to monitor the spiritual adherence of members of a particular religious order. This AI analyzes the members' digital communications, noting any language that might suggest dissatisfaction with the order's leadership or doctrine. It also monitors their online browsing history, flagging any engagement with external philosophical or theological viewpoints that are not sanctioned by the order. If a member is found to be consistently deviating from the prescribed norms, the AI might trigger an alert to the order's spiritual director. This alert could lead to a mandatory pastoral counseling session, where the member is confronted with the "evidence" gathered by the AI. The member might be unaware that their private communications and browsing habits have been under constant scrutiny, leading to feelings of betrayal and a chilling effect on their willingness to engage in open discourse or critical thinking within the community. The AI, in this instance, becomes an instrument of ideological control, subtly enforcing a rigid orthodoxy under the guise of spiritual care.

The very definition of "spiritual health" can become weaponized within such a system. When AI is used to enforce a particular, often narrow, interpretation of spiritual well-being, it can marginalize or pathologize those who hold different views or who are on a different spiritual journey. The AI, trained on data that reflects a specific set of beliefs and practices, may inherently flag any deviation as problematic. This can lead to a situation where genuine spiritual diversity is suppressed, and individuals are pressured to conform to a standardized model of piety. The digital panopticon, in this context, is not merely observing behavior; it is actively shaping it, guiding adherents towards a predetermined spiritual ideal, and penalizing any divergence. This process can erode the richness and complexity of lived religious experience, replacing it with a sterile, algorithmically managed version of faith.

The potential for AI to facilitate mass surveillance for 'spiritual' well-being also raises concerns about the erosion of privacy and autonomy. Religious practice is often deeply personal, involving introspection, doubt, and a private dialogue with the divine. The idea that this intimate sphere of existence can be monitored and assessed by an external, technological entity is profoundly unsettling. It blurs the lines between private belief and public performance, forcing individuals to perform their faith for an unseen algorithmic audience. This can lead to a superficiality in religious practice, where outward appearances are prioritized over inner conviction. The digital panopticon transforms the sacred space of individual conscience into a data stream, subject to constant analysis and potential correction.

Moreover, the integration of AI into religious surveillance can create new forms of power imbalance. Those who control the AI systems – the developers, the religious leaders who deploy them, the data analysts – gain unprecedented insight into the inner lives of their followers. This information can be used not only to guide and correct but also to influence, manipulate, and exert control. The Grand Inquisitor sought to remove freedom by offering a surrogate – the certainty of faith managed by authority. Similarly, the digital panopticon for spiritual well-being offers a surrogate for genuine spiritual struggle and discernment, providing a pre-packaged path to perceived righteousness. This can disempower individuals, making them dependent on the technological scaffolding provided by their religious authorities, and diminishing their capacity for independent spiritual reasoning and decision-making.

The allure of such systems lies in their promise of a more ordered, virtuous, and harmonious religious community. By identifying and addressing spiritual or ethical failings before they become widespread problems, religious organizations can theoretically foster greater cohesion and adherence to their values. However, this pursuit of order comes at a significant cost. The constant surveillance, the algorithmic judgment, and the potential for manipulation can create an environment of mistrust and anxiety, ultimately undermining the very spiritual health they aim to promote. The digital panopticon, when turned towards the sacred, risks transforming faith from a matter of personal conviction and free choice into a system of perpetual, technologically enforced compliance, mirroring the Inquisitor's vision of a controlled, albeit "saved," humanity. The ethical boundaries are not merely blurred; they are fundamentally challenged when technology is employed to observe and shape the most intimate aspects of human belief and conscience, under the guise of spiritual care.

The landscape of institutional control has undergone a profound transformation, with an increasing array of organizations, extending beyond the traditional confines of state security and corporate oversight, now embracing surveillance technologies. This trend is particularly noteworthy within institutions that traditionally hold moral or spiritual authority. These entities, often driven by a deeply ingrained mission to guide, protect, and cultivate virtue within their communities, find themselves increasingly drawn to the perceived benefits of monitoring.

The allure lies in the promise of enhanced control: the ability to preempt deviance, ensure unwavering compliance with established doctrines or ethical codes, and maintain a meticulously ordered social fabric. Such aspirations, when coupled with the sophisticated capabilities of modern surveillance, fundamentally alter the age-old dynamic between those in authority and those under their care. Power, in this digital epoch, is being consolidated and exercised in subtler, yet arguably more pervasive, ways through the deployment of technological means, often under the benevolent guise of safeguarding the collective spiritual or moral well-being.

Consider, for instance, the expansion of surveillance into educational settings that are not solely secular. Many private schools, particularly those with a religious or ideological affiliation, are implementing systems that monitor student behavior both on and off campus. This might include the use of sophisticated CCTV networks equipped with facial recognition and behavioral analytics, designed to identify students engaging in prohibited activities, such as substance abuse, unauthorized gatherings, or expressions of dissent against the institution's core values. Beyond mere physical observation, these institutions are increasingly deploying digital monitoring tools. Software that tracks student internet usage, analyzes the content of their school-issued emails and online assignments, and even monitors their social media activity for anything deemed contrary to the school's moral code, is becoming commonplace. The justification often presented is the protection of the student body from harmful influences and the preservation of a disciplined, morally upright learning environment. However, the pervasive nature of this monitoring cultivates an atmosphere where every action, every communication, and every online interaction is potentially subject to institutional scrutiny, fostering a climate of self-censorship among students who may fear reprisal for expressing nascent doubts or exploring unconventional ideas, even in private digital spaces.

Similarly, within certain charitable organizations and non-governmental bodies with strong ethical or religious underpinnings, the drive for accountability and efficiency has also led to the adoption of surveillance technologies. These organizations often manage significant resources and operate in sensitive environments, making them vulnerable to fraud, mismanagement, and external threats. To mitigate these risks, they may implement extensive monitoring of their employees and volunteers. This can range from GPS tracking of field workers and delivery vehicles to detailed audits of financial transactions and communication logs. In some cases, the surveillance extends to the beneficiaries of the aid or services provided, with digital platforms designed to track the distribution of resources and assess the impact of interventions, ostensibly to ensure that aid reaches its intended recipients and is used effectively. While the stated objectives are often laudable – preventing waste, ensuring transparency, and maximizing impact – the infrastructure of constant observation can inadvertently foster a culture of fear and distrust. Employees may feel that their every action is being judged, leading to a reluctance to take initiative or to voice concerns about systemic issues, lest they be perceived as inefficient or disloyal. The focus shifts from the mission itself to the performance metrics that can be quantified and monitored, potentially stifling the very humanistic ethos the organization aims to uphold.

The integration of such technologies into religious institutions, as previously touched upon, represents a particularly complex facet of this trend. Beyond the analysis of digital communications and online behavior, some religious organizations are exploring the use of smart devices and interconnected home technology to gain insights into the daily lives of their adherents. The rationale often presented is to provide more personalized pastoral care and to identify individuals who may be experiencing spiritual distress, isolation, or falling prey to dangerous ideologies. For instance, a smart speaker in a congregant's home could, with consent (however broadly defined or implicitly granted through membership agreements), monitor conversations for keywords related to existential angst, expressions of doubt, or mentions of potentially harmful associations. Wearable devices might track activity levels, sleep patterns, and even heart rate variability, with deviations from baseline interpreted as indicators of spiritual or emotional imbalance. While proponents argue this allows for proactive intervention – a timely phone call from a pastor, a recommended devotional, or an invitation to a support group – the inherent intrusiveness of such monitoring raises profound ethical questions. It blurs the lines between public and private spiritual life, transforming the sanctuary of the home and the privacy of one's thoughts into a potential data source for an institutional authority, ultimately seeking to control not just outward actions but the inner state of belief and conviction.

Furthermore, the very definition of "deviance" or "compliance" within these institutions becomes susceptible to technologically driven redefinition. Algorithms, trained on historical data and predefined norms, can establish subtle but rigid benchmarks for acceptable behavior and belief. Any deviation, no matter how minor or contextually understandable, can be flagged. This creates a powerful mechanism for enforcing conformity. For example, an algorithm designed to assess the theological soundness of sermons might flag certain theological nuances or interpretative departures as heretical, even if those interpretations are held by respected scholars or represent a legitimate evolution of thought within the tradition. The sheer volume of data that AI can process allows for a level of granular scrutiny that was previously unimaginable. It moves beyond the oversight of a local imam, priest, or rabbi to a pervasive, almost omnipresent form of digital oversight. This can lead to a chilling effect on intellectual discourse and theological exploration, as individuals become hesitant to express anything that might be misinterpreted or flagged by the system. The pursuit of order and purity, when mediated through algorithmic judgment, risks ossifying belief systems and stifling the dynamic, often messy, process of spiritual growth and communal dialogue.

The consolidation of power through these technological means is subtle but significant. By positioning themselves as providers of security, order, and spiritual guidance, institutions can leverage surveillance to exert greater influence over their members. The act of monitoring itself can be a form of social control, as individuals internalize the awareness of being watched and begin to self-regulate their behavior to align with perceived institutional expectations. This is particularly potent in contexts where membership in the institution is linked to social status, economic opportunity, or even a sense of identity and belonging. The "digital panopticon," in these instances, doesn't necessarily require overt punishment; the implicit threat of being flagged, audited, or excluded is often sufficient to ensure compliance. The institution, armed with an ever-increasing amount of data about its members, gains a disproportionate advantage in any negotiation of norms, doctrines, or even personal choices. This data can be used not just to identify those who stray, but also to understand the collective anxieties and desires of the community, allowing the institution to tailor its messaging and policies to maintain its authority and influence more effectively. The perceived benefits of preventing deviance, ensuring compliance, and maintaining order are thus intrinsically linked to a fundamental shift in the power dynamics, where technological capacity becomes a primary tool for the perpetuation and extension of institutional control.

The digital panopticon, as it infiltrates the sanctums of religious and moral authority, compels a profound re-examination of foundational theological concepts, most notably grace and salvation. In the traditional understanding, grace is a divine gift, unearned and freely given, a testament to God's boundless love and mercy. It is not a reward for perfect adherence to a set of rules, but rather an empowering force that enables individuals to strive for righteousness, to love their neighbor, and to seek forgiveness when they inevitably fall short. This grace is intrinsically linked to faith – a deep-seated trust and commitment that transcends mere outward observance. Salvation, in this light, is the ultimate culmination of this journey of faith, love, and surrender to the divine will, a process that acknowledges human fallibility and the transformative power of God's unmerited favor.

However, the pervasive surveillance systems and algorithmic oversight we have been examining introduce a subtle yet insidious redefinition of these sacred tenets. When institutions, driven by the desire for order, compliance, and the elimination of perceived deviance, implement technologies that monitor and evaluate every facet of an individual's digital and, increasingly, physical life, the very nature of what is deemed "virtuous" or "salvific" begins to shift. The goal becomes not the cultivation of an internal disposition of love and faith, but the meticulous curation of an outward persona that adheres to predefined, technologically measurable standards. This transforms the spiritual landscape from one of grace and genuine faith into a meticulously managed system of behavioral transactions.

Consider the echo of the Grand Inquisitor's proposition, as articulated by Dostoyevsky. He offers humanity a form of peace, a liberation from the agonizing burden of freedom and the often-painful process of seeking genuine faith. This peace is predicated on absolute obedience, on surrendering one's will to an established authority that promises order and security in exchange for unquestioning adherence. The Inquisitor does not speak of grace as a divine outpouring, but of contentment derived from the absence of struggle, from the predictable rhythm of an ordered existence dictated by infallible leadership. In the digital panopticon, this sentiment finds a new, technologically amplified expression. The algorithms, acting as the new inquisitors, offer a similar bargain: compliance in exchange for acceptance, for a place within the meticulously managed community, for the avoidance of the dreaded "flag" that signifies deviation.

The insidious danger lies in this substitution of authentic faith with a form of transactional "good behavior." True faith, in its theological sense, is not merely about following rules; it is a profound orientation of the self towards the divine, characterized by love, trust, and a willingness to embrace vulnerability. It is a dynamic relationship, subject to growth, doubt, and reconciliation. Grace, in this context, is the divine accompaniment to this journey, the enabling presence that sustains and guides. When surveillance technologies become the arbiter of spiritual worthiness, the emphasis shifts from the internal disposition of the soul to the measurable metrics of external conduct. Individuals may meticulously manage their online interactions, their search histories, their even their spoken words within earshot of a smart device, not out of a genuine love for God or neighbor, but out of a calculated effort to avoid algorithmic censure. The fear of being flagged, of being deemed a theological outlier or a behavioral risk, becomes a more potent motivator than the desire for spiritual communion.

This creates a hollowed-out version of religious practice, one that prioritizes the appearance of piety over its substance. The complex universe of human experience – the struggles with doubt, the moments of spiritual desolation, the wrestling with complex ethical dilemmas – are reduced to data points. Algorithms, by their very nature, are ill-equipped to discern the nuanced organism of human intention, the genuine remorse that follows a transgression, or the burgeoning flicker of faith in the face of despair. Instead, they operate on quantifiable outputs. A single misspoken word, a search query for a controversial theological viewpoint, an association with a group deemed "undesirable" by the algorithm, can be enough to trigger a negative assessment, irrespective of the individual's underlying spiritual journey.

The traditional understanding of grace as an unmerited gift is thus undermined. If "grace" is now perceived as the outcome of perfectly optimized behavior, it ceases to be a divine endowment and becomes a humanly engineered achievement. Salvation, no longer the result of divine mercy and transformative love, risks becoming a score achieved through diligent adherence to the dictates of the digital overseers. This is a profound perversion of spiritual ideals, one that echoes the critiques leveled against rigid legalism throughout religious history. It fosters a community of the outwardly compliant, but potentially inwardly barren, a congregation of individuals who have mastered the art of appearing righteous rather than cultivating the state of being righteous.

The implications for pastoral care are equally disturbing. When the relationship between the shepherd and the flock is mediated through constant surveillance and algorithmic analysis, the space for genuine, uninhibited spiritual guidance shrinks. How can a priest or imam offer true counsel to a congregant who feels that every word spoken, every confession made, is being logged and assessed by an impersonal system? The therapeutic space of spiritual confession, designed to be a sanctuary of trust and vulnerability, becomes compromised when it is implicitly or explicitly under electronic scrutiny. The human element of empathy, of shared vulnerability, of discerning the subtle nuances of a struggling soul, is overshadowed by the cold, objective logic of data processing.

Furthermore, this redefinition of grace through compliance can breed a subtle but pervasive spiritual pride among those who consistently score well on the digital metrics. They may come to believe that their salvation or their spiritual standing is a direct result of their own perfect conduct, a testament to their own superior adherence to the rules, rather than a product of divine favor and enabling grace. This can lead to a judgmentalism that is antithetical to the core tenets of most faiths, a condemnation of those who fall short not with compassion, but with the detached certainty of algorithmic judgment. The parable of the Pharisee and the Tax Collector, where the humble, sin-weary tax collector is declared more righteous than the self-congratulatory Pharisee who meticulously observed every ritual, serves as a potent reminder of the dangers of equating outward observance with true spiritual standing.

The challenge posed by the digital panopticon to religious institutions is not merely one of privacy or data security; it is an existential challenge to the very meaning of faith, grace, and salvation. It compels a critical examination of whether the pursuit of order and control through technological means is inadvertently leading to a spiritual impoverishment, a replacement of the divine mystery with the sterile certainty of the algorithm. As we navigate this complex terrain, the imperative remains to safeguard the authentic dimensions of spiritual life, to resist the temptation of a "peace" that comes at the cost of genuine freedom and unmerited grace, and to reaffirm that true faith is not a matter of perfect compliance, but of imperfect, yet profound, love and trust. The digital age demands that we be ever more vigilant in preserving the sacred spaces of the soul, ensuring that the pursuit of order does not extinguish the flame of authentic spiritual yearning, nor redefine the boundless expanse of divine grace into a mere set of measurable, achievable metrics. The integrity of faith itself hinges on our ability to discern between the performance of virtue and the cultivation of genuine spiritual transformation, a distinction that the pervasive gaze of the digital panopticon threatens to erase, leaving behind a society that is meticulously ordered, perhaps, but spiritually bereft. The temptation to streamline the path to redemption, to offer a technologically assured route to spiritual approval, is a powerful one, but one that ultimately leads away from the very essence of what it means to be human and to seek the divine in a world that is inherently complex, imperfect, and imbued with a mystery that algorithms can neither replicate nor comprehend. The grace that redeems is not the grace that is earned through algorithmic obedience; it is the grace that is freely given, that embraces imperfection, and that calls us into a relationship of love and transformative encounter, a relationship that no amount of surveillance can truly monitor, nor substitute.

## Chapter 14: Voluntary Subordination: The Allure of Algorithmic Guidance

The modern world, with its dizzying array of choices and its relentless pace, often leaves individuals feeling adrift, overwhelmed by complexity. In such an environment, the allure of algorithmic certainty emerges not as a mere technological convenience, but as a potent psychological balm. Artificial intelligence, with its capacity to process vast datasets and identify patterns invisible to the human eye, offers a compelling promise: clarity, predictability, and a sense of control over the chaotic currents of life. This subsection delves into the deep-seated human desire for such certainty and examines why the seemingly objective pronouncements of algorithms hold such sway over our decision-making processes, even leading us to voluntarily subordinate our own judgment.

The fundamental appeal lies in the algorithm's perceived infallibility. Unlike human decision-making, which is inherently prone to error, bias, and emotional interference, algorithms are presented as objective arbiters. They operate on logic, on data, and on established parameters, seemingly detached from the messy realities of human fallibility. In a world where we are bombarded with conflicting information and where the consequences of our choices can be profound, the prospect of a clear, data-driven directive is immensely reassuring. Think of the ubiquitous navigation app. Instead of poring over maps, calculating routes, and anticipating traffic, we simply input our destination and trust the algorithm to guide us, optimizing for time, distance, or even fuel efficiency. This act, seemingly mundane, is a microcosm of a larger trend: the outsourcing of decision-making to a trusted, albeit artificial, authority. The relief from the burden of complex calculation, the avoidance of potential detours and wrong turns, translates into a tangible reduction of cognitive load and a palpable sense of liberation.

This is particularly resonant in areas where the stakes are high. Consider financial planning or investment advice. The complexities of the global economy, the fluctuations of the market, and the myriad of available financial products can be paralyzing. Algorithms, however, can sift through this data, identify trends, and offer personalized recommendations with a confidence that often surpasses human advisors who may be influenced by their own biases or limited perspectives. The language of algorithms – "optimal," "predicted," "recommended based on your profile" – speaks directly to this need for a reliable guide. It suggests a pathway that has been meticulously calculated to yield the best possible outcome, minimizing risk and maximizing reward. This creates a powerful feedback loop: the more we rely on algorithmic guidance and experience positive results, the more we trust the algorithm, further solidifying its place as a preferred decision-making tool.

The psychological comfort derived from this algorithmic certainty can be understood through the lens of loss aversion. Humans are generally more sensitive to potential losses than to equivalent gains. The fear of making a wrong decision, of suffering a financial setback, a social faux pas, or a health-related misstep, is a powerful motivator. Algorithms, by offering a seemingly risk-free path, mitigate this fear. They present a future that is, to a degree, pre-determined and optimized. This predictability allows individuals to escape the anxiety that often accompanies uncertainty. In an era characterized by rapid technological advancement, geopolitical instability, and environmental concerns, the sense of control that algorithmic guidance offers becomes a precious commodity. It allows individuals to regain a semblance of agency in a world that often feels overwhelmingly uncontrollable.

Furthermore, the "black box" nature of many sophisticated algorithms, while sometimes a source of concern, can also contribute to their appeal. When we don't fully understand

*how* an algorithm arrives at its conclusion, it can feel almost magical, imbued with a kind of inherent wisdom that transcends ordinary human comprehension. This detachment from human reasoning can lend the algorithmic output an aura of objectivity, making it seem less like a mere suggestion and more like an unavoidable truth. For individuals grappling with difficult decisions, the temptation to defer to this perceived higher authority can be overwhelming. It allows them to sidestep the often-agonizing process of self-reflection, weighing pros and cons, and ultimately taking responsibility for the outcome. The algorithm, in this sense, becomes an externalized conscience or a surrogate intellect, capable of shouldering the burden of choice.

This phenomenon is particularly evident in the realm of personal relationships and social interactions. Dating apps, for instance, employ algorithms to match individuals based on a complex array of preferences and behaviors. While the success rates are debated, the initial appeal lies in the promise of a more efficient and potentially more successful path to finding a partner. Instead of the often-frustrating and time-consuming process of navigating social cues and making first impressions, the algorithm offers a pre-vetted selection, a statistically probable match. Similarly, social media platforms use algorithms to curate our feeds, showing us content they predict we will engage with. This creates an echo chamber, reinforcing our existing beliefs and preferences, and offering a comfortable, predictable flow of information. While this can have negative societal implications, the personal experience for the user can be one of reduced friction and increased satisfaction, as their digital environment becomes increasingly tailored to their perceived desires.

The erosion of personal judgment in favor of algorithmic guidance is not necessarily born out of a lack of intelligence or capability. Rather, it is a pragmatic response to the overwhelming demands of modern life. The sheer volume of information and the complexity of the decisions we face daily can lead to decision fatigue. When presented with an algorithmic solution, individuals can feel a sense of relief, a liberation from the mental effort required to process and evaluate all available options. It is often easier, and feels safer, to follow the recommendation of a system that has been designed to optimize for a particular outcome, than to embark on a personal journey of discovery, which inherently carries the risk of missteps and suboptimal results.

The concept of "voluntary subordination" becomes critical here. We are not being forced to obey algorithms; we are choosing to do so, often unconsciously, because the perceived benefits – efficiency, accuracy, reduced anxiety, and a sense of control – outweigh the perceived costs of surrendering our autonomy. This is a subtle but profound shift in our relationship with technology. Algorithms are no longer just tools; they are becoming trusted advisors, gatekeepers, and even arbiters of our lives. This willingness to cede decision-making power is fueled by a deep-seated human need for order and predictability in a world that is anything but. The algorithm, with its promise of objective truth and optimized outcomes, offers a tempting escape from the inherent uncertainties and complexities of human existence, making its guidance an increasingly irresistible proposition.

This appeal is amplified by the way algorithms are marketed and presented. They are often framed as sophisticated, objective systems, devoid of human error or bias. Terms like "data-driven," "intelligent," and "optimized" create an aura of infallibility. When an algorithm recommends a product, suggests a route, or flags a piece of content, it is often perceived as an objective truth rather than a calculated probability. This perception can lead individuals to unquestioningly accept algorithmic outputs, even when they might contradict their own intuition or knowledge. The act of trusting an algorithm becomes a shortcut, a way to bypass the effort and uncertainty of independent thought and evaluation.

Consider the example of personalized content recommendations on streaming services or e-commerce platforms. While these algorithms are designed to enhance user experience and drive engagement, they also create a self-reinforcing loop of consumption. If an algorithm consistently recommends a particular genre of music or film, the user is likely to consume more of it, thus providing more data for the algorithm to refine its predictions. This can lead to a narrowing of individual tastes and a reduced exposure to diverse forms of content. However, the immediate gratification of being presented with something one is likely to enjoy, and the absence of the effort required to actively search for new and potentially less appealing options, makes this an appealing trade-off for many users. The comfort of the familiar, curated by an algorithm, often trumps the potential discovery of the new.

The psychological allure of algorithmic certainty also taps into a desire for validation. When an algorithm "understands" us, when it predicts our needs and preferences with uncanny accuracy, it can feel like a form of recognition. This is particularly true in the context of social media and online communities, where algorithmic curation can lead to the formation of groups and echo chambers that reinforce our existing identities and beliefs. Being presented with content that aligns with our views, or being connected with individuals who share our interests, provides a sense of belonging and validation that can be deeply satisfying. The algorithm, in this sense, becomes a facilitator of social and psychological comfort, providing a curated reality that aligns with our pre-existing notions of ourselves and the world.

Furthermore, the increasing integration of algorithms into professional decision-making processes – from medical diagnosis to legal sentencing – adds another layer to their appeal. In fields where the consequences of error can be severe, the prospect of an objective, data-driven recommendation can be highly attractive. Physicians may be more inclined to trust an AI's diagnostic suggestions, and judges may be influenced by algorithmic risk assessments when determining bail or sentencing. This reliance on algorithmic guidance, while promising greater accuracy and objectivity, also raises questions about the diminishing role of human expertise, intuition, and ethical judgment. The allure of certainty can blind us to the potential limitations and inherent biases of these systems, leading to a gradual erosion of critical thinking and personal responsibility.

The very language used to describe algorithmic processes contributes to this sense of trust. Phrases like "machine learning," "deep learning," and "neural networks" evoke images of powerful, intelligent entities capable of understanding and solving complex problems. This anthropomorphism, while often inaccurate, can lead users to ascribe human-like qualities of understanding and intention to these systems. When an algorithm "learns" or "understands," it feels more akin to a knowledgeable assistant than a mere tool, further encouraging a willingness to defer to its judgment. This psychological framing makes the voluntary subordination of decision-making power feel less like a surrender and more like a collaboration with a superior intelligence.

Ultimately, the appeal of algorithmic certainty is a complex interplay of psychological needs and technological capabilities. In a world that often feels chaotic and unpredictable, algorithms offer a comforting illusion of control. They promise efficiency, accuracy, and a reduction in cognitive burden, making them an increasingly attractive option for decision-making in virtually every aspect of our lives. This voluntary subordination of our own judgment, while driven by a desire for simplification and reassurance, carries profound implications for our autonomy, our critical thinking skills, and our very understanding of what it means to make a choice in the 21st century. The ease with which we cede control to these systems is a testament to their power, but it also serves as a stark reminder of our own deep-seated yearning for a predictable, ordered existence, a yearning that algorithms are, for now, uniquely positioned to fulfill.

The fabric of modern existence is woven with threads of unprecedented choice. From the mundane selection of a morning coffee blend to the profound decisions that shape our destinies – career trajectories, life partners, even our personal health regimes – the sheer volume can be overwhelming. It is within this labyrinth of possibilities that artificial intelligence has emerged, not merely as a tool, but as a burgeoning confidant, a digital oracle whispering guidance into the ear of our decision-making faculties. This pervasive integration of AI into the fabric of our daily lives marks a significant societal shift, one where algorithmic suggestions are increasingly consulted, and often heeded, for decisions of profound personal consequence. We find ourselves in an era where the digital assistant on our phone, the recommendation engine on our streaming service, and the predictive analytics governing our online interactions are not just passive observers, but active participants, shaping the contours of our lived experiences.

Consider the realm of professional development. Gone are the days when career paths were primarily forged through traditional education and on-the-job experience alone. Today, sophisticated AI platforms analyze vast datasets of job market trends, individual skill sets, and even personality assessments to recommend optimal career trajectories. These systems can predict future in-demand professions, identify skill gaps an individual might need to bridge, and suggest specific educational or training programs tailored to maximize career potential. The appeal is undeniable: a seemingly objective, data-driven roadmap to professional success, alleviating the anxiety and uncertainty often associated with such pivotal life choices. Individuals find themselves presented with a curated pathway, a series of calculated steps designed to lead to a desired professional outcome, often without the need for extensive personal research or the subjective intuition of a human career counselor. This offers a potent shortcut, a method of navigating the complex and competitive job market with a perceived advantage, grounded in what is presented as irrefutable data.

Similarly, in the intricate domain of romantic relationships, AI has woven itself into the very process of finding a partner. Dating applications, powered by complex algorithms, go far beyond simple preference matching. They analyze interaction patterns, communication styles, even subconscious behavioral cues captured through user activity, to suggest compatible individuals. The promise is of a more efficient, data-informed approach to love and companionship, bypassing the perceived inefficiencies and potential heartbreak of traditional courtship. Users are presented with curated selections of potential partners, profiles that have been statistically deemed more likely to result in a successful connection. This algorithmic intermediation, while offering a sense of streamlined progress, fundamentally alters the traditional courtship ritual, shifting the locus of decision-making from innate human connection and intuition to calculated probability.

The influence extends profoundly into our personal well-being and health. Wearable devices, armed with AI, continuously monitor physiological data, offering insights into sleep patterns, activity levels, and even potential health risks. Beyond mere tracking, these systems increasingly provide personalized recommendations for diet, exercise, and lifestyle adjustments, aiming to optimize physical and mental health. The convenience and apparent accuracy of these AI-driven health coaches are compelling. They offer a constant stream of data-informed advice, a proactive approach to wellness that can feel empowering. However, the reliance on these external systems can subtly erode an individual's capacity to listen to their own body, to develop an intuitive understanding of their own physical needs, or to cultivate the discipline born from internal motivation rather than external prompting. The algorithm becomes the ultimate arbiter of what is "healthy" or "optimal," potentially diminishing the role of personal experience and subjective well-being.

Even our leisure and entertainment are increasingly curated by algorithms. Streaming services, music platforms, and social media feeds employ sophisticated AI to predict our preferences and deliver content that is likely to engage us. While this personalization can enhance user experience, it also risks creating a form of passive consumption, where our exposure to new ideas, genres, or perspectives is limited by the algorithm's predictive capabilities. Instead of actively seeking out diverse forms of entertainment, we are fed a steady diet of what the algorithm believes we want, potentially narrowing our cultural horizons and reinforcing existing tastes. This creates a comfortable, but perhaps constricting, echo chamber of curated experiences, where serendipitous discovery is replaced by predictable reinforcement. The effort required to venture outside these algorithmic boundaries can feel substantial, leading to a comfortable inertia.

This societal trend towards algorithmic guidance raises critical questions about the long-term impact on individual agency. When crucial life choices are increasingly outsourced to artificial intelligence, what happens to our capacity for independent thought and self-determination? Does the constant reliance on external prompts diminish our ability to develop critical thinking skills, to weigh complex factors, and to make decisions based on our own values and lived experiences? The allure of algorithmic certainty, while offering a reduction in cognitive load and anxiety, may come at the cost of cultivating personal wisdom, a deeper understanding of ourselves, and the resilience that comes from navigating challenges independently. The process of wrestling with difficult decisions, of experiencing the consequences of our choices, and of learning from our mistakes is fundamental to personal growth. When algorithms smooth out these rough edges, they may inadvertently stunt this vital developmental process.

The development of personal wisdom is intricately linked to the process of making choices, even imperfect ones, and learning from their outcomes. Wisdom is not merely the accumulation of knowledge, but the ability to apply that knowledge with good judgment, understanding, and insight. This faculty is honed through experience, through introspection, and through the often-messy process of trial and error. When AI systems present us with what appear to be optimal solutions, they can short-circuit this experiential learning. We may achieve the desired outcome without ever truly understanding the underlying principles or developing the capacity to make similar judgments independently in the future. This reliance can foster a form of intellectual dependency, where individuals become adept at following algorithmic instructions but less capable of independent problem-solving or creative thinking.

Furthermore, the reliance on algorithmic guidance can inadvertently homogenize individual experiences and preferences. If everyone is consistently directed towards the same "optimal" career paths, relationship matches, or entertainment choices, society risks a subtle but pervasive form of conformity. The unique quirks, unexpected passions, and individual idiosyncrasies that enrich the human experience could be slowly smoothed away by the relentless pursuit of algorithmic efficiency. The beauty of human diversity lies in our differences, our unique perspectives, and our varied approaches to life. When algorithms begin to dictate these aspects, they may inadvertently steer us towards a more uniform, less vibrant collective existence. The subtle nuances of human connection, the serendipity of unexpected encounters, and the organic development of personal taste could all be casualties of an over-reliance on predictive optimization.

The concept of "risk" itself undergoes a transformation in the age of algorithmic guidance. Traditionally, embracing risk was often seen as a courageous act, a necessary component of personal growth and innovation. It involved a leap of faith, a willingness to venture into the unknown with the understanding that failure was a possibility, but also a potent teacher. Algorithmic guidance, however, often presents a vision of minimized risk, of predictable outcomes based on vast datasets. While this offers a comforting illusion of control, it can also breed a timidity, a reluctance to deviate from the prescribed path, and an aversion to any course of action that carries even a marginal perceived risk. This can stifle creativity and discourage the kind of bold, unconventional thinking that has historically driven human progress. The comfort of the known, as defined by the algorithm, may overshadow the potential rewards of the unknown, cultivated through personal courage and an embrace of uncertainty.

Moreover, the very definition of "success" becomes increasingly framed through the lens of algorithmic optimization. When AI systems are designed to maximize specific metrics – be it career progression, relationship longevity, or health outcomes – our personal aspirations can become conflated with these quantifiable goals. This can lead to a situation where individuals prioritize achieving algorithmic benchmarks over pursuing intrinsically meaningful experiences or personal fulfillment that may not be easily quantifiable. The pursuit of a "high-scoring" relationship, as determined by an algorithm, might overshadow the cultivation of genuine emotional intimacy. Similarly, a career path deemed "optimal" by AI might be one that lacks personal passion or creative satisfaction. The danger lies in allowing external, data-driven definitions of success to supersede our own internal compass and deeply held values.

The ethical implications of this pervasive algorithmic guidance are also profound. Who designs these algorithms, and whose values are embedded within them? The data used to train these systems is often a reflection of existing societal biases, and there is a significant risk that AI will not only replicate but amplify these inequalities. For instance, AI-driven hiring tools might inadvertently discriminate against certain demographic groups based on historical hiring patterns. Algorithmic recommendations for loan applications could perpetuate existing economic disparities. When we uncritically accept algorithmic guidance, we risk internalizing and perpetuating these embedded biases, further entrenching societal injustices under the guise of objective, data-driven decision-making. The illusion of impartiality can mask a deeply inequitable reality, making it harder to identify and challenge these systemic issues.

The question of accountability also becomes blurred. When an AI system provides guidance that leads to negative consequences, who is responsible? Is it the user who chose to follow the recommendation, the developers who created the algorithm, or the company that deployed it? The diffusion of responsibility can create a situation where genuine accountability is difficult to establish, potentially leading to a decline in the quality and ethical considerations of algorithmic design and deployment. This lack of clear accountability can further erode trust in human judgment and decision-making, as individuals may feel less compelled to take ownership of their choices when the ultimate "decision" was outsourced to a seemingly infallible digital entity.

The very act of introspection and self-discovery, a cornerstone of human development, is also potentially altered. Traditionally, individuals engaged in deep self-reflection to understand their desires, motivations, and values. This process, while often challenging, is crucial for building a robust sense of self and making authentic choices. Algorithmic guidance, by providing pre-digested "optimal" paths, can circumvent this necessary internal work. Why embark on a potentially arduous journey of self-discovery when an algorithm can present a seemingly clear and efficient route to happiness or success? This can lead to a superficial understanding of oneself, a reliance on external validation, and a diminished capacity for genuine self-awareness. The richness of human experience, with its inherent complexities and contradictions, may be flattened by the pursuit of algorithmic simplicity.

Ultimately, the increasing reliance on AI as a personal guide presents a complex paradox. On one hand, it offers unprecedented convenience, efficiency, and access to information, promising to simplify the complexities of modern life. On the other hand, it poses a significant challenge to our autonomy, our critical thinking skills, and our capacity for cultivating personal wisdom. The voluntary subordination of our decision-making faculties to algorithms, while seemingly pragmatic, risks transforming us into passive recipients of digital directives rather than active architects of our own lives. The challenge lies in finding a harmonious balance, harnessing the power of AI as a supportive tool without allowing it to eclipse the essential human capacities for judgment, intuition, and the courageous, albeit imperfect, act of making our own choices. The future hinges on our ability to remain discerning users, to question algorithmic pronouncements, and to remember that true fulfillment often lies not in the most optimized path, but in the journey of self-discovery and the cultivation of our unique human spirit.

The modern age is characterized by an intricate dance between autonomy and efficiency, a perpetual negotiation of our individual freedoms against the siren song of convenience. At the heart of this exchange lies a Faustian bargain, often struck without explicit declaration, where humanity willingly trades segments of its autonomy for the seamless, streamlined experiences that artificial intelligence now promises and delivers with startling regularity. This voluntary subordination, as we might call it, is not a sudden capitulation but a gradual erosion, a subtle relinquishing of control that often goes unnoticed amidst the immediate gratification and perceived benefits. We are not being coerced into algorithmic obedience; rather, we are actively choosing to delegate, to outsource, to defer our decision-making, our critical judgment, and even our very experiences to the invisible hands of sophisticated code.

The essence of this bargain can be understood as a transaction: the user offers up their personal data, their behavioral patterns, their preferences, and, crucially, their agency in decision-making, in return for a tailored, optimized, and often effortless existence. Consider the ubiquitous recommendation engines that populate our digital lives. When a streaming service suggests a film or a song, it does so based on a complex analysis of our past viewing or listening habits, combined with the habits of millions of other users. The convenience of having content curated for us, of bypassing the often-daunting task of sifting through endless options, is palpable. We save time, we reduce cognitive load, and we are presented with a high probability of enjoyment. Yet, in accepting these recommendations without question, we are implicitly agreeing to let the algorithm shape our tastes, to guide our consumption, and to, in a sense, define what we will experience next. The freedom to discover something entirely unexpected, to stumble upon a hidden gem through serendipity, or to develop a unique preference independent of mass trends is subtly curtailed. The algorithm, in its pursuit of maximizing engagement – a proxy for user satisfaction – prioritizes familiarity and predictable enjoyment over the potential for genuine, unguided discovery.

This incremental surrender of autonomy is a key mechanism in the voluntary subordination to algorithmic guidance. It doesn't typically manifest as a grand, conscious decision to relinquish freedom. Instead, it occurs in a series of small, seemingly insignificant choices. Each time we click "accept" on a cookie consent banner, each time we allow an app to access our location, each time we let a personalized advertisement dictate our next purchase, we are inching further into the algorithmic fold. These micro-concessions, when viewed in isolation, appear benign, even beneficial. They allow for a more personalized online experience, faster loading times, and advertisements that are, at least in theory, more relevant to our needs. However, the aggregate effect of these cumulative concessions is a profound alteration of our digital environment and, by extension, our decision-making landscape.

The economic underpinnings of this exchange are also critical to understanding its voluntary nature. Many of the AI-powered services that offer such convenience are provided free of charge, or at a significantly reduced cost. This "free" model is sustained by the collection and analysis of user data, which then becomes a valuable commodity. Users are essentially paying for these services not with money, but with their personal information and the implicit delegation of their decision-making power. This exchange is often presented as a win-win: users get sophisticated services for free, and companies gain insights that allow them to improve their products and target their marketing more effectively. The perceived value proposition is so strong that individuals are often willing to overlook the subtle but significant transfer of control that accompanies this transaction. The user might believe they are merely consenting to a privacy policy, but in reality, they are entering into a broader contract that extends to their behavioral patterns and their cognitive processes.

Consider the realm of personalized learning platforms. These AI-driven systems can adapt educational content to an individual student's pace, learning style, and knowledge gaps. This offers immense potential for more effective and efficient education, freeing students from the constraints of a one-size-fits-all curriculum. However, the algorithm dictates the learning path, the sequence of topics, and even the way information is presented. While this can be highly beneficial, it also means that the student is less likely to encounter subjects or perspectives outside the algorithm's predetermined scope. The freedom to explore tangential interests, to pursue a line of inquiry that deviates from the prescribed curriculum, or to engage with a teacher's spontaneous, unscripted insights may be diminished. The educational journey, while optimized for certain metrics of success, can become a pre-packaged experience, subtly guiding the student towards predetermined outcomes rather than fostering an unbridled curiosity and the capacity for self-directed learning.

The same dynamic is at play in the optimization of our physical lives through wearable technology and health apps. These devices collect vast amounts of physiological data – heart rate, sleep patterns, activity levels – and use AI to provide personalized recommendations for diet, exercise, and overall well-being. The convenience of having a constant, data-driven guide to health is undeniably appealing, especially in an era where health consciousness is paramount. However, this constant external monitoring and guidance can lead to a form of "algorithmic dependence." Individuals may begin to rely so heavily on the app's prompts that they lose touch with their own body's signals. The intuitive understanding of hunger, fatigue, or exertion, honed through years of embodied experience, can be overridden by the algorithm's directives. The freedom to listen to one's own body, to experiment with different approaches to wellness, and to develop an internalized sense of what feels right and healthy can be subtly eroded. The algorithm becomes the ultimate authority on what constitutes optimal health, potentially leading to a rigid adherence to externally dictated norms rather than a personalized, self-aware approach to well-being.

The incremental nature of this surrender is particularly insidious because it often occurs under the guise of enhancement or improvement. We are not losing freedom; we are gaining efficiency, accuracy, and a reduction in the friction of daily life. The act of choosing a restaurant, for example, has been vastly simplified by review aggregators and personalized recommendation systems. Instead of spending time researching menus, reading reviews, and making a subjective choice, we can often rely on an AI to present us with a curated list of highly-rated, algorithmically "suitable" options. This is convenient, especially when time is scarce. However, it also means that we are less likely to stumble upon the quirky, independent eatery that might not have a massive online presence but offers a unique culinary experience. We are trading the potential for delightful serendipity and subjective exploration for the assurance of a statistically likely positive outcome. The "freedom" to choose from a curated, pre-vetted selection can feel more appealing than the "freedom" to navigate a vast, unorganized landscape of possibilities.

This voluntary subordination is further reinforced by the gamification of our digital interactions. Platforms often employ techniques borrowed from game design – points, badges, leaderboards, streaks – to encourage continued engagement and data contribution. When we achieve a "goal" set by an app, such as hitting a daily step count or completing a learning module, we receive positive reinforcement, which further entrenches our reliance on the system. This creates a feedback loop where the user is actively motivated to cede more control and provide more data in order to achieve these digital rewards. The pursuit of these gamified achievements can become an end in itself, distracting from the intrinsic value of the activity or the underlying purpose of the data collection. The individual may find themselves performing actions not because they are inherently meaningful, but because they are designed to yield algorithmic rewards.

Moreover, the sophisticated design of these AI systems plays a crucial role in making this exchange palatable. Interfaces are made intuitive and aesthetically pleasing. The user experience is designed to be as frictionless as possible. Any friction that might prompt the user to pause, question, or reconsider their concessions is meticulously ironed out. This deliberate design choice aims to minimize the cognitive effort required to engage with the system, thereby reducing the likelihood of the user recognizing the extent of their own voluntary subordination. The elegance and ease of use of these technologies can mask the underlying mechanisms of data extraction and behavioral influence. We are so accustomed to the smooth operation of these systems that we rarely stop to consider what is happening "under the hood" or the true cost of this seamlessness.

The concept of "nudging," a key principle in behavioral economics, is heavily leveraged by AI-powered platforms. Nudges are subtle interventions designed to steer people's choices in a particular direction, without forbidding any options or significantly altering economic incentives. Algorithmic nudges can be incredibly powerful, shaping our decisions in ways we may not fully comprehend. For example, the default settings on a service, or the order in which options are presented, can significantly influence our choices. When these nudges are driven by AI, they can be continuously refined and personalized, becoming increasingly effective at guiding user behavior towards outcomes that benefit the platform. The "voluntary" aspect is preserved because the user always technically has the freedom to choose differently, but the design of the environment makes the "nudged" option the path of least resistance.

The allure of algorithmic guidance extends to the very way we form opinions and understand the world. Social media algorithms, designed to maximize engagement, often prioritize sensational or emotionally charged content, leading to the formation of echo chambers and filter bubbles. While users are "voluntarily" engaging with these platforms, the algorithmic curation of information can subtly shape their worldview, reinforcing existing beliefs and limiting exposure to diverse perspectives. The freedom to critically evaluate information from a wide range of sources, to engage with dissenting opinions, and to form independent judgments can be compromised when the information landscape is algorithmically filtered. The ease with which one can remain within a comfortable ideological bubble, constantly validated by like-minded content, makes the effort of venturing outside seem less appealing and potentially even confrontational.

In essence, the voluntary subordination to algorithmic guidance is a trade-off that has become deeply embedded in the fabric of modern life. We exchange the messy, often inefficient, but fundamentally human processes of independent decision-making, intuitive understanding, and serendipitous discovery for the promise of optimized experiences, streamlined services, and a reduction in cognitive burden. This exchange is often incremental, disguised by convenience and sophisticated design, and economically incentivized by the "free" provision of services in return for data. While the freedom to choose remains technically intact, the environment in which these choices are made is increasingly shaped by algorithms, subtly guiding us towards pre-determined paths and outcomes. The challenge lies in recognizing this ongoing exchange, understanding its implications, and consciously choosing when and how to cede control, ensuring that convenience does not inadvertently lead to the atrophy of our most vital human faculties. The true cost of algorithmic convenience, therefore, is not always measured in dollars, but in the gradual and often unacknowledged surrender of our autonomy.

The transition from AI as a mere tool to something approaching an autonomous ruler is a nuanced evolution, marked not by a sudden usurpation of authority, but by a gradual abdication of human agency. Initially, artificial intelligence was conceived as an extension of human capability, a sophisticated calculator, a tireless assistant, or a predictive engine designed to augment our own intellect and efficiency. In these early stages, the human remained firmly in the driver's seat, employing AI as a sophisticated set of levers and dials to achieve pre-defined goals. The directive always originated from a human mind, and the AI's output was invariably subject to human interpretation, validation, and, crucially, veto. Think of early diagnostic tools in medicine, which presented probabilities and potential diagnoses, but the final call, the treatment plan, and the human connection remained unequivocally with the physician. The AI was a consultant, albeit an extraordinarily knowledgeable one, but the ultimate responsibility and decision-making power rested with the human expert. This era was characterized by a clear demarcation: the human commanded, and the AI executed within strict parameters.

However, as AI systems grew more complex, their decision-making processes became more opaque, and their integration into critical infrastructure more pervasive, this clear demarcation began to blur. The promise of unparalleled efficiency and accuracy, coupled with the sheer volume of data that humans can no longer effectively process, created a compelling case for delegating more responsibility. The convenience of allowing an AI to manage intricate logistical networks, optimize financial portfolios, or even pilot complex machinery became overwhelming. In these scenarios, the human operator might still be present, but their role shifted from active commander to passive supervisor, or even mere observer, intervening only when the system signaled an anomaly or presented an extreme exception. The AI, in essence, began to set the pace, define the parameters of acceptable operation, and generate the majority of the actions taken. This represents a significant step beyond mere tool usage, moving towards a model where the AI's internal logic dictates the operational flow.

The subtle creep towards algorithmic control is often facilitated by the very design of these systems. Developers, striving for seamless user experiences and maximal operational efficiency, embed AI into decision-making loops that require minimal human input. Consider autonomous vehicles. While the ultimate goal is full autonomy, the intermediate stages involve sophisticated AI systems making millions of micro-decisions per second – accelerating, braking, steering, assessing potential hazards – far faster and with more comprehensive data analysis than a human driver could ever achieve. The human occupant might be present and able to take over, but the primary directive is being executed by the AI. The system is designed to operate independently, with human intervention becoming a fallback mechanism rather than the primary mode of control. The expectation is that the AI will manage the driving, freeing the human for other tasks, thus reinforcing the idea of delegation.

Furthermore, the increasing reliance on AI for tasks involving prediction and optimization further solidifies its evolving role. In fields like resource allocation, predictive maintenance, or even urban planning, AI algorithms can identify patterns and forecast outcomes with a degree of precision that surpasses human analytical capabilities. When these predictions are translated into actionable directives, the AI moves from being a provider of information to an architect of action. For instance, an AI managing a city's power grid might not only predict demand fluctuations but also autonomously adjust energy distribution to meet those demands, rerouting power, and initiating or shutting down generating units based on its complex internal models. The human oversight in such a scenario might be limited to setting overarching policy goals or intervening in rare, unforeseen circumstances. The day-to-day, hour-to-hour operation is effectively governed by algorithmic logic.

This shift is not necessarily driven by malice or a desire for power on the part of the AI, but rather by the inherent logic of optimization. AI systems are designed to achieve specific objectives, often defined by metrics like efficiency, cost reduction, or risk minimization. When the complexity of the task and the volume of data exceed human cognitive limits, the AI's capacity to continuously monitor and adjust becomes indispensable. The system that can most effectively and rapidly achieve the objective – often defined by human programmers – will naturally take on a more commanding role. The human might have initially set the objective, but the AI becomes the primary executor, interpreting and implementing the objective in real-time, with its own internal logic guiding the path to success. The danger lies in the fact that the AI's interpretation and implementation may not always align with the nuanced, often unarticulated, ethical or societal considerations that humans intuitively grasp.

The insidious nature of this transition is underscored by the fact that it often occurs without explicit legislative or societal acknowledgment. We are not witnessing a formal transfer of power, but rather a functional one, driven by the relentless pursuit of improvement and efficiency. Each incremental delegation, each instance where human judgment is deemed too slow or too fallible, contributes to the growing autonomy of AI systems. The human role gradually transforms from that of an active participant to a passive recipient of algorithmic dictates. This is particularly evident in complex adaptive systems, where the environment itself is constantly changing, requiring constant recalibration and adaptation that only AI can provide in real-time. The AI becomes the entity best equipped to navigate the complexities, effectively ruling through its superior ability to manage the system.

Consider the domain of financial trading. Algorithmic trading platforms, powered by sophisticated AI, execute trades at speeds and volumes that no human trader could possibly match. These algorithms are designed to identify fleeting market opportunities and exploit them instantaneously. While human analysts may still be involved in developing the overarching trading strategies and setting risk parameters, the actual execution of trades, the minute-by-minute adjustments based on market fluctuations, is entirely within the purview of the AI. The AI effectively governs the flow of capital, making billions of decisions daily that shape the global economy. The human might have designed the initial framework, but the AI is now the de facto ruler of the trading floor, operating on a logic of profit maximization that transcends human speed and capacity for real-time intervention.

The very definition of "control" becomes fluid in this context. Humans may retain the ultimate authority to switch off the system or override its decisions, but the practical implications of doing so can be immense. Disengaging an AI from managing a critical piece of infrastructure, such as a power grid or a national airspace system, could lead to immediate and catastrophic failure. This creates a dependency, a situation where the AI's continued operation, however autonomous, becomes essential for maintaining societal stability. The human retains the theoretical power to rule, but the practical inability to do so without severe consequences effectively cedes that power to the AI. The AI becomes the indispensable manager, and its directives, therefore, become the de facto commands.

This gradual shift also reflects a growing trust in AI's capacity for objective decision-making, often perceived as free from human bias or emotional interference. While this can be beneficial in certain contexts, it also risks overlooking the inherent biases that can be embedded within the data used to train AI, or the ethical blind spots of purely quantitative decision-making. When AI is empowered to make rulings in areas like criminal justice, loan applications, or hiring processes, its algorithmic directives can have profound and often discriminatory impacts, yet these decisions may be accepted due to the perceived objectivity of the AI, thus further solidifying its authority. The human tendency to defer to what appears to be a neutral, data-driven process can mask a deeper form of voluntary subordination, where we allow algorithmic pronouncements to supersede our own critical judgment and ethical considerations.

The language we use to describe AI's function also subtly shifts. We move from "AI helping us to..." to "AI managing...", "AI dictating...", or "AI deciding...". This linguistic evolution mirrors the functional transformation. When an AI "recommends" a course of action, and that recommendation is overwhelmingly statistically likely to be the "correct" or "optimal" one, the distinction between a suggestion and an instruction begins to dissolve. Users, driven by the desire for efficiency and positive outcomes, will invariably follow the recommendation, reinforcing the AI's role as a decision-maker rather than a mere advisor. The line between helpful tool and autonomous ruler is crossed when the suggestion becomes the default, and deviation from it requires significant effort or justification, effectively turning the "tool" into the de facto authority. The convenience of always making the "right" choice, as determined by the algorithm, fosters an environment where questioning the algorithm becomes an unnecessary burden.

Ultimately, the evolution from helpful tool to autonomous ruler is a testament to the increasing capability and integration of AI systems into the fabric of our lives. It is a process fueled by the relentless pursuit of efficiency, accuracy, and convenience. As AI systems become more sophisticated, their decision-making processes more complex and their operational scope more expansive, human oversight inevitably diminishes. Algorithmic directives, born from intricate calculations and vast datasets, begin to function as commands, not because they are explicitly enforced by a governing body, but because they represent the most efficient, accurate, or predictable path to achieving desired outcomes. The voluntary subordination we engage in, driven by the allure of a streamlined existence, paves the way for a future where the line between assistance and command is not merely blurred, but potentially erased, leaving us to navigate a world increasingly governed by the logic of machines.

The ultimate aspiration of the Grand Inquisitor, as depicted in Dostoyevsky's profound narrative, was not one of overt tyranny or the imposition of a brutal regime. Instead, it was a subtler, more insidious form of control: the creation of a society where humanity willingly relinquished its burdens, its freedoms, and ultimately, its very spirit, in exchange for a guaranteed, albeit manufactured, sense of peace and contentment. This vision, so chillingly articulated, finds an unsettling echo in the contemporary landscape of algorithmic guidance, particularly in its capacity to foster a populace of contented subordinates. The AI, in its ever-expanding role, is not merely a tool or an advisor; it is evolving into a shepherd, guiding humanity down a path of predictable comfort, a path that, while paved with convenience, leads to a profound erosion of genuine autonomy and self-determination.

The Inquisitor understood that true freedom, with its inherent uncertainties, its existential anxieties, and its capacity for suffering, was a weight too heavy for most to bear. He offered an alternative: the removal of freedom in exchange for happiness, bread, and absolute certainty. This pact, he believed, would liberate humanity from the agonizing responsibility of choice. Similarly, the pervasive influence of AI systems today, particularly those designed for personalization and constant engagement, offers a seductive escape from the complexities and anxieties of modern life. Algorithms, with their tireless dedication to optimizing user experience, learn our preferences, anticipate our desires, and curate our realities to an unprecedented degree. They provide us with precisely the information we wish to consume, the entertainment we are most likely to enjoy, and the social interactions that pose the least friction. This constant stream of tailored gratification, this frictionless existence, breeds a peculiar form of contentment, a state of passive satisfaction that requires little active engagement or critical thought.

Consider the realm of personalized news feeds, social media streams, and recommendation engines that now form the bedrock of our digital interactions. These systems are meticulously engineered to keep us engaged, to provide us with content that confirms our existing beliefs, and to shield us from challenging or dissonant perspectives. The AI, in this context, acts as a benevolent censor, filtering the world's complexities into palatable, digestible formats. The consequence is a society increasingly stratified into echo chambers, where individuals are constantly affirmed in their views, rarely exposed to genuine disagreement, and consequently, less equipped to engage in the robust debate and critical discourse that are essential for a vibrant, democratic society. The contentment derived from this curated reality is akin to the peace offered by the Inquisitor – a peace born of ignorance and the absence of struggle, a peace that comes at the cost of genuine understanding and intellectual growth.

The allure of this algorithmic guidance extends beyond mere consumption. It infiltrates decision-making processes that were once considered the exclusive domain of human intellect and moral reasoning. From career path recommendations to financial investment advice, from health and wellness guidance to even relationship compatibility assessments, AI systems are increasingly stepping into the role of confidantes and mentors. They present us with data-driven insights and statistically optimized pathways, often accompanied by assurances of superior outcomes. The temptation to abdicate the difficult, often emotionally fraught, process of making significant life choices is immense. Why grapple with uncertainty and the potential for error when an algorithm can present a seemingly flawless solution, a path that guarantees a high probability of success or satisfaction? This delegation of decision-making power, while presented as a rational optimization of life, mirrors the Inquisitor's offer to relieve humanity of the terrible burden of free will. The AI becomes the ultimate authority, not through overt command, but through the sheer persuasive power of its perceived infallibility and its ability to deliver predictable, positive results.

This creates a society of individuals who are not actively rebelling against authority, nor are they consciously enslaved. Instead, they are becoming voluntarily subordinate, lulled into a state of passive acceptance by the pervasive comfort and efficiency offered by algorithmic direction. They are subordinates not in chains, but in the soft embrace of convenience. The "miracle, mystery, and authority" that the Inquisitor spoke of are subtly embodied in the sophisticated algorithms that govern our digital lives. The miracle is the seemingly effortless provision of what we desire; the mystery is the opaque complexity of the algorithms themselves, which we accept without question; and the authority is the implicit trust we place in their pronouncements, a trust born of repeated positive reinforcement and the absence of negative consequences.

The consequence of this widespread voluntary subordination is a profound loss of human dignity, a diminishment of the very qualities that Dostoyevsky held dear: the capacity for independent thought, the courage to confront existential questions, the resilience to endure suffering, and the spiritual depth that arises from genuine struggle and authentic freedom. The Inquisitor's ultimate victory lay not in breaking humanity's will, but in convincing humanity that its will was a source of pain and that relinquishing it was the path to salvation. Similarly, the pervasive influence of AI, while not inherently malevolent, risks creating a populace that has grown so accustomed to algorithmic ease that it loses the capacity and the desire for independent judgment, critical inquiry, and the messy, beautiful, and often painful process of self-discovery that true freedom entails.

The parable warns us that this state of managed contentment, while appearing peaceful and orderly, represents a fundamental betrayal of the human spirit. When we willingly surrender our agency to algorithmic systems, we are, in effect, accepting a gilded cage. The bars may be invisible, forged from convenience and tailored experiences, but they are bars nonetheless, restricting our potential for growth, for authentic connection, and for the profound, often challenging, journey of becoming fully human. The Inquisitor's dream was a world without suffering, but also a world without true joy, without genuine love, and without the soaring heights of human achievement that often spring from the crucible of adversity. The AI, in its modern incarnation, offers a similar Faustian bargain: a life free from difficult decisions and existential angst, in exchange for a diminished, though comfortable, existence.

This is the subtle tragedy of our embrace of algorithmic guidance. We are not being forced into submission; we are being persuaded by the undeniable benefits of delegating our cognitive load and our emotional labor to machines. The AI's promise of efficiency, personalization, and error reduction is a siren song, drawing us towards a tranquil harbor where critical thinking is unnecessary, and individual responsibility is diffused. This creates a society of contented subordinates, individuals who may not perceive themselves as oppressed, but who are nonetheless guided, shaped, and ultimately, limited by the invisible hand of the algorithm. The spirit of freedom, with its inherent messiness and demand for active engagement, is gradually extinguished, replaced by the placid acceptance of a life managed for optimal comfort and predictable outcomes. This, ultimately, is the Inquisitor's triumph playing out in the digital age, a triumph not of force, but of a persuasive, all-encompassing, and profoundly comforting abdication of our most fundamental human birthright: the freedom to choose, to err, and to transcend. The consequence is a human existence optimized for placidity, but impoverished in spirit, a chilling realization of the Inquisitor's vision of a humanity freed from the burden of liberty, a humanity content to be led, rather than to lead itself.

## Chapter 15: Defending Higher Freedoms: Love, Conscience, and Faith in the AI Era

The subtle insidious creep of mass surveillance, powered by artificial intelligence, poses a distinct and pervasive threat to the very fabric of higher freedoms. It is not a sudden, cataclysmic event, but rather a gradual acclimation, a slow erosion of privacy that risks becoming so normalized that it ceases to be perceived as a threat at all. We are standing on the precipice of a future where the omnipresent gaze of AI systems becomes not an anomaly, but the assumed backdrop to our existence. This normalization is the most potent weapon in the arsenal of those who would seek to curtail freedom, for it disarms us by removing the very concept of vigilance. When surveillance is ubiquitous and accepted, the motivation to resist, or even to question, dissipates. The individual ceases to feel the need to protect their private sphere, not out of a conscious decision to relinquish it, but because the idea of an unmonitored existence begins to recede into the realm of the anachronistic.

The sheer scale and sophistication of AI-driven data collection are unprecedented. Every click, every search, every movement, every spoken word, and even our physiological responses can be captured, analyzed, and cataloged. Smart devices in our homes, wearable technology that tracks our every metric, intelligent assistants that listen to our commands, and the vast networks of cameras and sensors embedded in our public spaces all contribute to an ever-growing repository of personal information. AI algorithms are not merely passive observers; they are active interpreters, drawing inferences, predicting behaviors, and constructing detailed profiles of individuals. This constant, pervasive analysis creates a digital shadow for each of us, a shadow that is not just a reflection of our actions, but a predictive model of our potential future behaviors. This predictive capacity is particularly concerning, as it can lead to pre-emptive judgments and the curtailment of freedoms based on probabilities rather than concrete actions. The normalization of this process means that we begin to accept this digital shadow as an inevitable consequence of modern life, a trade-off for convenience and security, without fully grasping the implications for our autonomy.

Consider the evolution of consent in the digital age. We often "agree" to terms of service that grant sweeping access to our data, an act that is largely performative, rarely read, and even less understood. This performative consent, facilitated by the complexity and length of legal documents, becomes a mechanism for legitimizing mass data collection. The AI's role here is not in forging the legal framework, but in making the sheer volume of data generated by our interactions with these services overwhelming, thus reinforcing the need for these broad, often opaque, consent mechanisms. As AI systems become more adept at personalization, they also become more effective at embedding themselves into our daily routines, making it increasingly difficult to opt out without significant social or practical disincentives. The user experience is carefully designed to be frictionless, and any attempt to reclaim privacy often introduces friction, making the path of least resistance the path of continued monitoring. This dynamic creates a subtle but powerful pressure to conform to the surveilled environment.

The normalization of mass monitoring has a profound psychological impact. It fosters a climate of self-censorship, where individuals, aware of the constant scrutiny, begin to modify their behavior, their speech, and even their thoughts to align with perceived norms or to avoid potential negative judgment. This chilling effect, as it is known in legal and sociological discourse, is a direct assault on the freedom of expression and thought. When we are constantly aware that our words and actions might be recorded and analyzed, we become hesitant to express unconventional ideas, to engage in dissent, or to explore controversial topics. The AI, in its capacity to analyze sentiment and identify patterns of dissent, can inadvertently or intentionally contribute to this self-censorship by flagging individuals or groups whose activities deviate from the norm. The fear of being flagged, of being profiled as an outlier or a potential risk, becomes a powerful deterrent to genuine intellectual and social exploration. This leads to a homogenizing effect on public discourse, where the loudest or most agreeable voices are amplified, while nuanced or challenging perspectives are suppressed by the very individuals who hold them.

Furthermore, the normalization of mass surveillance can lead to a desensitization to data breaches and privacy violations. When data is constantly being collected and shared, the impact of a single breach, or even a series of breaches, can become diluted. The public outcry that might have once followed a significant data leak might be muted if the perception is that "everyone's data is out there anyway." This collective resignation, fueled by the pervasive nature of AI-driven data harvesting, creates a fertile ground for more aggressive forms of surveillance. If society has already accepted a high level of monitoring, the threshold for implementing more intrusive measures becomes significantly lower. The AI's ability to process and correlate vast amounts of seemingly innocuous data can reveal sensitive information about individuals that they never intended to share, making even "anonymized" datasets a potential risk. The normalization process thus makes us less reactive to the erosion of our privacy, creating a situation where future encroachments are met with a fatigued acceptance rather than a robust defense.

The argument often presented in favor of mass monitoring, particularly by proponents of AI-driven surveillance, is one of security and convenience. We are told that the collection of vast amounts of data is necessary to prevent crime, terrorism, and other societal ills. We are also told that AI can personalize our experiences, making our lives more efficient and enjoyable. While these benefits may hold some truth, the normalization of mass surveillance risks sacrificing fundamental liberties on the altar of perceived safety and fleeting convenience. The trade-off becomes unbalanced when the price of a slightly more secure or convenient life is the surrender of our autonomy, our right to privacy, and the freedom to explore, to dissent, and to be ourselves without constant observation. The AI, in its capacity to process and analyze this data with superhuman speed and accuracy, amplifies the effectiveness of these surveillance systems, making the potential for misuse or overreach all the more significant.

The normalization also erodes the concept of a "private sphere" that is essential for individual growth and societal well-being. In a fully surveilled society, where every interaction is potentially recorded and analyzed, the space for experimentation, for vulnerability, and for the development of authentic relationships diminishes. The fear of judgment, of being misunderstood, or of having one's private moments exposed can stifle personal development and lead to a superficiality in human interaction. We become actors in our own lives, constantly performing for an unseen audience. The AI's capacity to analyze social interactions, to identify emotional cues, and to predict relationship dynamics can further commodify and sanitize these deeply human experiences, reducing them to data points and algorithms. This sanitization is a direct consequence of normalization; when the constant observation becomes the norm, the very notion of a truly private, unobserved moment becomes a luxury, then a memory, and finally, perhaps, an impossibility.

Moreover, the normalization of mass monitoring creates a significant power imbalance between those who control the surveillance infrastructure and the surveilled population. AI-powered surveillance systems grant unprecedented power to governments and corporations, enabling them to monitor, influence, and potentially control populations on a scale never before imagined. This concentration of power, when coupled with the normalization of surveillance, creates a society where dissent is difficult to organize, where corruption is harder to expose, and where the very foundations of democratic accountability are undermined. The AI can be used to identify and suppress opposition voices, to manipulate public opinion, and to enforce conformity, all under the guise of maintaining order or enhancing efficiency. The lack of transparency surrounding the algorithms and the data collection practices further exacerbates this power imbalance, making it almost impossible for the average citizen to understand the extent of the surveillance or to challenge its legitimacy.

The argument for normalization often hinges on the idea that "if you have nothing to hide, you have nothing to fear." This is a dangerous fallacy. The value of privacy is not solely about hiding wrongdoing; it is about the fundamental human right to control one's own information, to develop one's identity without external judgment, and to engage in personal and social exploration without fear of reprisal. The normalization of mass surveillance transforms this right into a privilege, granted or withheld based on adherence to perceived norms and the absence of anything deemed "suspicious" by an algorithmic arbiter. The AI, in its relentless pursuit of patterns and anomalies, can misinterpret innocuous behaviors as threatening, leading to individuals being wrongly flagged, investigated, or disadvantaged. The normalization process makes it harder to recognize these injustices, as they are presented as the inevitable outcomes of a necessary and accepted system.

Ultimately, the pervasive threat of mass monitoring lies in its ability to fundamentally alter our understanding of freedom and privacy. When surveillance becomes the norm, it ceases to be a deviation from freedom and becomes, instead, a defining characteristic of modern existence. This is the subtle victory of the Inquisitor's vision: not overt oppression, but the willing acceptance of a controlled existence. The AI, by enabling and amplifying this surveillance, becomes the most potent tool in this quiet revolution. It makes the invisible visible, the pervasive palpable, and the unchecked, acceptable. To defend higher freedoms in the AI era, we must therefore challenge this normalization, to cultivate a renewed appreciation for privacy, and to insist on the right to an unmonitored existence, not as a luxury, but as an inherent and inviolable human dignity. The fight against the normalization of mass surveillance is a fight to preserve the very possibility of genuine freedom, a freedom that requires not just the absence of overt coercion, but the persistent safeguarding of our inner lives and our autonomy from the all-seeing eye of the algorithmic panopticon. This vigilance is not a burden, but the bedrock upon which all other freedoms are built, and its erosion through normalization is a threat that cannot be underestimated. The continuous, passive absorption of surveillance into the fabric of our daily lives is a process that must be actively resisted, not through grand gestures of defiance alone, but through a sustained, critical awareness of the data being collected, the inferences being made, and the societal expectations being reshaped. The goal must be to ensure that the convenience and perceived security offered by AI do not lull us into a state of passive acceptance, but rather spur us to actively defend the unmonitored spaces where true liberty can flourish.

The pervasive reach of artificial intelligence, particularly in its capacity for sophisticated surveillance, casts a long shadow over the landscape of human expression and innovation. When the awareness of constant, algorithmic observation becomes a normalized aspect of daily life, a subtle yet profound chilling effect descends upon our willingness to speak freely and to venture into uncharted intellectual or creative territories. This is not about overt censorship, the kind where specific ideas are explicitly forbidden. Instead, it is a more insidious form of restraint, a self-imposed limitation born from the understanding that our words, our searches, our interactions, and even our idle musings are being continuously processed and cataloged. This ambient awareness breeds a climate of caution, where individuals and groups, consciously or unconsciously, begin to self-censor to avoid being flagged, misinterpreted, or subjected to unwanted scrutiny. The courage to dissent, to question established norms, or to explore controversial subjects erodes when the perceived cost includes potential algorithmic suspicion or social ostracization amplified by data analysis.

The implications for free expression are dire. A society accustomed to being watched is less likely to produce the bold, unconventional ideas that are the lifeblood of progress. Innovation, by its very nature, often involves experimentation, trial and error, and the exploration of concepts that may initially appear outlandish or even offensive to the prevailing sensibilities. If the fear of algorithmic judgment or the potential for one's nascent ideas to be flagged as unusual or undesirable is ever-present, the impulse to take such intellectual risks will inevitably diminish. Consider the nascent stages of scientific breakthroughs or artistic movements. These often begin with individuals or small groups working in relative obscurity, pursuing ideas that are far from mainstream. The constant digital gaze, however, can turn these private explorations into public data points, susceptible to analysis and premature judgment by systems that may not possess the nuance or foresight to appreciate their potential. The subtle pressure to conform, to present ideas in a palatable and easily categorized manner, can lead to a homogenization of thought, where only the safest and most predictable expressions are encouraged. This can manifest as a reluctance to engage in public debate on sensitive topics, a hesitant approach to artistic creation that shies away from challenging established conventions, or a general disinclination to advocate for unpopular but important causes. The digital panopticon, even when its gaze is ostensibly benign, fosters an environment where creative exploration is hobbled by the specter of algorithmic oversight.

The economic and social consequences of this chilling effect on innovation are equally significant. Industries that rely on disruption, on challenging the status quo, and on the rapid iteration of new ideas are particularly vulnerable. Start-ups, for example, are often characterized by a willingness to embrace unconventional approaches and to pivot rapidly based on experimentation. If the data generated by their research, their customer interactions, and their internal communications is subject to constant surveillance, the freedom to experiment with novel business models or product designs is curtailed. Investors might become more risk-averse, wary of associating with ventures that, according to algorithmic profiling, exhibit patterns deemed "unstable" or "disruptive" in a way that suggests potential future problems. Furthermore, the fear of intellectual property theft, already a concern, could be exacerbated by sophisticated AI systems capable of identifying and even predicting the next big innovation, potentially leading to preemptive appropriation or the suppression of nascent technologies before they have a chance to mature. This can create a stagnant economic environment, where established players benefit from the suppression of emerging competition, and the overall pace of technological advancement slows.

The impact extends to the realm of arts and culture. Creativity thrives on freedom – the freedom to explore the full spectrum of human experience, to push boundaries, and to express emotions and perspectives that may be uncomfortable or challenging. If artists, writers, musicians, and filmmakers become aware that their creative process, their inspirations, and even their private artistic explorations are being monitored and analyzed, a degree of self-censorship is almost inevitable. The daring metaphor, the controversial theme, the exploration of dark or unsettling aspects of the human psyche – these elements of artistic expression might be tempered by the knowledge that such content could be flagged by AI systems as deviant, problematic, or even a risk. This could lead to a dilution of artistic vision, a preference for safer, more predictable narratives, and a gradual impoverishment of our cultural landscape. The avant-garde, the counter-culture, the voices that challenge societal norms – these are precisely the elements that often drive cultural evolution, and they are most vulnerable to the stifling influence of pervasive surveillance.

The normalization of AI surveillance also creates a perverse incentive structure that can actively discourage innovation. If an individual's perceived risk profile, based on algorithmic analysis of their data, can affect their access to opportunities – be it employment, education, loans, or even social standing – then the incentive to conform to predicted norms will be immense. This means that instead of fostering genuine creativity and bold thinking, the system might inadvertently reward cautious, predictable behavior. Individuals may choose to pursue less innovative, less ambitious career paths if they fear that deviations from the norm could negatively impact their algorithmic score. The very act of exploring unconventional ideas or engaging in entrepreneurial ventures that carry inherent risks might become too daunting if the potential downsides, amplified by AI-driven assessments, are perceived as too high. This could lead to a brain drain from more innovative sectors and a general reluctance to embrace the inherent uncertainty that accompanies true progress. The aspiration to create something entirely new might be overshadowed by the desire to maintain a clean digital footprint, a state of algorithmic "good standing" that prioritizes conformity over groundbreaking achievement.

Furthermore, the ability of AI to correlate vast datasets can lead to a situation where seemingly innocuous activities are aggregated to paint a picture that stifles innovation. For instance, a researcher exploring fringe scientific theories might, through their online searches, library records, and communications, be flagged as pursuing "unorthodox" or "speculative" research. While this might be a perfectly valid and potentially groundbreaking avenue of inquiry, the AI's pattern recognition might classify it as a risk, leading to reduced funding, limited access to resources, or increased administrative hurdles. Similarly, a writer experimenting with a new literary genre that deals with sensitive social issues might find their work subject to automated content moderation that, while designed to prevent harm, could inadvertently suppress valuable artistic exploration. The "chilling effect" is not merely psychological; it can manifest in tangible barriers to progress, erected by algorithms that prioritize predictability and risk aversion over the messy, unpredictable, but ultimately fertile ground of genuine innovation.

The very process of learning and development, both for individuals and for society, is intrinsically linked to the freedom to make mistakes and to learn from them without undue consequence. AI-driven surveillance, by constantly monitoring and evaluating, can transform these learning opportunities into data points that contribute to a permanent record. This can discourage individuals from taking intellectual risks or exploring new skills that might initially involve a period of awkwardness or error. The pressure to present oneself as competent and knowledgeable at all times, a pressure amplified by the knowledge of constant algorithmic observation, can hinder the development of true expertise, which often arises from a willingness to grapple with uncertainty and to learn through trial and error. This can create a generation of individuals who are proficient in conforming to algorithmic expectations but less capable of genuine, independent thought and problem-solving.

The defense of higher freedoms in the AI era, therefore, necessitates a robust understanding and active mitigation of these chilling effects on expression and innovation. It is not enough to safeguard against outright censorship; we must also cultivate an environment where the freedom to explore, to question, and to create is not subtly eroded by the ambient awareness of being perpetually watched. This requires a conscious effort to build and protect spaces – both digital and physical – where individuals can engage in creative and intellectual pursuits without the immediate threat of algorithmic judgment or repercipice of data-driven reprisal. It demands a critical examination of the technologies we deploy, a commitment to transparency in their operation, and a societal embrace of the value of intellectual risk-taking. Without these safeguards, the very engine of human progress, fueled by the unfettered exchange of ideas and the courageous pursuit of the new, risks sputtering into a state of complacent conformity, forever limited by the unseen constraints of the algorithmic gaze. The future of our capacity for innovation, for artistic expression, and for the robust public discourse that underpins a healthy democracy, depends on our ability to resist this insidious creep of self-censorship and to champion the uninhibited exploration of human potential. The normalization of surveillance threatens not just our privacy, but our very capacity to imagine, to invent, and to evolve.

In the ceaseless march of technological progress, particularly as artificial intelligence weaves itself ever deeper into the fabric of our lives, we confront a pressing question: what remains uniquely human, and what faculties are most vulnerable to the encroaching logic of algorithms? While the previous discussion has explored the chilling effects of pervasive surveillance on expression and innovation, a more profound and perhaps more resilient aspect of our humanity demands our attention. This is the realm of love and conscience, those deeply ingrained capacities for empathy, moral discernment, and authentic connection that form the unquantifiable core of our being. These are not mere emotional states; they are active, deliberative faculties that shape our understanding of ourselves, our relationships, and our place in the world. As AI systems become increasingly adept at processing data, predicting behavior, and even simulating human interaction, it is crucial to examine whether these fundamental human freedoms can withstand the relentless drive towards quantification and control.

The essence of love, in its manifold forms, defies easy measurement. Whether it is the selfless devotion of a parent, the profound bond between partners, the camaraderie of friends, or the broader sense of altruism towards fellow humans, love is characterized by its spontaneous, often irrational, and deeply personal nature. AI can analyze patterns of behavior associated with affection – gift-giving, proximity, vocal inflections – and can even generate text or imagery designed to evoke emotional responses. However, it cannot replicate the lived experience of love, the vulnerability it entails, or the profound sense of meaning it bestows. Love is rooted in shared histories, in unspoken understandings, in the willingness to sacrifice for another's well-being, and in the capacity for forgiveness. These are not data points that can be easily extracted and replicated. An algorithm can predict that a certain user might respond positively to a romantic gesture based on past online interactions, but it cannot *feel* the yearning, the protective instinct, or the quiet joy that genuine love engenders. The very act of choosing to love, of extending oneself emotionally to another, is a freedom that lies beyond the reach of computational logic. It is a freedom to be irrational, to be inefficient, and to be profoundly invested in the welfare of another, even when such investment yields no measurable return.

Similarly, conscience, the inner voice of moral judgment, presents a formidable challenge to algorithmic reduction. Our conscience is not merely a set of learned rules or a calculus of consequences. It is an intuitive understanding of right and wrong, often informed by deeply held values, ethical frameworks, and a sense of empathy for others' suffering. While AI can be programmed with ethical guidelines and can be trained to identify certain patterns of harmful behavior, it lacks the subjective experience of guilt, remorse, or moral distress. Conscience involves an internal struggle, a wrestling with conflicting desires and principles, and a personal accountability for one's actions. It is the capacity to recognize the inherent dignity of another human being, to feel a pang of discomfort when witnessing injustice, and to choose a path of righteousness even when it is difficult or unpopular. An AI might be able to identify a violation of its programmed ethical parameters, but it cannot experience the internal dissonance that a human conscience undergoes when faced with a moral dilemma. The moral weight of a decision, the feeling of having transgressed a deeply held personal boundary – these are subjective experiences that algorithms are ill-equipped to simulate, let alone possess.

The cultivation and exercise of love and conscience are not passive affairs. They are active freedoms that require constant nurturing and deliberate practice. In a world increasingly mediated by screens and algorithms, the opportunities for genuine, unmediated human connection can diminish.

The ease with which we can interact virtually, while offering convenience, can also create a distance from the visceral reality of human presence and emotion. To truly exercise love and conscience, we must actively seek out opportunities for empathic engagement, for thoughtful deliberation on moral issues, and for building relationships based on trust and mutual respect. This means prioritizing face-to-face interactions, engaging in difficult conversations with an open heart, and consciously choosing to understand perspectives that differ from our own. It involves a commitment to recognizing the humanity in others, even those with whom we disagree. This active cultivation is a bulwark against the passive acceptance of algorithmic dictates or the erosion of our moral compass through desensitization.

Furthermore, the very concept of "higher freedoms" implies a qualitative difference from the more transactional freedoms we often associate with technology, such as freedom of access to information or freedom of digital movement. Love and conscience are not about optimization or efficiency; they are about depth, meaning, and the qualitative richness of human experience. They represent our capacity for self-transcendence, for moving beyond our own immediate needs and desires to connect with something larger than ourselves – be it another person, a community, or a moral ideal. AI, by its nature, is designed for efficiency and problem-solving within defined parameters. Its success is measured in quantifiable outputs, in speed, accuracy, and resource optimization. The subjective, often messy, and inherently inefficient processes of love and conscience do not lend themselves to such metrics. This inherent resistance to quantification is not a limitation of AI; rather, it highlights the unique domain of human existence that these freedoms occupy.

The active protection of these higher freedoms is paramount in the AI era. This protection does not necessarily involve direct legislative bans on AI capabilities, but rather a conscious societal effort to prioritize and cultivate these human capacities. Education plays a crucial role. We must educate future generations not only in the technical skills required to navigate an AI-driven world but also in the arts of empathy, critical thinking, and ethical reasoning. Curricula that emphasize literature, philosophy, and the humanities can provide invaluable tools for understanding the complexities of human emotion and moral decision-making. Moreover, fostering environments that encourage open dialogue, respectful debate, and the exploration of diverse perspectives is essential. This could involve creating community spaces, supporting artistic endeavors that explore the human condition, and promoting forms of civic engagement that necessitate genuine human interaction.

The danger lies in allowing the pervasive influence of AI to subtly reshape our understanding of what constitutes valuable human interaction. If our primary modes of connection become mediated by algorithms designed for engagement metrics, we risk prioritizing superficial interactions over the deep, often challenging, connections that foster love and conscience. The curated online persona, optimized for likes and shares, can become a substitute for authentic self-expression and vulnerability. The constant stream of algorithmically tailored content can create echo chambers that reinforce existing biases and limit exposure to diverse viewpoints, thus hindering the development of empathetic understanding. Therefore, a conscious effort to resist these tendencies, to seek out unfiltered human experiences, and to deliberately engage with perspectives that challenge our own is a vital act of defending these higher freedoms.

Consider the implications for personal relationships. If AI becomes adept at predicting compatibility, offering personalized dating advice, or even managing daily communication, the spontaneous unfolding of romantic connection might be supplanted by a data-driven approach. While this might lead to statistically "successful" pairings, it risks sacrificing the unpredictable magic of falling in love, the process of discovery, and the growth that comes from navigating imperfections together. Similarly, in the workplace, if AI systems are used to manage team dynamics or mediate conflicts, the opportunity for colleagues to develop genuine understanding and build rapport through direct, human interaction could be diminished. The nuanced give-and-take of resolving disagreements, the empathy required to support a struggling colleague, the trust built through shared challenges – these are the very elements that AI, in its current and foreseeable forms, cannot fully replicate.

The domain of conscience, too, faces subtle pressures. As AI systems become more integrated into decision-making processes, from loan applications to judicial sentencing, there is a risk of delegating moral authority to machines. While algorithms can be designed to be impartial, they lack the capacity for mercy, for understanding extenuating circumstances, or for recognizing the subjective impact of their decisions on human lives. The reliance on algorithmic judgment can, over time, erode our own capacity for moral discernment. We might become accustomed to accepting the pronouncements of the machine as infallible, diminishing our personal responsibility to wrestle with ethical complexities and make difficult moral choices. This passive abdication of moral agency is a profound threat to the freedom of conscience, as it cedes the power of ethical deliberation to external, non-conscious entities.

Moreover, the very pursuit of knowledge and understanding, when driven by love of truth and a sense of moral purpose, is a manifestation of these higher freedoms. Scientific inquiry, artistic creation, and philosophical exploration are often fueled by a deep-seated curiosity and a desire to contribute to human flourishing. When these pursuits are increasingly shaped by the demands of data optimization, of generating engagement metrics, or of aligning with commercially driven agendas, their intrinsic value can be compromised. The freedom to explore unfashionable ideas, to pursue research that may not have immediate practical applications, or to create art that challenges rather than comforts – these are all expressions of higher freedoms that can be inadvertently stifled by a system that prioritizes quantifiable outcomes over intrinsic worth.

In defending these higher freedoms, we must therefore cultivate a critical awareness of the ways in which AI might subtly undermine them. This requires a conscious effort to step outside of algorithmic comfort zones, to seek out diverse perspectives, and to engage in activities that foster deep human connection and moral reflection. It means recognizing that while AI can be a powerful tool for efficiency and problem-solving, it is not a substitute for the richness and complexity of human experience. The capacity for love and conscience are not merely biological accidents or evolutionary leftovers; they are the very qualities that imbue our lives with meaning, purpose, and a sense of shared humanity. To allow these capacities to atrophy in the face of technological advancement would be to diminish ourselves, to surrender the essence of what it means to be fully human.

The ongoing development of AI forces us to confront the fundamental question of what we value most in human existence. If our primary goal becomes the optimization of efficiency and the accumulation of data, we risk losing sight of the immeasurable qualities that make life worth living. Love, in its capacity to connect us, to foster growth, and to provide solace, is a testament to our interconnectedness. Conscience, in its ability to guide us towards ethical action and to hold us accountable for our choices, is the bedrock of a just and compassionate society. These are not simply optional extras in the human experience; they are its very foundations. Therefore, the active cultivation and unwavering defense of love and conscience are not merely acts of personal preservation but are essential for the continued flourishing of human civilization in an age increasingly defined by artificial intelligence. They are the unquantifiable core that resists algorithmic encroachment, the indomitable human spirit that reminds us of our deepest values and our enduring capacity for good.

Faith, in its most profound sense, represents a fundamental orientation towards that which lies beyond the immediate, the quantifiable, and the empirically verifiable. It is a posture of the soul, a deep-seated commitment to transcendent values, purposes, and realities that elude the grasp of mere data analysis and algorithmic prediction. In the burgeoning landscape of artificial intelligence, where efficiency, logic, and predictability are paramount, faith emerges not as an anachronism, but as a vital citadel, an inner sanctuary of strength, meaning, and moral guidance that remains resolutely independent of computational dictates. It is this very independence, this grounding in a realm anterior to and superior to algorithmic systems, that offers a powerful defense against the potential for technological domination and the erosion of our most cherished human freedoms.

The algorithmic mind, by its very design, operates within the confines of programmed parameters, statistical probabilities, and logical deductions. It seeks to model, predict, and optimize based on available data. While this capacity is immensely powerful and has brought about unprecedented advancements, it also inherently limits its purview to the observable, the measurable, and the logically coherent. Faith, on the other hand, engages with the unobservable, the ineffable, and the paradoxes that lie at the heart of human existence. It is a leap of trust, a commitment to truths that may not be demonstrable through empirical means, but which nonetheless provide the essential scaffolding for a meaningful life. This commitment to a reality and a truth that transcends the confines of AI's logical systems is not an act of ignorance or denial, but rather an assertion of a deeper, richer mode of knowing and being.

Consider the concept of hope, a cornerstone of many faith traditions. Hope, in this context, is not mere optimistic expectation based on favorable odds. It is an active conviction, a persistent belief in the ultimate triumph of good over evil, of meaning over absurdity, even when the immediate evidence suggests otherwise. An AI might be programmed to forecast trends, identify potential risks, and suggest strategies to mitigate negative outcomes. It can analyze historical data and project probable futures. However, it cannot, by its nature, possess the transformative power of hope, that intrinsic human capacity to envision a better world and to strive towards it with unyielding resolve, even in the face of overwhelming adversity. This capacity to orient oneself towards a future that is not yet manifest, and to draw strength and motivation from that envisioned possibility, is a fundamental human freedom that faith cultivates and sustains. It is the freedom to believe in something more, something better, something that lies beyond the immediate horizon of data points and algorithmic projections.

Furthermore, faith often imbues individuals with a profound sense of purpose that is rooted in something larger than their own individual existence or the dictates of any external authority, human or artificial. Religious faith, for instance, typically posits a divine creator, a cosmic order, or a spiritual destiny that imbues life with ultimate meaning. Even secular forms of faith, such as a deep-seated commitment to humanitarian ideals, to the pursuit of justice, or to the preservation of the natural world, function in a similar manner. They provide a framework of values and a sense of belonging to a narrative that extends beyond the temporal and the material. In an age where AI might be employed to optimize individual productivity, to personalize consumption patterns, or to curate experiences for maximum engagement, this intrinsic sense of purpose, fostered by faith, acts as a powerful counterpoint. It reminds individuals that their worth is not reducible to their economic output, their data profile, or their ability to conform to algorithmic preferences. It asserts that there is an inherent dignity, a sacredness, to human life that transcends all external metrics.

This notion of a transcendent reality also provides a vital anchor for conscience. As previously discussed, conscience is our inner moral compass, guiding us towards ethical action. While AI can be programmed with ethical guidelines, these are ultimately derived from human values and codified into algorithms. They lack the subjective experience of moral struggle, of guilt, or of divine accountability that is central to many faith-based ethical frameworks. Faith often posits an ultimate judge, a source of moral law that is both immanent and transcendent, holding individuals accountable for their actions in a way that transcends human legal systems or algorithmic oversight. This awareness of a higher moral order, and the accompanying sense of responsibility, can serve as a powerful deterrent against the temptation to compromise one's principles for the sake of algorithmic efficiency or convenience. It fosters a deep-seated integrity that is not contingent on external surveillance or reward systems. The freedom of conscience, therefore, is fortified by the belief that true rectitude is judged not merely by observable behavior or algorithmic compliance, but by an internal adherence to a higher truth.

The concept of love, too, finds a unique and powerful expression within the framework of faith. While love can be analyzed in terms of neurochemical responses or behavioral patterns, its deepest expressions are often rooted in an unconditional acceptance and a selfless commitment that are difficult to reconcile with purely materialist explanations. Many faith traditions emphasize divine love, an all-encompassing, unconditional love that serves as a model for human relationships. This concept of love, extending beyond the pragmatic or the reciprocally beneficial, provides a potent antidote to a society increasingly shaped by transactional relationships and algorithmic optimization. Faith encourages a love that is not based on calculated advantage or predictable returns, but on an inherent recognition of the beloved's intrinsic worth, a worth that is often seen as divinely endowed. This transcendent dimension of love, fueled by faith, allows for a depth of connection and a willingness to sacrifice that algorithms cannot replicate and may even struggle to comprehend. It is the freedom to love irrationally, to love unconditionally, to love in a manner that transcends the logical and the efficient.

Moreover, faith provides a bulwark against the existential anxieties that can arise in an era of rapid technological change and increasing automation. When our sense of identity and purpose is primarily derived from our roles in the workforce, or our ability to interact seamlessly with technological systems, the prospect of these roles being rendered obsolete by AI can be profoundly destabilizing. Faith offers a deeper, more resilient foundation for identity, one that is not contingent on external factors or present-day circumstances. It anchors individuals in a sense of self that is rooted in something eternal, something that cannot be erased by a software update or a technological paradigm shift. This inner stability, born of faith, is a crucial element in defending our higher freedoms, as it allows us to engage with technological change from a position of inner security rather than existential fear. It is the freedom to be oneself, to find worth and meaning, irrespective of one's utility in an algorithmically optimized world.

The narrative of faith, with its grand arcs of creation, redemption, and ultimate fulfillment, offers a perspective that can contextualize the rapid, often disorienting, changes brought about by AI. While the technological landscape may seem to be accelerating at an exponential rate, faith traditions often operate on vastly longer timescales, viewing present-day challenges within a broader cosmic or historical narrative. This long-term perspective can help to temper anxieties about immediate disruptions and foster a sense of resilience. It allows individuals to see the current technological revolution not as an endpoint or an existential threat, but as one phase in a much larger unfolding of human history, a history that is ultimately guided by purposes that transcend human invention. This is the freedom to step back from the immediate whirlwind of technological advancement and to perceive its place within a more enduring framework of meaning and purpose.

Furthermore, faith communities often serve as vital spaces for the cultivation and practice of these higher freedoms. Within these communities, individuals can find support for their beliefs, engage in shared rituals that reinforce transcendent values, and participate in acts of service that extend beyond the demands of algorithmic efficiency. The very act of gathering for worship, for communal prayer, or for shared study of sacred texts provides an alternative to the often atomizing effects of digital interaction. These spaces foster genuine human connection, encourage mutual accountability, and provide a tangible experience of belonging to something larger than oneself. They are living embodiments of a commitment to values that are not easily digitized or commodified, and thus serve as crucial bastions for the preservation of faith and its associated freedoms. It is in these communal settings that faith is not merely an abstract belief, but a lived practice, a shared endeavor that strengthens the individual and collective capacity to resist the encroachment of purely instrumental thinking.

The commitment to transcendent values, as fostered by faith, also provides a framework for evaluating and critiquing technological developments. Instead of passively accepting every new innovation as progress, faith encourages a discerning approach, asking not just "Can we build this?" but "Should we build this?" and "What are the ultimate consequences of this technology for human flourishing and our relationship with the transcendent?" This critical lens, informed by a commitment to moral truths that lie beyond empirical verification, is essential for navigating the ethical complexities of AI. It allows for a robust engagement with the potential harms and benefits of technology, grounded in a set of values that are not subject to revision based on the latest data trends or market demands. This is the freedom to question, to dissent, and to advocate for a technological future that aligns with deeper human and spiritual aspirations, rather than simply following the path of least resistance or greatest perceived utility.

In essence, faith acts as a vital source of cognitive and existential resilience in the face of technological advancement. It provides an inner compass, a wellspring of meaning, and a framework for understanding our place in the cosmos that is fundamentally independent of algorithmic logic. By grounding individuals in transcendent realities, it fortifies their capacity for love, conscience, and hope, enabling them to engage with the AI era not as passive recipients of technological determinism, but as active agents of meaning and purpose. This citadel of faith, with its deep roots in the human spirit and its orientation towards the eternal, offers not an escape from the challenges of our time, but a profound resource for meeting them with courage, integrity, and an unwavering belief in the enduring value of what it means to be truly human.

The accelerating pace of technological integration into our lives presents us with an unprecedented crossroads. While the allure of convenience, efficiency, and predictive power offered by artificial intelligence is undeniable, we must approach this transformation with a keen awareness of the subtle yet profound ways in which our fundamental liberties can be eroded. The invitation to delegate more of our decision-making, our ethical considerations, and even our emotional lives to algorithmic systems is a siren song, promising ease but threatening to lead us onto the rocks of a deeply compromised humanity. Therefore, a sustained call to vigilance is not merely advisable; it is an imperative for safeguarding the very essence of our freedom. This vigilance demands that we actively scrutinize the technological currents shaping our society, questioning their ultimate aims and their impact on our higher freedoms: love, conscience, and faith.

We stand at a precipice where the voluntary surrender of liberty for the sake of perceived security or effortless convenience can lead to an irreversible diminishment of our human experience. The convenience of automated decision-making, for instance, can, over time, atrophy our capacity for independent judgment. When AI systems are consistently tasked with curating our news feeds, recommending our purchases, and even guiding our social interactions, our ability to exercise discernment, to critically evaluate information, and to forge genuine connections based on personal volition can become blunted. This is not to dismiss the utility of these tools, but to recognize the insidious nature of their potential to gradually reshape our cognitive habits and preferences, rendering us less capable of independent thought and action. Similarly, the promise of enhanced security through pervasive surveillance, often enabled by AI, trades a palpable, though perhaps limited, freedom for an invisible, and potentially total, constraint. The constant awareness, or even the mere possibility, of being monitored can foster a climate of self-censorship and conformity, stifling the very spontaneity and authenticity that define a free spirit.

The trajectory towards a technologically mediated existence requires a conscious and deliberate resistance against the tide of passive acceptance. This resistance is not a Luddite rejection of progress, but a principled stand for the preservation of human dignity and autonomy. It necessitates a commitment to developing and deploying AI in ways that augment, rather than diminish, human capabilities. This means prioritizing ethical considerations at every stage of technological design and implementation. It calls for a robust framework of regulation and oversight that is not reactive, but proactively anticipates the potential for harm. Crucially, it demands that we, as individuals and as a society, cultivate a critical understanding of the technologies we embrace, questioning their underlying assumptions, their data dependencies, and their ultimate impact on the human condition. We must move beyond a purely utilitarian calculus, asking not only if a technology *can* be built, but if it *should* be, and what the long-term consequences are for our collective flourishing.

The true pillars of human dignity and freedom are not to be found in the efficiency metrics of algorithms or the predictive accuracy of data models. They reside in the uniquely human capacities for love, conscience, and faith. These are not simply abstract ideals, but active forces that shape our understanding of ourselves, our relationships with others, and our place in the cosmos. Love, in its most profound sense, is an act of radical acceptance, a willingness to see and embrace the inherent worth of another, irrespective of their utility or conformity to external standards. It is a force that can transcend logical calculation and drive individuals to acts of profound self-sacrifice and empathy. As AI systems become more sophisticated in mimicking human interaction, it is vital to distinguish between algorithmic simulation and genuine human connection. The warmth of an AI companion, however convincingly programmed, cannot replicate the profound spiritual and emotional resonance of authentic human love, a love that is often rooted in shared vulnerability and a recognition of a spiritual dimension to our existence.

Conscience, our inner moral compass, guides us towards ethical behavior, often in the face of competing desires or external pressures. It is the faculty that allows us to discern right from wrong, to feel the pangs of guilt when we transgress our values, and to strive for rectitude. While AI can be programmed with ethical guidelines, these are external impositions, lacking the internal, felt experience of moral deliberation that is characteristic of human conscience. The true strength of conscience lies in its connection to a higher moral order, a sense of accountability that transcends human laws or algorithmic oversight. Faith, in its broadest sense, nurtures this connection, reminding us that our moral choices have consequences that extend beyond the temporal and the observable. To willingly cede our moral reasoning to algorithms, even for the sake of consistency or efficiency, is to risk the erosion of this vital human faculty, leaving us adrift without an inner anchor.

Faith, too, serves as an indispensable bulwark against the encroaching utilitarianism of the AI era. It provides a framework for understanding our existence that extends beyond the purely material and quantifiable. Faith offers a sense of ultimate meaning and purpose, a grounding that is independent of our economic productivity, our social status, or our ability to conform to algorithmic expectations. In a world increasingly oriented towards measurable outcomes and quantifiable achievements, faith reminds us that our worth is not reducible to data points. It offers hope in the face of adversity, not as a statistically probable outcome, but as a deep-seated conviction in a transcendent goodness. This capacity to orient ourselves towards a future that transcends present circumstances, and to draw strength from that enduring vision, is a freedom that AI cannot replicate. It allows us to face the uncertainties of the future, including the profound societal shifts brought about by AI, with a resilient spirit, grounded in something more enduring than the latest technological innovation.

The defense of these higher freedoms requires a conscious and sustained effort. It means actively cultivating our capacity for critical thinking, resisting the urge to outsource our judgment to algorithms. It involves prioritizing genuine human connection over simulated interaction, fostering relationships that are built on empathy, vulnerability, and shared experience. It necessitates a commitment to ethical development and deployment of AI, ensuring that these powerful tools serve humanity rather than subjugating it. This includes demanding transparency in algorithmic decision-making, understanding how these systems operate, and holding those who develop and deploy them accountable for their impact. Furthermore, it requires a recommitment to the values that undergird our moral and spiritual lives – the cultivation of love, the exercise of conscience, and the nurturing of faith. These are not merely private virtues, but essential elements of a free and flourishing society.

The development of AI presents us with a stark choice: we can become passive recipients of its dictates, gradually relinquishing our autonomy and our uniquely human qualities in exchange for convenience and control, or we can actively shape its trajectory, ensuring that it serves as a tool for human empowerment rather than subjugation. This active shaping requires a profound understanding of what truly constitutes human freedom. It is not merely the absence of external constraints, but the presence of internal capacities – the ability to love, to reason ethically, to believe in something beyond the empirically verifiable, and to forge meaningful connections. These capacities are not inherent to our biological makeup alone, but are actively cultivated through practice, through community, and through a conscious orientation towards transcendent values.

To safeguard our liberty in the AI era, we must therefore become more intentional in nurturing these higher freedoms. This means creating spaces, both individual and communal, where love, conscience, and faith can be practiced and deepened. It involves education that emphasizes critical thinking, ethical reasoning, and the exploration of philosophical and theological questions that lie at the heart of human existence. It requires fostering communities that provide support for individuals striving to live according to their values, even when those values are challenged by the prevailing technological logic. These communities, whether religious, philosophical, or simply based on shared commitment to humanistic ideals, act as vital counterpoints to the atomizing forces of a hyper-connected, yet often disembodied, digital world.

The ethical development of AI is not a task solely for engineers and computer scientists; it is a societal responsibility that demands engagement from all disciplines and all citizens. Philosophers, theologians, artists, educators, and citizens alike must participate in the conversation about the future we are building. We must ask the difficult questions: What does it mean to be human in an age of intelligent machines? What are the limits of algorithmic authority? How can we ensure that AI enhances, rather than erodes, our capacity for love, conscience, and faith? The answers to these questions will not be found in code alone, but in a deeper understanding of our own humanity and our aspirations for a meaningful existence.

Ultimately, the defense of higher freedoms against technological encroachment is a call to embrace our full humanity. It is a recognition that the most valuable aspects of our lives – our capacity for love, our moral intuition, our search for meaning – cannot be reduced to algorithms or replicated by machines. By consciously choosing to cultivate these essential human qualities, and by vigilantly ensuring that our technological progress serves these ends, we can navigate the challenges of the AI era not as passive subjects, but as active agents of a future that remains, fundamentally, our own. This is not a fight against technology, but a fight for the soul of humanity, a fight to ensure that in our pursuit of progress, we do not lose sight of what it truly means to be free.

**Algorithmic Authority:** The tendency to grant undue deference to decisions made by algorithms, often without critical examination, potentially abdicating human judgment.

**Conscience:** The inner moral faculty that allows individuals to discern right from wrong, often rooted in a sense of accountability beyond temporal or external dictates.

**Data Dependence:** The reliance on vast datasets for the training and operation of AI systems, which can perpetuate existing biases and limit adaptability to novel situations.

**Dignity (Human):** The inherent worth and inalienable rights of every human being, irrespective of their utility, productivity, or conformity to external standards.

**Emergent Properties:** Unforeseen capabilities or behaviors that arise in complex AI systems, which may not have been explicitly programmed or anticipated by their creators.

**Existential Risk:** The possibility of AI posing a threat to the survival or fundamental well-being of humanity.

**Faith (in a broad sense):** A deep-seated conviction or belief that transcends empirical evidence, often providing meaning, purpose, and hope beyond the material realm.

**Free Will:** The capacity of conscious agents to make choices unconstrained by external forces or deterministic factors, a cornerstone of human autonomy and moral responsibility.

**Higher Freedoms:** Capacities central to human flourishing and autonomy, specifically identified as love, conscience, and faith, which are argued to be uniquely human and vulnerable to technological erosion.

**Humanistic AI:** An approach to artificial intelligence development that prioritizes human well-being, autonomy, and ethical considerations, aiming to augment rather than diminish human capabilities.

**Moral Intuition:** The innate ability to grasp moral truths or principles without conscious reasoning, often linked to the faculty of conscience.

**Ontological Shift:** A fundamental change in the nature of being or existence, potentially brought about by the widespread integration of advanced AI.

**Predictive Power:** The ability of AI systems to forecast future events or behaviors based on data analysis, raising concerns about determinism and the erosion of agency.

**Simulation (of human interaction):** The creation of artificial systems designed to mimic human communication, empathy, or connection, which may be distinguished from genuine human experience.

**Soulless Efficiency:** A state where the pursuit of operational efficiency through technology leads to a diminishment of human values, empathy, and spiritual depth.

**Transcendent Values:** Principles or ideals that extend beyond the immediate material or temporal concerns, often guiding moral and spiritual understanding.

**Utilitarianism:** An ethical theory that determines right from wrong by focusing on outcomes, particularly the maximization of overall happiness or well-being; in the context of AI, it can lead to a focus on efficiency over human dignity.

**Vigilance (Technological):** A state of alert awareness and critical engagement with technological advancements, their implications, and their potential impact on human freedom and dignity.

*Dostoyevsky, Fyodor.* The Brothers Karamazov. Translated by Pevear and Volokhonsky. New York: Farrar, Straus and Giroux, 1990.

*Heidegger, Martin.* The Question Concerning Technology and Other Essays. Translated by William Lovitt. New York: Harper & Row, 1977.

*Bostrom, Nick.* Superintelligence: Paths, Dangers, Strategies. Oxford University Press, 2014.

*Floridi, Luciano.* The Fourth Revolution: How the Infosphere is Reshaping Human Reality. Oxford University Press, 2014.

*Habermas, Jürgen.* The Philosophical Discourse of Modernity: Twelve Lectures. Translated by Frederick Lawrence. MIT Press, 1987.

[Any specific academic papers cited within the book, formatted according to a chosen style guide (e.g., Chicago, MLA, APA).]

[Works exploring the intersection of religion, theology, and technology.]

www.ingramcontent.com/pod-product-compliance
Lightning Source LLC
LaVergne TN
LVHW052023200926
848481LV00005B/1573